From Wonder to Wisdom

An Introduction to Philosophy through Classic Texts

Joseph R. Kirkland, J.D.

University of Michigan Dearborn

Kendall Hunt
publishing company

Cover image © 2014 Shutterstock, Inc.

Kendall Hunt
publishing company

www.kendallhunt.com
Send all inquiries to:
4050 Westmark Drive
Dubuque, IA 52004-1840

Copyright © 2014 by Kendall Hunt Publishing Company

ISBN 978-1-4652-5576-1

Printed in the United States of America
10 9 8 7 6 5 4 3 2 1

*For Robert and Carol Kirkland who made everything possible,
and for Kerri Kirkland who makes everything worth it.*

Contents

"There is a special service which the study of philosophy may render: . . . a study, by means of philosophy, of life-experience. But this experience is already overlaid and saturated with the products of the reflection of past generations and bygone ages. It is filled with interpretations, classifications, due to sophisticated thought, which have become incorporated into what seems to be fresh, naïve, empirical material. It would take more wisdom than is possessed by the wisest historical scholar to track all of these absorbed borrowings to their original sources. If we may for the moment call these materials *prejudices* (even if they are true, as long as their source and authority is unknown), then philosophy is a critique of prejudices.

These incorporated results of past reflection, welded into the genuine materials of first-hand experience, may become organs of enrichment if they are detected and reflected upon. If they are not detected, they often obfuscate and distort. Clarification and emancipation follow when they are detected and cast out; and one great object of philosophy is to accomplish this task."

—John Dewey, *Experience and Nature*

CHAPTER ONE

From Wonder to Wisdom

"The possession of knowledge does not kill the sense of wonder and mystery. There is always more mystery. I have no fear of clarity."

– Anais Nin[i]

"Sponges grow in the ocean. That just kills me. I wonder how much deeper the ocean would be if that didn't happen."

– Steven Wright[ii]

Few things induce a jolt of genuine wonder quite like a solitary confrontation with the night sky and its dazzling canopy of stars. Dwarfed by this, the barest fraction of the celestial scene actually visible from Earth, we may even find ourselves overwhelmed, our thoughts turning to questions quite unlike those that preoccupy us in the mundane trenches of daily daytime life: Where did this all come from? What, if anything, does it mean? Why are we even here? Encounters like this should remind us that, plainly put, the world we inhabit is both very big and very old. The numbers required to describe both its size and its age are so immense, in fact, as to be virtually incomprehensible. The latest scientific evidence suggests that our universe contains roughly 170 billion galaxies. Our own familiar Sun is but one of some 300 billion stars in our home galaxy, the Milky Way. As for its age, our current calculations place the birth of the universe an unfathomably distant 13.8 billion years ago. Our home planet formed relatively recently some 4.5 billion years ago, while human beings themselves—a veritable blip on the cosmic timeline—did not emerge until (only!) approximately 200,000 years ago.[iii]

Faced with the enormity of the task of explaining the enormity of the universe, author and astronomer **Carl Sagan** (1934-1996) devised a useful model for putting all of these hilariously large numbers into perspective by employing a sense of scale with which we are more familiar: the calendar.[iv] Imagine that the universe is but one year old. Thus, each calendar month would correspond to a little more than one billion years of cosmic history. Per this model, the Big Bang occurs at the stroke of midnight, ushering in New Year's Day, while the Milky Way galaxy does not appear until several months later, sometime in March. The Sun, the Earth, and the other planets in our solar system appear in August, with single-celled life forms arising on Earth sometime in late September. The mass extinction of the dinosaurs does not occur until very late in our cosmic calendar: December 29th, in fact. As for us? Modern humans finally emerge at the fashionably late hour of 11:54 PM on New Year's Eve, with the invention of writing, for example, following at a mere fifteen seconds to midnight. Let us assume that you will be fortunate enough to live to the ripe old age of eighty. Your lifespan in these cosmic calendar terms? A scant sixteen hundredths of a second, and that's if you're lucky. Understandably, this kind of cosmic perspective can unnerve as well as inspire. In contemplating the sheer vastness and age of an indifferent cosmos relative to our own miniscule corner of it and time in it, the French philosopher and mathematician **Blaise Pascal** (1623–1662) once confessed, "The eternal silence of these infinite spaces terrifies me." Perhaps part of the jolt we feel in facing the cosmic expanse is precisely due to that peculiar blend of terror and wonder. Little wonder, then, that our thoughts so often turn to profound, deep, *philosophical* questions, in light of confrontations and contemplations such as these.

3

Plato of Athens, perhaps the most influential philosopher who ever lived, once wrote, "The feeling of wonder shows that you are a philosopher, since wonder is the true beginning of philosophy."[v] His student **Aristotle**, arguably the second most influential philosopher known to history, concurred: "It is through wonder that men now begin and originally began to philosophize."[vi] Since its formal Western inception some twenty-five centuries ago in ancient Greece, the wonderful has remained both the impetus for and the domain of philosophy. Nowhere, perhaps, is this clearer than in the popular imagination and its conception of what philosophy involves. Ask a random person for an example of a philosophical question and, bemused reactions aside, you're most likely to elicit a gloss on some perennial "Big Question" concerning what the great and late author **Douglas Adams** once memorably described as "the question of Life, the Universe, and Everything." It is true that philosophers traffic in the so-called "Big Questions," questions including but most certainly not limited to: Does God exist and can we know that? What is the nature of good and evil, right and wrong? Why, for that matter, is there so much evil in the world if, as some profess, it is the creation of a benevolent deity? Are moral values and principles merely the product of the conventions of our respective cultures, or are some such values and principles valid for human beings in general? What can we human beings really know about the world we happen to find ourselves in? Moreover, what if anything could we possibly come to know about realities allegedly beyond our own? What makes a law or a custom—or a society for that matter—just? Indeed, what is a truly fair way in which to organize society, and, not just ours, but any society whatsoever? This is but a small sampling of some admittedly "big" philosophical questions. At the same time, however, philosophers also ask a great many deceptively "small" questions in the service of answering the larger ones. This text is an opportunity for you to wonder alongside some of the most brilliant and influential philosophical minds who have ever lived, to wander in their footsteps as they interrogate matters both profound and pragmatic, and to discover that, while its historical roots may lie buried in the ruins of centuries-gone antiquity, philosophy and its central questions remain a vital component of what it means to be human and to live life well.

To philosophize in the proper sense of the word, however, is not merely to exhibit a perfunctory curiosity about things or simply to engage in idle speculation about matters abstruse. Nor is it to adopt a general approach to a particular field or endeavor. Thus, while we may speak loosely in other contexts of having a "philosophy of this" or a "philosophy of that," as an academic discipline, **philosophy** involves the rigorous and critical analysis of fundamental problems, concepts, and values, as well as the analysis of our reasons for accepting some positions while rejecting others concerning these matters. As logicians might say, then, wonder is a necessary but not a sufficient condition for philosophy which, of course, is not unique in addressing problems, concepts, or values *per se*. One way to grasp the distinctive nature of philosophy and its methods—that is, to grasp what makes philosophy *philosophy*—is to contrast it with that from which it grew: namely, myth.

FROM MYTHOS TO LOGOS

"One time a cop pulled me over for running a stop sign. He said, 'Didn't you see the stop sign?'
I said, 'Yeah, but I don't believe everything I read.'"

—Steven Wright[vii]

As a historical matter, the tendrils of ancient Greek philosophy emerged gradually from the fertile soil of ancient Greek mythology. From the ancient Greek word *mythos* meaning a story or a tale (think here of the words "fable" or "legend" in English), mythology functioned for the ancient Greeks in much the same way that myth has functioned for countless human cultures throughout history. In surveying myths the world over we typically find, among other things, cosmogonies (i.e., legendary accounts of the creation of the world), descriptions of the foibles, predilections, and misadventures of various gods and demigods, and some of the first more or less systematic attempts to provide supernatural explanations for ostensibly natural phenomena (e.g., lightning is the product of a jealous and angry Zeus hurling electric bolts from high atop Mount Olympus, the legendary abode of the Greek divinities). Unlike the myths from which it grew, however, ancient Greek philosophy ultimately came to represent a different way of addressing questions of fundamental problems, concepts, and values altogether. This departure, as we shall see, quite literally changed history.

Myths are, by and large, accepted (if at all) on the basis of claimed authority alone: perhaps the authority of the myth-maker or, more typically, that of the divinities credited with inspiring a given poet to wax mythological on a particular subject or theme. Hesiod, the famed ancient Greek poet and author of the seminal texts *Theogony* and *Works and Days* (and contemporary of Greek myth-maker Homer of *Iliad* and *Odyssey* fame), opens the former with an assertion of his indirect authority. The nine divine Muses (and daughters of Zeus) are directly cited as both his inspiration and the source of his authority—i.e., the reason why we should trust and accept his particular *mythos*:

> From the Heliconian Muses let us begin to sing, who hold the great and holy mount of Helicon, and dance on soft feet about the deep-blue spring and the altar of the almighty son of Cronos, and, when they have washed their tender bodies in Permessus or in the Horse's Spring or Olmeius, make their fair, lovely dances upon highest Helicon and move with vigorous feet.
>
> Thence they arise and go abroad by night, veiled in thick mist, and utter their song with lovely voice, praising Zeus the aegis-holder and queenly Hera of Argos who walks on golden sandals and the daughter of Zeus the aegis-holder bright-eyed Athene, and Phoebus Apollo, and Artemis who delights in arrows, and Poseidon the earth-holder who shakes the earth, and reverend Themis and quick-glancing Aphrodite, and Hebe with the crown of gold, and fair Dione, Leto, Iapetus, and Cronos the crafty counsellor, Eos and great Helius and bright Selene, Earth too, and great Oceanus, and dark Night, and the holy race of all the other deathless ones that are forever.
>
> And one day they taught Hesiod glorious song while he was shepherding his lambs under holy Helicon, and this word first the goddesses said to me—the Muses of Olympus, daughters of Zeus who holds the aegis: "Shepherds of the wilderness, wretched things of shame, mere bellies, we know how to speak many false things as though they were true; but we know, when we will, to utter true things."
>
> So said the ready-voiced daughters of great Zeus, and they plucked and gave me a rod, a shoot of sturdy laurel, a marvelous thing, and breathed into me a divine voice to celebrate things that shall be and things there were aforetime; and they bade me sing of the race of the blessed gods that are eternally . . .[viii]

He goes on like this at some length. The point, however, is that Hesiod is essentially trumpeting his credentials in this passage. He is transformed from humble shepherd to poet of divine inspiration, brandishing the sturdy laurel staff, gifted to him by the Muses, as the symbol of his having been selected (by the very daughters of Zeus himself, no less!) specifically for the task of the telling of divine things. It is in light of this claim and the indirect authority it is supposed to bestow that Hesiod believes his audience should treat and take his account seriously. Such is the case with myth, by and large, in general.

The earliest philosophers in this tradition, on the other hand, gradually attempted to forge a different method of inquiry into and explanation of, among other things, natural phenomena. Known as the **Pre-Socratics** (for they lived either before or contemporaneous with Socrates of Athens, who was born sometime around the year 470 BCE and was executed by his fellow Athenians in 399 BCE), these very first Western philosophers sought a rationally grounded, as opposed to merely mythical, account of the first principle of all things. Traditionally, Western philosophy is said to have begun in the port town of Miletus (located on the Ionian coast of the Mediterranean Sea in present-day Turkey) when the astronomer and mathematician **Thales** (c.624–c.546 BCE) successfully predicted a solar eclipse in the year 585 BCE. His apparent penchant for wandering eyes upon the skies while doing his wondering is also the source of quite possibly the first "absent-minded philosophy professor" joke in Western history. As Plato relates the story in his dialogue *Theaetetus*:

> While he was studying the stars and looking upwards, [Thales] fell into a well, and a neat, witty Thracian servant girl jeered at him, they say, because he was so eager to know the things in the sky that he could not see what was there before him at his very feet.[ix]

While perhaps the first, Thales was certainly not the last philosopher to be mocked for a concern with ethereal things while paying too little heed to the so-called "real world." In any event, Thales is most significant in the history of philosophy, however, for his apparent contention that all of reality could be reduced to some one basic substance. This position is called **monism**: the idea that reality is fundamentally unitary in nature—that is, the claim that reality is composed of one substance, or that it obeys one principle, or that it is one entity or process, *et cetera*.

What is the one thing from which everything is composed? Thales seemed to argue that all is (or rests upon) water. In positing water as the fundamental substance from which all things are made, he was both invoking a natural (as opposed to supernatural) explanation of natural phenomena and providing an account for which the evidence could be weighed and assessed. Instead of suggesting (demanding?) that we accept his account on the grounds that the gods had assured him that, say, water was the fundamental element or "building block" of reality, we can imagine (and occasionally *have* to imagine, as with the Pre-Socratics we are often dealing with interpreting mere fragments of texts and/or their mention in later writers' interpretations of their views) some of the possible reasons Thales may have cited in defense of his theory that "all is water." Liquid water, after all, is a (pardon the pun) fairly fluid kind of thing. With relatively small variations in temperature it can assume the shape of either a solid or a gas. It occupies a majority of the surface of the Earth and constitutes a majority of the human body, as well. Without water, life itself—at least on this planet—is literally impossible. Also recall that Thales hailed from a port town: its proximity to the sea permitted Miletus to, at one point, become a thriving commercial hub. Anyone from a coastal city can tell you how much the flow and ebb of life there is affected by the presence and properties of the sea. It stands to reason, then, that Thales had several good reasons to suspect that water is quite possibly the one thing that all things ultimately have in common.

The ancient Greek word for "reason"—in this sense of a rational account or explanation—is ***logos***. Whereas a *mythos* represents a story or tale, *logos* for the ancient Greeks referred to (among other things) both a rational account or explanation and the distinctively human ability to engage in reasoned discourse on a variety of matters. Aristotle characterized this particular conception of *logos* thusly:

> In Aristotle's view, human beings are set apart from the other animals not by their capacity for self-expression, but rather by their capacity for rational speech (*logos*). Man possesses more than mere voice (*phone*); he can do more than just intimate that he feels pleasure or pain. Thus his humanity is in no way constituted by his ability to speak out, to get a load off his chest, to give vent to his spleen. He could just as well accomplish a purge of emotion by the inarticulate utterance of the beast. For Aristotle, *logos* is something more refined than the capacity to make private feelings public: it enables the human being to perform as no other animal can; it makes it possible for him to perceive and make clear to others through reasoned discourse the difference between what is advantageous and what is harmful, between what is just and what is unjust, and between what is good and what is evil.[x]

Thus, one way to characterize the gradual emergence of Greek philosophy from Greek myth is to frame it as the gradual triumph of *logos* over *mythos*, of a slow but steady transition from a concern with the transmission of fables (*mythoi*) claiming divine warrant to the pursuit of a knowledge of fundamental concepts and values based on reasoned arguments (*logoi*). Etymologically speaking, our English word "logic" stems from the Greek *logos*, and one could argue that logic is the native tongue of philosophy itself. Relatedly, our common English suffix for "the science or the study of" something ("-ology") comes from the selfsame root. While other disciplines including the arts, theology, and so forth clearly address fundamental concepts and values as well, the manner in which philosophy as a discipline does so is what it is arguably distinctive: namely, in the weighing and assessment of various logical arguments for and against various positions on these matters. We see this in the exchange of arguments between the very first philosophers in the Western tradition, and we see it in contemporary philosophical inquiry and discourse as well. For further information on the nature of logical arguments and how best to assess them, please consult *Appendix A: An Introduction to Logical Argument*.

FROM WONDER TO WISDOM

> *"Why is it, 'A penny for your thoughts,' but, 'You have to put your two cents in.'? Somebody's making a penny."*
>
> —Steven Wright[xi]

We have seen that two of the most influential philosophers to have ever lived (i.e., Plato and Aristotle) both claimed that philosophy has its origins in wonder. But we have also seen that as ancient Greek philosophy emerged from ancient Greek myth, it began to adopt its own methods and adapt to the conditions in which it emerged. A *logos*-based approach to questions of fundamental concepts and values was now here and something to be reckoned with, one way or another. So where, then, did the wondering of the first philosophers actually lead them? A clue hides in the very word for the discipline itself. Some historians suspect that the Pre-Socratic philosopher **Pythagoras** (c. 570 BCE–c. 495 BCE)—yes, the Pythagoras of geometric fame—may have been the person who coined the term "philosopher," which in ancient Greek means not "one who wonders," but rather "lover of wisdom." This is an admittedly unusual job description! You can imagine the response you would likely elicit if you introduced yourself to someone and, when queried about your line of work, proclaimed that you were a "professional wisdom-lover." By way of contrast, the title "biologist" does not mean "lover of biology" any more than "physicist" means "lover of physics." While the philosopher's original job description, etymologically speaking, may strike you as more than a little bizarre, it does merit a closer read.

The prefix "philo-" in English refers to having a strong affinity or preference for something. If we think of this affinity in terms of what it typically leads to, namely, the pursuit of that which we prefer, then "to philosophize" can mean something like "to pursue wisdom." Understood in this way, the first philosophers came to see themselves as those in pursuit of wisdom. Far from an arrogant claim of having attained a wise state, to identify as a philosopher involves the admission, implicit or otherwise, that one has yet to attain wisdom, if ever. Think of the police, for example, in hot pursuit of a suspect in a procedural crime drama: if the police are still "in pursuit" then they most certainly have not apprehended their suspect yet. Thus, if we frame the "love of wisdom" as the "pursuit of wisdom," then the philosopher would have to concede, at least initially, that wisdom represents a goal and not a starting point. When we turn to Socrates of Athens in the next chapter, we will encounter this notion in terms of something like humility, not the general trait of being humble so much as **intellectual humility**. Philosophers begin with the admission that they are not fully wise, that they do not "have all of the answers," that there is much in fact about which they are currently ignorant or confused. This kind of humility is not a celebration of ignorance so much as a necessary first step if we truly care about trying to correct the pockets of ignorance and inconsistency within our own beliefs about, for example, what is real, what is true, what is good, what is just, and so forth. After all, the kind of person who pursues wisdom as a goal presumably wants to, at minimum, correct any misconceptions they may have regarding these (and, of course, other) crucial ideas and ideals.

Appropriately, the four aforementioned concepts and/or values (i.e., reality, truth, goodness, and justice) can also be used to represent four of the major areas of specialization or emphasis within philosophy. For while it is true, etymologically speaking, that philosophy is the love or pursuit of wisdom, we should not exactly expect toga-clad professors of philosophy hunting after that elusive catch "wisdom" up and down the halls of philosophy departments today. That is because philosophy is not immune from the pressures of specialization and professionalization at work in most major fields of intellectual inquiry. While there admittedly are "general practitioners" in many fields, it is nonetheless true that specialization rules the day. Think here of a field like psychology wherein you can study human psychology in general (perhaps in the context of an introductory course), but at the same time courses are offered and important intellectual work is done in a host of specialized branches: for example, clinical psychology, child psychology, social psychology, behavioral psychology, and so forth. Philosophers in academia tend to specialize as well, and we can identify at least four major areas of specialization ("branches of philosophy") in terms of some of the major concepts and values addressed in each:

- **METAPHYSICS** → reality / existence / being, etc.
- **EPISTEMOLOGY** → knowledge / truth / evidence / belief, etc.
- **ETHICS** → goodness / rightness / virtue, etc.
- **POLITICAL PHILOSOPHY** → justice / fairness / equality, etc.

There are other areas of specialization within philosophy beyond these four main branches. They include **aesthetics** (the philosophy of art and beauty) and the aforementioned **logic** (the philosophy of correct reasoning)—though many Western philosophers would be more prone to describe logic not so much as just another branch on the metaphorical tree, but so much as the very trunk or roots of philosophy. Moreover, there are various branches in philosophy wherein other particular fields or areas of intellectual inquiry are subjected to philosophical analysis. These include the **philosophy of law**, the **philosophy of religion**, the **philosophy of science**, and the **philosophy of language**, for example. What unites these diverse forms of specialization is a shared methodology that focuses on the assessment of reasoned arguments concerning whatever particular issue is being analyzed, discussed, or debated, that is, to seek for those accounts or explanations that are supported in turn by the strongest *logoi*.

KNOWLEDGE VERSUS WISDOM

> *A cop stopped me for speeding. He said, "Why were you going so fast?" I said, "See this thing my foot is on? It's called an accelerator. When you push down on it, it sends more gas to the engine. The whole car just takes right off. And see this thing? This steers it."*
>
> —Steven Wright[xii]

If philosophy begins with wonder and leads those who practice it to pursue wisdom, one way or another, it is a fair and perfectly philosophical question to ask: what is wisdom? As with many of the fundamental concepts philosophers subject to close analysis, there is widespread disagreement on what wisdom may ultimately be or mean. Nonetheless, one way to help us achieve a bit more clarity is to contrast it with that which it is not, namely, knowledge. Ever since Plato composed the dialogue *Theaetetus*, many Western philosophers have defined **knowledge** as something like **justified true belief**. Here "belief" functions something like the word "opinion," in that it refers to a person giving their mental assent to a particular claim. For example, I believe that it is true that it snowed last night. Why do I believe that? Because I am looking out the window as I type these words and see my street blanketed in mounds of fluffy whiteness. For a belief, even a true one, to be considered knowledge, however, it must be supported by good reasons and/or evidence. This is what philosophers mean, generally speaking, by the terms **justification** or **warrant**. After all, if I believe a claim is true without good reasons for believing it to be true, I cannot properly claim to have *known* that it was true. Maybe I made a lucky guess! For example, if you meet someone for the first time and correctly guess their name (without gathering any information beforehand), it makes no sense to claim that you *knew* their name, at least not until they tell you, or show you their driver's license, or provide some sort of good reason for believing it to be true. You should notice, here, that "belief" in philosophy functions very broadly as an epistemological concept. Whereas in other contexts a reference to "our beliefs" may signify something like our most profound, or cherished, or deeply held personal beliefs, one's beliefs in the general epistemic sense can be quite mundane indeed. I am not exactly ready to die for my belief, say, that it snowed last night. As you may imagine, one of the most pressing areas of epistemology involves the analysis of what kind of justification is necessary for belief to count as knowledge.

We should be careful not to conflate knowledge with wisdom, however. If to know something is to have something like a justified true belief that a claim is true, then it should be clear that knowledge, much like belief, is a very broad epistemological concept indeed. By way of illustration, let us assume that I decide to quit my job at this very moment and dedicate the rest of my days to memorizing the entries in the phonebook. [**Editor's note:** the "phonebook" was apparently an ancient artifact that earlier cultures employed to record the names, addresses, and phone numbers of the residents in a particular area. Recent archaeological evidence suggests that these records were kept on trees that had been pulped and often dyed a distinctive shade of yellow.] What is more, let us suppose that I succeed in this endeavor. As I lay on my deathbed, I recite by rote each entry in the phonebook in order and with unerring precision. Surrounded by the few remaining friends and loved ones I have failed to alienate as a result of my peculiar vocational change, I utter with my final breath the dramatic words: "Zbigniew Zyskowksi, 4855 Commonwealth St., 313-555-1212! Gah! Ack! Blargh! Forsooth!" and then expire. Is it fair to say that, upon dying, I had amassed a vast amount of knowledge concerning, in this instance, the contents of the phone book? Of course. Would anyone who truly cared about me or my well-being have counseled me to cease all other pursuits and dedicate my entire life to the pursuit of such knowledge? Of course not. Those who cared would rightfully mourn, among other things, the grave waste of potential and a lifetime squandered. "What a fool, and what a foolish thing to have done," we imagine even otherwise sympathetic observers noting sadly, as they lift the sheet over my face a final time.

Why is that? If wisdom is knowledge, then how could the pursuit of knowledge be foolish? The short answer is that one can know a great many things about a great deal of things that, in the end, do not amount to much. If, say, memorizing the contents of the phonebook would be an unwise way in which to spend one's time, much less one's life, then wisdom—whatever it may be—cannot be reduced to knowledge or the pursuit thereof alone. Nor should we err in the opposite direction and presume there is no connection whatsoever between the knowledgeable person and the wise person. While they may be distinct concepts, they are nonetheless related concepts. Let us imagine that you find yourself in the throes of an apparently intractable romantic dilemma. You call up a dear friend who has been known to dispense sage and useful advice to others when it comes to matters of the heart. However, in this instance she fails to answer her phone for whatever reason, and so you leave a lengthy message detailing all of the specifics of your current predicament and urging her to call you back as soon as she can with advice on how to proceed in this delicate situation. Unfortunately, while she does receive your message and does return your call, the message you left was so garbled that she is only able to make out every other word of your message. In light of the (now misleading) information she has access to, what are the chances that she will be able to dispense useful, much less wise, counsel? From this and other examples like it, we may conclude that knowledge, then, is a necessary but not a sufficient condition for wisdom.

Applicability. Relevance. Significance. These are precisely the sort of qualities that are absent in the case of our phonebook example and difficult to achieve in the case of our garbled voicemail example. Perhaps the wise person is, among other things, precisely the sort of person who is able to apply what they know in practical circumstances and in a way which is of some real relevance or significance to our lives more broadly speaking. The wise person does not just merely know a great deal; rather, the wise woman or man is able to bring their knowledge to bear on matters that *matter*. Our age has been dubbed the Information Age, but a case could be made that it is actually the Information Overload Age. With an unimaginable amount of information now available at our fingertips and a world of distractions around us, the need for genuine wisdom is more pressing than ever. Consider each of the following readings, then, an opportunity. Each reading contained herein is an opportunity to explore with rigor and depth some of the most probing questions we can ask, as we, like so many human beings before us, struggle to direct our oft-elusive feelings of genuine wonder toward something approaching genuine wisdom.

NOTES

i *The Diary of Anais Nin*, Vol. 1: 1931-1934. Mariner Books (1969), p. 155.
ii www.wright-house.com/steven-wright/steven-wright-jokes.html
iii http://wmap.gsfc.nasa.gov/universe/uni_age.html
iv Carl Sagan. *The Dragons of Eden*. Random House (2012)
v *Theateteus*. 155c-d
vi *Metaphysics*. Book 1, Section 982b
vii www.wright-house.com/steven-wright/steven-wright-jokes.html
viii *Theogony*. Trans. by Hugh G. Evelyn-White (1914), lines 1-34
ix *Theateteus*. 174a
x Paul Rahe. *Republics Ancient and Modern: The Ancient Regime in Classical Greece*. The University of North Carolina Press (1994).
xi www.wright-house.com/steven-wright/steven-wright-jokes.html
xii www.wright-house.com/steven-wright/steven-wright-jokes.html

CHAPTER TWO

Socrates on Wisdom and Justice

Image © Anastasios71, 2014. Used under license from Shutterstock, Inc.

— Socrates (470–399 BCE)

SELECTED READINGS

- ▶ *Euthyphro*—Plato
- ▶ *Apology*—Plato
- ▶ *Crito*—Plato
- ▶ "The Death of Socrates" from *Phaedo*—Plato

Euthyphro

Plato
(Translated by Benjamin Jowett and edited by Joseph R. Kirkland)

PERSONS OF THE DIALOGUE: Socrates, Euthyphro
SCENE: The Porch of the King Archon

EUTHYPHRO: Why have you left the Lyceum, Socrates? and what are you doing in the Porch of the King Archon? Surely you cannot be concerned in a suit before the King, like myself?

SOCRATES: Not in a suit, Euthyphro; impeachment is the word which the Athenians use.

EUTHYPHRO: What! I suppose that someone has been prosecuting you, for I cannot believe that you are the prosecutor of another.

SOCRATES: Certainly not.

EUTHYPHRO: Then someone else has been prosecuting you?

SOCRATES: Yes.

EUTHYPHRO: And who is he?

SOCRATES: A young man who is little known, Euthyphro; and I hardly know him: his name is Meletus, and he is of the deme of Pitthis. Perhaps you may remember his appearance; he has a beak, and long straight hair, and a beard which is ill grown.

EUTHYPHRO: No, I do not remember him, Socrates. But what is the charge which he brings against you?

SOCRATES: What is the charge? Well, a very serious charge, which shows a good deal of character in the young man, and for which he is certainly not to be despised. He says he knows how the youth are corrupted and who are their corruptors. I fancy that he must be a wise man, and seeing that I am the reverse of a wise man, he has found me out, and is going to accuse me of corrupting his young friends. And of this our mother the state is to be the judge. Of all our political men he is the only one who seems to me to begin in the right way, with the cultivation of virtue in youth; like a good husbandman, he makes the young shoots his first care, and clears away us who are the destroyers of them. This is only the first step; he will afterwards attend to the elder branches; and if he goes on as he has begun, he will be a very great public benefactor.

EUTHYPHRO: I hope that he may; but I rather fear, Socrates, that the opposite will turn out to be the truth. My opinion is that in attacking you he is simply aiming a blow at the foundation of the state. But in what way does he say that you corrupt the young?

SOCRATES: He brings a wonderful accusation against me, which at first hearing excites surprise: he says that I am a poet or maker of gods, and that I invent new gods and deny the existence of old ones; this is the ground of his indictment.

EUTHYPHRO: I understand, Socrates; he means to attack you about the familiar sign which occasionally, as you say, comes to you. He thinks that you are a neologian, and he is going to have you up before the court for this. He knows that such a charge is readily received by the world, as I myself know too well; for when I speak in the assembly about divine things, and foretell the future to them, they laugh at me and think me a madman. Yet every word that I say is true. But they are jealous of us all; and we must be brave and go at them.

SOCRATES: Their laughter, friend Euthyphro, is not a matter of much consequence. For a man may be thought wise; but the Athenians, I suspect, do not much trouble themselves about him until he begins to impart his wisdom to others, and then for some reason or other, perhaps, as you say, from jealousy, they are angry.

EUTHYPHRO: I am never likely to try their temper in this way.

SOCRATES: I dare say not, for you are reserved in your behavior, and seldom impart your wisdom. But I have a benevolent habit of pouring out myself to everybody, and would even pay for a listener, and I am afraid that the Athenians may think me too talkative. Now if, as I was saying, they would only laugh at me, as you say that they laugh at you, the time might pass gaily enough in the court; but perhaps they may be in earnest, and then what the end will be you soothsayers only can predict.

EUTHYPHRO: I dare say that the affair will end in nothing, Socrates, and that you will win your cause; and I think that I shall win my own.

SOCRATES: And what is your suit, Euthyphro? Are you the pursuer or the defendant?

EUTHYPHRO: I am the pursuer.

SOCRATES: Of whom?

EUTHYPHRO: You will think me mad when I tell you.

SOCRATES: Why, has the fugitive wings?

EUTHYPHRO: Nay, he is not very volatile at his time of life.

SOCRATES: Who is he?

EUTHYPHRO: My father.

SOCRATES: Your *father*, my good man!?

EUTHYPHRO: Yes.

SOCRATES: And of what is he accused?

EUTHYPHRO: Of murder, Socrates.

SOCRATES: By the powers, Euthyphro! how little does the common herd know of the nature of right and truth. A man must be an extraordinary man, and have made great strides in wisdom, before he could have seen his way to bring such an action.

EUTHYPHRO: Indeed, Socrates, he must.

SOCRATES: I suppose that the man whom your father murdered was one of your relatives—clearly he was; for if he had been a stranger you would never have thought of prosecuting him.

EUTHYPHRO: I am amused, Socrates, at your making a distinction between one who is a relation and one who is not a relation; for surely the pollution is the same in either case, if you knowingly associate with the murderer when you ought to clear yourself and him by proceeding against him. The real question is whether the murdered man has been justly slain. If justly, then your duty is to let the matter alone; but if unjustly, then even if the murderer lives under the same roof with you and eats at the same table, proceed against him. Now the man who is dead was a poor dependent of mine who worked for us as a field laborer on our farm in Naxos, and one day in a fit of drunken passion he got into a quarrel with one of our domestic servants and slew him. My father bound him hand and foot and threw him into a ditch, and then sent to Athens to ask

of a diviner what he should do with him. Meanwhile he never attended to him and took no care about him, for he regarded him as a murderer; and thought that no great harm would be done even if he did die. Now this was just what happened. For such was the effect of cold and hunger and chains upon him, that before the messenger returned from the diviner, he was dead. And my father and family are angry with me for taking the part of the murderer and prosecuting my father. They say that he did not kill him, and that if he did, the dead man was but a murderer, and I ought not to take any notice, for that a son is impious who prosecutes a father. Which shows, Socrates, how little they know what the gods think about piety and impiety.

SOCRATES: Good heavens, Euthyphro! And is your knowledge of religion and of things pious and impious so very exact, that, supposing the circumstances to be as you state them, you are not afraid lest you too may be doing an impious thing in bringing an action against your father?

EUTHYPHRO: The best of Euthyphro, and that which distinguishes him, Socrates, from other men, is his exact knowledge of all such matters. What should I be good for without it?

SOCRATES: Rare friend! I think that I cannot do better than be your disciple. Then before the trial with Meletus comes on I shall challenge him, and say that I have always had a great interest in religious questions, and now, as he charges me with rash imaginations and innovations in religion, I have become your disciple. You, Meletus, as I shall say to him, acknowledge Euthyphro to be a great theologian, and sound in his opinions; and if you approve of him you ought to approve of me, and not have me into court; but if you disapprove, you should begin by indicting him who is my teacher, and who will be the ruin, not of the young, but of the old; that is to say, of myself whom he instructs, and of his old father whom he admonishes and chastises. And if Meletus refuses to listen to me, but will go on, and will not shift the indictment from me to you, I cannot do better than repeat this challenge in the court.

EUTHYPHRO: Yes, indeed, Socrates; and if he attempts to indict me I am mistaken if I do not find a flaw in him; the court shall have a great deal more to say to him than to me.

SOCRATES: And I, my dear friend, knowing this, am desirous of becoming your disciple. For I observe that no one appears to notice you—not even this Meletus;

but his sharp eyes have found me out at once, and he has indicted me for impiety. And therefore, I adjure you to tell me the nature of piety and impiety, which you said that you knew so well, and of murder, and of other offences against the gods. What are they? Is not piety in every action always the same? And impiety, again—is it not always the opposite of piety, and also the same with itself, having, as impiety, one notion which includes whatever is impious?

EUTHYPHRO: To be sure, Socrates.

SOCRATES: And what is piety, and what is impiety?

EUTHYPHRO: Piety is doing as I am doing; that is to say, prosecuting anyone who is guilty of murder, sacrilege, or of any similar crime—whether he be your father or mother, or whoever he may be—that makes no difference; and not to prosecute them is impiety. And please to consider, Socrates, what a notable proof I will give you of the truth of my words, a proof which I have already given to others:—of the principle, I mean, that the impious, whoever he may be, ought not to go unpunished. For do not men regard Zeus as the best and most righteous of the gods?—and yet they admit that he bound his father (Cronos) because he wickedly devoured his sons, and that he too had punished his own father (Uranus) for a similar reason, in a nameless manner. And yet when I proceed against my father, they are angry with me. So inconsistent are they in their way of talking when the gods are concerned, and when I am concerned.

SOCRATES: May not this be the reason, Euthyphro, why I am charged with impiety—that I cannot away with these stories about the gods? and therefore I suppose that people think me wrong. But, as you who are well informed about them approve of them, I cannot do better than assent to your superior wisdom. What else can I say, confessing as I do, that I know nothing about them? Tell me, for the love of Zeus, whether you really believe that they are true.

EUTHYPHRO: Yes, Socrates; and things more wonderful still, of which the world is in ignorance.

SOCRATES: And do you really believe that the gods fought with one another, and had dire quarrels, battles, and the like, as the poets say, and as you may see represented in the works of great artists? The temples are full of them; and notably the robe of Athene, which is carried up to the Acropolis at the great Panathenaea, is embroidered with them. Are all these tales of the gods true, Euthyphro?

EUTHYPHRO: Yes, Socrates; and, as I was saying, I can tell you, if you would like to hear them, many other things about the gods which would quite amaze you.

SOCRATES: I dare say; and you shall tell me them at some other time when I have leisure. But just at present I would rather hear from you a more precise answer, which you have not as yet given, my friend, to the question: What is 'piety'? When asked, you only replied, Doing as you do, charging your father with murder.

EUTHYPHRO: And what I said was true, Socrates.

SOCRATES: No doubt, Euthyphro; but you would admit that there are many other pious acts?

EUTHYPHRO: There are.

SOCRATES: Remember that I did not ask you to give me two or three examples of piety, but to explain the general idea which makes all pious things to be pious. Do you not recollect that there was one idea which made the impious impious, and the pious pious?

EUTHYPHRO: I remember.

SOCRATES: Tell me what is the nature of this idea, and then I shall have a standard to which I may look, and by which I may measure actions, whether yours or those of any one else, and then I shall be able to say that such and such an action is pious, such another impious.

EUTHYPHRO: I will tell you, if you like.

SOCRATES: I should very much like.

EUTHYPHRO: Piety, then, is that which is dear to the gods, and impiety is that which is not dear to them.

SOCRATES: Very good, Euthyphro; you have now given me the sort of answer which I wanted. But whether what you say is true or not I cannot as yet tell, although I make no doubt that you will prove the truth of your words.

EUTHYPHRO: Of course.

SOCRATES: Come, then, and let us examine what we are saying. That thing or person which is dear to the gods is pious, and that thing or person which is hateful to the gods is impious, these two being the extreme opposites of one another. Was not that said?

EUTHYPHRO: It was.

SOCRATES: And well said?

EUTHYPHRO: Yes, Socrates, I thought so; it was certainly said.

SOCRATES: And further, Euthyphro, the gods were admitted to have enmities and hatreds and differences?

EUTHYPHRO: Yes, that was also said.

SOCRATES: And what sort of difference creates enmity and anger? Suppose for example that you and I, my good friend, differ about a number; do differences of this sort make us enemies and set us at variance with one another? Do we not go at once to arithmetic, and put an end to them by a sum?

EUTHYPHRO: True.

SOCRATES: Or suppose that we differ about magnitudes, do we not quickly end the differences by measuring?

EUTHYPHRO: Very true.

SOCRATES: And we end a controversy about heavy and light by resorting to a weighing machine?

EUTHYPHRO: To be sure.

SOCRATES: But what differences are there which cannot be thus decided, and which therefore make us angry and set us at enmity with one another? I dare say the answer does not occur to you at the moment, and therefore I will suggest that these enmities arise when the matters of difference are the just and unjust, good and evil, honorable and dishonorable. Are not these the points about which men differ, and about which when we are unable satisfactorily to decide our differences, you and I and all of us quarrel, when we do quarrel?

EUTHYPHRO: Yes, Socrates, the nature of the differences about which we quarrel is such as you describe.

SOCRATES: And the quarrels of the gods, noble Euthyphro, when they occur, are of a like nature?

EUTHYPHRO: Certainly they are.

SOCRATES: They have differences of opinion, as you say, about good and evil, just and unjust, honorable and dishonorable: there would have been no quarrels among them, if there had been no such differences—would there now?

EUTHYPHRO: You are quite right.

SOCRATES: Does not every man love that which he deems noble and just and good, and hate the opposite of them?

EUTHYPHRO: Very true.

SOCRATES: But, as you say, people regard the same things, some as just and others as unjust,—about these they dispute; and so there arise wars and fighting among them.

EUTHYPHRO: Very true.

SOCRATES: Then the same things are hated by the gods and loved by the gods, and are both hateful and dear to them?

EUTHYPHRO: True.

SOCRATES: And upon this view the same things, Euthyphro, will be pious and also impious?

EUTHYPHRO: So I should suppose.

SOCRATES: Then, my friend, I remark with surprise that you have not answered the question which I asked. For I certainly did not ask you to tell me what action is both pious and impious: but now it would seem that what is loved by the gods is also hated by them. And therefore, Euthyphro, in thus chastising your father you may very likely be doing what is agreeable to Zeus but disagreeable to Cronos or Uranus, and what is acceptable to Hephaestus but unacceptable to Hera, and there may be other gods who have similar differences of opinion.

EUTHYPHRO: But I believe, Socrates, that all the gods would be agreed as to the propriety of punishing a murderer: there would be no difference of opinion about that.

SOCRATES: Well, but speaking of men, Euthyphro, did you ever hear any one arguing that a murderer or any sort of evil-doer ought to be let off?

EUTHYPHRO: I should rather say that these are the questions which they are always arguing, especially in courts of law: they commit all sorts of crimes, and there is nothing which they will not do or say in their own defense.

SOCRATES: But do they admit their guilt, Euthyphro, and yet say that they ought not to be punished?

EUTHYPHRO: No; they do not.

SOCRATES: Then there are some things which they do not venture to say and do: for they do not venture to argue that the guilty are to be unpunished, but they deny their guilt, do they not?

EUTHYPHRO: Yes.

SOCRATES: Then they do not argue that the evil-doer should not be punished, but they argue about the fact of who the evil-doer is, and what he did and when?

EUTHYPHRO: True.

SOCRATES: And the gods are in the same case, if as you assert they quarrel about just and unjust, and some of them say while others deny that injustice is done among them. For surely neither God nor man will ever venture to say that the doer of injustice is not to be punished?

EUTHYPHRO: That is true, Socrates, in the main.

SOCRATES: But they join issue about the particulars—gods and men alike; and, if they dispute at all, they dispute about some act which is called in question, and which by some is affirmed to be just, by others to be unjust. Is not that true?

EUTHYPHRO: Quite true.

SOCRATES: Well then, my dear friend Euthyphro, do tell me, for my better instruction and information, what proof have you that in the opinion of all the gods a servant who is guilty of murder, and is put in chains by the master of the dead man, and dies because he is put in chains before he who bound him can learn from the interpreters of the gods what he ought to do with him, dies unjustly; and that on behalf of such an one a son ought to proceed against his father and accuse him of murder. How would you show that all the gods absolutely agree in approving of his act? Prove to me that they do, and I will applaud your wisdom as long as I live.

EUTHYPHRO: It will be a difficult task; but I could make the matter very clear indeed to you.

SOCRATES: I understand; you mean to say that I am not so quick of apprehension as the judges: for to them you will be sure to prove that the act is unjust, and hateful to the gods.

EUTHYPHRO: Yes indeed, Socrates; at least if they will listen to me.

SOCRATES: But they will be sure to listen if they find that you are a good speaker. There was a notion that came into my mind while you were speaking; I said to myself: 'Well, and what if Euthyphro does prove to me that all the gods regarded the death of the serf as unjust, how do I know anything more of the nature of piety and impiety? for granting that this action may be hateful to the gods, still piety and impiety are not adequately defined by these distinctions, for that which is hateful to the gods has been shown to be also pleasing and dear to them.' And therefore, Euthyphro, I do not ask you to prove this; I will suppose, if you like, that all the gods condemn and abominate such an action. But I will amend the definition so far as to say that what all the gods hate is impious, and what they love pious or holy; and what some of them love and others hate is both or neither. Shall this be our definition of piety and impiety?

EUTHYPHRO: Why not, Socrates?

SOCRATES: Why not! certainly, as far as I am concerned, Euthyphro, there is no reason why not. But whether this admission will greatly assist you in the task of instructing me as you promised, is a matter for you to consider.

EUTHYPHRO: Yes, I should say that what all the gods love is pious and holy, and the opposite which they all hate, impious.

SOCRATES: Ought we to enquire into the truth of this, Euthyphro, or simply to accept the mere statement on our own authority and that of others? What do you say?

EUTHYPHRO: We should enquire; and I believe that the statement will stand the test of enquiry.

SOCRATES: We shall know better, my good friend, in a little while. The point which I should first wish to understand is whether the pious or holy is beloved by the gods because it is holy, or holy because it is beloved of the gods.

EUTHYPHRO: I do not understand your meaning, Socrates.

SOCRATES: I will endeavor to explain: we, speak of carrying and we speak of being carried, of leading and being led, seeing and being seen. You know that in all such cases there is a difference, and you know also in what the difference lies?

EUTHYPHRO: I think that I understand.

SOCRATES: And is not that which is beloved distinct from that which loves?

EUTHYPHRO: Certainly.

SOCRATES: Well; and now tell me, is that which is carried in this state of carrying because it is carried, or for some other reason?

EUTHYPHRO: No; that is the reason.

SOCRATES: And the same is true of what is led and of what is seen?

EUTHYPHRO: True.

SOCRATES: And a thing is not seen because it is visible, but conversely, visible because it is seen; nor is a thing led because it is in the state of being led, or carried because it is in the state of being carried, but the converse of this. And now I think, Euthyphro, that my meaning will be intelligible; and my meaning is, that any state of action or passion implies previous action or passion. It does not become because it is becoming, but it is in a state of becoming because it becomes; neither does it suffer because it is in a state of suffering, but it is in a state of suffering because it suffers. Do you not agree?

EUTHYPHRO: Yes.

SOCRATES: Is not that which is loved in some state either of becoming or suffering?

EUTHYPHRO: Yes.

SOCRATES: And the same holds as in the previous instances; the state of being loved follows the act of being loved, and not the act the state.

EUTHYPHRO: Certainly.

SOCRATES: And what do you say of piety, Euthyphro: is not piety, according to your definition, loved by all the gods?

EUTHYPHRO: Yes.

SOCRATES: Because it is pious or holy, or for some other reason?

EUTHYPHRO: No, that is the reason.

SOCRATES: It is loved because it is holy, not holy because it is loved?

EUTHYPHRO: Yes.

SOCRATES: And that which is dear to the gods is loved by them, and is in a state to be loved of them because it is loved of them?

EUTHYPHRO: Certainly.

SOCRATES: Then that which is dear to the gods, Euthyphro, is not holy, nor is that which is holy loved of God, as you affirm; but they are two different things.

EUTHYPHRO: How do you mean, Socrates?

SOCRATES: I mean to say that the holy has been acknowledged by us to be loved of God because it is holy, not to be holy because it is loved.

EUTHYPHRO: Yes.

SOCRATES: But that which is dear to the gods is dear to them because it is loved by them, not loved by them because it is dear to them.

EUTHYPHRO: True.

SOCRATES: But, friend Euthyphro, if that which is holy is the same with that which is dear to God, and is loved because it is holy, then that which is dear to God would have been loved as being dear to God; but if that which is dear to God is dear to him because loved by him, then that which is holy would have been holy because loved by him. But now you see that the reverse is the case, and that they are quite different from one another. For one (i.e., *theophiles*) is of a kind to be loved cause it is loved, and the other (i.e., *osion*) is loved because it is of a kind to be loved. Thus you appear to me, Euthyphro, when I ask you what is the essence of holiness, to offer an attribute only, and not the essence—the attribute of being loved by all the gods. But you still refuse to explain to me the nature of holiness. And therefore, if you please, I will ask you not to hide your treasure, but to tell me once more what holiness or piety really is, whether dear to the gods or not (for that is a matter about which we will not quarrel); and what is impiety?

EUTHYPHRO: I really do not know, Socrates, how to express what I mean. For somehow or other our arguments, on whatever ground we rest them, seem to turn round and walk away from us.

SOCRATES: Your words, Euthyphro, are like the handiwork of my ancestor Daedalus; and if I were the sayer or propounder of them, you might say that my arguments walk away and will not remain fixed where they are placed because I am a descendant of his. But now, since these notions are your own, you must find some other gibe, for they certainly, as you yourself allow, show an inclination to be on the move.

EUTHYPHRO: Nay, Socrates, I shall still say that you are the Daedalus who sets arguments in motion; not I, certainly, but you make them move or go round, for they would never have stirred, as far as I am concerned.

SOCRATES: Then I must be a greater than Daedalus: for whereas he only made his own inventions to move,

I move those of other people as well. And the beauty of it is, that I would rather not. For I would give the wisdom of Daedalus, and the wealth of Tantalus, to be able to detain them and keep them fixed. But enough of this. As I perceive that you are lazy, I will myself endeavor to show you how you might instruct me in the nature of piety; and I hope that you will not grudge your labor. Tell me, then—Is not that which is pious necessarily just?

EUTHYPHRO: Yes.

SOCRATES: And is, then, all which is just pious? Or is that which is pious all just, but that which is just, only in part and not all, pious?

EUTHYPHRO: I do not understand you, Socrates.

SOCRATES: And yet I know that you are as much wiser than I am, as you are younger. But, as I was saying, revered friend, the abundance of your wisdom makes you lazy. Please to exert yourself, for there is no real difficulty in understanding me. What I mean I may explain by an illustration of what I do not mean. The poet [Stasinus] sings—

"Of Zeus, the author and creator of all these things, You will not tell: for where there is fear there is also reverence."

Now I disagree with this poet. Shall I tell you in what respect?

EUTHYPHRO: By all means.

SOCRATES: I should not say that where there is fear there is also reverence; for I am sure that many persons fear poverty and disease, and the like evils, but I do not perceive that they reverence the objects of their fear.

EUTHYPHRO: Very true.

SOCRATES: But where reverence is, there is fear; for he who has a feeling of reverence and shame about the commission of any action, fears and is afraid of an ill reputation.

EUTHYPHRO: No doubt.

SOCRATES: Then we are wrong in saying that where there is fear there is also reverence; and we should say, where there is reverence there is also fear. But there is not always reverence where there is fear; for fear is a more extended notion, and reverence is a part of fear, just as the odd is a part of number, and number is a more extended notion than the odd. I suppose that you follow me now?

EUTHYPHRO: Quite well.

SOCRATES: That was the sort of question which I meant to raise when I asked whether the just is always the pious, or the pious always the just; and whether there may not be justice where there is not piety; for justice is the more extended notion of which piety is only a part. Do you dissent?

EUTHYPHRO: No, I think that you are quite right.

SOCRATES: Then, if piety is a part of justice, I suppose that we should enquire what part? If you had pursued the enquiry in the previous cases; for instance, if you had asked me what is an even number, and what part of number the even is, I should have had no difficulty in replying, a number which represents a figure having two equal sides. Do you not agree?

EUTHYPHRO: Yes, I quite agree.

SOCRATES: In like manner, I want you to tell me what part of justice is piety or holiness, that I may be able to tell Meletus not to do me injustice, or indict me for impiety, as I am now adequately instructed by you in the nature of piety or holiness, and their opposites.

EUTHYPHRO: Piety or holiness, Socrates, appears to me to be that part of justice which attends to the gods, as there is the other part of justice which attends to men.

SOCRATES: That is good, Euthyphro; yet still there is a little point about which I should like to have further information: What is the meaning of "attention"? For attention can hardly be used in the same sense when applied to the gods as when applied to other things. For instance, horses are said to require attention, and not every person is able to attend to them, but only a person skilled in horsemanship. Is it not so?

EUTHYPHRO: Certainly.

SOCRATES: I should suppose that the art of horsemanship is the art of attending to horses?

EUTHYPHRO: Yes.

SOCRATES: Nor is every one qualified to attend to dogs, but only the huntsman?

EUTHYPHRO: True.

SOCRATES: And I should also conceive that the art of the huntsman is the art of attending to dogs?

EUTHYPHRO: Yes.

SOCRATES: As the art of the ox-herd is the art of attending to oxen?

EUTHYPHRO: Very true.

SOCRATES: In like manner holiness or piety is the art of attending to the gods?—that would be your meaning, Euthyphro?

EUTHYPHRO: Yes.

SOCRATES: And is not attention always designed for the good or benefit of that to which the attention is given? As in the case of horses, you may observe that when attended to by the horseman's art they are benefited and improved, are they not?

EUTHYPHRO: True.

SOCRATES: As the dogs are benefited by the huntsman's art, and the oxen by the art of the ox-herd, and all other things are tended or attended for their good and not for their hurt?

EUTHYPHRO: Certainly, not for their hurt.

SOCRATES: But for their good?

EUTHYPHRO: Of course.

SOCRATES: And does piety or holiness, which has been defined to be the art of attending to the gods, benefit or improve them? Would you say that when you do a holy act you make any of the gods better?

EUTHYPHRO: No, no; that was certainly not what I meant.

SOCRATES: And I, Euthyphro, never supposed that you did. I asked you the question about the nature of the attention, because I thought that you did not.

EUTHYPHRO: You do me justice, Socrates; that is not the sort of attention which I mean.

SOCRATES: Good: but I must still ask: what is this attention to the gods which is called piety?

EUTHYPHRO: It is such, Socrates, as servants show to their masters.

SOCRATES: I understand—a sort of ministration to the gods.

EUTHYPHRO: Exactly.

SOCRATES: Medicine is also a sort of ministration or service, having in view the attainment of some object—would you not say of health?

EUTHYPHRO: I should.

SOCRATES: Again, there is an art which ministers to the ship-builder with a view to the attainment of some result?

EUTHYPHRO: Yes, Socrates, with a view to the building of a ship.

SOCRATES: As there is an art which ministers to the house-builder with a view to the building of a house?

EUTHYPHRO: Yes.

SOCRATES: And now tell me, my good friend, about the art which ministers to the gods: what work does that help to accomplish? For you must surely know if, as you say, you are of all men living the one who is best instructed in religion.

EUTHYPHRO: And I speak the truth, Socrates.

SOCRATES: Tell me then, oh tell me—what is that fair work which the gods do by the help of our ministrations?

EUTHYPHRO: Many and fair, Socrates, are the works which they do.

SOCRATES: Why, my friend, and so are those of a general. But the chief of them is easily told. Would you not say that victory in war is the chief of them?

EUTHYPHRO: Certainly.

SOCRATES: Many and fair, too, are the works of the husbandman, if I am not mistaken; but his chief work is the production of food from the earth?

EUTHYPHRO: Exactly.

SOCRATES: And of the many and fair things done by the gods, which is the chief or principal one?

EUTHYPHRO: I have told you already, Socrates, that to learn all these things accurately will be very tiresome. Let me simply say that piety or holiness is learning how to please the gods in word and deed, by prayers and sacrifices. Such piety is the salvation of families and states, just as the impious, which is unpleasing to the gods, is their ruin and destruction.

SOCRATES: I think that you could have answered in much fewer words the chief question which I asked, Euthyphro, if you had chosen. But I see plainly that you are not disposed to instruct me—clearly not: else why, when we reached the point, did you turn aside? Had you only answered me I should have truly learned of you by this time the nature of piety. Now, as the asker of a question is necessarily dependent on the answerer, whither he leads I must follow; and can only ask again, what is the pious, and what is piety? Do you mean that they are a sort of science of praying and sacrificing?

EUTHYPHRO: Yes, I do.

SOCRATES: And sacrificing is giving to the gods, and prayer is asking of the gods?

EUTHYPHRO: Yes, Socrates.

SOCRATES: Upon this view, then, piety is a science of asking and giving?

EUTHYPHRO: You understand me capitally, Socrates.

SOCRATES: Yes, my friend; the reason is that I am a votary of your science, and give my mind to it, and therefore nothing which you say will be thrown away upon me. Please then to tell me, what is the nature of this service to the gods? Do you mean that we prefer requests and give gifts to them?

EUTHYPHRO: Yes, I do.

SOCRATES: Is not the right way of asking to ask of them what we want?

EUTHYPHRO: Certainly.

SOCRATES: And the right way of giving is to give to them in return what they want of us. There would be no meaning in an art which gives to any one that which he does not want.

EUTHYPHRO: Very true, Socrates.

SOCRATES: Then piety, Euthyphro, is an art which gods and men have of doing business with one another?

EUTHYPHRO: That is an expression which you may use, if you like.

SOCRATES: But I have no particular liking for anything but the truth. I wish, however, that you would tell me what benefit accrues to the gods from our gifts. There is no doubt about what they give to us; for there is no good thing which they do not give; but how we can give any good thing to them in return is far from being equally clear. If they give everything and we give nothing, that must be an affair of business in which we have very greatly the advantage of them.

EUTHYPHRO: And do you imagine, Socrates, that any benefit accrues to the gods from our gifts?

SOCRATES: But if not, Euthyphro, what is the meaning of gifts which are conferred by us upon the gods?

EUTHYPHRO: What else, but tributes of honor; and, as I was just now saying, what pleases them?

SOCRATES: Piety, then, is pleasing to the gods, but not beneficial or dear to them?

EUTHYPHRO: I should say that nothing could be dearer.

SOCRATES: Then once more the assertion is repeated that piety is dear to the gods?

EUTHYPHRO: Certainly.

SOCRATES: And when you say this, can you wonder at your words not standing firm, but walking away? Will you accuse me of being the Daedalus who makes them walk away, not perceiving that there is another and far greater artist than Daedalus who makes them go round in a circle, and he is yourself; for the argument, as you will perceive, comes round to the same point. Were we not saying that the holy or pious was not the same with that which is loved of the gods? Have you forgotten?

EUTHYPHRO: I quite remember.

SOCRATES: And are you not saying that what is loved of the gods is holy; and is not this the same as what is dear to them—do you see?

EUTHYPHRO: True.

SOCRATES: Then either we were wrong in our former assertion; or, if we were right then, we are wrong now.

EUTHYPHRO: One of the two must be true.

SOCRATES: Then we must begin again and ask: What is piety? That is an enquiry which I shall never be weary of pursuing as far as in me lies; and I entreat you not to scorn me, but to apply your mind to the utmost, and tell me the truth. For, if any man knows, you are he; and therefore I must detain you, like Proteus, until you tell. If you had not certainly known the nature of piety and impiety, I am confident that you would never, on behalf of a serf, have charged your aged father with murder. You would not have run such a risk of doing wrong in the sight of the gods, and you would have had too much respect for the opinions of men. I am sure, therefore, that you know the nature of piety and impiety. Speak out then, my dear Euthyphro, and do not hide your knowledge.

EUTHYPHRO: Another time, Socrates; for I am in a hurry, and must go now.

SOCRATES: Alas! My companion, and will you leave me in despair? I was hoping that you would instruct me in the nature of piety and impiety; and then I might have cleared myself of Meletus and his indictment. I would have told him that I had been enlightened by Euthyphro, and had given up rash innovations and speculations, in which I indulged only through ignorance, and that now I am about to lead a better life.

[The Dialogues of Plato. Trans. By Benjamin Jowett (London: Macmillan, 1891).]

Apology

Plato

(Translated by Benjamin Jowett and edited by Joseph R. Kirkland)

PERSONS OF THE DIALOGUE: Socrates, Meletus
SCENE: The Trial of Socrates

SOCRATES: How you, O Athenians, have been affected by my accusers, I cannot tell; but I know that they almost made me forget who I was—so persuasively did they speak; and yet they have hardly uttered a word of truth. But of the many falsehoods told by them, there was one which quite amazed me;—I mean when they said that you should be upon your guard and not allow yourselves to be deceived by the force of my eloquence. To say this, when they were certain to be detected as soon as I opened my lips and proved myself to be anything but a great speaker, did indeed appear to me most shameless—unless by the force of eloquence they mean the force of truth; for if such is their meaning, I admit that I am eloquent. But in how different a way from theirs! Well, as I was saying, they have scarcely spoken the truth at all; but from me you shall hear the whole truth: not, however, delivered after their manner in a set oration duly ornamented with words and phrases. No, by heaven! but I shall use the words and arguments which occur to me at the moment; for I am confident in the justice of my cause (Or, I am certain that I am right in taking this course.): at my age I ought not to be appearing before you, O men of Athens, in the character of a juvenile orator—let no one expect it of me. And I must beg of you to grant me a favor:—If I defend myself in my accustomed manner, and you hear me using the words which I have been in the habit of using in the agora, at the tables of the money-changers, or anywhere else, I would ask you not to be surprised, and not to interrupt me on this account. For I am more than seventy years of age, and appearing now for the first time in a court of law, I am quite a stranger to the language of the place; and therefore I would have you regard me as if I were really a stranger, whom you would excuse if he spoke in his native tongue, and after the fashion of his country:— Am I making an unfair request of you? Never mind the manner, which may or may not be good; but think only of the truth of my words, and give heed to that: let the speaker speak truly and the judge decide justly.

And first, I have to reply to the older charges and to my first accusers, and then I will go on to the later ones. For of old I have had many accusers, who have accused me falsely to you during many years; and I am more afraid of them than of Anytus and his associates, who are dangerous, too, in their own way. But far more dangerous are the others, who began when you were children, and took possession of your minds with their falsehoods, telling of one Socrates, a wise man, who speculated about the heaven above, and searched into the earth beneath, and made the worse appear the better cause. The disseminators of this tale are the accusers whom I dread; for their hearers are apt to fancy that such enquirers do not believe in the existence of the gods. And they are many, and their charges against me are of ancient date, and they were made by them in the days when you were more impressible than you are now—in childhood, or it may have been in youth— and the cause when heard went by default, for there was none to answer. And hardest of all, I do not know and cannot tell the names of my accusers; unless in the chance case of a Comic poet. All who from envy and malice have persuaded you—some of them having first convinced themselves—all this class of men are most difficult to deal with; for I cannot have them up here, and cross-examine them, and therefore I must simply fight with shadows in my own defense, and argue when there is no one who answers. I will ask you then to assume with me, as I was saying, that my opponents are of two kinds; one recent, the other ancient: and I hope that you will see the propriety of my answering the latter first, for these accusations you heard long before the others, and much oftener.

Well, then, I must make my defense, and endeavor to clear away in a short time, a slander which has lasted a long time. May I succeed, if to succeed be for my good and yours, or likely to avail me in my cause! The task is not an easy one; I quite understand the nature of it. And so leaving the outcome with the god, in obedience to the law I will now make my defense.

I will begin at the beginning, and ask: what is the accusation which has given rise to the slander of me, and in fact has encouraged Meletus to level this charge against me? Well, what do the slanderers say? They shall be my prosecutors, and I will sum up their words in an affidavit: 'Socrates is an evil-doer, and a curious person, who searches into things under the earth and in heaven, and he makes the worse appear the better cause; and he teaches the aforesaid doctrines to others.' Such is the nature of the accusation: it is just what you have yourselves seen in the comedy of Aristophanes who has introduced a character whom he calls Socrates, going about and saying that he walks in air, and talking a deal of nonsense concerning matters of which I do not pretend to know either much or little—not that I mean to speak disparagingly of any one who is a student of natural philosophy. I should be very sorry if Meletus could bring so grave a charge against me. But the simple truth is, O Athenians, that I have nothing to do with physical speculations. Very many of those here present are witnesses to the truth of this, and to them I appeal. Speak then, you who have heard me, and tell your neighbors whether any of you have ever known me to hold forth in few words or in many upon such matters.

[The crowd is silent.]

You hear their answer. And from what they say of this part of the charge you will be able to judge of the truth of the rest.

There is as little foundation for the report that I am a teacher and take money [i.e., a sophist]; this accusation has no more truth in it than the other. Although, if a man were really able to instruct mankind, to receive money for giving instruction would, in my opinion, be an honor to him. There is Gorgias of Leontium, and Prodicus of Ceos, and Hippias of Elis, who travel to all of the cities, and are able to persuade the young men to leave their own citizens by whom they might be taught for nothing, and come to them whom they not only pay, but are thankful if they may be allowed to pay them. There is at this time a Parian philosopher residing in Athens, of whom I have heard; and I came to hear of him in this way:—I came across a man who has spent a world of money on the Sophists, namely Callias, the son of Hipponicus, and knowing that he had sons, I asked him: "Callias," I said, "if your two sons were foals or calves, there would be no difficulty in finding someone to put over them; we should hire a trainer of horses, or a farmer probably, who would improve and perfect them in their own proper virtue and excellence; but as they are human beings, whom are you thinking of placing over them? Is there anyone who understands human and political virtue? You must

have thought about the matter, for you have sons; is there any one?" "There is," he said. "Who is he?" said I; "and of what country? and what does he charge?" "Evenus the Parian," he replied; "he is the man, and his charge is five minae." Happy is Evenus, I said to myself, if he really has this wisdom, and teaches at such a moderate charge. Had I the same, I should have been very proud and conceited; but the truth is that I have no knowledge of the kind.

I dare say, Athenians, that someone among you will reply, "Yes, Socrates, but what is the origin of these accusations which are brought against you; there must have been something strange which you have been doing? All these rumors and this talk about you would never have arisen if you had been like other men: tell us, then, what is the cause of them, for we should be sorry to judge hastily of you." Now I regard this as a fair challenge, and I will endeavor to explain to you the reason why I am called wise and have such an evil reputation. Please pay attention, then. And although some of you may think that I am joking, I declare that I will tell you the entire truth. Men of Athens, this reputation of mine has come of a certain sort of wisdom which I possess. If you ask me what kind of wisdom, I reply, wisdom such as may perhaps be attained by man, for to that extent I am inclined to believe that I am wise; whereas the persons of whom I was speaking have a superhuman wisdom which I may fail to describe, because I have it not myself; and he who says that I have, speaks falsely, and is taking away my character. And here, O men of Athens, I must beg you not to interrupt me, even if I seem to say something extravagant. For the word which I will speak is not mine. I will refer you to a witness who is worthy of credit; that witness shall be [Apollo] the god of Delphi—he will tell you about my wisdom, if I have any, and of what sort it is. You must have known Chaerephon; he was early a friend of mine, and also a friend of yours, for he shared in the recent exile of the people, and returned with you. Well, Chaerephon, as you know, was very impetuous in all his doings, and he went to Delphi and boldly asked the oracle to tell him whether—as I was saying, I must beg you not to interrupt—he asked the oracle to tell him whether anyone was wiser than I was, and the Pythian prophetess answered that there was no man wiser. Chaerephon is dead himself; but his brother, who is in court, will confirm the truth of what I am saying.

Why do I mention this? Because I am going to explain to you why I have such an evil reputation. When I heard the answer, I said to myself, "What can the god mean? And what is the interpretation of his riddle? For I know that I have no wisdom, small or great. What then can he mean when he says that I am the wisest of men? And yet he is a god, and cannot lie; that would be against his nature." After long consideration, I thought of a method of trying the question. I reflected that if I could only find a man wiser than myself, then I might go to the god with a refutation in my hand. I should say to him, "Here is a man who is wiser than I am; but you said that I was the wisest." Accordingly I went to one who had the reputation of wisdom, and observed him—his name I need not mention; he was a politician whom I selected for examination—and the result was as follows: When I began to talk with him, I could not help thinking that he was not really wise, although he was thought wise by many, and still wiser by himself; and thereupon I tried to explain to him that he thought himself wise, but was not really wise; and the consequence was that he hated me, and his enmity was shared by several who were present and heard me. So I left him, saying to myself, as I went away: Well, although I do not suppose that either of us knows anything [about what is] really beautiful and good, I am better off than he is,—for he knows nothing, and thinks that he knows; I neither know nor think that I know. In this latter particular, then, I seem to have slightly the advantage of him. Then I went to another who had still higher pretensions to wisdom, and my conclusion was exactly the same. Whereupon I made another enemy of him, and of many others besides him.

Then I went to one man after another, being not unconscious of the enmity which I provoked, and I lamented and feared this: but necessity was laid upon me,—the word of the god, I thought, ought to be considered first. And I said to myself, Go I must to all who appear to know, and find out the meaning of the oracle. And I swear to you, Athenians, by the dog I swear!—for I must tell you the truth—the result of my mission was just this: I found that the men most in repute were all but the most foolish; and that others less esteemed were really wiser and better. I will tell you the tale of my wanderings and of the 'Herculean' labors, as I may call them, which I endured only to find at last the oracle irrefutable. After the politicians, I went to the poets; tragic, dithyrambic, and all sorts. And there, I said to myself, you will be instantly detected; now you will find out that you are more ignorant than they are. Accordingly, I took them some of the most elaborate passages in their own writings, and asked what was the meaning of them—thinking that

they would teach me something. Will you believe me? I am almost ashamed to confess the truth, but I must say that there is hardly a person present who would not have talked better about their poetry than they did themselves. Then I knew that not by wisdom do poets write poetry, but by a sort of genius and inspiration; they are like diviners or soothsayers who also say many fine things, but do not understand the meaning of them. The poets appeared to me to be much in the same case; and I further observed that upon the strength of their poetry they believed themselves to be the wisest of men in other things in which they were not wise. So I departed, conceiving myself to be superior to them for the same reason that I was superior to the politicians.

At last I went to the artisans. I was conscious that I knew nothing at all, as I may say, and I was sure that they knew many fine things; and here I was not mistaken, for they did know many things of which I was ignorant, and in this they certainly were wiser than I was. But I observed that even the good artisans fell into the same error as the poets;—because they were good workmen they thought that they also knew all sorts of high matters, and this defect in them overshadowed their wisdom; and therefore I asked myself on behalf of the oracle, whether I would like to be as I was, neither having their knowledge nor their ignorance, or like them in both; and I made answer to myself and to the oracle that I was better off as I was.

This inquisition has led to my having many enemies of the worst and most dangerous kind, and has led also to much slander. And I am called wise, for my hearers always imagine that I myself possess the wisdom which I find wanting in others: but the truth is, O men of Athens, that the god only is wise; and by his answer he intends to show that the wisdom of men is worth little or nothing; he is not speaking of Socrates, he is only using my name by way of illustration, as if he said, "He, O men, is the wisest, who, like Socrates, knows that his wisdom is in truth worth nothing." And so I go about the world, obedient to the god, and search and make enquiry into the wisdom of anyone, whether citizen or stranger, who appears to be wise; and if he is not wise, then in vindication of the oracle I show him that he is not wise; and my occupation quite absorbs me, and I have no time to give either to any public matter of interest or to any concern of my own, indeed I am in utter poverty by reason of my devotion to the god.

There is another thing:—young men of the richer classes, who have not much to do, come about me of their own accord; they like to hear the pretenders examined, and they often imitate me, and proceed to examine others; there are plenty of persons, as they quickly discover, who think that they know something, but really know little or nothing; and then those who are examined by them instead of being angry with themselves are angry with me: This confounded Socrates, they say; this villainous misleader of youth!—and then if somebody asks them, Why, what evil does he practice or teach? they do not know, and cannot tell; but in order that they may not appear to be at a loss, they repeat the ready-made charges which are used against all philosophers about teaching things up in the clouds and under the earth, and having no gods, and making the worse appear the better cause; for they do not like to confess that their pretense of knowledge has been detected—which is the truth; and as they are numerous and ambitious and energetic, and are drawn up in battle array and have persuasive tongues, they have filled your ears with their loud and inveterate slander. And this is the reason why my three accusers, Meletus and Anytus and Lycon, have set upon me; Meletus, who has a quarrel with me on behalf of the poets; Anytus, on behalf of the craftsmen and politicians; Lycon, on behalf of the rhetoricians: and as I said at the beginning, I cannot expect to get rid of such a mass of slander all in a moment. And this, O men of Athens, is the truth and the whole truth; I have concealed nothing, I have dissembled nothing. And yet, I know that my plainness of speech makes them hate me, and what is their hatred but a proof that I am speaking the truth?— Hence has arisen the prejudice against me; and this is the reason of it, as you will find out either in this or in any future enquiry.

I have said enough in my defense against the first class of my accusers; I turn to the second class. They are headed by Meletus, that good man and true lover of his country, as he calls himself. Against these, too, I must try to make a defense:—Let their affidavit be read: it contains something of this kind: It says that Socrates is a doer of evil, who corrupts the youth; and who does not believe in the gods of the state, but has other new divinities of his own. Such is the charge; and now let us examine the particular counts. He says that I am a doer of evil and corrupt the youth; but I say, O men of Athens, that Meletus is a doer of evil, in that he pretends to be in earnest when he is only in jest, and is so eager to bring men to trial from a pretended zeal and interest about matters in which he really never had the smallest interest. And the truth of this I will endeavor to prove to you.

Come hither, Meletus, and let me ask a question of you. You think a great deal about the improvement of youth?

Meletus: Yes, I do.

Socrates: Tell the judges, then, who is their improver; for you must know, as you have taken the pains to discover their corrupter, and are citing and accusing me before them. Speak, then, and tell the judges who their improver is.—Observe, Meletus, that you are silent, and have nothing to say. But is not this rather disgraceful, and a very considerable proof of what I was saying, that you have no interest in the matter? Speak up, friend, and tell us who their improver is.

MELETUS: The laws.

SOCRATES: But that, my good sir, is not my meaning. I want to know who the person is, who, in the first place, knows the laws.

MELETUS: The judges, Socrates, who are present in court.

SOCRATES: What, do you mean to say, Meletus, that they are able to instruct and improve youth?

MELETUS: Certainly they are.

SOCRATES: What, all of them, or some only and not others?

MELETUS: All of them.

SOCRATES: By the goddess Hera, that is good news! There are plenty of improvers, then. And what do you say of the audience,—do they improve them?

MELETUS: Yes, they do.

SOCRATES: And the senators?

MELETUS: Yes, the senators improve them.

SOCRATES: But perhaps the members of the assembly corrupt them?—or do they too improve them?

MELETUS: They improve them.

Then every Athenian improves and elevates them; all with the exception of myself; and I alone am their corrupter? Is that what you affirm?

MELETUS: That is what I stoutly affirm.

SOCRATES: I am very unfortunate if you are right. But suppose I ask you a question: How about horses? Does one man do them harm and all the world good?

Is not the exact opposite the truth? One man is able to do them good, or at least not many;—the trainer of horses, that is to say, does them good, and others who have to do with them rather injure them? Is not that true, Meletus, of horses, or of any other animals? Most assuredly it is; whether you and Anytus say yes or no. Happy indeed would be the condition of youth if they had one corrupter only, and all the rest of the world were their improvers. But you, Meletus, have sufficiently shown that you never had a thought about the young: your carelessness is seen in your not caring about the very things which you bring against me.

And now, Meletus, I will ask you another question—by Zeus I will: Which is better, to live among bad citizens, or among good ones? Answer, friend, I say; the question is one which may be easily answered. Do not the good do their neighbors good, and the bad do them evil?

MELETUS: Certainly.

SOCRATES: And is there anyone who would rather be injured than benefited by those who live with him? Answer, my good friend, the law requires you to answer—does anyone like to be injured?

MELETUS: Certainly not.

SOCRATES: And when you accuse me of corrupting and deteriorating the youth, do you allege that I corrupt them intentionally or unintentionally?

MELETUS: Intentionally, I say.

SOCRATES: But you have just admitted that the good do their neighbors good, and the evil do them evil. Now, is that a truth which your superior wisdom has recognized thus early in life, and am I, at my age, in such darkness and ignorance as not to know that if a man with whom I have to live is corrupted by me, I am very likely to be harmed by him; and yet I corrupt him, and intentionally, too—so you say, although neither I nor any other human being is ever likely to be convinced by you. But either I do not corrupt them, or I corrupt them unintentionally; and on either view of the case you lie. If my offence is unintentional, the law has no cognizance of unintentional offences: you ought to have taken me privately, and warned and admonished me; for if I had been better advised, I should have left off doing what I only did unintentionally—no doubt I should; but you would have nothing to say to me and refused to teach me. And now you bring me up in this court, which is a place not of instruction, but of punishment.

It will be very clear to you, Athenians, as I was saying, that Meletus has no care at all, great or small, about the matter. But still I should like to know, Meletus, in what I am affirmed to corrupt the young. I suppose you mean, as I infer from your indictment, that I teach them not to acknowledge the gods which the state acknowledges, but some other new divinities or spiritual agencies in their stead. These are the lessons by which I corrupt the youth, as you say.

MELETUS: Yes, that I say emphatically.

SOCRATES: Then, by the gods, Meletus, of whom we are speaking, tell me and the court, in somewhat plainer terms, what you mean! for I do not as yet understand whether you affirm that I teach other men to acknowledge some gods, and therefore that I do believe in gods, and am not an entire atheist—this you do not lay to my charge,—but only you say that they are not the same gods which the city recognizes—the charge is that they are different gods. Or, do you mean that I am an atheist simply, and a teacher of atheism?

MELETUS: I mean the latter—that you are a complete atheist.

SOCRATES: What an extraordinary statement! Why do you think so, Meletus? Do you mean that I do not believe in the godhead of the sun or moon, like other men?

I assure you, judges, that he does not: for he says that the sun is stone, and the moon earth.

Friend Meletus, you think that you are accusing Anaxagoras: and you have but a bad opinion of the judges, if you fancy them illiterate to such a degree as not to know that these doctrines are found in the books of Anaxagoras the Clazomenian, which are full of them. And so, forsooth, the youth are said to be taught them by Socrates, when there are not unfrequently exhibitions of them at the theatre; and they might pay their money, and laugh at Socrates if he pretends to father these extraordinary views. And so, Meletus, you really think that I do not believe in any god?

MELETUS: I swear by Zeus that you believe absolutely in none at all.

SOCRATES: Nobody will believe you, Meletus, and I am pretty sure that you do not believe yourself. I cannot help thinking, men of Athens, that Meletus is reckless and impudent, and that he has written this indictment in a spirit of mere wantonness and youthful bravado. Has he not compounded a riddle, thinking to try me? He said to himself:—I shall see whether the wise Socrates will discover my facetious contradiction, or whether I shall be able to deceive him and the rest of them. For he certainly does appear to me to contradict himself in the indictment as much as if he said that Socrates is guilty of not believing in the gods, and yet of believing in them—but this is not like a person who is in earnest.

I should like you, O men of Athens, to join me in examining what I conceive to be his inconsistency; and do you, Meletus, answer. And I must remind the audience of my request that they would not make a disturbance if I speak in my accustomed manner:

Did ever man, Meletus, believe in the existence of human things, and not of human beings?

[Meletus protests.]

I wish, men of Athens, that he would answer, and not be always trying to get up an interruption. Did ever any man believe in horsemanship, and not in horses? Or in flute-playing, and not in flute-players? No, my friend; I will answer to you and to the court, as you refuse to answer for yourself. There is no man who ever did. But now please to answer the next question: Can a man believe in spiritual and divine agencies, and not in spirits or demigods?

MELETUS: He cannot.

SOCRATES: How lucky I am to have extracted that answer, by the assistance of the court! But then you swear in the indictment that I teach and believe in divine or spiritual agencies (new or old, no matter for that); at any rate, I believe in spiritual agencies,—so you say and swear in the affidavit; and yet if I believe in divine beings, how can I help believing in spirits or demigods;—must I not? To be sure I must; and therefore I may assume that your silence gives consent. Now what are spirits or demigods? Are they not either gods or the sons of gods?

MELETUS: Certainly they are.

SOCRATES: But this is what I call the facetious riddle invented by you: the demigods or spirits are gods, and you say first that I do not believe in gods, and then again that I do believe in gods; that is, if I believe in demigods. For if the demigods are the illegitimate sons of gods, whether by the nymphs or by any other mothers, of whom they are said to be the sons—what human being will ever believe that there are no gods if they are the sons of gods? You might as well affirm the existence of mules, and deny that of horses and asses. Such nonsense, Meletus, could only have been intended by you to make trial of me. You have put this into the indictment because you had nothing real of which to accuse me. But no one who has a particle of understanding will ever be convinced by you that the same men can believe in divine and superhuman things, and yet not believe that there are gods and demigods and heroes.

I have said enough in answer to the charge of Meletus: any elaborate defense is unnecessary, but I know only too well how many are the enmities which I have incurred, and this is what will be my destruction if I am destroyed;—not Meletus, nor yet Anytus, but the envy and detraction of the world, which has been the death of many good men, and will probably be the death of many more; there is no danger of my being the last of them.

Someone will say: And are you not ashamed, Socrates, of a course of life which is likely to bring you to an untimely end? To him I may fairly answer: There you are mistaken: a man who is good for anything ought not to calculate the chance of living or dying; he ought only to consider whether in doing anything he is doing right or wrong—acting the part of a good man or of a bad. Whereas, upon your view, the heroes who fell at Troy were not good for much, and the son of Thetis above all, who altogether despised danger in comparison with disgrace; and when he was so eager to slay Hector, his goddess mother said to him, that if he avenged his companion Patroclus, and slew Hector, he would die himself—'Fate,' she said, in these or the like words, 'waits for you next after Hector;' he, receiving this warning, utterly despised danger and death, and instead of fearing them, feared rather to live in dishonor, and not to avenge his friend. 'Let me die forthwith,' he replies, 'and be avenged of my enemy, rather than abide here by the beaked ships, a laughing-stock and a burden of the earth.' Had Achilles any thought of death and danger? For wherever a man's place is, whether the place which he has chosen or that in which he has been placed by a commander, there he ought to remain in the hour of danger; he should not think of death or of anything but of disgrace. And this, O men of Athens, is a true saying.

Strange, indeed, would be my conduct, O men of Athens, if I who, when I was ordered by the generals whom you chose to command me at Potidaea and Amphipolis and Delium, remained where they placed me, like any other man, facing death—if now, when, as I conceive and imagine, the god orders me to fulfil the philosopher's mission of searching into myself and other men, I were to desert my post through fear of death, or any other fear; that would indeed be strange, and I might justly be arraigned in court for denying the existence of the gods, if I disobeyed the oracle because I was afraid of death, fancying that I was wise when I was not wise. For the fear of death is indeed the pretense of wisdom, and not real wisdom, being a pretense of knowing the unknown; and no one knows whether death, which men in their fear apprehend to be the greatest evil, may not be the greatest good. Is not this ignorance of a disgraceful sort, the ignorance which is the conceit that a man knows what he does not know? And in this respect only I believe myself to differ from men in general, and may perhaps claim to be wiser than they are:—that whereas I know but little of the world below, I do not suppose that I know: but I do know that injustice and disobedience to a better, whether god or man, is evil and dishonorable, and I will never fear or avoid a possible good rather than a certain evil. And therefore if you let me go now, and are not convinced by Anytus, who said that since I had been prosecuted I must be put to death; (or if not that I ought never to have been prosecuted at all); and that if I escape now, your sons will all be utterly ruined by listening to my words—if you say to me, Socrates, this time we will not mind Anytus, and you shall be let off, but upon one condition, that you are not to enquire and speculate in this way anymore, and that if you are caught doing so again you shall die;—if this was the condition on which you let me go, I should reply: Men of Athens, I honor and love you; but I shall obey the god rather than you, and while I have life and strength I shall never cease from the practice and teaching of philosophy, exhorting any one whom I meet and saying to him after my manner: You, my friend,—a citizen of the great and mighty and wise city of Athens,—are you not ashamed of heaping up the greatest amount of money and honor and reputation, and caring so little about wisdom and truth and the greatest improvement of the soul, which you never regard or heed at all? And if the person with whom I am arguing, says: Yes, but I do care; then I do not leave him or let him go at once; but I proceed to interrogate and examine and cross-examine him, and if I think that he has no virtue in him, but only says that he has, I reproach him with undervaluing the greater, and overvaluing the less. And I shall repeat the same words to every one whom I meet, young and old, citizen and alien, but especially to the citizens, inasmuch as they are my brethren. For know that this is the command of the god; and I believe that no greater good has ever

happened in the state than my service to the god. For I do nothing but go about persuading you all, old and young alike, not to take thought for your persons or your properties, but first and chiefly to care about the greatest improvement of the soul. I tell you that virtue is not given by money, but that from virtue comes money and every other good of man, public as well as private. This is my teaching, and if this is the doctrine which corrupts the youth, I am a mischievous person. But if any one says that this is not my teaching, he is speaking an untruth. Wherefore, O men of Athens, I say to you, do as Anytus bids or not as Anytus bids, and either acquit me or not; but whichever you do, understand that I shall never alter my ways, not even if I have to die many times.

Men of Athens, do not interrupt, but hear me; there was an understanding between us that you should hear me to the end: I have something more to say, at which you may be inclined to cry out; but I believe that to hear me will be good for you, and therefore I beg that you will not cry out. I would have you know, that if you kill such a one as I am, you will injure yourselves more than you will injure me. Nothing will injure me, not Meletus nor yet Anytus—they cannot, for a bad man is not permitted to injure a better than himself. I do not deny that Anytus may, perhaps, kill him, or drive him into exile, or deprive him of civil rights; and he may imagine, and others may imagine, that he is inflicting a great injury upon him: but there I do not agree. For the evil of doing as he is doing—the evil of unjustly taking away the life of another—is greater far.

And now, Athenians, I am not going to argue for my own sake, as you may think, but for yours, that you may not sin against the god by condemning me, who am his gift to you. For if you kill me you will not easily find a successor to me, who, if I may use such a ludicrous figure of speech, am a sort of gadfly, given to the state by the god; and the state is a great and noble steed who is tardy in his motions owing to his very size, and requires to be stirred into life. I am that gadfly which god has attached to the state, and all day long and in all places am always fastening upon you, arousing and persuading and reproaching you. You will not easily find another like me, and therefore I would advise you to spare me. I dare say that you may feel out of temper (like a person who is suddenly awakened from sleep), and you think that you might easily strike me dead as Anytus advises, and then you would sleep on for the remainder of your lives, unless god in his care of you sent you another gadfly. When I say that I am given to you by god, the proof of my mission is this:—if I had been like other men, I should not have neglected all my own concerns or patiently seen the neglect of them during all these years, and have been doing yours, coming to you individually like a father or elder brother, exhorting you to regard virtue; such conduct, I say, would be unlike human nature. If I had gained anything, or if my exhortations had been paid, there would have been some sense in my doing so; but now, as you will perceive, not even the impudence of my accusers dares to say that I have ever exacted or sought pay of any one; of that they have no witness. And I have a sufficient witness to the truth of what I say—my poverty.

Someone may wonder why I go about in private giving advice and busying myself with the concerns of others, but do not venture to come forward in public and advise the state. I will tell you why. You have heard me speak at sundry times and in diverse places of an oracle or sign which comes to me, and is the divinity which Meletus ridicules in the indictment. This sign, which is a kind of voice, first began to come to me when I was a child; it always forbids but never commands me to do anything which I am going to do. This is what deters me from being a politician. And rightly, as I think. For I am certain, O men of Athens, that if I had engaged in politics, I should have perished long ago, and done no good either to you or to myself. And do not be offended at my telling you the truth: for the truth is, that no man who goes to war with you or any other multitude, honestly striving against the many lawless and unrighteous deeds which are done in a state, will save his life; he who will fight for the right, if he would live even for a brief space, must have a private station and not a public one.

I can give you convincing evidence of what I say, not words only, but what you value far more—actions. Let me relate to you a passage of my own life which will prove to you that I should never have yielded to injustice from any fear of death, and that 'as I should have refused to yield' I must have died at once. I will tell you a tale of the courts, not very interesting perhaps, but nevertheless true. The only office of state which I ever held, O men of Athens, was that of senator: the tribe Antiochis, which is my tribe, had the presidency at the trial of the generals who had not taken up the bodies of the slain after the battle of Arginusae; and you proposed to try them in a body, contrary to law, as you all thought afterwards; but at the time I was the only one of the Prytanes who was opposed to the illegality, and I gave my vote against you; and when the orators threatened to impeach and arrest me, and you called and shouted, I made up my mind that I would run the risk, having law and justice with me, rather than take part in your injustice because I feared imprisonment and death. This happened in the days of the democracy. But when the oligarchy of the Thirty was in power, they sent for me and four others into the rotunda, and bade us bring Leon the Salaminian from Salamis, as they wanted to put him to death. This was a specimen of the sort of commands which they were always giving with the view of implicating as many as possible in their crimes; and then I showed, not in word only but in deed, that, if I may be allowed to use such an expression, I cared not a straw for death, and that my great and only care was lest I should do an unrighteous or unholy thing. For the strong arm of that oppressive power did not frighten me into doing wrong; and when we came out of the rotunda the other four went to Salamis and fetched Leon, but I went quietly home. For which I might have lost my life, had not the power of the Thirty shortly afterwards come to an end. And many will witness to my words.

Now do you really imagine that I could have survived all these years, if I had led a public life, supposing that like a good man I had always maintained the right and had made justice, as I ought, the first thing? No indeed, men of Athens, neither I nor any other man. But I have been always the same in all my actions, public as well as private, and never have I yielded any base compliance to those who are slanderously termed my disciples, or to any other. Not that I have any regular disciples. But if any one likes to come and hear me while I am pursuing my mission, whether he be young or old, he is not excluded. Nor do I converse only with those who pay; but any one, whether he be rich or poor, may ask and answer me and listen to my words; and whether he turns out to be a bad man or a good one, neither result can be justly imputed to me; for I never taught or professed to teach him anything. And if any one says that he has ever learned or heard anything from me in private which all the world has not heard, let me tell you that he is lying.

But I shall be asked: Why do people delight in continually conversing with you? I have told you already, Athenians, the whole truth about this matter: they like to hear the cross-examination of the pretenders to wisdom; there is amusement in it. Now this duty of cross-examining other men has been imposed upon me by god; and has been signified to me by oracles, visions, and in every way in which the will of divine power was ever intimated to anyone. This is true, O Athenians, or, if not true, would be soon refuted. If I am or have been corrupting the youth, those of them who are now grown up and have become sensible that I gave them bad advice in the days of their youth should come forward as accusers, and take their revenge; or if they do not like to come themselves, some of their relatives, fathers, brothers, or other kinsmen, should say what evil their families have suffered at my hands. Now is their time. Many of them I see in the court. There is Crito, who is of the same age and of the same deme with myself, and there is Critobulus his son, whom I also see. Then again there is Lysanias of Sphettus, who is the father of Aeschines—he is present; and also there is Antiphon of Cephisus, who is the father of Epigenes; and there are the brothers of several who have associated with me. There is Nicostratus the son of Theosdotides, and the brother of Theodotus (now Theodotus himself is dead, and therefore he, at any rate, will not seek to stop him); and there is Paralus the son of Demodocus, who had a brother Theages; and Adeimantus the son of Ariston, whose brother Plato is present; and Aeantodorus, who is the brother of Apollodorus, whom I also see. I might mention a great many others, some of whom Meletus should have produced as witnesses in the course of his speech; and let him still produce them, if he has forgotten—I will make way for him. And let him say, if he has any testimony of the sort which he can produce. Nay, Athenians, the very opposite is the truth. For all these are ready to witness on behalf of the corrupter, of the injurer of their kindred, as Meletus and Anytus call me; not the corrupted youth only—there might have been a motive for that—but their uncorrupted elder relatives. Why should they too support me with their testimony? Why, indeed, except for the sake of truth and justice, and because they know that I am speaking the truth, and that Meletus is a liar.

Well, Athenians, this and the like of this is all the defense which I have to offer. Yet a word more. Perhaps there may be someone who is offended at me, when he calls to mind how he himself on a similar, or even a less serious occasion, prayed and entreated the judges with many tears, and how he produced his children in court, which was a moving spectacle, together with a host of relations and friends; whereas I, who am probably in danger of my life, will do none of these things. The contrast may occur to his mind, and he may be set against me, and vote in anger because he is displeased at me on this account. Now if there be such a person among you,—mind, I do not say that there is,—to him I

may fairly reply: My friend, I am a man, and like other men, a creature of flesh and blood, and not 'of wood or stone,' as Homer says; and I have a family, yes, and sons, O Athenians, three in number, one almost a man, and two others who are still young; and yet I will not bring any of them hither in order to petition you for an acquittal. And why not? Not from any self-assertion or want of respect for you. Whether I am or am not afraid of death is another question, of which I will not now speak. But, having regard to public opinion, I feel that such conduct would be discreditable to myself, and to you, and to the whole state. One who has reached my years, and who has a name for wisdom, ought not to demean himself. Whether this opinion of me be deserved or not, at any rate the world has decided that Socrates is in some way superior to other men. And if those among you who are said to be superior in wisdom and courage, and any other virtue, demean themselves in this way, how shameful is their conduct! I have seen men of reputation, when they have been condemned, behaving in the strangest manner: they seemed to fancy that they were going to suffer something dreadful if they died, and that they could be immortal if you only allowed them to live; and I think that such are a dishonor to the state, and that any stranger coming in would have said of them that the most eminent men of Athens, to whom the Athenians themselves give honor and command, are no better than women. And I say that these things ought not to be done by those of us who have a reputation; and if they are done, you ought not to permit them; you ought rather to show that you are far more disposed to condemn the man who gets up a doleful scene and makes the city ridiculous, than him who holds his peace.

But, setting aside the question of public opinion, there seems to be something wrong in asking a favor of a judge, and thus procuring an acquittal, instead of informing and convincing him. For his duty is, not to make a present of justice, but to give judgment; and he has sworn that he will judge according to the laws, and not according to his own good pleasure; and we ought not to encourage you, nor should you allow yourselves to be encouraged, in this habit of perjury—there can be no piety in that. Do not then require me to do what I consider dishonorable and impious and wrong, especially now, when I am being tried for impiety on the indictment of Meletus. For if, O men of Athens, by force of persuasion and entreaty I could overpower your oaths, then I should be teaching you to believe that there are no gods, and in defending should simply convict myself of the charge of not believing in them. But that is not so—far otherwise. For I do believe that there are gods, and in a sense higher than that in which any of my accusers believe in them. And to you and to god I commit my cause, to be determined by you as is best for you and me.

[The jury votes to convict Socrates.]

There are many reasons why I am not grieved, O men of Athens, at the vote of condemnation. I expected it, and am only surprised that the votes are so nearly equal; for I had thought that the majority against me would have been far larger; but now, had thirty votes gone over to the other side, I should have been acquitted. And I may say, I think, that I have escaped Meletus. I may say more; for without the assistance of Anytus and Lycon, any one may see that he would not have had a fifth part of the votes, as the law requires, in which case he would have incurred a fine of a thousand drachmae.

And so he proposes death as the penalty. And what shall I propose on my part, O men of Athens? Clearly that which is my due. And what is my due? What return shall be made to the man who has never had the wit to be idle during his whole life; but has been careless of what the many care for—wealth, and family interests, and military offices, and speaking in the assembly, and magistracies, and plots, and parties. Reflecting that I was really too honest a man to be a politician and live, I did not go where I could do no good to you or to myself; but where I could do the greatest good privately to every one of you, thither I went, and sought to persuade every man among you that he must look to himself, and seek virtue and wisdom before he looks to his private interests, and look to the state before he looks to the interests of the state; and that this should be the order which he observes in all his actions. What shall be done to such a one? Doubtless some good thing, O men of Athens, if he has his reward; and the good should be of a kind suitable to him. What would be a reward suitable to a poor man who is your benefactor, and who desires leisure that he may instruct you? There can be no reward so fitting as maintenance in the Prytaneum, O men of Athens, a reward which he deserves far more than the citizen who has won the prize at Olympia in the horse or chariot race, whether the chariots were drawn by two horses or by many. For I am in want, and he has enough; and he only gives you the appearance of happiness, and I give you the reality. And if I am to estimate the penalty fairly, I should say that maintenance in the Prytaneum is the just return.

Perhaps you think that I am braving you in what I am saying now, as in what I said before about the tears and prayers. But this is not so. I speak rather because I am convinced that I never intentionally wronged any one, although I cannot convince you—the time has been too short; if there were a law at Athens, as there is in other cities, that a capital cause should not be decided in one day, then I believe that I should have convinced you. But I cannot in a moment refute great slanders; and, as I am convinced that I never wronged another, I will assuredly not wrong myself. I will not say of myself that I deserve any evil, or propose any penalty. Why should I? because I am afraid of the penalty of death which Meletus proposes? When I do not know whether death is a good or an evil, why should I propose a penalty which would certainly be an evil? Shall I say imprisonment? And why should I live in prison, and be the slave of the magistrates of the year—of the Eleven? Or shall the penalty be a fine, and imprisonment until the fine is paid? There is the same objection. I should have to lie in prison, for money I have none, and cannot pay. And if I say exile (and this may possibly be the penalty which you will affix), I must indeed be blinded by the love of life, if I am so irrational as to expect that when you, who are my own citizens, cannot endure my discourses and words, and have found them so grievous and odious that you will have no more of them, others are likely to endure me. No indeed, men of Athens, that is not very likely. And what a life should I lead, at my age, wandering from city to city, ever changing my place of exile, and always being driven out! For I am quite sure that wherever I go, there, as here, the young men will flock to me; and if I drive them away, their elders will drive me out at their request; and if I let them come, their fathers and friends will drive me out for their sakes.

Someone will say: Yes, Socrates, but cannot you hold your tongue, and then you may go into a foreign city, and no one will interfere with you? Now I have great difficulty in making you understand my answer to this. For if I tell you that to do as you say would be a disobedience to the god, and therefore that I cannot hold my tongue, you will not believe that I am serious; and if I say again that daily to discourse about virtue, and of those other things about which you hear me examining myself and others, is the greatest good of man, and that the unexamined life is not worth living, you are still less likely to believe me. Yet I say what is true, although a thing of which it is hard for me to persuade you. Also, I have never been accustomed to think that I deserve to suffer any harm. Had I money I might have estimated the offence at what I was able to pay, and not have been much the worse. But I have none, and therefore I must ask you to proportion the fine to my means. Well, perhaps I could afford a mina, and therefore I propose that penalty: Plato, Crito, Critobulus, and Apollodorus, my friends here, bid me say thirty minae, and they will be the sureties. Let thirty minae be the penalty; for which sum they will be ample security to you.

[The jury condemns Socrates to death.]

Not much time will be gained, O Athenians, in return for the evil name which you will get from the detractors of the city, who will say that you killed Socrates, a wise man; for they will call me wise, even although I am not wise, when they want to reproach you. If you had waited a little while, your desire would have been fulfilled in the course of nature. For I am far advanced in years, as you may perceive, and not far from death. I am speaking now not to all of you, but only to those who have condemned me to death. And I have another thing to say to them: you think that I was convicted because I had no words of the sort which would have procured my acquittal—I mean, if I had thought fit to leave nothing undone or unsaid. Not so; the deficiency which led to my conviction was not of words—certainly not. But I had not the boldness or impudence or inclination to address you as you would have liked me to do, weeping and wailing and lamenting, and saying and doing many things which you have been accustomed to hear from others, and which, as I maintain, are unworthy of me. I thought at the time that I ought not to do anything common or mean when in danger: nor do I now repent of the style of my defense; I would rather die having spoken after my manner, than speak in your manner and live. For neither in war nor yet at law ought I or any man to use every way of escaping death. Often in battle there can be no doubt that if a man will throw away his arms, and fall on his knees before his pursuers, he may escape death; and in other dangers there are other ways of escaping death, if a man is willing to say and do anything. The difficulty, my friends, is not to avoid death, but to avoid unrighteousness; for that runs faster than death. I am old and move slowly, and the slower runner has overtaken me, and my accusers are keen and quick, and the faster runner, who is unrighteousness, has overtaken them. And now I depart hence condemned by you to suffer the penalty of death,—they too go their ways condemned by the truth to suffer the penalty of villainy and wrong; and I must abide by my award—let them abide by theirs. I suppose that these things may be regarded as fated,—and I think that they are well.

And now, O men who have condemned me, I would fain prophesy to you; for I am about to die, and in the hour of death men are gifted with prophetic power. And I prophesy to you who are my murderers, that immediately after my departure punishment far heavier than you have inflicted on me will surely await you. Me you have killed because you wanted to escape the accuser, and not to give an account of your lives. But that will not be as you suppose: far otherwise. For I say that there will be more accusers of you than there are now; accusers whom hitherto I have restrained: and as they are younger they will be more inconsiderate with you, and you will be more offended at them. If you think that by killing men you can prevent someone from censuring your evil lives, you are mistaken; that is not a way of escape which is either possible or honorable; the easiest and the noblest way is not to be disabling others, but to be improving yourselves. This is the prophecy which I utter before my departure to the judges who have condemned me.

Friends, who would have acquitted me, I would like also to talk with you about the thing which has come to pass, while the magistrates are busy, and before I go to the place at which I must die. Stay then a little, for we may as well talk with one another while there is time. You are my friends, and I should like to show you the meaning of this event which has happened to me. O my judges—for you I may truly call judges—I should like to tell you of a wonderful circumstance. Hitherto the divine faculty of which the internal oracle is the source has constantly been in the habit of opposing me even about trifles, if I was going to make a slip or error in any matter; and now as you see there has come upon me that which may be thought, and is generally believed to be, the last and worst evil. But the oracle made no sign of opposition, either when I was leaving my house in the morning, or when I was on my way to the court, or while I was speaking, at anything which I was going to say; and yet I have often been stopped in the middle of a speech, but now in nothing I either said or did touching the matter in hand has the oracle opposed me. What do I take to be the explanation of this silence? I will tell you. It is an intimation that what has happened to me is a good, and that those of us who think that death is an evil are in error. For the customary sign would surely have opposed me had I been going to evil and not to good.

Let us reflect in another way, and we shall see that there is great reason to hope that death is a good; for one of two things—either death is a state of nothingness and utter unconsciousness, or, as men say, there is a change and migration of the soul from this world to another. Now if you suppose that there is no consciousness, but a sleep like the sleep of him who is undisturbed even by dreams, death will be an unspeakable gain. For if a person were to select the night in which his sleep was undisturbed even by dreams, and were to compare with this the other days and nights of his life, and then were to tell us how many days and nights he had passed in the course of his life better and more pleasantly than this one, I think that any man, I will not say a private man, but even the great king will not find many such days or nights, when compared with the others. Now if death be of such a nature, I say that to die is gain; for eternity is then only a single night. But if death is the journey to another place, and there, as men say, all the dead abide, what good, O my friends and judges, can be greater than this? If indeed when the pilgrim arrives in the world below, he is delivered from the professors of justice in this world, and finds the true judges who are said to give judgment there, Minos and Rhadamanthus and Aeacus and Triptolemus, and other sons of the gods who were righteous in their own life, that pilgrimage will be worth making. What would not a man give if he might converse with Orpheus and Musaeus and Hesiod and Homer? Nay, if this be true, let me die again and again. I myself, too, shall have a wonderful interest in there meeting and conversing with Paramedic, and Ajax the son of Telamon, and any other ancient hero who has suffered death through an unjust judgment; and there will be no small pleasure, as I think, in comparing my own sufferings with theirs. Above all, I shall then be able to continue my search into true and false knowledge; as in this world, so also in the next; and I shall find out who is wise, and who pretends to be wise, and is not. What would not a man give, O judges, to be able to examine the leader of the great Trojan expedition; or Odysseus or Sisyphus, or numberless others, men and women too! What infinite delight would there be in conversing with them and asking them questions! In another world they do not put a man to death for asking questions: assuredly not. For besides being happier than we are, they will be immortal, if what is said is true.

Wherefore, O judges, be of good cheer about death, and know of a certainty, that no evil can happen to a good man, either in life or after death. He and his are not neglected by the gods; nor has my own approaching end happened by mere chance. But I see clearly that the time had arrived when it was better for me to die and be released from trouble; wherefore the oracle gave no sign. For which reason, also, I am not angry with my condemners, or with my accusers; they have done me no harm, although they did not mean to do me any good; and for this I may gently blame them.

Still I have a favor to ask of them. When my sons are grown up, I would ask you, O my friends, to punish them; and I would have you trouble them, as I have troubled you, if they seem to care about riches, or anything, more than about virtue; or if they pretend to be something when they are really nothing,—then reprove them, as I have reproved you, for not caring about that for which they ought to care, and thinking that they are something when they are really nothing. And if you do this, both I and my sons will have received justice at your hands.

The hour of departure has arrived, and we go our ways—I to die, and you to live. Which is better only god knows.

[The Dialogues of Plato. Trans. By Benjamin Jowett (London: Macmillan, 1891).]

Crito

Plato

(Translated by Benjamin Jowett and edited by Joseph R. Kirkland)

PERSONS OF THE DIALOGUE: Socrates, Crito
SCENE: The Prison of Socrates

SOCRATES: Why have you come at this hour, Crito? It must be quite early?

CRITO: Yes, certainly.

SOCRATES: What is the exact time?

CRITO: The dawn is breaking.

SOCRATES: I wonder why the keeper of the prison would let you in.

CRITO: He knows me, because I often come, Socrates; moreover, I have done him a kindness.

SOCRATES: And are you only just arrived?

CRITO: No, I came some time ago.

SOCRATES: Then why did you sit and say nothing, instead of at once awakening me?

CRITO: I should not have liked myself, Socrates, to be in such great trouble and unrest as you are—indeed I should not: I have been watching with amazement your peaceful slumbers; and for that reason I did not awake you, because I wished to minimize the pain. I have always thought you to be of a happy disposition; but never did I see anything like the easy, tranquil manner in which you bear this calamity.

SOCRATES: Why, Crito, when a man has reached my age he ought not to be repining at the approach of death.

CRITO: And yet other old men find themselves in similar misfortunes, and age does not prevent them from repining.

SOCRATES: That is true. But you have not told me why you come at this early hour.

CRITO: I come to bring you a message which is sad and painful; not, as I believe, to yourself, but to all of us who are your friends, and saddest of all to me.

SOCRATES: What? Has the ship come from Delos, on the arrival of which I am to die?

CRITO: No, the ship has not actually arrived, but she will probably be here today, as persons who have come from Sunium tell me that they have left her there; and therefore tomorrow, Socrates, will be the last day of your life.

SOCRATES: Very well, Crito; if such is the will of the god, I am willing; but my belief is that there will be a delay of a day.

CRITO: Why do you think so?

SOCRATES: I will tell you. I am to die on the day after the arrival of the ship?

CRITO: Yes; that is what the authorities say.

SOCRATES: But I do not think that the ship will be here until tomorrow; this I infer from a vision which I had last night, or rather only just now, when you fortunately allowed me to sleep.

CRITO: And what was the nature of the vision?

SOCRATES: There appeared to me the likeness of a woman, fair and comely, clothed in bright raiment, who called to me and said: "O Socrates, the third day hence to fertile Phthia shalt thou go."

CRITO: What a singular dream, Socrates!

SOCRATES: There can be no doubt about the meaning, Crito, I think.

CRITO: Yes; the meaning is only too clear. But, oh! My beloved Socrates, let me entreat you once more to take my advice and escape. For if you die I shall not only lose a friend who can never be replaced, but there is another evil: people who do not know you and me will believe that I might have saved you if I had been willing to give money, but that I did not care. Now, can there be a worse disgrace than this—that I should be thought to value money more than the life of a friend? For the many will not be persuaded that I wanted you to escape, and that you refused.

SOCRATES: But why, my dear Crito, should we care about the opinion of the many? Good men, and they are the only persons who are worth considering, will think of these things truly as they occurred.

CRITO: But you see, Socrates, that the opinion of the many must be regarded, for what is now happening shows that they can do the greatest evil to anyone who has lost their good opinion.

SOCRATES: I only wish it were so, Crito; and that the many could do the greatest evil; for then they would also be able to do the greatest good—and what a fine thing this would be! But in reality they can do neither; for they cannot make a man either wise or foolish; and whatever they do is the result of chance.

CRITO: Well, I will not dispute with you; but please to tell me, Socrates, whether you are not acting out of regard to me and your other friends: are you not afraid that if you escape from prison we may get into trouble with the informers for having stolen you away, and lose either the whole or a great part of our property; or that even a worse evil may happen to us? Now, if you fear on our account, be at ease; for in order to save you, we ought surely to run this, or even a greater risk; be persuaded, then, and do as I say.

SOCRATES: Yes, Crito, that is one fear which you mention, but by no means the only one.

CRITO: Fear not—there are persons who are willing to get you out of prison at no great cost; and as for the informers, they are far from being exorbitant in their demands—a little money will satisfy them. My means, which are certainly ample, are at your service, and if you have a scruple about spending all mine, here are strangers who will give you the use of theirs; and one of them, Simmias the Theban, has brought a large sum of money for this very purpose; and Cebes and many others are prepared to spend their money in helping you to escape. I say, therefore, do not hesitate on our account, and do not say, as you did in the court that you will have a difficulty in knowing what to do with yourself anywhere else. For men will love you in other places to which you may go, and not in Athens only; there are friends of mine in Thessaly, if you would like to go to them, who will value and protect you, and no Thessalian will give you any trouble. Nor can I think that you are at all justified, Socrates, in betraying your own life when you might be saved; in acting thus you are playing into the hands of your enemies, who are hurrying on your destruction. And further I should say that you are deserting your own children; for you might bring them up and educate them; instead of which you go away and leave them, and they will have to take their chance; and if they do not meet with the usual fate of orphans, there will be small thanks to you. No man

should bring children into the world who is unwilling to persevere to the end in their nurture and education. But you appear to be choosing the easier part, not the better and manlier, which would have been more becoming in one who professes to care for virtue in all his actions, like yourself. And indeed, I am ashamed not only of you, but of us who are your friends, when I reflect that the whole business will be attributed entirely to our want of courage. The trial need never have come on, or might have been managed differently; and this last act, or crowning folly, will seem to have occurred through our negligence and cowardice, who might have saved you, if we had been good for anything; and you might have saved yourself, for there was no difficulty at all. See now, Socrates, how sad and discreditable are the consequences, both to us and you. Make up your mind then, or rather have your mind already made up, for the time of deliberation is over, and there is only one thing to be done, which must be done this very night, and, if we delay at all, will be no longer practicable or possible; I beseech you therefore, Socrates, be persuaded by me, and do as I say.

SOCRATES: Dear Crito, your zeal is invaluable, if a right one; but if wrong, the greater the zeal, the greater the danger; and therefore we ought to consider whether I shall or shall not do as you say. For I am and always have been one of those natures who must be guided by reason, whatever the reason may be which upon reflection appears to me to be the best; and now that this chance has befallen me, I cannot repudiate my own words: the principles which I have hitherto honored and revered I still honor, and unless we can at once find other and better principles, I am certain not to agree with you; no, not even if the power of the multitude could inflict many more imprisonments, confiscations, deaths, frightening us like children with hobgoblin terrors. What will be the fairest way of considering the question? Shall I return to your old argument about the opinions of men?—we were saying that some of them are to be regarded, and others not. Now were we right in maintaining this before I was condemned? And has the argument which was once good now proved to be talk for the sake of talking—mere childish nonsense? That is what I want to consider with your help, Crito:—whether, under my present circumstances, the argument appears to be in any way different or not; and is to be allowed by me or disallowed. That argument, which, as I believe, is maintained by many persons of authority, was to the effect, as I was saying, that the opinions of some men are to be regarded, and of other men not to be regarded. Now you, Crito, are not going to die tomorrow—at least, there is no human probability of this—and therefore you are disinterested and not liable to be deceived by the circumstances in which you are placed. Tell me then, whether I am right in saying that some opinions, and the opinions of some men only, are to be valued, and that other opinions, and the opinions of other men, are not to be valued. I ask you whether I was right in maintaining this?

CRITO: Certainly.

SOCRATES: The good are to be regarded, and not the bad?

CRITO: Yes.

SOCRATES: And the opinions of the wise are good, and the opinions of the unwise are evil?

CRITO: Certainly.

SOCRATES: And what was said about another matter? Is the pupil who devotes himself to the practice of gymnastics supposed to attend to the praise and blame and opinion of every man, or of one man only—his physician or trainer, whoever he may be?

CRITO: Of one man only.

SOCRATES: And he ought to fear the censure and welcome the praise of that one only, and not of the many?

CRITO: Clearly so.

SOCRATES: And he ought to act and train, and eat and drink in the way which seems good to his single master who has understanding, rather than according to the opinion of all other men put together?

CRITO: True.

SOCRATES: And if he disobeys and disregards the opinion and approval of the one, and regards the opinion of the many who have no understanding, will he not suffer evil?

CRITO: Certainly he will.

SOCRATES: And what will the evil be, whither tending and what affecting, in the disobedient person?

CRITO: Clearly, affecting the body; that is what is destroyed by the evil.

SOCRATES: Very good; and is not this true, Crito, of other things which we need not separately enumerate? In questions of just and unjust, fair and foul, good and

evil, which are the subjects of our present consultation, ought we to follow the opinion of the many and to fear them; or the opinion of the one man who has understanding? Ought we not to fear and reverence him more than all the rest of the world: and if we desert him shall we not destroy and injure that principle in us which may be assumed to be improved by justice and deteriorated by injustice—there is such a principle?

CRITO: Certainly there is, Socrates.

SOCRATES: Take a parallel instance:—if, acting under the advice of those who have no understanding, we destroy that which is improved by health and is deteriorated by disease, would life be worth having? And that which has been destroyed is—the body?

CRITO: Yes.

SOCRATES: Could we live, having an evil and corrupted body?

CRITO: Certainly not.

SOCRATES: And will life be worth having, if that higher part of man be destroyed, which is improved by justice and depraved by injustice? Do we suppose that principle, whatever it may be in man, which has to do with justice and injustice, to be inferior to the body?

CRITO: Certainly not.

SOCRATES: More honorable than the body?

CRITO: Far more.

SOCRATES: Then, my friend, we must not regard what the many say of us; but what he, the one man who has understanding of just and unjust, will say, and what the truth will say. And therefore you begin in error when you advise that we should regard the opinion of the many about just and unjust, good and evil, honorable and dishonorable.—"Well," someone will say, "but the many can kill us."

CRITO: Yes, Socrates; that will clearly be the answer.

SOCRATES: And it is true; but still I find with surprise that the old argument is unshaken as ever. And I should like to know whether I may say the same of another proposition—that not life, but a good life, is to be chiefly valued?

CRITO: Yes, that also remains unshaken.

SOCRATES: And a good life is equivalent to a just and honorable one—that holds also?

CRITO: Yes, it does.

SOCRATES: From these premises I proceed to argue the question whether I ought or ought not to try and escape without the consent of the Athenians: and if I am clearly right in escaping, then I will make the attempt; but if not, I will abstain. The other considerations which you mention, of money and loss of character and the duty of educating one's children, are, I fear, only the doctrines of the multitude, who would be as ready to restore people to life, if they were able, as they are to put them to death—and with as little reason. But now, since the argument has thus far prevailed, the only question which remains to be considered is whether we shall do rightly either in escaping or in suffering others to aid in our escape and paying them in money and thanks, or whether in reality we shall not do rightly; and if the latter, then death or any other calamity which may ensue on my remaining here must not be allowed to enter into the calculation.

CRITO: I think that you are right, Socrates; how then shall we proceed?

SOCRATES: Let us consider the matter together, and do you either refute me if you can, and I will be convinced; or else cease, my dear friend, from repeating to me that I ought to escape against the wishes of the Athenians: for I highly value your attempts to persuade me to do so, but I may not be persuaded against my own better judgment. And now please to consider my first position, and try how you can best answer me.

CRITO: I will.

SOCRATES: Are we to say that we are never intentionally to do wrong, or that in one way we ought and in another way we ought not to do wrong, or is doing wrong always evil and dishonorable, as I was just now saying, and as has been already acknowledged by us? Are all our former admissions which were made within a few days to be thrown away? And have we, at our age, been earnestly discoursing with one another all our life long only to discover that we are no better than children? Or, in spite of the opinion of the many, and in spite of consequences whether better or worse, shall we insist on the truth of what was then said, that injustice is always an evil and dishonor to him who acts unjustly? Shall we say so or not?

CRITO: Yes.

SOCRATES: Then we must do no wrong?

CRITO: Certainly not.

SOCRATES: Nor, when injured, injure in return, as the many imagine; for we must injure no one at all?

CRITO: Clearly not.

SOCRATES: Again, Crito, may we do evil?

CRITO: Surely not, Socrates.

SOCRATES: And what of doing evil in return for evil, which is the morality of the many—is that just or not?

CRITO: Not just.

SOCRATES: For doing evil to another is the same as injuring him?

CRITO: Very true.

SOCRATES: Then we ought not to retaliate or render evil for evil to anyone, whatever evil we may have suffered from him. But I would have you consider, Crito, whether you really mean what you are saying. For this opinion has never been held, and never will be held, by any considerable number of persons; and those who are agreed and those who are not agreed upon this point have no common ground, and can only despise one another when they see how widely they differ. Tell me, then, whether you agree with and assent to my first principle, that neither injury nor retaliation nor warding off evil by evil is ever right. And shall that be the premise of our argument? Or do you decline and dissent from this? For so I have ever thought, and continue to think; but, if you are of another opinion, let me hear what you have to say. If, however, you remain of the same mind as formerly, I will proceed to the next step.

CRITO: You may proceed, for I have not changed my mind.

SOCRATES: Then I will go on to the next point, which may be put in the form of a question: Ought a man to do what he admits to be right, or ought he to betray the right?

CRITO: He ought to do what he thinks right.

SOCRATES: But if this is true, what is the application? In leaving the prison against the will of the Athenians, do I wrong any? Or rather do I not wrong those whom I ought least to wrong? Do I not desert the principles which were acknowledged by us to be just—what do you say?

CRITO: I cannot tell, Socrates; for I do not know.

SOCRATES: Then consider the matter in this way: Imagine that I am about to play truant (you may call the proceeding by any name which you like), and the laws and the government come and interrogate me: "Tell us,

Socrates," they say; "what are you about? Are you not going by an act of yours to overturn us—the laws, and the whole state, as far as in you lies? Do you imagine that a state can subsist and not be overthrown, in which the decisions of law have no power, but are set aside and trampled upon by individuals?" What will be our answer, Crito, to these and the like words? Anyone, and especially a rhetorician, will have a good deal to say on behalf of the law which requires a sentence to be carried out. He will argue that this law should not be set aside; and shall we reply, "Yes; but the state has injured us and given an unjust sentence." Suppose I say that?

CRITO: Very good, Socrates.

SOCRATES: "And was that our agreement with you?" the law would answer; "or were you to abide by the sentence of the state?" And if I were to express my astonishment at their words, the law would probably add: "Answer, Socrates, instead of opening your eyes—you are in the habit of asking and answering questions. Tell us,—What complaint have you to make against us which justifies you in attempting to destroy us and the state? In the first place did we not bring you into existence? Your father married your mother by our aid and begat you. Say whether you have any objection to urge against those of us who regulate marriage?' None, I should reply. "Or against those of us who after birth regulate the nurture and education of children, in which you also were trained? Were not the laws, which have the charge of education, right in commanding your father to train you in music and gymnastic?" "Right," I should reply. "Well then, since you were brought into the world and nurtured and educated by us, can you deny in the first place that you are our child and slave, as your fathers were before you? And if this is true you are not on equal terms with us; nor can you think that you have a right to do to us what we are doing to you. Would you have any right to strike or revile or do any other evil to your father or your master, if you had one, because you have been struck or reviled by him, or received some other evil at his hands? You would not say this. And because we think right to destroy you, do you think that you have any right to destroy us in return, and your country as far as in you lies? Will you, O professor of true virtue, pretend that you are justified in this? Has a philosopher like you failed to discover that our country is more to be valued and higher and holier far than mother or father or any ancestor, and more to be regarded in the eyes of the gods and of men of understanding? Also to be soothed, and gently and reverently entreated when angry, even

more than a father, and either to be persuaded, or if not persuaded, to be obeyed? And when we are punished by her, whether with imprisonment or stripes, the punishment is to be endured in silence; and if she lead us to wounds or death in battle, thither we follow as is right; neither may anyone yield or retreat or leave his rank, but whether in battle or in a court of law, or in any other place, he must do what his city and his country order him; or he must change their view of what is just: and if he may do no violence to his father or mother, much less may he do violence to his country." What answer shall we make to this, Crito? Do the laws speak truly, or do they not?

CRITO: I think that they do.

SOCRATES: Then the laws will say: "Consider, Socrates, if we are speaking truly that in your present attempt you are going to do us an injury. For, having brought you into the world, and nurtured and educated you, and given you and every other citizen a share in every good which we had to give, we further proclaim to any Athenian by the liberty which we allow him, that if he does not like us when he has become of age and has seen the ways of the city, and made our acquaintance, he may go where he pleases and take his goods with him. None of us laws will forbid him or interfere with him. Anyone who does not like us and the city, and who wants to emigrate to a colony or to any other city, may go where he likes, retaining his property. But he who has experience of the manner in which we order justice and administer the state, and still remains, has entered into an implied contract that he will do as we command him. And he who disobeys us is, as we maintain, thrice wrong; first, because in disobeying us he is disobeying his parents; secondly, because we are the authors of his education; thirdly, because he has made an agreement with us that he will duly obey our commands; and he neither obeys them nor convinces us that our commands are unjust; and we do not rudely impose them, but give him the alternative of obeying or convincing us;—that is what we offer, and he does neither. These are the sort of accusations to which, as we were saying, you, Socrates, will be exposed if you accomplish your intentions; you, above all other Athenians."

Suppose now I ask why I rather than anybody else? They will justly retort upon me that I above all other men have acknowledged the agreement. "There is clear proof," they will say, "Socrates, that we and the city were not displeasing to you. Of all Athenians you have been the most constant resident in the city, which, as you never leave, you may be supposed to love. For you never went out of the city either to see the games, except once when you went to the Isthmus, or to any other place unless when you were on military service; nor did you travel as other men do. Nor had you any curiosity to know other states or their laws: your affections did not go beyond us and our state; we were your especial favorites, and you acquiesced in our government of you; and here in this city you begat your children, which is a proof of your satisfaction. Moreover, you might in the course of the trial, if you had liked, have fixed the penalty at banishment; the state which refuses to let you go now would have let you go then. But you pretended that you preferred death to exile, and that you were not unwilling to die. And now you have forgotten these fine sentiments, and pay no respect to us the laws, of whom you are the destroyer; and are doing what only a miserable slave would do, running away and turning your back upon the compacts and agreements which you made as a citizen. And first of all answer this very question: Are we right in saying that you agreed to be governed according to us in deed, and not in word only? Is that true or not?" How shall we answer, Crito? Must we not assent?

CRITO: We cannot help it, Socrates.

SOCRATES: Then will they not say: "You, Socrates, are breaking the covenants and agreements which you made with us at your leisure, not in any haste or under any compulsion or deception, but after you have had seventy years to think of them, during which time you were at liberty to leave the city, if we were not to your mind, or if our covenants appeared to you to be unfair. You had your choice, and might have gone either to Lacedaemon or Crete, both which states are often praised by you for their good government, or to some other Hellenic or foreign state. Whereas you, above all other Athenians, seemed to be so fond of the state, or, in other words, of us, her laws (and who would care about a state which has no laws?), that you never stirred out of her; the lame, the blind, the maimed were not more stationary in her than you were. And now you run away and forsake your agreements. Not so, Socrates, if you will take our advice; do not make yourself ridiculous by escaping out of the city."

"For just consider, if you transgress and err in this sort of way, what good will you do either to yourself or to your friends? That your friends will be driven into exile and deprived of citizenship, or will lose their property, is tolerably certain; and you yourself, if you fly to one of the neighboring cities, as, for example, Thebes or Megara, both of which are well governed, will come to

them as an enemy, Socrates, and their government will be against you, and all patriotic citizens will cast an evil eye upon you as a subverter of the laws, and you will confirm in the minds of the judges the justice of their own condemnation of you. For he who is a corrupter of the laws is more than likely to be a corrupter of the young and foolish portion of mankind. Will you then flee from well-ordered cities and virtuous men? And is existence worth having on these terms? Or will you go to them without shame, and talk to them, Socrates? And what will you say to them? What you say here about virtue and justice and institutions and laws being the best things among men? Would that be decent of you? Surely not. But if you go away from well-governed states to Crito's friends in Thessaly, where there is great disorder and license, they will be charmed to hear the tale of your escape from prison, set off with ludicrous particulars of the manner in which you were wrapped in a goatskin or some other disguise, and metamorphosed as the manner is of runaways; but will there be no one to remind you that in your old age you were not ashamed to violate the most sacred laws from a miserable desire of a little more life? Perhaps not, if you keep them in a good temper; but if they are out of temper you will hear many degrading things; you will live, but how?—as the flatterer of all men, and the servant of all men; and doing what?—eating and drinking in Thessaly, having gone abroad in order that you may get a dinner. And where will be your fine sentiments about justice and virtue? Say that you wish to live for the sake of your children—you want to bring them up and educate them—will you take them into Thessaly and deprive them of Athenian citizenship? Is this the benefit which you will confer upon them? Or are you under the impression that they will be better cared for and educated here if you are still alive, although absent from them; for your friends will take care of them? Do you fancy that if you are an inhabitant of Thessaly they will take care of them, and if you are an inhabitant of the other world that they will not take care of them? Nay; but if they who call themselves friends are good for anything, they will—to be sure they will."

"Listen, then, Socrates, to us who have brought you up. Think not of life and children first, and of justice afterwards, but of justice first, that you may be justified before the princes of the world below. For neither will you nor any that belong to you be happier or holier or more just in this life, or happier in another, if you do as Crito bids. Now you depart in innocence, a sufferer and not a doer of evil; a victim, not of the laws, but of men. But if you go forth, returning evil for evil, and injury for injury, breaking the covenants and agreements which you have made with us, and wronging those whom you ought least of all to wrong, that is to say, yourself, your friends, your country, and us, we shall be angry with you while you live, and our brethren, the laws in the world below, will receive you as an enemy; for they will know that you have done your best to destroy us. Listen, then, to us and not to Crito."

This, dear Crito, is the voice which I seem to hear murmuring in my ears, like the sound of the flute in the ears of the mystic; that voice, I say, is humming in my ears, and prevents me from hearing any other. And I know that anything more which you may say will be vain. Yet speak, if you have anything to say.

CRITO: I have nothing to say, Socrates.

SOCRATES: Leave me then, Crito, to fulfil the will of the god, and to follow whither he leads.

[The Dialogues of Plato. Trans. By Benjamin Jowett (London: Macmillan, 1891).*]*

"The Death of Socrates" from *Phaedo*

Plato

(Translated by Benjamin Jowett and edited by Joseph R. Kirkland)

SOCRATES: A man of sense ought not to say, nor will I be very confident, that the description which I have given of the soul and her mansions is exactly true. But I do say that, inasmuch as the soul is shown to be immortal, he may venture to think, not improperly or unworthily, that something of the kind is true. The venture is a glorious one, and he ought to comfort himself with words like these, which is the reason why I lengthen out the tale. Wherefore, I say, let a man be of good cheer about his soul, who having cast away the pleasures and ornaments of the body as alien to him and working harm rather than good, has sought after the pleasures of knowledge; and has arrayed the soul, not in some foreign attire, but in her own proper jewels, temperance, and justice, and courage, and nobility, and truth—in these adorned she is ready to go on her journey to the world below, when her hour comes. You, Simmias and Cebes, and all other men, will depart at some time or other. Me already, as the tragic poet would say, the voice of fate calls. Soon I must drink the poison; and I think that I had better repair to the bath first, in order that the women may not have the trouble of washing my body after I am dead.

[**PHAEDO:** When he was done speaking, Crito said]

CRITO: And have you any commands for us, Socrates—anything to say about your children, or any other matter in which we can serve you?

SOCRATES: Nothing particular, Crito: only, as I have always told you, take care of yourselves; that is a service which you may be ever rendering to me and mine and to all of us, whether you promise to do so or not. But if you have no thought for yourselves, and care not to walk according to the rule which I have prescribed for you, not now for the first time, however much you may profess or promise at the moment, it will be of no avail.

CRITO: We will do our best: And in what way shall we bury you?

SOCRATES: In any way that you like; but you must get hold of me, and take care that I do not run away from you.

[**PHAEDO:** Then he turned to us, and added with a smile]

SOCRATES: I cannot make Crito believe that I am the same Socrates who have been talking and conducting the argument; he fancies that I am the other Socrates whom he will soon see, a dead body—and he asks, How shall he bury me? And though I have spoken many words in the endeavor to show that when I have drunk the poison I shall leave you and go to the joys of the blessed,—these words of mine, with which I was comforting you and myself, have had, as I perceive, no effect upon Crito. And therefore I want you to be surety for me to him now, as at the trial he was surety to the judges for me: but let the promise be of another sort; for he was surety for me to the judges that I would remain, and you must be my surety to him that I shall not remain, but go away and depart; and then he will suffer less at my death, and not be grieved when he sees my body being burned or buried. I would not have him sorrow at my hard lot, or say at the burial, 'Thus we lay out Socrates,' or, 'Thus we follow him to the grave or bury him'; for false words are not only evil in themselves, but they infect the soul with evil. Be of good cheer, then, my dear Crito, and say that you are burying my body only, and do with that whatever is usual, and what you think best.

[**PHAEDO:** When he had spoken these words, he arose and went into a chamber to bathe; Crito followed him and told us to wait. So we remained behind, talking and thinking of the subject of discourse, and also of the greatness of our sorrow; he was like a father of whom we were being bereaved, and we were about to pass the rest of our lives as orphans. When he had taken the bath his children were brought to him—(he had two young sons and an elder one); and the women of his family also came, and he talked to them and gave them a few directions in the presence of Crito; then he dismissed them and returned to us.

Now the hour of sunset was near, for a good deal of time had passed while he was within. When he came out, he sat down with us again after his bath, but not much was said. Soon the jailer, who was the servant of the Eleven, entered and stood by him.]

JAILER: To you, Socrates, whom I know to be the noblest and gentlest and best of all who ever came to

41

this place, I will not impute the angry feelings of other men, who rage and swear at me, when, in obedience to the authorities, I bid them drink the poison—indeed, I am sure that you will not be angry with me; for others, as you are aware, and not I, are to blame. And so fare you well, and try to bear lightly what must needs be—you know my errand.

[Then bursting into tears he turned away and went out. Socrates looked at him and said]

SOCRATES: I return your good wishes, and will do as you bid.

[Turning to us, he said]

SOCRATES: How charming the man is: since I have been in prison he has always been coming to see me, and at times he would talk to me, and was as good to me as could be, and now see how generously he sorrows on my account. We must do as he says, Crito; and therefore let the cup be brought, if the poison is prepared: if not, let the attendant prepare some.

CRITO: Yet, the sun is still upon the hill-tops, and I know that many a one has taken the draught late, and after the announcement has been made to him, he has eaten and drunk, and enjoyed the society of his beloved; do not hurry—there is time enough.

SOCRATES: Yes, Crito, and they of whom you speak are right in so acting, for they think that they will be gainers by the delay; but I am right in not following their example, for I do not think that I should gain anything by drinking the poison a little later; I should only be ridiculous in my own eyes for sparing and saving a life which is already forfeit. Please then to do as I say, and not to refuse me.

[**PHAEDO:** Crito made a sign to the servant, who was standing by; and he went out, and having been absent for some time, returned with the jailer carrying the cup of poison.]

SOCRATES: You, my good friend, who are experienced in these matters, shall give me directions how I am to proceed.

JAILER: You have only to walk about until your legs are heavy, and then to lie down, and the poison will act.

[At the same time he handed the cup to Socrates, who in the easiest and gentlest manner, without the least

fear or change of color or feature, looking at the man with all his eyes, Echecrates, as his manner was, took the cup and said]

SOCRATES: What do you say about making a libation out of this cup to any god? May I, or not?

JAILER: We only prepare, Socrates, just so much as we deem enough.

SOCRATES: I understand: but I may and must ask the gods to prosper my journey from this to the other world—even so—and so be it according to my prayer.

[**PHAEDO:** Then raising the cup to his lips, quite readily and cheerfully he drank off the poison. And hitherto most of us had been able to control our sorrow; but now when we saw him drinking, and saw too that he had finished the draught, we could no longer forbear, and in spite of myself my own tears were flowing fast; so that I covered my face and wept, not for him, but at the thought of my own calamity in having to part from such a friend. Nor was I the first; for Crito, when he found himself unable to restrain his tears, had got up, and I followed; and at that moment, Apollodorus, who had been weeping all the time, broke out in a loud and passionate cry which made cowards of us all. Socrates alone retained his calmness.]

SOCRATES: What is this strange outcry? I sent away the women mainly in order that they might not misbehave in this way, for I have been told that a man should die in peace. Be quiet, then, and have patience.

PHAEDO: When we heard his words we were ashamed, and refrained our tears; and he walked about until, as he said, his legs began to fail, and then he lay on his back, according to the directions, and the man who gave him the poison now and then looked at his feet and legs; and after a while he pressed his foot hard, and asked him if he could feel; No; and then his leg, and so upwards and upwards, and showed us that he was cold and stiff. And he felt them himself, and said]

SOCRATES: When the poison reaches the heart, that will be the end.

[**PHAEDO:** He was beginning to grow cold about the groin, when he uncovered his face, for he had covered himself up, and said—they were his last words—]

SOCRATES: Crito, I owe a rooster to Asclepius; will you remember to pay the debt?

CRITO: The debt shall be paid; is there anything else?

[**PHAEDO:** There was no answer to this question; but in a minute or two a movement was heard, and the attendants uncovered him; his eyes were set, and Crito closed his eyes and mouth.

Such was the end, Echecrates, of our friend; concerning whom I may truly say, that of all the men of his time whom I have known, he was the wisest and justest and best.]

[The Dialogues of Plato. Trans. By Benjamin Jowett (London: Macmillan, 1891).]

CHAPTER THREE

Plato on Enlightenment and the Soul

Image © Dimitrios, 2014. Used under license from Shutterstock, Inc.

Plato (428–347 BCE)

SELECTED READINGS

"The Allegory of the Cave" from
The Republic – Book VII

Plato

(Translated by Benjamin Jowett and edited by Joseph R. Kirkland)

SOCRATES: Now let me depict how far our human nature is enlightened or unenlightened: Imagine human beings living in an underground cavern, with the mouth of the cave open towards the light and reaching deep into the den. Here they have been from childhood, with their legs and necks chained so that they cannot move and can only see in front of them, being prevented by the chains from turning their heads around. Above and behind them a fire is blazing at a distance, and between the fire and the prisoners there is a raised way with a low wall built alongside it, like the screen which marionette players have in front of them, above which they show their puppets.

GLAUCON: I see.

SOCRATES: Now imagine there are men passing along the wall carrying all sorts of vessels, and statues and figures of animals made of wood and stone and various materials, which appear above the wall. Some of them are talking, while others remain silent.

GLAUCON: You have shown me a strange image, and strange prisoners.

SOCRATES: They are like ourselves. Do they not see only their own shadows, or the shadows of one another, which the fire throws on the opposite wall of the cave?

GLAUCON: True, how could they see anything but the shadows if they were never allowed to move their heads?

SOCRATES: And as for the objects which are being carried in like manner, they would only see their shadows as well?

GLAUCON: Yes.

SOCRATES: And if the prisoners were able to converse with one another, would they not suppose that they were naming what was actually before them?

GLAUCON: Very true.

SOCRATES: And suppose further that the prison had an echo which came from the other side, would they not be sure to believe that, when one of the passers-by spoke, the voice which they heard came from the passing shadow?

GLAUCON: No question.

SOCRATES: To them the truth would be literally nothing but the shadows of the images.

GLAUCON: That is certain.

SOCRATES: And now look again, and see what will naturally follow if the prisoners are released and cured of their error. At first, when any of them is liberated and compelled suddenly to stand up and turn his neck round and walk and look towards the light, he will suffer sharp pains. The glare will distress him, and he will be unable to see the realities of which in his former state he had seen the shadows; and then imagine someone now saying to him that what he saw before was an illusion, but that now, when he is approaching nearer to being and his eye is turned towards more real existence, he has a clearer vision,—what will be his reply? And you may further imagine that his instructor is pointing to the objects as they pass and requiring him to name them,—will he not be perplexed? Will he not believe that the shadows which he formerly saw are truer than the objects which are now shown to him?

GLAUCON: Far truer.

SOCRATES: And if he is compelled to look straight at the light, will he not have a pain in his eyes which will make him turn away to take refuge in those objects of vision he can see, and which he will take to be in reality clearer than the things which are now being shown to him?

GLAUCON: True.

SOCRATES: And suppose once more, that he is reluctantly dragged up a steep and rugged ascent, and held fast until he is forced into the presence of the sun itself, is he not likely to be pained and irritated? When he approaches the light his eyes will be dazzled, and he will not be able to see anything at all of what are now called realities.

GLAUCON: Not right away, no.

SOCRATES: He will require time to grow accustomed to the sight of the upper world. First he will see the shadows of objects best, next the reflections of men and other objects in the water, and then the objects themselves. Then he will gaze upon the light of the moon and the stars and the spangled heaven, and he will see the sky and the stars by night better than the sun or the light of the sun by day?

GLAUCON: Certainly.

SOCRATES: Last of all he will be able to see the sun, and not mere reflections of it in the water, but he will see it in its own proper place, and not in another; and he will contemplate it as it is.

GLAUCON: Certainly.

SOCRATES: He will then proceed to argue that it is the sun who gives the season and the years and is the guardian of all that is in the visible world, and in a certain way the cause of all things which he and his fellows have been accustomed to behold?

GLAUCON: Clearly he would first see the sun and then reason about it.

SOCRATES: And when he remembered his old home, and the "wisdom" of the cave and his fellow-prisoners, do you not suppose that he would celebrate his new circumstances and pity them?

GLAUCON: Certainly, he would.

SOCRATES: And if they were in the habit of conferring honors among themselves on those who were quickest to observe the passing shadows and to remark which of them went before, and which followed after, and which were together; and who were therefore best able to draw conclusions as to which shadows would come next, do you think that he would care for such honors and glories, or envy the possessors of them? Would he not say with Homer: "Better to be the poor servant of a poor master," and to endure anything rather than think as they do and live after their manner?

GLAUCON: Yes, I think that he would rather suffer anything than entertain these false notions and live in their miserable manner.

SOCRATES: Imagine once more such a person coming suddenly out of the sun and returning to the depths of the cave; would he not be certain to have his eyes full of darkness?

GLAUCON: To be sure.

SOCRATES: And if there were a contest, and he had to compete in measuring the shadows with the prisoners who had never moved out of the den, while his sight was still weak, and before his eyes had become steady (and the time which would be needed to acquire this new habit of sight might be very considerable), would he not be ridiculous? Men would say of him that up he went and down he came without his eyes; and that it was better not even to think of ascending; and if any one tried to free another and lead him up to the light, let them only catch the offender, and they would put him to death.

GLAUCON: No question.

SOCRATES: This entire allegory you may now append, dear Glaucon, to the previous argument; the prison-house is the world of sight, the light of the fire is the sun, and you will not misapprehend me if you interpret the journey upwards to be the ascent of the soul into the intellectual world according to my poor belief, which, at your desire, I have expressed—whether rightly or wrongly God knows. But, whether true or false, my opinion is that in the world of knowledge the idea of good appears last of all, and is seen only with an effort; and, when seen, is also inferred to be the universal author of all things beautiful and right, parent of light and of the lord of light in this visible world, and the immediate source of reason and truth in the intellectual; and that this is the power upon which he who would act rationally either in public or private life must have his eye fixed.

GLAUCON: I agree as far as I am able to understand you.

SOCRATES: Moreover you must not wonder that those who attain to this beatific vision are unwilling to descend to human affairs; for their souls are ever hastening into the upper world where they desire to dwell; which desire of theirs is very natural, if our allegory may be trusted.

GLAUCON: Yes, very natural.

SOCRATES: And is there anything surprising in one who passes from divine contemplations to the evil state of man, misbehaving himself in a ridiculous manner; if, while his eyes are blinking and before he has become accustomed to the surrounding darkness, he is compelled to fight in courts of law, or in other places, about the images or the shadows of images of justice, and is endeavoring to meet the conceptions of those who have never yet seen absolute justice?

GLAUCON: Anything but surprising.

SOCRATES: Anyone who has common sense will remember that the bewilderments of the eyes are of two kinds, and arise from two causes, either from coming out of the light or from going into the light, which is true of the mind's eye, quite as much as of the bodily eye; and he who remembers this when he sees any one whose vision is perplexed and weak, will not be too ready to laugh; he will first ask whether that soul of man has come out of the brighter life, and is unable to see because unaccustomed to the dark, or having turned from darkness to the day is dazzled by excess of light. And he will count the one happy in his condition and state of being, and he will pity the other; or, if he have a mind to laugh at the soul which comes from below into the light, there will be more reason in this than in the laugh which greets him who returns from above out of the light into the den.

GLAUCON: That is a very just distinction.

SOCRATES: But then, if I am right, certain professors of education must be wrong when they say that they can put a knowledge into the soul which was not there before, like sight into blind eyes.

GLAUCON: They undoubtedly say this.

SOCRATES: Whereas, our argument shows that the power and capacity of learning exists in the soul already; and that just as the eye was unable to turn from darkness to light without the whole body, so too the instrument of knowledge can only by the movement of the whole soul be turned from the world of becoming into that of being, and learn by degrees to endure the sight of being, and of the brightest and best of being, or in other words, of the good.

[The Dialogues of Plato. *Trans. By Benjamin Jowett (London: Macmillan, 1891).]*

Phaedo

Plato

(Translated by Benjamin Jowett and edited by Joseph R. Kirkland)

PERSONS OF THE DIALOGUE: Phaedo, Socrates,
Apollodorus, Simmias, Cebes, Crito, and a Jailer
SCENE: The Prison of Socrates

ECHECRATES: Were you yourself, Phaedo, in the prison with Socrates on the day when he drank the poison?

PHAEDO: Yes, Echecrates, I was.

ECHECRATES: I should so like to hear about his death. What did he say in his last hours? We were informed that he died by taking poison, but no one knew anything more; for no Phliasian ever goes to Athens now, and it is a long time since any stranger from Athens has found his way hither; so that we had no clear account.

PHAEDO: Did you not hear of the proceedings at the trial?

...

ECHECRATES: What was the manner of his death, Phaedo? What was said or done? And which of his friends were with him? Or did the authorities forbid them to be present—so that he had no friends near him when he died?

PHAEDO: No; there were several of them with him.

ECHECRATES: If you have nothing to do, I wish that you would tell me what passed, as exactly as you can.

PHAEDO: I have nothing at all to do, and will try to gratify your wish. To be reminded of Socrates is always the greatest delight to me, whether I speak myself or hear another speak of him.

ECHECRATES: You will have listeners who are of the same mind with you, and I hope that you will be as exact as you can.

PHAEDO: I had a singular feeling at being in his company. For I could hardly believe that I was present at the death of a friend, and therefore I did not pity him, Echecrates; he died so fearlessly, and his words and bearing were so noble and gracious, that to me he appeared blessed. I thought that in going to the other world he could not be without a divine call, and that he would be happy, if any man ever was, when he arrived there, and therefore I did not pity him as might have seemed natural at such an hour. But I had not the pleasure which I usually feel in philosophical discourse (for philosophy was the theme of which we spoke). I was pleased, but in the pleasure there was also a strange admixture of pain; for I reflected that he was soon to die, and this double feeling was shared by us all; we were laughing and weeping by turns, especially the excitable Apollodorus—you know the sort of man?

ECHECRATES: Yes.

PHAEDO: He was quite beside himself; and I and all of us were greatly moved.

ECHECRATES: Who were present?

PHAEDO: Of native Athenians there were, besides Apollodorus, Critobulus and his father Crito, Hermogenes, Epigenes, Aeschines, Antisthenes; likewise Ctesippus of the deme of Paeania, Menexenus, and some others; Plato, if I am not mistaken, was ill.

ECHECRATES: Were there any strangers?

PHAEDO: Yes, there were; Simmias the Theban, and Cebes, and Phaedondes; Euclid and Terpison, who came from Megara.

ECHECRATES: And was Aristippus there, and Cleombrotus?

PHAEDO: No, they were said to be in Aegina.

ECHECRATES: Anyone else?

PHAEDO: I think that these were nearly all.

ECHECRATES: Well, and what did you talk about?

PHAEDO: I will begin at the beginning, and endeavor to repeat the entire conversation. On the previous days we had been in the habit of assembling early in the morning at the court in which the trial took place, and which is not far from the prison. There we used to wait talking with one another until the opening of the doors (for they were not opened very early); then we went in and generally passed the day with Socrates. On the last morning we assembled sooner than usual, having heard on the day before when we quitted the prison in the evening that the sacred ship had come from Delos, and so we arranged to meet very early at the accustomed place. On our arrival the jailer who answered the door, instead of admitting us, came out and told us to stay until he called us.

JAILER: For the Eleven are now with Socrates; they are taking off his chains, and giving orders that he is to die today.

[He soon returned and said that we might come in. On entering we found Socrates just released from chains, and Xanthippe, whom you know, sitting by him, and holding his child in her arms. When she saw us she uttered a cry and said, as women will]

XANTHIPPE: O Socrates, this is the last time that either you will converse with your friends, or they with you!

[Socrates turned to Crito and said]

SOCRATES: Crito, let someone take her home.

[Some of Crito's people accordingly led her away, crying out and beating herself. And when she was gone, Socrates, sitting up on the couch, bent and rubbed his leg, saying, as he was rubbing]

SOCRATES: How singular is the thing called pleasure, and how curiously related to pain, which might be thought to be the opposite of it; for they are never present to a man at the same instant, and yet he who pursues either is generally compelled to take the other; their bodies are two, but they are joined by a single head. And I cannot help thinking that if Aesop had remembered them, he would have made a fable about God trying to reconcile their strife, and how, when he could not, he fastened their heads together; and this is the reason why when one comes the other follows, as I know by my own experience now, when after the pain in my leg which was caused by the chain pleasure appears to succeed.

CEBES: I am glad, Socrates, that you have mentioned the name of Aesop. For it reminds me of a question which has been asked by many, and was asked of me only the day before yesterday by Evenus the poet—he will be sure to ask it again, and therefore if you would like me to have an answer ready for him, you may as well tell me

what I should say to him:—he wanted to know why you, who never before wrote a line of poetry, now that you are in prison are turning Aesop's fables into verse, and also composing that hymn in honor of Apollo.

SOCRATES: Tell him, Cebes, what is the truth—that I had no idea of rivalling him or his poems; to do so, as I knew, would be no easy task. But I wanted to see whether I could purge away a scruple which I felt about the meaning of certain dreams. In the course of my life I have often had intimations in dreams 'that I should compose music.' The same dream came to me sometimes in one form, and sometimes in another, but always saying the same or nearly the same words: 'Cultivate and make music,' said the dream. And hitherto I had imagined that this was only intended to exhort and encourage me in the study of philosophy, which has been the pursuit of my life, and is the noblest and best of music. The dream was bidding me do what I was already doing, in the same way that the competitor in a race is bidden by the spectators to run when he is already running. But I was not certain of this, for the dream might have meant music in the popular sense of the word, and being under sentence of death, and the festival giving me a respite, I thought that it would be safer for me to satisfy the scruple, and, in obedience to the dream, to compose a few verses before I departed. And first I made a hymn in honor of the god of the festival, and then considering that a poet, if he is really to be a poet, should not only put together words, but should invent stories, and that I have no invention, I took some fables of Aesop, which I had ready at hand and which I knew—they were the first I came upon—and turned them into verse. Tell this to Evenus, Cebes, and bid him be of good cheer; say that I would have him come after me if he be a wise man, and not tarry; and that to-day I am likely to be going, for the Athenians say that I must.

SIMMIAS: What a message for such a man! Having been a frequent companion of his I should say that, as far as I know him, he will never take your advice unless he is obliged.

SOCRATES: Why, is not Evenus a philosopher?

SIMMIAS: I think that he is.

SOCRATES: Then he, or any man who has the spirit of philosophy, will be willing to die, but he will not take his own life, for that is held to be unlawful.

[**PHAEDO:** Here he changed his position, and put his legs off the couch on to the ground, and during the rest of the conversation he remained sitting.]

CEBES: Why do you say that a man ought not to take his own life, but that the philosopher will be ready to follow the dying?

SOCRATES: And have you, Cebes and Simmias, who are the disciples of Philolaus, never heard him speak of this?

CEBES: Yes, but his language was obscure, Socrates.

SOCRATES: My words, too, are only an echo; but there is no reason why I should not repeat what I have heard: and indeed, as I am going to another place, it is very meet for me to be thinking and talking of the nature of the pilgrimage which I am about to make. What can I do better in the interval between this and the setting of the sun?

CEBES: Then tell me, Socrates, why is suicide held to be unlawful? As I have certainly heard Philolaus, about whom you were just now asking, affirm when he was staying with us at Thebes: and there are others who say the same, although I have never understood what was meant by any of them.

SOCRATES: Do not lose heart, and the day may come when you will understand. I suppose that you wonder why, when other things which are evil may be good at certain times and to certain persons, death is to be the only exception, and why, when a man is better dead, he is not permitted to be his own benefactor, but must wait for the hand of another.

CEBES: Very true, laughing gently and speaking in his native Boeotian.

SOCRATES: I admit the appearance of inconsistency in what I am saying; but there may not be any real inconsistency after all. There is a doctrine whispered in secret that man is a prisoner who has no right to open the door and run away; this is a great mystery which I do not quite understand. Yet I too believe that the gods are our guardians, and that we are a possession of theirs. Do you not agree?

CEBES: Yes, I quite agree.

SOCRATES: And if one of your own possessions, an ox or an ass, for example, took the liberty of putting himself out of the way when you had given no intimation of your wish that he should die, would you not be angry with him, and would you not punish him if you could?

CEBES: Certainly.

SOCRATES: Then, if we look at the matter thus, there may be reason in saying that a man should wait, and not take his own life until God summons him, as he is now summoning me.

CEBES: Yes, Socrates, there seems to be truth in what you say. And yet how can you reconcile this seemingly true belief that God is our guardian and we his possessions, with the willingness to die which we were just now attributing to the philosopher? That the wisest of men should be willing to leave a service in which they are ruled by the gods who are the best of rulers, is not reasonable; for surely no wise man thinks that when set at liberty he can take better care of himself than the gods take of him. A fool may perhaps think so—he may argue that he had better run away from his master, not considering that his duty is to remain to the end, and not to run away from the good, and that there would be no sense in his running away. The wise man will want to be ever with him who is better than himself. Now this, Socrates, is the reverse of what was just now said; for upon this view the wise man should sorrow and the fool rejoice at passing out of life.

[**PHAEDO:** The earnestness of Cebes seemed to please Socrates.]

SOCRATES: Here is a man who is always inquiring, and is not so easily convinced by the first thing which he hears.

SIMMIAS: And certainly, the objection which he is now making does appear to me to have some force. For what can be the meaning of a truly wise man wanting to fly away and lightly leave a master who is better than himself? And I rather imagine that Cebes is referring to you; he thinks that you are too ready to leave us, and too ready to leave the gods whom you acknowledge to be our good masters.

SOCRATES: Yes. There is reason in what you say. And so you think that I ought to answer your indictment as if I were in a court?

SIMMIAS: We should like you to do so.

SOCRATES: Then I must try to make a more successful defense before you than I did when before the judges. For I am quite ready to admit, Simmias and Cebes, that I ought to be grieved at death, if I were not persuaded in the first place that I am going to other gods who are wise and good (of which I am as certain as I can be of any such matters), and secondly (though I am not so sure of this last) to men departed, better than those whom I leave behind; and therefore I do not grieve as I might have done, for I have good hope that there is yet something remaining for the dead, and as has been said of old, some far better thing for the good than for the evil.

SIMMIAS: But do you mean to take away your thoughts with you, Socrates? Will you not impart them to us?—for they are a benefit in which we too are entitled to share. Moreover, if you succeed in convincing us, that will be an answer to the charge against yourself.

SOCRATES: I will do my best. But you must first let me hear what Crito wants; he has long been wishing to say something to me.

CRITO: Only this, Socrates: the attendant who is to give you the poison has been telling me, and he wants me to tell you, that you are not to talk much, talking, he says, increases heat, and this is apt to interfere with the action of the poison; persons who excite themselves are sometimes obliged to take a second or even a third dose.

SOCRATES: Then let him mind his business and be prepared to give the poison twice or even thrice if necessary; that is all.

CRITO: I knew quite well what you would say, but I was obliged to satisfy him.

SOCRATES: Never mind him.

And now, O my judges, I desire to prove to you that the real philosopher has reason to be of good cheer when he is about to die, and that after death he may hope to obtain the greatest good in the other world. And how this may be, Simmias and Cebes, I will endeavor to explain. For I deem that the true votary of philosophy is likely to be misunderstood by other men; they do not perceive that he is always pursuing death and dying; and if this be so, and he has had the desire of death all his life long, why when his time comes should he repine at that which he has been always pursuing and desiring?

SIMMIAS: [laughingly, though not in a laughing humor] You have made me laugh, Socrates; for I cannot help thinking that the many when they hear your words will say how truly you have described philosophers, and our people at home will likewise say that the life which philosophers desire is in reality death, and that they have found them out to be deserving of the death which they desire.

SOCRATES: And they are right, Simmias, in thinking so, with the exception of the words 'they have found them out'; for they have not found out either what is the nature of that death which the true philosopher deserves, or how he deserves or desires death. But enough of them:—let us discuss the matter among ourselves: Do we believe that there is such a thing as death?

SIMMIAS: To be sure.

SOCRATES: Is it not the separation of soul and body? And to be dead is the completion of this; when the soul exists in herself, and is released from the body and the body is released from the soul, what is this but death?

SIMMIAS: Just so.

SOCRATES: There is another question, which will probably throw light on our present inquiry if you and I can agree about it:—Ought the philosopher to care about the pleasures—if they are to be called pleasures—of eating and drinking?

SIMMIAS: Certainly not.

SOCRATES: And what about the pleasures of love—should he care for them?

SIMMIAS: By no means.

SOCRATES: And will he think much of the other ways of indulging the body, for example, the acquisition of costly raiment, or sandals, or other adornments of the body? Instead of caring about them, does he not rather despise anything more than nature needs? What do you say?

SIMMIAS: I should say that the true philosopher would despise them.

SOCRATES: Would you not say that he is entirely concerned with the soul and not with the body? He would like, as far as he can, to get away from the body and to turn to the soul.

SIMMIAS: Quite true.

SOCRATES: In matters of this sort philosophers, above all other men, may be observed in every sort of way to dissever the soul from the communion of the body.

SIMMIAS: Very true.

SOCRATES: Whereas, Simmias, the rest of the world are of opinion that to him who has no sense of pleasure and no part in bodily pleasure, life is not worth having; and that he who is indifferent about them is as good as dead.

SIMMIAS: That is also true.

SOCRATES: What again shall we say of the actual acquirement of knowledge?—is the body, if invited to share in the enquiry, a hinderer or a helper? I mean to say, have sight and hearing any truth in them? Are they not, as the poets are always telling us, inaccurate witnesses? And yet, if even they are inaccurate and indistinct, what is to be said of the other senses?—for you will allow that they are the best of them?

SIMMIAS: Certainly.

SOCRATES: Then when does the soul attain truth?—for in attempting to consider anything in company with the body she is obviously deceived.

SIMMIAS: True.

SOCRATES: Then must not true existence be revealed to her in thought, if at all?

SIMMIAS: Yes.

SOCRATES: And thought is best when the mind is gathered into herself and none of these things trouble her—neither sounds nor sights nor pain nor any pleasure,—when she takes leave of the body, and has as little as possible to do with it, when she has no bodily sense or desire, but is aspiring after true being?

SIMMIAS: Certainly.

SOCRATES: And in this the philosopher dishonors the body; his soul runs away from his body and desires to be alone and by herself?

SIMMIAS: That is true.

SOCRATES: Well, but there is another thing, Simmias: Is there or is there not an absolute justice?

SIMMIAS: Assuredly there is.

SOCRATES: And an absolute beauty and absolute good?

SIMMIAS: Of course.

SOCRATES: But did you ever behold any of them with your eyes?

SIMMIAS: Certainly not.

SOCRATES: Or did you ever reach them with any other bodily sense?—and I speak not of these alone, but of absolute greatness, and health, and strength, and of the essence or true nature of everything. Has the reality of them ever been perceived by you through the bodily organs? Or rather, is not the nearest approach to the knowledge of their several natures made by him who so orders his intellectual vision as to have the most exact conception of the essence of each thing which he considers?

SIMMIAS: Certainly.

SOCRATES: And he attains to the purest knowledge of them who goes to each with the mind alone, not introducing or intruding in the act of thought sight or any other sense together with reason, but with the very light of the mind in her own clearness searches into the very truth of each; he who has got rid, as far as he can, of eyes and ears and, so to speak, of the whole body, these being in his opinion distracting elements which when they infect the soul hinder her from acquiring truth and knowledge—who, if not he, is likely to attain the knowledge of true being?

SIMMIAS: What you say has a wonderful truth in it, Socrates.

SOCRATES: And when real philosophers consider all these things, will they not be led to make a reflection which they will express in words something like the following? 'Have we not found,' they will say, 'a path of thought which seems to bring us and our argument to the conclusion, that while we are in the body, and while the soul is infected with the evils of the body, our desire will not be satisfied? And our desire is of the truth. For the body is a source of endless trouble to us by reason of the mere requirement of food; and is liable also to diseases which overtake and impede us in the search after true being: it fills us full of loves, and lusts, and fears, and fancies of all kinds, and endless foolery, and in fact, as men say, takes away from us the power of thinking at all. Whence come wars, and fighting, and factions? Whence but from the body and the lusts of the body? Wars are occasioned by the love of money, and money has to be acquired for the sake and in the service of the body; and by reason of all these impediments we have no time to give to philosophy; and, last and worst of all, even if we are at leisure and betake ourselves to some speculation, the body is always breaking in upon us, causing turmoil and confusion in our enquiries, and so amazing us that we are prevented from seeing the truth. It has been proved to us by experience that if we would have pure knowledge of anything we must be quit of the body—the soul in herself must behold things in themselves: and then we shall attain the wisdom which we desire, and of which we say that we are lovers, not while we live, but after death; for if while in company with the body, the soul cannot have pure knowledge, one of two things follows—either knowledge is not to be attained at all, or, if at all, after death. For then, and not till then, the soul will be parted from the body and exist in herself alone. In this present life, I reckon that we make the nearest approach to knowledge when we have the least possible intercourse or communion with the body, and are not surfeited with the bodily nature, but keep ourselves pure until the hour when God himself is pleased to release us. And thus having got rid of the foolishness of the body we shall be pure and hold converse with the pure, and know of ourselves the clear light everywhere, which is no other than the light of truth. For the impure are not permitted to approach the pure. These are the sort of words, Simmias, which the true lovers of knowledge cannot help saying to one another, and thinking. You would agree; would you not?

SIMMIAS: Undoubtedly, Socrates.

SOCRATES: But, O my friend, if this is true, there is great reason to hope that, going whither I go, when I have come to the end of my journey, I shall attain that which has been the pursuit of my life. And therefore I go on my way rejoicing, and not I only, but every other man who believes that his mind has been made ready and that he is in a manner purified.

SIMMIAS: Certainly.

SOCRATES: And what is purification but the separation of the soul from the body, as I was saying before; the habit of the soul gathering and collecting herself into herself from all sides out of the body; the dwelling in her own place alone, as in another life, so also in this, as far as she can;—the release of the soul from the chains of the body?

SIMMIAS: Very true.

SOCRATES: And this separation and release of the soul from the body is termed death?

SIMMIAS: To be sure.

SOCRATES: And the true philosophers, and they only, are ever seeking to release the soul. Is not the separation and release of the soul from the body their especial study?

SIMMIAS: That is true.

SOCRATES: And, as I was saying at first, there would be a ridiculous contradiction in men studying to live as nearly as they can in a state of death, and yet repining when it comes upon them.

SIMMIAS: Clearly.

SOCRATES: And the true philosophers, Simmias, are always occupied in the practice of dying, wherefore also to them least of all men is death terrible. Look at the matter thus:—if they have been in every way the enemies of the body, and are wanting to be alone with the soul, when this desire of theirs is granted, how inconsistent would they be if they trembled and repined, instead of rejoicing at their departure to that place where, when they arrive, they hope to gain that which in life they desired—and this was wisdom—and at the same time to be rid of the company of their enemy. Many a man has been willing to go to the world below animated by the hope of seeing there an earthly love, or wife, or son, and conversing with them. And will he who is a true lover of wisdom, and is strongly persuaded in like manner that only in the world below he can worthily enjoy her, still repine at death? Will he not depart with joy? Surely he will, O my friend, if he be a true philosopher. For he will have a firm conviction that there and there only, he can find wisdom in her purity. And if this be true, he would be very absurd, as I was saying, if he were afraid of death.

SIMMIAS: He would, indeed.

SOCRATES: And when you see a man who is repining at the approach of death, is not his reluctance a sufficient proof that he is not a lover of wisdom, but a lover of the body, and probably at the same time a lover of either money or power, or both?

SIMMIAS: Quite so.

SOCRATES: And is not courage, Simmias, a quality which is especially characteristic of the philosopher?

SIMMIAS: Certainly.

SOCRATES: There is temperance again, which even by the vulgar is supposed to consist in the control and regulation of the passions, and in the sense of superiority to them—is not temperance a virtue belonging to those only who despise the body, and who pass their lives in philosophy?

SIMMIAS: Most assuredly.

SOCRATES: For the courage and temperance of other men, if you will consider them, are really a contradiction.

SIMMIAS: How so?

SOCRATES: Well, you are aware that death is regarded by men in general as a great evil.

SIMMIAS: Very true.

SOCRATES: And do not courageous men face death because they are afraid of yet greater evils?

SIMMIAS: That is quite true.

SOCRATES: Then all but the philosophers are courageous only from fear, and because they are afraid; and yet that a man should be courageous from fear, and because he is a coward, is surely a strange thing.

SIMMIAS: Very true.

SOCRATES: And are not the temperate exactly in the same case? They are temperate because they are intemperate—which might seem to be a contradiction, but is nevertheless the sort of thing which happens with this foolish temperance. For there are pleasures which they are afraid of losing; and in their desire to keep them, they abstain from some pleasures, because they are overcome by others; and although to be conquered by pleasure is called by men intemperance, to them the conquest of pleasure consists in being conquered by pleasure. And that is what I mean by saying that, in a sense, they are made temperate through intemperance.

SIMMIAS: Such appears to be the case.

SOCRATES: Yet the exchange of one fear or pleasure or pain for another fear or pleasure or pain, and of the greater for the less, as if they were coins, is not the exchange of virtue. O, my blessed Simmias, is there not one true coin for which all things ought to be exchanged?—and that is wisdom; and only in exchange for this, and in company with this, is anything truly bought or sold, whether courage or temperance or justice. And is not all true virtue the companion of wisdom, no matter what fears or pleasures or other similar goods or evils may or may not attend her? But the virtue which is made up of these goods, when they are severed from wisdom and exchanged with one another, is a shadow of virtue only, nor is there any freedom or health or truth in her; but in the true exchange there is a purging away of all these things, and temperance, and justice, and courage, and wisdom herself are the purgation of them. The founders of the mysteries would appear to have had a real meaning, and were not talking nonsense when they intimated in a figure long ago that he who passes unsanctified and uninitiated into the world below will lie in a slough, but that he who arrives there after initiation and purification will dwell with the gods. For 'many,' as they say in the mysteries, 'are the thyrsus-bearers, but few are the mystics,'—meaning, as I interpret the words, 'the true philosophers.' In the number of whom, during my whole life, I have been seeking, according to my ability, to find a place;—whether I have sought in a right way or not, and whether I have succeeded or not, I shall truly know in a little while, if God will, when I myself arrive in the other world—such is my belief. And therefore I maintain that I am right, Simmias and Cebes, in not grieving or repining at parting from you and my masters in this world, for I believe that I shall equally find good masters and friends in another world. But most men do not believe this saying; if then I succeed in convincing you by my defense better than I did the Athenian judges, it will be well.

CEBES: I agree, Socrates, in the greater part of what you say. But in what concerns the soul, men are apt to be incredulous; they fear that when she has left the body her place may be nowhere, and that on the very day of death she may perish and come to an end—immediately on her release from the body, issuing forth dispersed like smoke or air and in her flight vanishing away into nothingness. If she could only be collected into herself after she has obtained release from the evils of which you are speaking, there would be good reason to hope, Socrates, that what you say is true. But surely it requires a great deal of argument and many proofs to show that when the man is dead his soul yet exists, and has any force or intelligence.

SOCRATES: True, Cebes. And shall I suggest that we converse a little of the probabilities of these things?

CEBES: I am sure that I should greatly like to know your opinion about them.

SOCRATES: I reckon that no one who heard me now, not even if he were one of my old enemies, the Comic poets, could accuse me of idle talking about matters in which I have no concern:—If you please, then, we will proceed with the inquiry.

Suppose we consider the question whether the souls of men after death are or are not in the world below. There comes into my mind an ancient doctrine which affirms that they go from hence into the other world, and returning hither, are born again from the dead. Now if it be true that the living come from the dead, then our souls must exist in the other world, for if not, how could they have been born again? And this would be conclusive, if there were any real evidence that the living are only born from the dead; but if this is not so, then other arguments will have to be adduced.

CEBES: Very true.

SOCRATES: Then let us consider the whole question, not in relation to man only, but in relation to animals generally, and to plants, and to everything of which there is generation, and the proof will be easier. Are not all things which have opposites generated out of their opposites? I mean such things as good and evil, just and unjust—and there are innumerable other opposites which are generated out of opposites. And I want to show that in all opposites there is of necessity a similar alternation; I mean to say, for example, that anything which becomes greater must become greater after being less.

CEBES: True.

SOCRATES: And that which becomes less must have been once greater and then have become less.

CEBES: Yes.

SOCRATES: And the weaker is generated from the stronger, and the swifter from the slower.

CEBES: Very true.

SOCRATES: And the worse is from the better, and the more just is from the more unjust.

CEBES: Of course.

SOCRATES: And is this true of all opposites? And are we convinced that all of them are generated out of opposites?

CEBES: Yes.

SOCRATES: And in this universal opposition of all things, are there not also two intermediate processes which are ever going on, from one to the other opposite, and back again; where there is a greater and a less there is also an intermediate process of increase and diminution, and that which grows is said to wax, and that which decays to wane?

CEBES: Yes.

SOCRATES: And there are many other processes, such as division and composition, cooling and heating, which equally involve a passage into and out of one another. And this necessarily holds of all opposites, even though not always expressed in words—they are really generated out of one another, and there is a passing or process from one to the other of them?

CEBES: Very true.

SOCRATES: Well, and is there not an opposite of life, as sleep is the opposite of waking?

CEBES: True.

SOCRATES: And what is it?

CEBES: Death.

SOCRATES: And these, if they are opposites, are generated the one from the other, and have there their two intermediate processes also?

CEBES: Of course.

SOCRATES: Now, I will analyze one of the two pairs of opposites which I have mentioned to you, and also its intermediate processes, and you shall analyze the other to me. One of them I term sleep, the other waking. The state of sleep is opposed to the state of waking, and out of sleeping waking is generated, and out of waking, sleeping; and the process of generation is in the one case falling asleep, and in the other waking up. Do you agree?

CEBES: I entirely agree.

SOCRATES: Then, suppose that you analyze life and death to me in the same manner. Is not death opposed to life?

CEBES: Yes.

SOCRATES: And they are generated one from the other?

CEBES: Yes.

SOCRATES: What is generated from the living?

CEBES: The dead.

SOCRATES: And what from the dead?

CEBES: I can only say in answer—the living.

SOCRATES: Then the living, whether things or persons, Cebes, are generated from the dead?

CEBES: That is clear.

SOCRATES: Then the inference is that our souls exist in the world below?

CEBES: That is true.

SOCRATES: And one of the two processes or generations is visible—for surely the act of dying is visible?

CEBES: Surely.

SOCRATES: What then is to be the result? Shall we exclude the opposite process? And shall we suppose nature to walk on one leg only? Must we not rather assign to death some corresponding process of generation?

CEBES: Certainly.

SOCRATES: And what is that process?

CEBES: Return to life.

SOCRATES: And return to life, if there be such a thing, is the birth of the dead into the world of the living?

CEBES: Quite true.

SOCRATES: Then here is a new way by which we arrive at the conclusion that the living come from the dead, just as the dead come from the living; and this, if true, affords a most certain proof that the souls of the dead exist in some place out of which they come again.

CEBES: Yes, Socrates, the conclusion seems to flow necessarily out of our previous admissions.

SOCRATES: And that these admissions were not unfair, Cebes, may be shown, I think, as follows: If generation were in a straight line only, and there were no compensation or circle in nature, no turn or return of elements into their opposites, then you know that all things would at last have the same form and pass into the same state, and there would be no more generation of them.

CEBES: What do you mean?

SOCRATES: A simple thing enough, which I will illustrate by the case of sleep. You know that if there were no alternation of sleeping and waking, the tale of the sleeping Endymion would in the end have no meaning, because all other things would be asleep, too, and he would not be distinguishable from the rest. Or if there were composition only, and no division of substances, then the chaos of Anaxagoras would come again. And in like manner, my dear Cebes, if all things which partook of life were to die, and after they were dead remained in the form of death, and did not come to life again, all would at last die, and nothing would be alive—what other result could there be? For if the living spring from any other things, and they too die, must not all things at last be swallowed up in death?

CEBES: There is no escape, Socrates, and to me your argument seems to be absolutely true.

SOCRATES: Yes, Cebes, it is and must be so, in my opinion; and we have not been deluded in making these admissions; but I am confident that there truly is such a thing as living again, and that the living spring from the dead, and that the souls of the dead are in existence, and that the good souls have a better portion than the evil.

CEBES: Your favorite doctrine, Socrates, that knowledge is simply recollection, if true, also necessarily implies a previous time in which we have learned that which we now recollect. But this would be impossible unless our soul had been in some place before existing in the form of man; here then is another proof of the soul's immortality.

SIMMIAS: But tell me, Cebes, interposing, what arguments are urged in favor of this doctrine of recollection. I am not very sure at the moment that I remember them.

CEBES: One excellent proof is afforded by questions. If you put a question to a person in a right way, he will give a true answer of himself, but how could he do this unless there were knowledge and right reason already in him? And this is most clearly shown when he is taken to a diagram or to anything of that sort.

SOCRATES: But if you are still incredulous, Simmias, I would ask you whether you may not agree with me when you look at the matter in another way;—I mean, if you are still incredulous as to whether knowledge is recollection.

SIMMIAS: Incredulous I am not, but I want to have this doctrine of recollection brought to my own recollection, and, from what Cebes has said, I am beginning to recollect and be convinced; but I should still like to hear what you were going to say.

SOCRATES: This is what I would say: we should agree, if I am not mistaken, that what a man recollects he must have known at some previous time.

SIMMIAS: Very true.

SOCRATES: And what is the nature of this knowledge or recollection? I mean to ask, Whether a person who, having seen or heard or in any way perceived anything, knows not only that, but has a conception of something else which is the subject, not of the same but of some other kind of knowledge, may not be fairly said to recollect that of which he has the conception?

SIMMIAS: What do you mean?

SOCRATES: I mean what I may illustrate by the following instance:—The knowledge of a lyre is not the same as the knowledge of a man?

SIMMIAS: True.

SOCRATES: And yet what is the feeling of lovers when they recognize a lyre, or a garment, or anything else which the beloved has been in the habit of using?

Do not they, from knowing the lyre, form in the mind's eye an image of the youth to whom the lyre belongs? And this is recollection. In like manner anyone who sees Simmias may remember Cebes; and there are endless examples of the same thing.

SIMMIAS: Endless, indeed.

SOCRATES: And recollection is most commonly a process of recovering that which has been already forgotten through time and inattention.

SIMMIAS: Very true.

SOCRATES: Well; and may you not also from seeing the picture of a horse or a lyre remember a man? And from the picture of Simmias, you may be led to remember Cebes?

SIMMIAS: True.

SOCRATES: Or you may also be led to the recollection of Simmias himself?

SIMMIAS: Quite so.

SOCRATES: And in all these cases, the recollection may be derived from things either like or unlike?

SIMMIAS: It may be.

SOCRATES: And when the recollection is derived from like things, then another consideration is sure to arise, which is—whether the likeness in any degree falls short or not of that which is recollected?

SIMMIAS: Very true.

SOCRATES: And shall we proceed a step further, and affirm that there is such a thing as equality, not of one piece of wood or stone with another, but that, over and above this, there is absolute equality? Shall we say so?

SIMMIAS: Say so, yes, and swear to it with all the confidence in life.

SOCRATES: And do we know the nature of this absolute essence?

SIMMIAS: To be sure.

SOCRATES: And whence did we obtain our knowledge? Did we not see equalities of material things, such as pieces of wood and stones, and gather from them the idea of an equality which is different from them? For you will acknowledge that there is a difference. Or look at the matter in another way:—Do not the same pieces of wood or stone appear at one time equal, and at another time unequal?

SIMMIAS: That is certain.

SOCRATES: But are real equals ever unequal? Or is the idea of equality the same as of inequality?

SIMMIAS: Impossible, Socrates.

SOCRATES: Then these (so-called) equals are not the same with the idea of equality?

SIMMIAS: I should say, clearly not, Socrates.

SOCRATES: And yet from these equals, although differing from the idea of equality, you conceived and attained that idea?

SIMMIAS: Very true.

SOCRATES: Which might be like, or might be unlike them?

SIMMIAS: Yes.

SOCRATES: But that makes no difference; whenever from seeing one thing you conceived another, whether like or unlike, there must surely have been an act of recollection?

SIMMIAS: Very true.

SOCRATES: But what would you say of equal portions of wood and stone, or other material equals? And what is the impression produced by them? Are they equals in the same sense in which absolute equality is equal? Or do they fall short of this perfect equality in a measure?

SIMMIAS: Yes, in a very great measure too.

SOCRATES: And must we not allow, that when I or any one, looking at any object, observes that the thing which he sees aims at being some other thing, but falls short of, and cannot be, that other thing, but is inferior, he who makes this observation must have had a previous knowledge of that to which the other, although similar, was inferior?

SIMMIAS: Certainly.

SOCRATES: And has not this been our own case in the matter of equals and of absolute equality?

SIMMIAS: Precisely.

SOCRATES: Then we must have known equality previously to the time when we first saw the material equals, and reflected that all these apparent equals strive to attain absolute equality, but fall short of it?

SIMMIAS: Very true.

SOCRATES: And we recognize also that this absolute equality has only been known, and can only be known, through the medium of sight or touch, or of some other of the senses, which are all alike in this respect?

SIMMIAS: Yes, Socrates, as far as the argument is concerned, one of them is the same as the other.

SOCRATES: From the senses then is derived the knowledge that all sensible things aim at an absolute equality of which they fall short?

SIMMIAS: Yes.

SOCRATES: Then before we began to see or hear or perceive in any way, we must have had a knowledge of absolute equality, or we could not have referred to that standard the equals which are derived from the senses?—for to that they all aspire, and of that they fall short.

SIMMIAS: No other inference can be drawn from the previous statements.

SOCRATES: And did we not see and hear and have the use of our other senses as soon as we were born?

SIMMIAS: Certainly.

SOCRATES: Then we must have acquired the knowledge of equality at some previous time?

SIMMIAS: Yes.

SOCRATES: That is to say, before we were born, I suppose?

SIMMIAS: True.

SOCRATES: And if we acquired this knowledge before we were born, and were born having the use of it, then we also knew before we were born and at the instant of birth not only the equal or the greater or the less, but all other ideas; for we are not speaking only of equality, but of beauty, goodness, justice, holiness, and of all which we stamp with the name of essence in the dialectical process, both when we ask and when we answer questions. Of all this we may certainly affirm that we acquired the knowledge before birth?

SIMMIAS: We may.

SOCRATES: But if, after having acquired, we have not forgotten what in each case we acquired, then we must always have come into life having knowledge, and shall always continue to know as long as life lasts—for knowing is the acquiring and retaining knowledge and not forgetting. Is not forgetting, Simmias, just the losing of knowledge?

SIMMIAS: Quite true, Socrates.

SOCRATES: But if the knowledge which we acquired before birth was lost by us at birth, and if afterwards by the use of the senses we recovered what we previously knew, will not the process which we call learning be a recovering of the knowledge which is natural to us, and may not this be rightly termed recollection?

SIMMIAS: Very true.

SOCRATES: So much is clear—that when we perceive something, either by the help of sight, or hearing, or some other sense, from that perception we are able to obtain a notion of some other thing like or unlike which is associated with it but has been forgotten. Whence, as I was saying, one of two alternatives follows:—either we had this knowledge at birth, and continued to know through life; or, after birth, those who are said to learn only remember, and learning is simply recollection.

SIMMIAS: Yes, that is quite true, Socrates.

SOCRATES: And which alternative, Simmias, do you prefer? Had we the knowledge at our birth, or did we recollect the things which we knew previously to our birth?

SIMMIAS: I cannot decide at the moment.

SOCRATES: At any rate you can decide whether he who has knowledge will or will not be able to render an account of his knowledge? What do you say?

SIMMIAS: Certainly, he will.

SOCRATES: But do you think that every man is able to give an account of these very matters about which we are speaking?

SIMMIAS: Would that they could, Socrates, but I rather fear that tomorrow, at this time, there will no longer be any one alive who is able to give an account of them such as ought to be given.

SOCRATES: Then you are not of opinion, Simmias, that all men know these things?

SIMMIAS: Certainly not.

SOCRATES: They are in process of recollecting that which they learned before?

SIMMIAS: Certainly.

SOCRATES: But when did our souls acquire this knowledge?—not since we were born as men?

SIMMIAS: Certainly not.

SOCRATES: And therefore, previously?

SIMMIAS: Yes.

SOCRATES: Then, Simmias, our souls must also have existed without bodies before they were in the form of man, and must have had intelligence.

SIMMIAS: Unless indeed you suppose, Socrates, that these notions are given us at the very moment of birth; for this is the only time which remains.

SOCRATES: Yes, my friend, but if so, when do we lose them? For they are not in us when we are born—that is admitted. Do we lose them at the moment of receiving them, or if not at what other time?

SIMMIAS: No, Socrates, I perceive that I was unconsciously talking nonsense.

SOCRATES: Then may we not say, Simmias, that if, as we are always repeating, there is an absolute beauty, and goodness, and an absolute essence of all things; and if to this, which is now discovered to have existed in our former state, we refer all our sensations, and with this compare them, finding these ideas to be pre-existent and our inborn possession—then our souls must have had a prior existence, but if not, there would be no force in the argument? There is the same proof that these ideas must have existed before we were born, as that our souls existed before we were born; and if not the ideas, then not the souls.

SIMMIAS: Yes, Socrates; I am convinced that there is precisely the same necessity for the one as for the other; and the argument retreats successfully to the position that the existence of the soul before birth cannot be separated from the existence of the essence of which you speak. For there is nothing which to my mind is so patent as that beauty, goodness, and the other notions of which you were just now speaking, have a most real and absolute existence; and I am satisfied with the proof.

SOCRATES: Well, but is Cebes equally satisfied? For I must convince him too.

SIMMIAS: I think that Cebes is satisfied: although he is the most incredulous of mortals, yet I believe that he is sufficiently convinced of the existence of the soul before birth. But that after death the soul will continue to exist is not yet proven even to my own satisfaction. I cannot get rid of the feeling of the many to which Cebes was referring—the feeling that when the man dies the soul will be dispersed, and that this may be the extinction of her. For admitting that she may have been born elsewhere, and framed out of other elements, and was in existence before entering the human body, why after having entered in and gone out again may she not herself be destroyed and come to an end?

CEBES: Very true, Simmias; about half of what was required has been proven; to wit, that our souls existed before we were born:—that the soul will exist after death as well as before birth is the other half of which the proof is still wanting, and has to be supplied; when that is given the demonstration will be complete.

SOCRATES: But that proof, Simmias and Cebes, has been already given, if you put the two arguments together—I mean this and the former one, in which we admitted that everything living is born of the dead. For if the soul exists before birth, and in coming to life and being born can be born only from death and dying, must she not after death continue to exist, since she has to be born again?—Surely the proof which you desire has been already furnished. Still I suspect that you and Simmias would be glad to probe the argument further. Like children, you are haunted with a fear that when the soul leaves the body, the wind may really blow her away and scatter her; especially if a man should happen to die in a great storm and not when the sky is calm.

CEBES: [smiling] Then, Socrates, you must argue us out of our fears—and yet, strictly speaking, they are not our fears, but there is a child within us to whom death is a sort of hobgoblin; him too we must persuade not to be afraid when he is alone in the dark.

SOCRATES: Let the voice of the charmer be applied daily until you have charmed away the fear.

CEBES: And where shall we find a good charmer of our fears, Socrates, when you are gone?

SOCRATES: Hellas is a large place, Cebes, and has many good men, and there are barbarous races not a few: seek for him among them all, far and wide, sparing neither pains nor money; for there is no better way of spending your money. And you must seek among yourselves too; for you will not find others better able to make the search.

CEBES: The search shall certainly be made. And now, if you please, let us return to the point of the argument at which we digressed.

SOCRATES: By all means; what else should I please?

CEBES: Very good.

SOCRATES: Must we not ask ourselves what that is which, as we imagine, is liable to be scattered, and about which we fear? And what again is that about which we have no fear? And then we may proceed further to enquire whether that which suffers dispersion is or is not of the nature of soul—our hopes and fears as to our own souls will turn upon the answers to these questions.

CEBES: Very true.

SOCRATES: Now the compound or composite may be supposed to be naturally capable, as of being compounded, so also of being dissolved; but that which is uncompounded, and that only, must be, if anything is, indissoluble.

CEBES: Yes; I should imagine so.

SOCRATES: And the uncompounded may be assumed to be the same and unchanging, whereas the compound is always changing and never the same.

CEBES: I agree.

SOCRATES: Then now let us return to the previous discussion. Is that idea or essence, which in the dialectical process we define as essence or true existence—whether essence of equality, beauty, or anything else—are these essences, I say, liable at times to some degree of change? Or are they each of them always what they are, having the same simple self-existent and unchanging forms, not admitting of variation at all, or in any way, or at any time?

CEBES: They must be always the same, Socrates.

SOCRATES: And what would you say of the many beautiful—whether men or horses or garments or any other things which are named by the same names and may be called equal or beautiful,—are they all unchanging and the same always, or quite the reverse? May they not rather be described as almost always changing and hardly ever the same, either with themselves or with one another?

CEBES: The latter, they are always in a state of change.

SOCRATES: And these you can touch and see and perceive with the senses, but the unchanging things you can only perceive with the mind—they are invisible and are not seen?

CEBES: That is very true.

SOCRATES: Well, then, let us suppose that there are two sorts of existences—one seen, the other unseen.

CEBES: Let us suppose them.

SOCRATES: The seen is the changing, and the unseen is the unchanging?

CEBES: That may be also supposed.

SOCRATES: And, further, is not one part of us body, another part soul?

CEBES: To be sure.

SOCRATES: And to which class is the body more alike and akin?

CEBES: Clearly to the seen—no one can doubt that.

SOCRATES: And is the soul seen or not seen?

CEBES: Not by man, Socrates.

SOCRATES: And what we mean by 'seen' and 'not seen' is that which is or is not visible to the eye of man?

CEBES: Yes, to the eye of man.

SOCRATES: And is the soul seen or not seen?

CEBES: Not seen.

SOCRATES: Unseen then?

CEBES: Yes.

SOCRATES: Then the soul is more like to the unseen, and the body to the seen?

CEBES: That follows necessarily, Socrates.

SOCRATES: And were we not saying long ago that the soul when using the body as an instrument of perception, that is to say, when using the sense of sight or hearing or some other sense (for the meaning of perceiving through the body is perceiving through the senses)—were we not saying that the soul too is then dragged by the body into the region of the changeable, and wanders and is confused; the world spins round her, and she is like a drunkard, when she touches change?

CEBES: Very true.

SOCRATES: But when returning into herself she reflects, then she passes into the other world, the region of purity, and eternity, and immortality, and unchangeableness, which are her kindred, and with them she ever lives, when she is by herself and is not let or hindered; then she ceases from her erring ways, and being in communion with the unchanging is unchanging. And this state of the soul is called wisdom?

CEBES: That is well and truly said, Socrates.

SOCRATES: And to which class is the soul more nearly alike and akin, as far as may be inferred from this argument, as well as from the preceding one?

CEBES: I think, Socrates, that, in the opinion of every one who follows the argument, the soul will be infinitely more like the unchangeable—even the most stupid person will not deny that.

SOCRATES: And the body is more like the changing?

CEBES: Yes.

SOCRATES: Yet once more consider the matter in another light: When the soul and the body are united, then nature orders the soul to rule and govern, and the body to obey and serve. Now which of these two functions is akin to the divine? And which to the mortal? Does not the divine appear to you to be that which naturally orders and rules, and the mortal to be that which is subject and servant?

CEBES: True.

SOCRATES: And which does the soul resemble?

CEBES: The soul resembles the divine, and the body the mortal—there can be no doubt of that, Socrates.

SOCRATES: Then reflect, Cebes: of all which has been said is not this the conclusion?—that the soul is in the very likeness of the divine, and immortal, and intellectual, and uniform, and indissoluble, and unchangeable; and that the body is in the very likeness of the human, and mortal, and unintellectual, and multiform, and dissoluble, and changeable. Can this, my dear Cebes, be denied?

CEBES: It cannot.

SOCRATES: But if it be true, then is not the body liable to speedy dissolution? And is not the soul almost or altogether indissoluble?

CEBES: Certainly.

SOCRATES: And do you further observe, that after a man is dead, the body, or visible part of him, which is lying in the visible world, and is called a corpse, and would naturally be dissolved and decomposed and dissipated, is not dissolved or decomposed at once, but may remain for a for some time, nay even for a long time, if the constitution be sound at the time of death, and the season of the year favorable? For the body when shrunk and embalmed, as the manner is in Egypt, may remain almost entire through infinite ages; and even in decay, there are still some portions, such as the bones and ligaments, which are practically indestructible:—Do you agree?

CEBES: Yes.

SOCRATES: And is it likely that the soul, which is invisible, in passing to the place of the true Hades, which like her is invisible, and pure, and noble, and on her way to the good and wise God, whither, if God will, my soul is also soon to go,—that the soul, I repeat, if this be her nature and origin, will be blown away and destroyed immediately on quitting the body, as the many say? That can never be, my dear Simmias and Cebes. The truth rather is, that the soul which is pure at departing and draws after her no bodily taint, having never voluntarily during life had connection with the body, which she is ever avoiding, herself gathered into herself;—and making such abstraction her perpetual study—which means that she has been a true disciple of philosophy; and therefore has in fact been always engaged in the practice of dying? For is not philosophy the practice of death?

CEBES: Certainly

SOCRATES: That soul, I say, herself invisible, departs to the invisible world—to the divine and immortal and rational: thither arriving, she is secure of bliss and is released from the error and folly of men, their fears and wild passions and all other human ills, and forever dwells, as they say of the initiated, in company with the gods. Is not this true, Cebes?

CEBES: Yes, beyond a doubt.

SOCRATES: But the soul which has been polluted, and is impure at the time of her departure, and is the companion and servant of the body always, and is in love with and fascinated by the body and by the desires and pleasures of the body, until she is led to believe that the truth only exists in a bodily form, which a man may touch and see and taste, and use for the purposes of his lusts,—the soul, I mean, accustomed to hate and fear and avoid the intellectual principle, which to the bodily eye is dark and invisible, and can be attained only by philosophy;—do you suppose that such a soul will depart pure and unalloyed?

CEBES: Impossible.

SOCRATES: She is held fast by the corporeal, which the continual association and constant care of the body have wrought into her nature.

CEBES: Very true.

SOCRATES: And this corporeal element, my friend, is heavy and weighty and earthy, and is that element of sight by which a soul is depressed and dragged down again into the visible world, because she is afraid of the invisible and of the world below—prowling about tombs and sepulchers, near which, as they tell us, are seen certain ghostly apparitions of souls which have not departed pure, but are cloyed with sight and therefore visible.

CEBES: That is very likely, Socrates.

SOCRATES: Yes, that is very likely, Cebes; and these must be the souls, not of the good, but of the evil, which are compelled to wander about such places in payment of the penalty of their former evil way of life; and they continue to wander until through the craving after the corporeal which never leaves them, they are imprisoned finally in another body. And they may be supposed to find their prisons in the same natures which they have had in their former lives.

CEBES: What natures do you mean, Socrates?

SOCRATES: What I mean is that men who have followed after gluttony, and wantonness, and drunkenness, and have had no thought of avoiding them, would pass into asses and animals of that sort. What do you think?

CEBES: I think such an opinion to be exceedingly probable.

SOCRATES: And those who have chosen the portion of injustice, and tyranny, and violence, will pass into wolves, or into hawks and kites;—whither else can we suppose them to go?

CEBES: Yes. With such natures, beyond question.

SOCRATES: And there is no difficulty, he said, in assigning to all of them places answering to their several natures and propensities?

CEBES: There is not.

SOCRATES: Some are happier than others; and the happiest both in themselves and in the place to which they go are those who have practiced the civil and social virtues which are called temperance and justice, and are acquired by habit and attention without philosophy and mind.

CEBES: Why are they the happiest?

SOCRATES: Because they may be expected to pass into some gentle and social kind which is like their own, such as bees or wasps or ants, or back again into the form of man, and just and moderate men may be supposed to spring from them.

CEBES: Very likely.

SOCRATES: No one who has not studied philosophy and who is not entirely pure at the time of his departure is allowed to enter the company of the Gods, but the lover of knowledge only. And this is the reason, Simmias and Cebes, why the true votaries of philosophy abstain from all fleshly lusts, and hold out against them and refuse to give themselves up to them,—not because they fear poverty or the ruin of their families, like the lovers of money, and the world in general; nor like the lovers of power and honor, because they dread the dishonor or disgrace of evil deeds.

CEBES: No, Socrates, that would not become them.

SOCRATES: No indeed, and therefore they who have any care of their own souls, and do not merely live molding and fashioning the body, say farewell to all this; they will not walk in the ways of the blind: and when philosophy offers them purification and release from evil, they feel that they ought not to resist her influence, and whither she leads they turn and follow.

CEBES: What do you mean, Socrates?

SOCRATES: I will tell you. The lovers of knowledge are conscious that the soul was simply fastened and glued to the body—until philosophy received her, she could only view real existence through the bars of a prison, not in and through herself; she was wallowing in the mire of every sort of ignorance; and by reason of lust had become the principal accomplice in her own captivity. This was her original state; and then, as I was saying, and as the lovers of knowledge are well aware, philosophy, seeing how terrible was her confinement, of which she was to herself the cause, received and gently comforted her and sought to release her, pointing out that the eye and the ear and the other senses are full of deception, and persuading her to retire from them, and abstain from all but the necessary use of them, and be gathered up and collected into herself, bidding her trust in herself and her own pure apprehension of pure existence, and to mistrust whatever comes to her through other channels and is subject to variation; for such things are visible and tangible, but what she sees in her own nature is intelligible and invisible. And the soul of the true philosopher thinks that she ought not to resist this deliverance, and therefore abstains from pleasures and desires and pains and fears, as far as she is able; reflecting that when a man has great joys or sorrows or fears or desires, he suffers from them, not merely the sort of evil which might be anticipated—as for example, the loss of his health or property which he has sacrificed to his lusts—but an evil greater far, which is the greatest and worst of all evils, and one of which he never thinks.

CEBES: What is it, Socrates?

SOCRATES: The evil is that when the feeling of pleasure or pain is most intense, every soul of man imagines the objects of this intense feeling to be then plainest and truest: but this is not so, they are really the things of sight.

CEBES: Very true.

SOCRATES: And is not this the state in which the soul is most enthralled by the body?

CEBES: How so?

SOCRATES: Why, because each pleasure and pain is a sort of nail which nails and rivets the soul to the body, until she becomes like the body, and believes that to be true which the body affirms to be true; and from agreeing with the body and having the same delights she is obliged to have the same habits and haunts, and is not likely ever to be pure at her departure to the world below, but is always infected by the body; and so she sinks into another body and there germinates and grows, and has therefore no part in the communion of the divine and pure and simple.

CEBES: Most true, Socrates.

SOCRATES: And this, Cebes, is the reason why the true lovers of knowledge are temperate and brave; and not for the reason which the world gives.

CEBES: Certainly not.

SOCRATES: Certainly not! The soul of a philosopher will reason in quite another way; she will not ask philosophy to release her in order that when released she may deliver herself up again to the thrall of pleasures and pains, doing a work only to be undone again, weaving instead of unweaving her Penelope's web. But she will calm passion, and follow reason, and dwell in the contemplation of her, beholding the true and divine [which is not matter of opinion], and thence deriving nourishment. Thus she seeks to live while she lives, and after death she hopes to go to her own kindred and to that which is like her, and to be freed from human ills. Never fear, Simmias and Cebes, that a soul which

has been thus nurtured and has had these pursuits, will at her departure from the body be scattered and blown away by the winds and be nowhere and nothing.

[**PHAEDO:** When Socrates was done speaking, for a considerable time there was silence; he himself appeared to be meditating, as most of us were, on what had been said; only Cebes and Simmias spoke a few words to one another. And Socrates observing them asked what they thought of the argument, and whether there was anything wanting?]

SOCRATES: For there are many points still open to suspicion and attack, if any one were disposed to sift the matter thoroughly. Should you be considering some other matter I say no more, but if you are still in doubt do not hesitate to say exactly what you think, and let us have anything better which you can suggest; and if you think that I can be of any use, allow me to help you.

SIMMIAS: I must confess, Socrates, that doubts did arise in our minds, and each of us was urging and inciting the other to put the question which we wanted to have answered and which neither of us liked to ask, fearing that our importunity might be troublesome under present at such a time.

SOCRATES: [smiling] O, Simmias, what are you saying? I am not very likely to persuade other men that I do not regard my present situation as a misfortune, if I cannot even persuade you that I am no worse off now than at any other time in my life. Will you not allow that I have as much of the spirit of prophecy in me as the swans? For they, when they perceive that they must die, having sung all their life long, do then sing more lustily than ever, rejoicing in the thought that they are about to go away to the god whose ministers they are. But men, because they are themselves afraid of death, slanderously affirm of the swans that they sing a lament at the last, not considering that no bird sings when cold, or hungry, or in pain, not even the nightingale, nor the swallow, nor yet the hoopoe; which are said indeed to tune a lay of sorrow, although I do not believe this to be true of them any more than of the swans. But because they are sacred to Apollo, they have the gift of prophecy, and anticipate the good things of another world, wherefore they sing and rejoice in that day more than they ever did before. And I too, believing myself to be the consecrated servant of the same God, and the fellow-servant of the swans, and thinking that I have received from my master gifts of prophecy which are not inferior to theirs, would not go out of life less merrily than the swans. Never mind then, if this be your only objection, but speak and ask anything which you like, while the eleven magistrates of Athens allow.

SIMMIAS: Very good, Socrates, then I will tell you my difficulty, and Cebes will tell you his. I feel myself, (and I daresay that you have the same feeling), how hard or rather impossible is the attainment of any certainty about questions such as these in the present life. And yet I should deem him a coward who did not prove what is said about them to the uttermost, or whose heart failed him before he had examined them on every side. For he should persevere until he has achieved one of two things: either he should discover, or be taught the truth about them; or, if this be impossible, I would have him take the best and most irrefragable of human theories, and let this be the raft upon which he sails through life—not without risk, as I admit, if he cannot find some word of God which will more surely and safely carry him. And now, as you bid me, I will venture to question you, and then I shall not have to reproach myself hereafter with not having said at the time what I think. For when I consider the matter, either alone or with Cebes, the argument does certainly appear to me, Socrates, to be not sufficient.

SOCRATES: I dare say, my friend, that you may be right, but I should like to know in what respect the argument is insufficient.

SIMMIAS: In this respect – Suppose a person to use the same argument about harmony and the lyre— might he not say that harmony is a thing invisible, incorporeal, perfect, divine, existing in the lyre which is harmonized, but that the lyre and the strings are matter and material, composite, earthy, and akin to mortality? And when someone breaks the lyre, or cuts and rends the strings, then he who takes this view would argue as you do, and on the same analogy, that the harmony survives and has not perished—you cannot imagine, he would say, that the lyre without the strings, and the broken strings themselves which are mortal remain, and yet that the harmony, which is of heavenly and immortal nature and kindred, has perished—perished before the mortal. The harmony must still be somewhere, and the wood and strings will decay before anything can happen to that. The thought, Socrates, must have occurred to your own mind that such is our conception of the soul; and that when the body is in a manner strung and held together by the elements of hot and cold, wet and dry, then the soul is the harmony or due proportionate admixture of them. But if so, whenever the strings of the body are unduly loosened or overstrained

through disease or other injury, then the soul, though most divine, like other harmonies of music or of works of art, of course perishes at once, although the material remains of the body may last for a considerable time, until they are either decayed or burnt. And if any one maintains that the soul, being the harmony of the elements of the body, is first to perish in that which is called death, how shall we answer him?

[**PHAEDO:** Socrates looked fixedly at us as his manner was, and said with a smile]

SOCRATES: Simmias has reason on his side; and why does not some one of you who is better able than myself answer him? For there is force in his attack upon me. But perhaps, before we answer him, we had better also hear what Cebes has to say that we may gain time for reflection, and when they have both spoken, we may either assent to them, if there is truth in what they say, or if not, we will maintain our position. Please to tell me then, Cebes, he said, what was the difficulty which troubled you?

CEBES: I will tell you. My feeling is that the argument is where it was, and open to the same objections which were urged before; for I am ready to admit that the existence of the soul before entering into the bodily form has been very ingeniously, and, if I may say so, quite sufficiently proven; but the existence of the soul after death is still, in my judgment, unproven. Now my objection is not the same as that of Simmias; for I am not disposed to deny that the soul is stronger and more lasting than the body, being of opinion that in all such respects the soul very far excels the body. Well, then, says the argument to me, why do you remain unconvinced?—When you see that the weaker continues in existence after the man is dead, will you not admit that the more lasting must also survive during the same period of time? Now I will ask you to consider whether the objection, which, like Simmias, I will express in a figure, is of any weight. The analogy which I will adduce is that of an old weaver, who dies, and after his death somebody says:—He is not dead, he must be alive;—see, there is the coat which he himself wove and wore, and which remains whole and undecayed. And then he proceeds to ask of someone who is incredulous, whether a man lasts longer, or the coat which is in use and wear; and when he is answered that a man lasts far longer, thinks that he has thus certainly demonstrated the survival of the man, who is the more lasting, because the less lasting remains. But that, Simmias, as I would beg you to remark, is a mistake;

any one can see that he who talks thus is talking non-sense. For the truth is, that the weaver aforesaid, having woven and worn many such coats, outlived several of them, and was outlived by the last; but a man is not therefore proved to be slighter and weaker than a coat. Now the relation of the body to the soul may be expressed in a similar figure; and any one may very fairly say in like manner that the soul is lasting, and the body weak and short-lived in comparison. He may argue in like manner that every soul wears out many bodies, especially if a man live many years. While he is alive the body deliquesces and decays, and the soul always weaves another garment and repairs the waste. But of course, whenever the soul perishes, she must have on her last garment, and this will survive her; and then at length, when the soul is dead, the body will show its native weakness, and quickly decompose and pass away. I would therefore rather not rely on the argument from superior strength to prove the continued existence of the soul after death. For granting even more than you affirm to be possible, and acknowledging not only that the soul existed before birth, but also that the souls of some exist, and will continue to exist after death, and will be born and die again and again, and that there is a natural strength in the soul which will hold out and be born many times—nevertheless, we may be still inclined to think that she will weary in the labors of successive births, and may at last succumb in one of her deaths and utterly perish; and this death and dissolution of the body which brings destruction to the soul may be unknown to any of us, for no one of us can have had any experience of it: and if so, then I maintain that he who is confident about death has but a foolish confidence, unless he is able to prove that the soul is altogether immortal and imperishable. But if he cannot prove the soul's immortality, he who is about to die will always have reason to fear that when the body is disunited, the soul also may utterly perish.

[PHAEDO: All of us, as we afterwards remarked to one another, had an unpleasant feeling at hearing what they said. When we had been so firmly convinced before, now to have our faith shaken seemed to introduce a confusion and uncertainty, not only into the previous argument, but into any future one; either we were incapable of forming a judgment, or there were no grounds of belief.

ECHECRATES: There I feel with you—by heaven I do, Phaedo, and when you were speaking, I was beginning to ask myself the same question: What argument can I ever trust again? For what could be more convincing than the argument of Socrates, which has now fallen into discredit? That the soul is a harmony is a doctrine which has always had a wonderful attraction for me, and, when mentioned, came back to me at once, as my own original conviction. And now I must begin again and find another argument which will assure me that when the man is dead the soul survives. Tell me, I implore you, how did Socrates proceed? Did he appear to share the unpleasant feeling which you mention? Or did he calmly meet the attack? And did he answer forcibly or feebly? Narrate what passed as exactly as you can.

PHAEDO: Often, Echecrates, I have wondered at Socrates, but never more than on that occasion. That he should be able to answer was nothing, but what astonished me was, first, the gentle and pleasant and approving manner in which he received the words of the young men, and then his quick sense of the wound which had been inflicted by the argument, and the readiness with which he healed it. He might be compared to a general rallying his defeated and broken army, urging them to accompany him and return to the field of argument.

ECHECRATES: What followed?

PHAEDO: You shall hear, for I was close to him on his right hand, seated on a sort of stool, and he on a couch which was a good deal higher. He stroked my head, and pressed the hair upon my neck—he had a way of playing with my hair; and then he said]

SOCRATES: Tomorrow, Phaedo, I suppose that these fair locks of yours will be severed.

PHAEDO: Yes, Socrates, I suppose that they will.

SOCRATES: Not so, if you will take my advice.

PHAEDO: What shall I do with them?

SOCRATES: Today, and not tomorrow, if this argument dies and we cannot bring it to life again, you and I will both shave our locks; and if I were you, and the argument got away from me, and I could not hold my ground against Simmias and Cebes, I would myself take an oath, like the Argives, not to wear hair any more until I had renewed the conflict and defeated them.

PHAEDO: Yes, but Heracles himself is said not to be a match for two.

SOCRATES: Summon me then, he said, and I will be your Iolaus until the sun goes down.

PHAEDO: I summon you, rather, not as Heracles summoning Iolaus, but as Iolaus might summon Heracles.

SOCRATES: That will do as well. But first let us take care that we avoid a danger.

PHAEDO: Of what nature?

SOCRATES: Lest we become misologists. No worse thing can happen to a man than this. For as there are misanthropists or haters of men, there are also misologists or haters of ideas, and both spring from the same cause, which is ignorance of the world. Misanthropy arises out of the too great confidence of inexperience;—you trust a man and think him altogether true and sound and faithful, and then in a little while he turns out to be false and knavish; and then another and another, and when this has happened several times to a man, especially when it happens among those whom he deems to be his own most trusted and familiar friends, and he has often quarreled with them, he at last hates all men, and believes that no one has any good in him at all. You must have observed this trait of character?

PHAEDO: I have.

SOCRATES: And is not the feeling discreditable? Is it not obvious that such an one having to deal with other men, was clearly without any experience of human nature; for experience would have taught him the true state of the case, that few are the good and few the evil, and that the great majority are in the interval between them.

PHAEDO: What do you mean?

SOCRATES: I mean, as you might say of the very large and very small, that nothing is more uncommon than a very large or very small man; and this applies generally to all extremes, whether of great and small, or swift and slow, or fair and foul, or black and white: and whether the instances you select be men or dogs or anything else, few are the extremes, but many are in the mean between them. Did you never observe this?

PHAEDO: Yes, I have.

SOCRATES: And do you not imagine that if there were a competition in evil, the worst would be found to be very few?

PHAEDO: Yes, that is very likely.

SOCRATES: Yes, that is very likely, although in this respect arguments are unlike men—there I was led on by you to say more than I had intended; but the point of comparison was, that when a simple man who has no skill in dialectics believes an argument to be true which he afterwards imagines to be false, whether really false or not, and then another and another, he has no longer any faith left, and great disputers, as you know, come to think at last that they have grown to be the wisest of mankind; for they alone perceive the utter unsoundness and instability of all arguments, or indeed, of all things, which, like the currents in the Euripus, are going up and down in never-ceasing ebb and flow.

PHAEDO: That is quite true.

SOCRATES: Yes, Phaedo, and how melancholy, if there be such a thing as truth or certainty or possibility of knowledge—that a man should have lighted upon some argument or other which at first seemed true and then turned out to be false, and instead of blaming himself and his own want of wit, because he is annoyed, should at last be too glad to transfer the blame from himself to arguments in general: and forever afterwards should hate and revile them, and lose truth and the knowledge of realities.

PHAEDO: Yes, indeed, I said; that is very melancholy.

SOCRATES: Let us then, in the first place, be careful of allowing or of admitting into our souls the notion that there is no health or soundness in any arguments at all. Rather say that we have not yet attained to soundness in ourselves, and that we must struggle manfully and do our best to gain health of mind—you and all other men having regard to the whole of your future life, and I myself in the prospect of death. For at this moment I am sensible that I have not the temper of a philosopher; like the vulgar, I am only a partisan. Now the partisan, when he is engaged in a dispute, cares nothing about the rights of the question, but is anxious only to convince his hearers of his own assertions. And the difference between him and me at the present moment is merely this—that whereas he seeks to convince his hearers that what he says is true, I am rather seeking to convince myself; to convince my hearers is a secondary matter with me. And do but see how much I gain by the argument. For if what I say is true, then I do well to be persuaded of the truth, but if there be nothing after death, still, during the short time that remains, I shall not distress my friends with lamentations, and my ignorance will not last, but will die with me, and therefore no harm will be done. This is the state of mind, Simmias and Cebes, in which I approach the argument. And I would ask you to be thinking of the truth and not of Socrates: agree with me, if I seem to you to be speaking the truth; or if not, withstand me might and main, that I may not deceive you as well as myself in my enthusiasm, and like the bee, leave my sting in you before I die.

SOCRATES: And now let us proceed. And first of all let me be sure that I have in my mind what you were saying. Simmias, if I remember rightly, has fears and misgivings whether the soul, although a fairer and diviner thing than the body, being as she is in the form of harmony, may not perish first. On the other hand, Cebes appeared to grant that the soul was more lasting than the body, but he said that no one could know whether the soul, after having worn out many bodies, might not perish herself and leave her last body behind her; and that this is death, which is the destruction not of the body but of the soul, for in the body the work of destruction is ever going on. Are not these, Simmias and Cebes, the points which we have to consider?

[**PHAEDO:** They both agreed to this statement of them. He proceeded.]

SOCRATES: And did you deny the force of the whole preceding argument, or of a part only?

SIMMIAS AND CEBES: Of a part only.

SOCRATES: And what did you think of that part of the argument in which we said that knowledge was recollection, and hence inferred that the soul must have previously existed somewhere else before she was enclosed in the body?

[**PHAEDO:** Cebes said that he had been wonderfully impressed by that part of the argument, and that his conviction remained absolutely unshaken. Simmias agreed, and added that he himself could hardly imagine the possibility of his ever thinking differently.]

SOCRATES: But, you will have to think differently, my Theban friend, if you still maintain that harmony is a compound, and that the soul is a harmony which is made out of strings set in the frame of the body; for you will surely never allow yourself to say that a harmony is prior to the elements which compose it.

SIMMIAS: Never, Socrates.

SOCRATES: But do you not see that this is what you imply when you say that the soul existed before she took the form and body of man, and was made up of elements which as yet had no existence? For harmony is not like the soul, as you suppose; but first the lyre, and the strings, and the sounds exist in a state of discord, and then harmony is made last of all, and perishes first. And how can such a notion of the soul as this agree with the other?

SIMMIAS: Not at all.

SOCRATES: And yet, there surely ought to be harmony in a discourse of which harmony is the theme.

SIMMIAS: There ought.

SOCRATES: But there is no harmony in the two propositions that knowledge is recollection, and that the soul is a harmony. Which of them will you retain?

SIMMIAS: I think that I have a much stronger faith, Socrates, in the first of the two, which has been fully demonstrated to me, than in the latter, which has not been demonstrated at all, but rests only on probable and plausible grounds; and is therefore believed by the many. I know too well that these arguments from probabilities are impostors, and unless great caution is observed in the use of them, they are apt to be deceptive—in geometry, and in other things too. But the doctrine of knowledge and recollection has been proven to me on trustworthy grounds; and the proof was that the soul must have existed before she came into the body, because to her belongs the essence of which the very name implies existence. Having, as I am convinced, rightly accepted this conclusion, and on sufficient grounds, I must, as I suppose, cease to argue or allow others to argue that the soul is a harmony.

Let me put the matter, Simmias, he said, in another point of view: Do you imagine that a harmony or any other composition can be in a state other than that of the elements, out of which it is compounded?

Certainly not.

Or do or suffer anything other than they do or suffer?

He agreed.

Then a harmony does not, properly speaking, lead the parts or elements which make up the harmony, but only follows them.

He assented.

For harmony cannot possibly have any motion, or sound, or other quality which is opposed to its parts.

That would be impossible, he replied.

And does not the nature of every harmony depend upon the manner in which the elements are harmonized?

I do not understand you, he said.

I mean to say that a harmony admits of degrees, and is more of a harmony, and more completely a harmony, when more truly and fully harmonized, to any extent which is possible; and less of a harmony, and less completely a harmony, when less truly and fully harmonized.

True.

But does the soul admit of degrees? or is one soul in the very least degree more or less, or more or less completely, a soul than another?

Not in the least.

Yet surely of two souls, one is said to have intelligence and virtue, and to be good, and the other to have folly and vice, and to be an evil soul: and this is said truly?

Yes, truly.

But what will those who maintain the soul to be a harmony say of this presence of virtue and vice in the soul?—will they say that here is another harmony, and another discord, and that the virtuous soul is harmonized, and herself being a harmony has another harmony within her, and that the vicious soul is inharmonical and has no harmony within her?

I cannot tell, replied Simmias; but I suppose that something of the sort would be asserted by those who say that the soul is a harmony.

And we have already admitted that no soul is more a soul than another; which is equivalent to admitting that harmony is not more or less harmony, or more or less completely a harmony?

Quite true.

And that which is not more or less a harmony is not more or less harmonized?

True.

And that which is not more or less harmonized cannot have more or less of harmony, but only an equal harmony?

Yes, an equal harmony.

Then one soul not being more or less absolutely a soul than another, is not more or less harmonized?

Exactly.

And therefore has neither more nor less of discord, nor yet of harmony?

She has not.

And having neither more nor less of harmony or of discord, one soul has no more vice or virtue than another, if vice be discord and virtue harmony?

Not at all more.

Or speaking more correctly, Simmias, the soul, if she is a harmony, will never have any vice; because a harmony, being absolutely a harmony, has no part in the inharmonical.

No.

And therefore a soul which is absolutely a soul has no vice?

How can she have, if the previous argument holds?

Then, if all souls are equally by their nature souls, all souls of all living creatures will be equally good?

I agree with you, Socrates, he said.

And can all this be true, think you? he said; for these are the consequences which seem to follow from the assumption that the soul is a harmony?

It cannot be true.

Once more, he said, what ruler is there of the elements of human nature other than the soul, and especially the wise soul? Do you know of any?

Indeed, I do not.

And is the soul in agreement with the affections of the body? or is she at variance with them? For example, when the body is hot and thirsty, does not the soul incline us against drinking? and when the body is hungry, against eating? And this is only one instance out of ten thousand of the opposition of the soul to the things of the body.

Very true.

But we have already acknowledged that the soul, being a harmony, can never utter a note at variance with the tensions and relaxations and vibrations and other affections of the strings out of which she is composed; she can only follow, she cannot lead them?

It must be so, he replied.

And yet do we not now discover the soul to be doing the exact opposite—leading the elements of which she is believed to be composed; almost always opposing and coercing them in all sorts of ways throughout life, sometimes more violently with the pains of medicine and gymnastic; then again more gently; now threatening, now admonishing the desires, passions, fears, as if talking to a thing which is not herself, as Homer in the Odyssee represents Odysseus doing in the words—

'He beat his breast, and thus reproached his heart: Endure, my heart; far worse hast thou endured!'

Do you think that Homer wrote this under the idea that the soul is a harmony capable of being led by the affections of the body, and not rather of a nature which should lead and master them—herself a far diviner thing than any harmony?

Yes, Socrates, I quite think so.

Then, my friend, we can never be right in saying that the soul is a harmony, for we should contradict the divine Homer, and contradict ourselves.

True, he said.

Thus much, said Socrates, of Harmonia, your Theban goddess, who has graciously yielded to us; but what shall I say, Cebes, to her husband Cadmus, and how shall I make peace with him?

I think that you will discover a way of propitiating him, said Cebes; I am sure that you have put the argument with Harmonia in a manner that I could never have expected. For when Simmias was mentioning his difficulty, I quite imagined that no answer could be given to him, and therefore I was surprised at finding that his argument could not sustain the first onset of yours, and not impossibly the other, whom you call Cadmus, may share a similar fate.

Nay, my good friend, said Socrates, let us not boast, lest some evil eye should put to flight the word which I am about to speak. That, however, may be left in the hands of those above, while I draw near in Homeric fashion, and try the mettle of your words. Here lies the point:—You want to have it proven to you that the soul is imperishable and immortal, and the philosopher who is confident in death appears to you to have but a vain and foolish confidence, if he believes that he will fare better in the world below than one who has led another sort of life, unless he can prove this; and you say that the demonstration of the strength and divinity of the soul, and of her existence prior to our becoming men, does not necessarily imply her immortality. Admitting the soul to be long-lived, and to have known and done much in a former state, still she is not on that account immortal; and her entrance into the human form may be a sort of disease which is the beginning of dissolution, and may at last, after the toils of life are over, end in that which is called death. And whether the soul enters into the body once only or many times, does not, as you say, make any difference in the fears of individuals.

For any man, who is not devoid of sense, must fear, if he has no knowledge and can give no account of the soul's immortality. This, or something like this, I suspect to be your notion, Cebes; and I designedly recur to it in order that nothing may escape us, and that you may, if you wish, add or subtract anything.

CEBES: But as far as I see at present, I have nothing to add or subtract: I mean what you say that I mean.

[**PHAEDO:** Socrates paused awhile, and seemed to be absorbed in reflection. At length he said:]

SOCRATES: You are raising a tremendous question, Cebes, involving the whole nature of generation and corruption, about which, if you like, I will give you my own experience; and if anything which I say is likely to avail towards the solution of your difficulty you may make use of it.

CEBES: I should very much like to hear what you have to say.

SOCRATES: Then I will tell you. When I was young, Cebes, I had a prodigious desire to know that department of philosophy which is called the investigation of nature; to know the causes of things, and why a thing is and is created or destroyed appeared to me to be a lofty profession; and I was always agitating myself with the consideration of questions such as these:—Is the growth of animals the result of some decay which the hot and cold principle contracts, as some have said? Is the blood the element with which we think, or the air, or the fire? or perhaps nothing of the kind—but the brain may be the originating power of the perceptions of hearing and sight and smell, and memory and opinion may come from them, and science may be based on memory and opinion when they have attained fixity. And then I went on to examine the corruption of them, and then to the things of heaven and earth, and at last I concluded myself to be utterly and absolutely incapable of these enquiries, as I will satisfactorily prove to you. For I was fascinated by them to such a degree that my eyes grew blind to things which I had seemed to myself, and also to others, to know quite well; I forgot what I had before thought self-evident truths; e.g. such a fact as that the growth of man is the result of eating and drinking; for when by the digestion of food flesh is added to flesh and bone to bone, and whenever there is an aggregation of congenial elements, the lesser bulk becomes larger and the small man great. Was not that a reasonable notion?

CEBES: Yes, I think so.

SOCRATES: Well; but let me tell you something more. There was a time when I thought that I understood the meaning of greater and less pretty well; and when I saw a great man standing by a little one, I fancied that one was taller than the other by a head; or one horse would appear to be greater than another horse: and still more clearly did I seem to perceive that ten is two more than eight, and that two cubits are more than one, because two is the double of one.

CEBES: And what is now your notion of such matters?

SOCRATES: I should be far enough from imagining that I knew the cause of any of them, by heaven I should; for I cannot satisfy myself that, when one is added to one, the one to which the addition is made becomes two, or that the two units added together make two by reason of the addition. I cannot understand how, when separated from the other, each of them was one and not two, and now, when they are brought together, the mere juxtaposition or meeting of them should be the cause of their becoming two: neither can I understand how the division of one is the way to make two; for then a different cause would produce the same effect,—as in the former instance the addition and juxtaposition of one to one was the cause of two, in this the separation and subtraction of one from the other would be the cause. Nor am I any longer satisfied that I understand the reason why one or anything else is either generated or destroyed or is at all, but I have in my mind some confused notion of a new method, and can never admit the other.

Then I heard someone reading from a book of Anaxagoras, that mind was the disposer and cause of all, and I was delighted at this notion, which appeared quite admirable, and I said to myself: If mind is the disposer, mind will dispose all for the best, and put each particular in the best place; and I argued that if any one desired to find out the cause of the generation or destruction or existence of anything, he must find out what state of being or doing or suffering was best for that thing, and therefore a man had only to consider the best for himself and others, and then he would also know the worse, since the same science comprehended both. And I rejoiced to think that I had found in Anaxagoras a teacher of the causes of existence such as I desired, and I imagined that he would tell me first whether the earth is flat or round; and whichever was true, he would proceed to explain the cause and the necessity of this being so, and then he would teach me the nature of the best and show that this was best; and if he said that

the earth was in the center, he would further explain that this position was the best, and I should be satisfied with the explanation given, and not want any other sort of cause. And I thought that I would then go on and ask him about the sun and moon and stars, and that he would explain to me their comparative swiftness, and their returnings and various states, active and passive, and how all of them were for the best. For I could not imagine that when he spoke of mind as the disposer of them, he would give any other account of their being as they are, except that this was best; and I thought that when he had explained to me in detail the cause of each and the cause of all, he would go on to explain to me what was best for each and what was good for all. These hopes I would not have sold for a large sum of money, and I seized the books and read them as fast as I could in my eagerness to know the better and the worse.

What expectations I had formed, and how grievously was I disappointed! As I proceeded, I found my philosopher altogether forsaking mind or any other principle of order, but having recourse to air, and ether, and water, and other eccentricities. I might compare him to a person who began by maintaining generally that mind is the cause of the actions of Socrates, but who, when he endeavored to explain the causes of my several actions in detail, went on to show that I sit here because my body is made up of bones and muscles; and the bones, as he would say, are hard and have joints which divide them, and the muscles are elastic, and they cover the bones, which have also a covering or environment of flesh and skin which contains them; and as the bones are lifted at their joints by the contraction or relaxation of the muscles, I am able to bend my limbs, and this is why I am sitting here in a curved posture—that is what he would say, and he would have a similar explanation of my talking to you, which he would attribute to sound, and air, and hearing, and he would assign ten thousand other causes of the same sort, forgetting to mention the true cause, which is, that the Athenians have thought fit to condemn me, and accordingly I have thought it better and more right to remain here and undergo my sentence; for I am inclined to think that these muscles and bones of mine would have gone off long ago to Megara or Boeotia—by the dog they would, if they had been moved only by their own idea of what was best, and if I had not chosen the better and nobler part, instead of playing truant and running away, of enduring any punishment which the state inflicts. There is surely a strange confusion of causes and conditions in all this.

It may be said, indeed, that without bones and muscles and the other parts of the body I cannot execute my purposes. But to say that I do as I do because of them, and that this is the way in which mind acts, and not from the choice of the best, is a very careless and idle mode of speaking. I wonder that they cannot distinguish the cause from the condition, which the many, feeling about in the dark, are always mistaking and misnaming. And thus one man makes a vortex all round and steadies the earth by the heaven; another gives the air as a support to the earth, which is a sort of broad trough. Any power which in arranging them as they are arranges them for the best never enters into their minds; and instead of finding any superior strength in it, they rather expect to discover another Atlas of the world who is stronger and more everlasting and more containing than the good;— of the obligatory and containing power of the good they think nothing; and yet this is the principle which I would fain learn if anyone would teach me. But as I have failed either to discover myself, or to learn of anyone else, the nature of the best, I will exhibit to you, if you like, what I have found to be the second best mode of enquiring into the cause.

CEBES: I should very much like to hear, he replied.

SOCRATES: I thought that as I had failed in the contemplation of true existence, I ought to be careful that I did not lose the eye of my soul; as people may injure their bodily eye by observing and gazing on the sun during an eclipse, unless they take the precaution of only looking at the image reflected in the water, or in some similar medium. So in my own case, I was afraid that my soul might be blinded altogether if I looked at things with my eyes or tried to apprehend them by the help of the senses. And I thought that I had better have recourse to the world of mind and seek there the truth of existence. I dare say that the simile is not perfect—for I am very far from admitting that he who contemplates existences through the medium of thought, sees them only 'through a glass darkly,' any more than he who considers them in action and operation. However, this was the method which I adopted: I first assumed some principle which I judged to be the strongest, and then I affirmed as true whatever seemed to agree with this, whether relating to the cause or to anything else; and that which disagreed I regarded as untrue. But I should like to explain my meaning more clearly, as I do not think that you as yet understand me.

CEBES: No indeed, not very well.

SOCRATES: There is nothing new in what I am about to tell you; but only what I have been always and everywhere repeating in the previous discussion and on other occasions: I want to show you the nature of that cause which has occupied my thoughts. I shall have to go back to those familiar words which are in the mouth of every one, and first of all assume that there is an absolute Beauty and Goodness and Greatness, and the like; grant me this, and I hope to be able to show you the nature of the cause, and to prove the immortality of the soul.

CEBES: You may proceed at once with the proof, for I grant you this.

SOCRATES: Well, then I should like to know whether you agree with me in the next step; for I cannot help thinking, if there be anything beautiful other than absolute Beauty should there be such, that it can be beautiful only in as far as it partakes of absolute Beauty—and I should say the same of everything. Do you agree in this notion of the cause?

CEBES: Yes, I agree.

SOCRATES: I know nothing and can understand nothing of any other of those wise causes which are alleged; and if a person says to me that the bloom of color, or form, or any such thing is a source of beauty, I leave all that, which is only confusing to me, and simply and singly, and perhaps foolishly, hold and am assured in my own mind that nothing makes a thing beautiful but the presence and participation of Beauty in whatever way or manner obtained; for as to the manner I am uncertain, but I stoutly contend that by Beauty all beautiful things become beautiful. This appears to me to be the safest answer which I can give, either to myself or to another, and to this I cling, in the persuasion that this principle will never be overthrown, and that to myself or to anyone who asks the question, I may safely reply, that by Beauty beautiful things become beautiful. Do you not agree with me?

CEBES: I do.

SOCRATES: And that by Greatness only great things become great and greater *greater*, and by Smallness the less become less?

CEBES: True.

SOCRATES: Then if a person were to remark that A is taller by a head than B, and B less by a head than A, you would refuse to admit his statement, and would stoutly contend that what you mean is only that the greater is greater by, and by reason of, greatness, and the less is less only by, and by reason of, smallness;

and thus you would avoid the danger of saying that the greater is greater and the less *less* by the measure of the head, which is the same in both, and would also avoid the monstrous absurdity of supposing that the greater man is greater by reason of the head, which is small. You would be afraid to draw such an inference, would you not?

CEBES: [laughing] Indeed, I should.

SOCRATES: In like manner you would be afraid to say that ten exceeded eight by, and by reason of, two; but would say by, and by reason of, number; or you would say that two cubits exceed one cubit not by a half, but by magnitude? For there is the same liability to error in all these cases.

CEBES: Very true.

SOCRATES: Again, would you not be cautious of affirming that the addition of one to one, or the division of one, is the cause of two? And you would loudly asseverate that you know of no way in which anything comes into existence except by participation in its own proper essence, and consequently, as far as you know, the only cause of two is the participation in Duality—this is the way to make two, and the participation in Oneness is the way to make one. You would say: I will let alone puzzles of division and addition—wiser heads than mine may answer them; inexperienced as I am, and ready to start, as the proverb says, at my own shadow, I cannot afford to give up the sure ground of a principle. And if any one assails you there, you would not mind him, or answer him, until you had seen whether the consequences which follow agree with one another or not, and when you are further required to give an explanation of this principle, you would go on to assume a higher principle, and a higher, until you found a resting-place in the best of the higher; but you would not confuse the principle and the consequences in your reasoning, like the Eristics—at least if you wanted to discover real existence. Not that this confusion signifies to them, who never care or think about the matter at all, for they have the wit to be well pleased with themselves however great may be the turmoil of their ideas. But you, if you are a philosopher, will certainly do as I say.

SIMMIAS AND CEBES: What you say is most true.

[**ECHECRATES:** Yes, Phaedo; and I do not wonder at their assenting. Anyone who has the least sense will acknowledge the wonderful clearness of Socrates' reasoning.

PHAEDO: Certainly, Echecrates; and such was the feeling of the whole company at the time.

ECHECRATES: Yes, and equally of ourselves, who were not of the company, and are now listening to your recital. But what followed?

PHAEDO: After all this had been admitted, and they had that ideas exist, and that other things participate in them and derive their names from them, Socrates, if I remember rightly, said]

SOCRATES: This is your way of speaking; and yet when you say that Simmias is greater than Socrates and less than Phaedo, do you not predicate of Simmias both greatness and smallness?

SIMMIAS: Yes, I do.

SOCRATES: But still you allow that Simmias does not really exceed Socrates, as the words may seem to imply, because he is Simmias, but by reason of the size which he has; just as Simmias does not exceed Socrates because he is Simmias, any more than because Socrates is Socrates, but because he has smallness when compared with the greatness of Simmias?

SIMMIAS: True.

SOCRATES: And if Phaedo exceeds him in size, this is not because Phaedo is Phaedo, but because Phaedo has Greatness relatively to Simmias, who is comparatively smaller?

SIMMIAS: That is true.

SOCRATES: And therefore Simmias is said to be great, and is also said to be small, because he is in a mean between them, exceeding the smallness of the one by his greatness, and allowing the greatness of the other to exceed his smallness. [laughing] I am speaking like a book, but I believe that what I am saying is true.

[**PHAEDO:** Simmias assented.]

SOCRATES: I speak as I do because I want you to agree with me in thinking, not only that absolute Greatness will never be great and also small, but that greatness in us or in the concrete will never admit the small or admit of being exceeded: instead of this, one of two things will happen, either the greater will fly or retire before the opposite, which is the less, or at the approach of the less has already ceased to exist; but will not, if allowing or admitting of smallness, be changed by that; even as I, having received and admitted smallness when compared with Simmias, remain just as I was, and am the same small person. And as the idea of Greatness cannot condescend ever to be or become small, in like manner the smallness in us cannot be or become great; nor can any other opposite which remains the same ever be or become its own opposite, but either passes away or perishes in the change.

CEBES: That is quite my notion.

[**PHAEDO:** Hereupon one of the company, though I do not exactly remember which of them, said: "In heaven's name, is not this the direct contrary of what was admitted before—that out of the greater came the less and out of the less the greater, and that opposites were simply generated from opposites; but now this principle seems to be utterly denied."

Socrates inclined his head to the speaker and listened.]

SOCRATES: I like your courage in reminding us of this. But you do not observe that there is a difference in the two cases. For then we were speaking of opposites in the concrete, and now of the essential opposite which, as is affirmed, neither in us nor in nature can ever be at variance with itself: then, my friend, we were speaking of things in which opposites are inherent and which are called after them, but now about the opposites which are inherent in them and which give their name to them; and these essential opposites will never, as we maintain, admit of generation into or out of one another. At the same time, turning to Cebes, he said: Are you at all disconcerted, Cebes, at our friend's objection?

CEBES: No, I do not feel so; and yet I cannot deny that I am often disturbed by objections.

SOCRATES: Then we are agreed after all that the opposite will never in any case be opposed to itself?

CEBES: To that we are quite agreed.

SOCRATES: Yet once more let me ask you to consider the question from another point of view, and see whether you agree with me:—There is a thing which you term heat, and another thing which you term cold?

CEBES: Certainly.

SOCRATES: But are they the same as fire and snow?

CEBES: Most assuredly not.

SOCRATES: Heat is a thing different from fire, and cold is not the same with snow?

CEBES: Yes.

SOCRATES: And yet you will surely admit, that when snow, as was before said, is under the influence of heat, they will not remain snow and heat; but at the advance of the heat, the snow will either retire or perish?

CEBES: Very true.

SOCRATES: And the fire too at the advance of the cold will either retire or perish; and when the fire is under the influence of the cold, they will not remain as before, fire and cold.

CEBES: That is true.

SOCRATES: And in some cases the name of the idea is not only attached to the idea in an eternal connection, but anything else which, not being the idea, exists only in the form of the idea, may also lay claim to it. I will try to make this clearer by an example:—The odd number is always called by the name of Odd?

CEBES: Very true.

SOCRATES: But is this the only thing which is called odd? Are there not other things which have their own name, and yet are called odd, because, although not the same as Oddness, they are never without Oddness?— that is what I mean to ask—whether numbers such as the number three are not of the class of Odd. And there are many other examples: would you not say, for example, that three may be called by its proper name, and also be called Odd, which is not the same with three? and this may be said not only of three but also of five, and of every alternate number—each of them without being Oddness is odd, and in the same way two and four, and the other series of alternate numbers, has every number even, without being evenness. Do you agree?

CEBES: Of course.

SOCRATES: Then now mark the point at which I am aiming:—not only do essential opposites exclude one another, but also concrete things, which, although not in themselves opposed, contain opposites; these, I say, likewise reject the idea which is opposed to that which is contained in them, and when it approaches them they either perish or withdraw. For example; Will not the number three endure annihilation or anything sooner than be converted into an even number, while remaining three?

CEBES: Very true.

SOCRATES: And yet, the number two is certainly not opposed to the number three?

CEBES: It is not.

SOCRATES: Then not only do opposite ideas repel the advance of one another, but also there are other natures which repel the approach of opposites.

CEBES: Very true.

SOCRATES: Suppose that we endeavor, if possible, to determine what these are.

CEBES: By all means.

SOCRATES: Are they not, Cebes, such as compel the things of which they have possession, not only to take their own form, but also the form of some opposite?

CEBES: What do you mean?

SOCRATES: I mean, as I was just now saying, and as I am sure that you know, that those things which are possessed by the number three must not only be three in number, but must also be odd.

CEBES: Quite true.

SOCRATES: And on this Oddness, of which the number three has the impress, the opposite idea will never intrude?

CEBES: No.

SOCRATES: And this impress was given by the odd principle?

CEBES: Yes.

SOCRATES: And to the Odd is opposed the Even?

CEBES: True.

SOCRATES: Then the idea of the Even number will never arrive at three?

CEBES: No.

SOCRATES: Then three has no part in the Even?

CEBES: None.

SOCRATES: Then the triad or number three is uneven?

CEBES: Very true.

SOCRATES: To return then to my distinction of natures which are not opposed, and yet do not admit opposites—as, in the instance given, three, although not opposed to the even, does not any the more admit of the even, but always brings the opposite into play on the other side; or as two does not receive the odd,

or fire the cold—from these examples (and there are many more of them) perhaps you may be able to arrive at the general conclusion, that not only opposites will not receive opposites, but also that nothing which brings the opposite will admit the opposite of that which it brings, in that to which it is brought. And here let me recapitulate—for there is no harm in repetition. The number five will not admit the nature of the even, any more than ten, which is the double of five, will admit the nature of the odd. The double has another opposite, and is not strictly opposed to the odd, but nevertheless rejects the odd altogether. Nor again will parts in the ratio 3:2, nor any fraction in which there is a half, nor again in which there is a third, admit the notion of the whole, although they are not opposed to the whole: You will agree?

CEBES: Yes, I entirely agree and go along with you in that.

SOCRATES: And now let us begin again; and do not you answer my question in the words in which I ask it: let me have not the old safe answer of which I spoke at first, but another equally safe, of which the truth will be inferred by you from what has been just said. I mean that if anyone asks you 'what that is, of which the inherence makes the body hot,' you will reply not heat (this is what I call the safe and stupid answer), but fire, a far superior answer, which we are now in a condition to give. Or if anyone asks you 'why a body is diseased,' you will not say from disease, but from fever; and instead of saying that oddness is the cause of odd numbers, you will say that the monad is the cause of them: and so of things in general, as I dare say that you will understand sufficiently without my adducing any further examples.

CEBES: Yes, I quite understand you.

SOCRATES: Tell me, then, what is that of which the inherence will render the body alive?

CEBES: The soul.

SOCRATES: And is this always the case?

CEBES: Yes, of course.

SOCRATES: Then whatever the soul possesses, to that she comes bearing life?

CEBES: Yes, certainly.

SOCRATES: And is there any opposite to life?

CEBES: There is.

SOCRATES: And what is that?

CEBES: Death.

SOCRATES: Then the soul, as has been acknowledged, will never receive the opposite of what she brings.

CEBES: Impossible.

SOCRATES: And now, what did we just now call that principle which repels the Even?

CEBES: The Odd.

SOCRATES: And that principle which repels the musical, or the just?

CEBES: The unmusical, and the unjust.

SOCRATES: And what do we call the principle which does not admit of death?

CEBES: The immortal.

SOCRATES: And does the soul admit of death?

CEBES: No.

SOCRATES: Then the soul is immortal?

CEBES: Yes.

SOCRATES: And may we say that this has been proven?

CEBES: Yes, abundantly proven, Socrates.

SOCRATES: Supposing that the Odd were imperishable, must not three be imperishable?

CEBES: Of course.

SOCRATES: And if that which is cold were imperishable, when the warm principle came attacking the snow, must not the snow have retired whole and unmelted—for it could never have perished, nor could it have remained and admitted the heat?

CEBES: True.

SOCRATES: Again, if the uncooling or warm principle were imperishable, the fire when assailed by cold would not have perished or have been extinguished, but would have gone away unaffected?

CEBES: Certainly.

SOCRATES: And the same may be said of the immortal: if the immortal is also imperishable, the soul when attacked by death cannot perish; for the preceding argument shows that the soul will not admit of death, or

ever be dead, any more than three or the odd number will admit of the even, or fire or the heat in the fire, of the cold. Yet a person may say: 'But although the odd will not become even at the approach of the even, why may not the odd perish and the even take the place of the odd?' Now to him who makes this objection, we cannot answer that the odd principle is imperishable; for this has not been acknowledged, but if this had been acknowledged, there would have been no difficulty in contending that at the approach of the even the odd principle and the number three took their departure; and the same argument would have held good of fire and heat and any other thing.

CEBES: Very true.

SOCRATES: And the same may be said of the immortal: if the immortal is also imperishable, then the soul will be imperishable as well as immortal; but if not, some other proof of her imperishableness will have to be given.

CEBES: No other proof is needed; for if the immortal, being eternal, is liable to perish, then nothing is imperishable.

SOCRATES: Yes, and yet all men will agree that God, and the essential form of life, and the immortal in general, will never perish.

CEBES: Yes, all men—that is true; and what is more, gods, if I am not mistaken, as well as men.

SOCRATES: Seeing then that the immortal is indestructible, must not the soul, if she is immortal, be also imperishable?

CEBES: Most certainly.

SOCRATES: Then when death attacks a man, the mortal portion of him may be supposed to die, but the immortal retires at the approach of death and is preserved safe and sound?

CEBES: True.

SOCRATES: Then, Cebes, beyond question, the soul is immortal and imperishable, and our souls will truly exist in another world!

CEBES: I am convinced, Socrates, and have nothing more to object; but if my friend Simmias, or anyone else, has any further objection to make, he had better speak out, and not keep silence, since I do not know to what other season he can defer the discussion, if there is anything which he wants to say or to have said.

SIMMIAS: But I have nothing more to say; nor can I see any reason for doubt after what has been said. But I still feel and cannot help feeling uncertain in my own mind, when I think of the greatness of the subject and the feebleness of man.

SOCRATES: Yes, Simmias, that is well said: and I may add that first principles, even if they appear certain, should be carefully considered; and when they are satisfactorily ascertained, then, with a sort of hesitating confidence in human reason, you may, I think, follow the course of the argument; and if that be plain and clear, there will be no need for any further enquiry.

SIMMIAS: Very true.

SOCRATES: But then, O my friends, if the soul is really immortal, what care should be taken of her, not only in respect of the portion of time which is called life, but of eternity! And the danger of neglecting her from this point of view does indeed appear to be awful. If death had only been the end of all, the wicked would have had a good bargain in dying, for they would have been happily quit not only of their body, but of their own evil together with their souls. But now, inasmuch as the soul is manifestly immortal, there is no release or salvation from evil except the attainment of the highest virtue and wisdom. For the soul when on her progress to the world below takes nothing with her but nurture and education; and these are said greatly to benefit or greatly to injure the departed, at the very beginning of his journey thither.

[The Dialogues of Plato. Trans. By Benjamin Jowett (London: Macmillan, 1891).]

CHAPTER FOUR

Aristotle on Virtue, Habit, and Happiness

Image © Panos Karas, 2014. Used under license from Shutterstock, Inc.

Aristotle (384–322 BCE)

SELECTED READINGS

▶ *Nicomachean Ethics*—Aristotle

Nicomachean Ethics

Aristotle
(Translated by W.D. Ross and edited by Joseph R. Kirkland)

BOOK ONE

1.

Every art and every inquiry, and similarly every action and pursuit, is thought to aim at some good; and for this reason the good has rightly been declared to be that at which all things aim. But a certain difference is found among ends; some are activities, others are products apart from the activities that produce them. Where there are ends apart from the actions, it is the nature of the products to be better than the activities. Now, as there are many actions, arts, and sciences, their ends also are many; the end of the medical art is health, that of shipbuilding a vessel, that of strategy victory, that of economics wealth. But where such arts fall under a single capacity – as bridle-making and the other arts concerned with the equipment of horses fall under the art of riding, and this and every military action under strategy, in the same way other arts fall under yet others – in all of these the ends of the master arts are to be preferred to all the subordinate ends; for it is for the sake of the former that the latter are pursued. It makes no difference whether the activities themselves are the ends of the actions, or something else apart from the activities, as in the case of the sciences just mentioned.

2.

If, then, there is some end of the things we do, which we desire for its own sake (everything else being desired for the sake of this), and if we do not choose everything for the sake of something else (for at that rate the process would go on to infinity, so that our desire would be empty and vain), clearly this must be the good and the chief good. Will not the knowledge of it, then, have a great influence on life? Shall we not, like archers who have a mark to aim at, be more likely to hit upon what is right? If so, we must try, in outline at least, to determine what it is, and of which of the sciences or capacities it is the object. It would seem to belong to the most authoritative art and that which is most truly the master art. And politics appears to be of this nature; for it is this that ordains which of the sciences should be studied in a state, and which each class of citizens should learn and up to what point they should learn them; and

we see even the most highly esteemed of capacities to fall under this, e.g. strategy, economics, rhetoric; now, since politics uses the rest of the sciences, and since, again, it legislates as to what we are to do and what we are to abstain from, the end of this science must include those of the others, so that this end must be the good for man. For even if the end is the same for a single man and for a state, that of the state seems at all events something greater and more complete whether to attain or to preserve; though it is worthwhile to attain the end merely for one man, it is finer and more godlike to attain it for a nation or for city-states. These, then, are the ends at which our inquiry aims, since it is political science, in one sense of that term.

3.

Our discussion will be adequate if it has as much clearness as the subject-matter admits of, for precision is not to be sought for alike in all discussions, any more than in all the products of the crafts. Now fine and just actions, which political science investigates, admit of much variety and fluctuation of opinion, so that they may be thought to exist only by convention, and not by nature. And goods also give rise to a similar fluctuation because they bring harm to many people; for before now men have been undone by reason of their wealth, and others by reason of their courage. We must be content, then, in speaking of such subjects and with such premises to indicate the truth roughly and in outline, and in speaking about things which are only for the most part true and with premises of the same kind to reach conclusions that are no better. In the same spirit, therefore, should each type of statement be received; for it is the mark of an educated man to look for precision in each class of things just so far as the nature of the subject admits; it is evidently equally foolish to accept probable reasoning from a mathematician and to demand from a rhetorician scientific proofs.

Now each man judges well the things he knows, and of these he is a good judge. And so the man who has been educated in a subject is a good judge of that subject, and the man who has received an all-round education is a good judge in general. Hence a young man is not a proper hearer of lectures on political science; for he is inexperienced in the actions that occur in life, but its discussions start from these and are about these; and, further, since he tends to follow his passions, his study will be vain and unprofitable, because the end aimed at is not knowledge but action. And it makes no difference whether he is young in years or youthful in character; the defect does not depend on time, but on his living, and pursuing each successive object, as passion directs. For to such persons, as to the incontinent, knowledge brings no profit; but to those who desire and act in accordance with a rational principle knowledge about such matters will be of great benefit.

These remarks about the student, the sort of treatment to be expected, and the purpose of the inquiry, may be taken as our preface.

4.

Let us resume our inquiry and state, in view of the fact that all knowledge and every pursuit aims at some good, what it is that we say political science aims at and what is the highest of all goods achievable by action. Verbally there is very general agreement; for both the general run of men and people of superior refinement say that it is happiness, and identify living well and doing well with being happy; but with regard to what happiness is they differ, and the many do not give the same account as the wise. For the former think it is some plain and obvious thing, like pleasure, wealth, or honor; they differ, however, from one another- and often even the same man identifies it with different things, with health when he is ill, with wealth when he is poor; but, conscious of their ignorance, they admire those who proclaim some great ideal that is above their comprehension. Now some thought that apart from these many goods there is another which is self-subsistent and causes the goodness of all these as well. To examine all the opinions that have been held were perhaps somewhat fruitless; enough to examine those that are most prevalent or that seem to be arguable.

Let us not fail to notice, however, that there is a difference between arguments from and those to the first principles. For Plato, too, was right in raising this question and asking, as he used to do, 'are we on the way from or to the first principles?' There is a difference, as there is in a race-course between the course from the judges to the turning-point and the way back. For, while we must begin with what is known, things are objects of knowledge in two senses- some to us, some without qualification. Presumably, then, we must begin with things known to us. Hence anyone who is to listen intelligently to lectures about what is noble and just, and generally, about the subjects of political science must have been brought up in good habits. For the fact is the starting-point, and if this is sufficiently plain to him, he will not at the start need the reason as well; and the man who has been well brought up has or can easily get starting points. And as for him who neither has nor can get them, let him hear the words of Hesiod:

> Far best is he who knows all things himself;
> Good, he that hearkens when men counsel
> right; But he who neither knows, nor lays to
> heart Another's wisdom, is a useless wight.

5.

Let us, however, resume our discussion from the point at which we digressed. To judge from the lives that men lead, most men, and men of the most vulgar type, seem (not without some ground) to identify the good, or happiness, with pleasure; which is the reason why they love the life of enjoyment. For there are, we may say, three prominent types of life- that just mentioned, the political, and thirdly the contemplative life. Now the mass of mankind are evidently quite slavish in their tastes, preferring a life suitable to beasts, but they get some ground for their view from the fact that many of those in high places share the tastes of Sardanapallus. A consideration of the prominent types of life shows that people of superior refinement and of active disposition identify happiness with honor; for this is, roughly speaking, the end of the political life. But it seems too superficial to be what we are looking for, since it is thought to depend on those who bestow honor rather than on him who receives it, but the good we divine to be something proper to a man and not easily taken from him. Further, men seem to pursue honor in order that they may be assured of their goodness; at least it is by men of practical wisdom that they seek to be honored, and among those who know them, and on the ground of their virtue; clearly, then, according to them, at any rate, virtue is better. And perhaps one might even suppose this to be, rather than honor, the end of the political life. But even this appears somewhat incomplete; for possession of virtue seems actually compatible with being asleep, or with lifelong inactivity, and, further, with the greatest sufferings and misfortunes; but a man who was living so no one would call happy, unless he were maintaining a thesis at all costs. But enough of this; for the subject has been sufficiently treated even in the current discussions. Third comes the contemplative life, which we shall consider later.

The life of money-making is one undertaken under compulsion, and wealth is evidently not the good we are seeking; for it is merely useful and for the sake of something else. And so one might rather take the aforementioned objects to be ends; for they are loved for themselves. But it is evident that not even these are ends; yet many arguments have been thrown away in support of them. Let us leave this subject, then.

6.

We had perhaps better consider the universal good and discuss thoroughly what is meant by it, although such an inquiry is made an uphill one by the fact that the Forms have been introduced by friends of our own. Yet it would perhaps be thought to be better, indeed to be our duty, for the sake of maintaining the truth even to destroy what touches us closely, especially as we are philosophers or lovers of wisdom; for, while both are dear, piety requires us to honor truth above our friends.

The men who introduced this doctrine did not posit Ideas of classes within which they recognized priority and posteriority (which is the reason why they did not maintain the existence of an Idea embracing all numbers); but the term 'good' is used both in the category of substance and in that of quality and in that of relation, and that which is per se, i.e. substance, is prior in nature to the relative (for the latter is like an off shoot and accident of being); so that there could not be a common Idea set over all these goods. Further, since 'good' has as many senses as 'being' (for it is predicated both in the category of substance, as of God and of reason, and in quality, i.e. of the virtues, and in quantity, i.e. of that which is moderate, and in relation, i.e. of the useful, and in time, i.e. of the right opportunity, and in place, i.e. of the right locality and the like), clearly it cannot be something universally present in all cases and single; for then it could not have been predicated in all the categories but in one only. Further, since of the things answering to one Idea there is one science, there would have been one science of all the goods; but as it is there are many sciences even of the things that fall under one category, e.g. of opportunity, for opportunity in war is studied by strategics and in disease by medicine, and the moderate in food is studied by medicine and in exercise by the science of gymnastics. And one might ask the question, what in the world they mean by 'a thing itself', is (as is the case) in 'man himself'

and in a particular man the account of man is one and the same. For in so far as they are man, they will in no respect differ; and if this is so, neither will 'good itself' and particular goods, in so far as they are good. But again it will not be good any the more for being eternal, since that which lasts long is no whiter than that which perishes in a day. The Pythagoreans seem to give a more plausible account of the good, when they place the one in the column of goods; and it is they that Speusippus seems to have followed.

But let us discuss these matters elsewhere; an objection to what we have said, however, may be discerned in the fact that the Platonists have not been speaking about all goods, and that the goods that are pursued and loved for themselves are called good by reference to a single Form, while those which tend to produce or to preserve these somehow or to prevent their contraries are called so by reference to these, and in a secondary sense. Clearly, then, goods must be spoken of in two ways, and some must be good in themselves, the others by reason of these. Let us separate, then, things good in themselves from things useful, and consider whether the former are called good by reference to a single Idea. What sort of goods would one call good in themselves? Is it those that are pursued even when isolated from others, such as intelligence, sight, and certain pleasures and honors? Certainly, if we pursue these also for the sake of something else, yet one would place them among things good in themselves. Or is nothing other than the Idea of good good in itself? In that case the Form will be empty. But if the things we have named are also things good in themselves, the account of the good will have to appear as something identical in them all, as that of whiteness is identical in snow and in white lead. But of honor, wisdom, and pleasure, just in respect of their goodness, the accounts are distinct and diverse. The good, therefore, is not some common element answering to one Idea.

But what then do we mean by the good? It is surely not like the things that only chance to have the same name. Are goods one, then, by being derived from one good or by all contributing to one good, or are they rather one by analogy? Certainly as sight is in the body, so is reason in the soul, and so on in other cases. But perhaps these subjects had better be dismissed for the present; for perfect precision about them would be more appropriate to another branch of philosophy. And similarly with regard to the Idea; even if there is some one good which is universally predicable of goods or is capable of separate and independent existence, clearly it could not be achieved or attained by man; but we are now seeking something attainable. Perhaps, however, some one might think it worthwhile to recognize this with a view to the goods that are attainable and achievable; for having this as a sort of pattern we shall know better the goods that are good for us, and if we know them shall attain them. This argument has some plausibility, but seems to clash with the procedure of the sciences; for all of these, though they aim at some good and seek to supply the deficiency of it, leave on one side the knowledge of the good. Yet that all the exponents of the arts should be ignorant of, and should not even seek, so great an aid is not probable. It is hard, too, to see how a weaver or a carpenter will be benefited in regard to his own craft by knowing this 'good itself', or how the man who has viewed the Idea itself will be a better doctor or general thereby. For a doctor seems not even to study health in this way, but the health of man, or perhaps rather the health of a particular man; it is individuals that he is healing. But enough of these topics.

7.

Let us again return to the good we are seeking, and ask what it can be. It seems different in different actions and arts; it is different in medicine, in strategy, and in the other arts likewise. What then is the good of each? Surely that for whose sake everything else is done. In medicine this is health, in strategy victory, in architecture a house, in any other sphere something else, and in every action and pursuit the end; for it is for the sake of this that all men do whatever else they do. Therefore, if there is an end for all that we do, this will be the good achievable by action, and if there are more than one, these will be the goods achievable by action.

So the argument has by a different course reached the same point; but we must try to state this even more clearly. Since there are evidently more than one end, and we choose some of these (e.g., wealth, flutes, and in general instruments) for the sake of something else, clearly not all ends are final ends; but the chief good is evidently something final. Therefore, if there is only one final end, this will be what we are seeking, and if there are more than one, the most final of these will be what we are seeking. Now we call that which is in itself worthy of pursuit more final than that which is worthy of pursuit for the sake of something else, and that which is never desirable for the sake of something else more final than the things that are desirable both in themselves and for the sake of that other thing, and therefore we call final without qualification that which

is always desirable in itself and never for the sake of something else.

Now such a thing happiness, above all else, is held to be; for this we choose always for self and never for the sake of something else, but honor, pleasure, reason, and every virtue we choose indeed for themselves (for if nothing resulted from them we should still choose each of them), but we choose them also for the sake of happiness, judging that by means of them we shall be happy. Happiness, on the other hand, no one chooses for the sake of these, nor, in general, for anything other than itself.

From the point of view of self-sufficiency the same result seems to follow; for the final good is thought to be self-sufficient. Now by self-sufficient we do not mean that which is sufficient for a man by himself, for one who lives a solitary life, but also for parents, children, wife, and in general for his friends and fellow citizens, since man is born for citizenship. But some limit must be set to this; for if we extend our requirement to ancestors and descendants and friends' friends we are in for an infinite series. Let us examine this question, however, on another occasion; the self-sufficient we now define as that which when isolated makes life desirable and lacking in nothing; and such we think happiness to be; and further we think it most desirable of all things, without being counted as one good thing among others- if it were so counted it would clearly be made more desirable by the addition of even the least of goods; for that which is added becomes an excess of goods, and of goods the greater is always more desirable. Happiness, then, is something final and self-sufficient, and is the end of action.

Presumably, however, to say that happiness is the chief good seems a platitude, and a clearer account of what it is still desired. This might perhaps be given, if we could first ascertain the function of man. For just as for a flute-player, a sculptor, or an artist, and, in general, for all things that have a function or activity, the good and the 'well' is thought to reside in the function, so would it seem to be for man, if he has a function. Have the carpenter, then, and the tanner certain functions or activities, and has man none? Is he born without a function? Or as eye, hand, foot, and in general each of the parts evidently has a function, may one lay it down that man similarly has a function apart from all these? What then can this be? Life seems to be common even to plants, but we are seeking what is peculiar to man. Let us exclude, therefore, the life of nutrition and growth. Next there would be a life of perception, but it also seems to be common even to the horse, the ox, and every animal. There remains, then, an active life of the element that has a rational principle; of this, one part has such a principle in the sense of being obedient to one, the other in the sense of possessing one and exercising thought. And, as 'life of the rational element' also has two meanings, we must state that life in the sense of activity is what we mean; for this seems to be the more proper sense of the term. Now if the function of man is an activity of soul which follows or implies a rational principle, and if we say 'so-and-so-and 'a good so-and-so' have a function which is the same in kind, e.g. a lyre, and a good lyre-player, and so without qualification in all cases, eminence in respect of goodness being added to the name of the function (for the function of a lyre-player is to play the lyre, and that of a good lyre-player is to do so well): if this is the case, and we state the function of man to be a certain kind of life, and this to be an activity or actions of the soul implying a rational principle, and the function of a good man to be the good and noble performance of these, and if any action is well performed when it is performed in accordance with the appropriate excellence: if this is the case, human good turns out to be activity of soul in accordance with virtue, and if there are more than one virtue, in accordance with the best and most complete.

But we must add 'in a complete life.' For one swallow does not make a summer, nor does one day; and so too one day, or a short time, does not make a man blessed and happy.

Let this serve as an outline of the good; for we must presumably first sketch it roughly, and then later fill in the details. But it would seem that any one is capable of carrying on and articulating what has once been well outlined, and that time is a good discoverer or partner in such a work; to which facts the advances of the arts are due; for any one can add what is lacking. And we must also remember what has been said before, and not look for precision in all things alike, but in each class of things such precision as accords with the subject-matter, and so much as is appropriate to the inquiry. For a carpenter and a geometer investigate the right angle in different ways; the former does so in so far as the right angle is useful for his work, while the latter inquires what it is or what sort of thing it is; for he is a spectator of the truth. We must act in the same way, then, in all other matters as well, that our main task may not be subordinated to minor questions. Nor must we demand the cause in all matters alike; it is enough in some

cases that the fact be well established, as in the case of the first principles; the fact is the primary thing or first principle. Now of first principles we see some by induction, some by perception, some by a certain habituation, and others too in other ways. But each set of principles we must try to investigate in the natural way, and we must take pains to state them definitely, since they have a great influence on what follows. For the beginning is thought to be more than half of the whole, and many of the questions we ask are cleared up by it.

8.

We must consider it, however, in the light not only of our conclusion and our premises, but also of what is commonly said about it; for with a true view all the data harmonize, but with a false one the facts soon clash. Now goods have been divided into three classes, and some are described as external, others as relating to soul or to body; we call those that relate to soul most properly and truly goods, and psychical actions and activities we class as relating to soul. Therefore our account must be sound, at least according to this view, which is an old one and agreed on by philosophers. It is correct also in that we identify the end with certain actions and activities; for thus it falls among goods of the soul and not among external goods. Another belief which harmonizes with our account is that the happy man lives well and does well; for we have practically defined happiness as a sort of good life and good action. The characteristics that are looked for in happiness seem also, all of them, to belong to what we have defined happiness as being. For some identify happiness with virtue, some with practical wisdom, others with a kind of philosophic wisdom, others with these, or one of these, accompanied by pleasure or not without pleasure; while others include also external prosperity. Now some of these views have been held by many men and men of old, others by a few eminent persons; and it is not probable that either of these should be entirely mistaken, but rather that they should be right in at least some one respect or even in most respects.

With those who identify happiness with virtue or some one virtue our account is in harmony; for to virtue belongs virtuous activity. But it makes, perhaps, no small difference whether we place the chief good in possession or in use, in state of mind or in activity. For the state of mind may exist without producing any good result, as in a man who is asleep or in some other way quite inactive, but the activity cannot; for one who has the activity will of necessity be acting, and acting well.

And as in the Olympic Games it is not the most beautiful and the strongest that are crowned but those who compete (for it is some of these that are victorious), so those who act win, and rightly win, the noble and good things in life.

Their life is also in itself pleasant. For pleasure is a state of soul, and to each man that which he is said to be a lover of is pleasant; e.g. not only is a horse pleasant to the lover of horses, and a spectacle to the lover of sights, but also in the same way just acts are pleasant to the lover of justice and in general virtuous acts to the lover of virtue. Now for most men their pleasures are in conflict with one another because these are not by nature pleasant, but the lovers of what is noble find pleasant the things that are by nature pleasant; and virtuous actions are such, so that these are pleasant for such men as well as in their own nature. Their life, therefore, has no further need of pleasure as a sort of adventitious charm, but has its pleasure in itself. For, besides what we have said, the man who does not rejoice in noble actions is not even good; since no one would call a man just who did not enjoy acting justly, nor any man liberal who did not enjoy liberal actions; and similarly in all other cases. If this is so, virtuous actions must be in themselves pleasant. But they are also good and noble, and have each of these attributes in the highest degree, since the good man judges well about these attributes; his judgment is such as we have described. Happiness then is the best, noblest, and most pleasant thing in the world, and these attributes are not severed as in the inscription at Delos:

> Most noble is that which is most just, and best
> is health / But most pleasant is it to win what
> we love.

> For all these properties belong to the best activities; and these, or one- the best- of these, we identify with happiness.

Yet evidently, as we said, it needs the external goods as well; for it is impossible, or not easy, to do noble acts without the proper equipment. In many actions we use friends and riches and political power as instruments; and there are some things the lack of which takes the luster from happiness, as good birth, goodly children, beauty; for the man who is very ugly in appearance or ill-born or solitary and childless is not very likely to be happy, and perhaps a man would be still less likely if he had thoroughly bad children or friends or had lost good children or friends by death. As we said, then, happiness seems to need this sort of prosperity in addition; for which reason some identify happiness with good fortune, though others identify it with virtue.

9.

For this reason also the question is asked, whether happiness is to be acquired by learning or by habituation or some other sort of training, or comes in virtue of some divine providence or again by chance. Now if there is any gift of the gods to men, it is reasonable that happiness should be given by the gods, and most surely gods-given of all human things inasmuch as it is the best. But this question would perhaps be more appropriate to another inquiry; happiness seems, however, even if it is not god-sent but comes as a result of virtue and some process of learning or training, to be among the most godlike things; for that which is the prize and end of virtue seems to be the best thing in the world, and something godlike and blessed.

It will also on this view be very generally shared; for all who are not maimed as regards their potentiality for virtue may win it by a certain kind of study and care. But if it is better to be happy thus than by chance, it is reasonable that the facts should be so, since everything that depends on the action of nature is by nature as good as it can be, and similarly everything that depends on art or any rational cause, and especially if it depends on the best of all causes. To entrust to chance what is greatest and most noble would be a very defective arrangement.

The answer to the question we are asking is plain also from the definition of happiness; for it has been said to be a virtuous activity of soul, of a certain kind. Of the remaining goods, some must necessarily pre-exist as conditions of happiness, and others are naturally co-operative and useful as instruments. And this will be found to agree with what we said at the outset; for we stated the end of political science to be the best end, and political science spends most of its pains on making the citizens to be of a certain character, viz. good and capable of noble acts.

It is natural, then, that we call neither ox nor horse nor any other of the animals happy; for none of them is capable of sharing in such activity. For this reason also a boy is not happy; for he is not yet capable of such acts, owing to his age; and boys who are called happy are being congratulated by reason of the hopes we have for them. For there is required, as we said, not only complete virtue but also a complete life, since many changes occur in life, and all manner of chances, and the most prosperous may fall into great misfortunes in old age, as is told of Priam in the Trojan Cycle; and one who has experienced such chances and has ended wretchedly no one calls happy.

10.

Must no one at all, then, be called happy while he lives; must we, as Solon says, see the end? Even if we are to lay down this doctrine, is it also the case that a man is happy when he is dead? Or is not this quite absurd, especially for us who say that happiness is an activity? But if we do not call the dead man happy, and if Solon does not mean this, but that one can then safely call a man blessed as being at last beyond evils and misfortunes, this also affords matter for discussion; for both evil and good are thought to exist for a dead man, as much as for one who is alive but not aware of them; e.g. honors and dishonors and the good or bad fortunes of children and in general of descendants. And this also presents a problem; for though a man has lived happily up to old age and has had a death worthy of his life, many reverses may befall his descendants- some of them may be good and attain the life they deserve, while with others the opposite may be the case; and clearly too the degrees of relationship between them and their ancestors may vary indefinitely. It would be odd, then, if the dead man were to share in these changes and become at one time happy, at another wretched; while it would also be odd if the fortunes of the descendants did not for some time have some effect on the happiness of their ancestors.

But we must return to our first difficulty; for perhaps by a consideration of it our present problem might be solved. Now if we must see the end and only then call a man happy, not as being happy but as having been so before, surely this is a paradox, that when he is happy the attribute that belongs to him is not to be truly predicated of him because we do not wish to call living men happy, on account of the changes that may befall them, and because we have assumed happiness to be something permanent and by no means easily changed, while a single man may suffer many turns of fortune's wheel. For clearly if we were to keep pace with his fortunes, we should often call the same man happy and again wretched, making the happy man out to be chameleon and insecurely based. Or is this keeping pace with his fortunes quite wrong? Success or failure in life does not depend on these, but human life, as we said, needs these as mere additions, while virtuous activities or their opposites are what constitute happiness or the reverse.

The question we have now discussed confirms our definition. For no function of man has so much permanence as virtuous activities (these are thought to be more durable even than knowledge of the sciences), and of these themselves the most valuable are more durable because those who are happy spend their life most readily and most continuously in these; for this seems to be the reason why we do not forget them. The attribute in question, then, will belong to the happy man, and he will be happy throughout his life; for always, or by preference to everything else, he will be engaged in virtuous action and contemplation, and he will bear the chances of life most nobly and altogether decorously, if he is 'truly good' and 'foursquare beyond reproach'.

Now many events happen by chance, and events differing in importance; small pieces of good fortune or of its opposite clearly do not weigh down the scales of life one way or the other, but a multitude of great events if they turn out well will make life happier (for not only are they themselves such as to add beauty to life, but the way a man deals with them may be noble and good), while if they turn out ill they crush and maim happiness; for they both bring pain with them and hinder many activities. Yet even in these nobility shines through, when a man bears with resignation many great misfortunes, not through insensibility to pain but through nobility and greatness of soul.

If activities are, as we said, what gives life its character, no happy man can become miserable; for he will never do the acts that are hateful and mean. For the man who is truly good and wise, we think, bears all the chances life becomingly and always makes the best of circumstances, as a good general makes the best military use of the army at his command and a good shoemaker makes the best shoes out of the hides that are given him; and so with all other craftsmen. And if this is the case, the happy man can never become miserable; though he will not reach blessedness, if he meet with fortunes like those of Priam.

Nor, again, is he many-colored and changeable; for neither will he be moved from his happy state easily or by any ordinary misadventures, but only by many great ones, nor, if he has had many great misadventures, will he recover his happiness in a short time, but if at all, only in a long and complete one in which he has attained many splendid successes.

When then should we not say that he is happy who is active in accordance with complete virtue and is sufficiently equipped with external goods, not for some chance period but throughout a complete life? Or must we add 'and who is destined to live thus and die as befits his life'? Certainly the future is obscure to us, while happiness, we claim, is an end and something in every way final. If so, we shall call happy those among living men in whom these conditions are, and are to be, fulfilled- but happy men. So much for these questions.

11.

That the fortunes of descendants and of all a man's friends should not affect his happiness at all seems a very unfriendly doctrine, and one opposed to the opinions men hold; but since the events that happen are numerous and admit of all sorts of difference, and some come more near to us and others less so, it seems a long - nay, an infinite - task to discuss each in detail; a general outline will perhaps suffice. If, then, as some of a man's own misadventures have a certain weight and influence on life while others are, as it were, lighter, so too there are differences among the misadventures of our friends taken as a whole, and it makes a difference whether the various suffering befall the living or the dead (much more even than whether lawless and terrible deeds are presupposed in a tragedy or done on the stage), this difference also must be taken into account; or rather, perhaps, the fact that doubt is felt whether the dead share in any good or evil. For it seems, from these considerations, that even if anything whether good or evil penetrates to them, it must be something weak and negligible, either in itself or for them, or if not, at least it must be such in degree and kind as not to make happy those who are not happy nor to take away their blessedness from those who are. The good or bad fortunes of friends, then, seem to have some effects on the dead, but effects of such a kind and degree as neither to make the happy unhappy nor to produce any other change of the kind.

12.

These questions having been definitely answered, let us consider whether happiness is among the things that are praised or rather among the things that are prized; for clearly it is not to be placed among potentialities. Everything that is praised seems to be praised because it is of a certain kind and is related somehow to something else; for we praise the just or brave man and in general both the good man and virtue itself because of the actions and functions involved, and we praise the strong man, the good runner, and so on, because he is of a certain kind and is related in a certain way to something good and important. This is clear also from the praises of the gods; for it seems absurd that the gods should be referred to our standard, but this is done because praise involves a reference, to something else. But if if praise is for things such as we have described, clearly what applies to the best things is not praise, but something greater and better, as is indeed obvious; for what we do to the gods and the most godlike of men is to call them blessed and happy. And so too with good things; no one praises happiness as he does justice, but rather calls it blessed, as being something more divine and better.

Eudoxus also seems to have been right in his method of advocating the supremacy of pleasure; he thought that the fact that, though a good, it is not praised indicated it to be better than the things that are praised, and that this is what God and the good are; for by reference to these all other things are judged. Praise is appropriate to virtue, for as a result of virtue men tend to do noble deeds, but encomia are bestowed on acts, whether of the body or of the soul. But perhaps nicety in these matters is more proper to those who have made a study of encomia; to us it is clear from what has been said that happiness is among the things that are prized and perfect. It seems to be so also from the fact that it is a first principle; for it is for the sake of this that we all do all that we do, and the first principle and cause of goods is, we claim, something prized and divine.

13.

Since happiness is an activity of soul in accordance with perfect virtue, we must consider the nature of virtue; for perhaps we shall thus see better the nature of happiness. The true student of politics, too, is thought to have studied virtue above all things; for he wishes to make his fellow citizens good and obedient to the laws. As an example of this we have the lawgivers of the Cretans and the Spartans, and any others of the kind that there may have been. And if this inquiry belongs to political science, clearly the pursuit of it will be in accordance with our original plan. But clearly the virtue we must study is human virtue; for the good we were seeking was human good and the happiness human happiness. By human virtue we mean not that of the body but that of the soul; and happiness also we call an activity of soul. But if this is so, clearly the student of politics must know somehow the facts about soul, as the man who is to heal the eyes or the body as a whole must know about the eyes or the body; and all the more since politics is more prized and better than medicine; but even among doctors the best educated spend much labor on acquiring knowledge of the body. The student of politics, then, must study the soul, and must study it with these objects in view, and do so just to the extent which is sufficient for the questions we are discussing; for further precision is perhaps something more laborious than our purposes require.

Some things are said about it, adequately enough, even in the discussions outside our school, and we must use these; e.g. that one element in the soul is irrational and one has a rational principle. Whether these are separated as the parts of the body or of anything divisible are, or are distinct by definition but by nature inseparable, like convex and concave in the circumference of a circle, does not affect the present question.

Of the irrational element one division seems to be widely distributed, and vegetative in its nature, I mean that which causes nutrition and growth; for it is this kind of power of the soul that one must assign to all nurslings and to embryos, and this same power to full-grown creatures; this is more reasonable than to assign some different power to them. Now the excellence of this seems to be common to all species and not specifically human; for this part or faculty seems to function most in sleep, while goodness and badness are least manifest in sleep (whence comes the saying that the happy are not better off than the wretched for half their lives; and this happens naturally enough, since sleep is an inactivity of the soul in that respect in which it is called good or bad), unless perhaps to a small extent some of the movements actually penetrate to the soul, and in this respect the dreams of good men are better than those of ordinary people. Enough of this subject, however; let us leave the nutritive faculty alone, since it has by its nature no share in human excellence.

There seems to be also another irrational element in the soul-one which in a sense, however, shares in a rational principle. For we praise the rational principle of the continent man and of the incontinent, and the part of their soul that has such a principle, since it urges them aright and towards the best objects; but there is found in them also another element naturally opposed to the rational principle, which fights against and resists that principle. For exactly as paralyzed limbs when we intend to move them to the right turn on the contrary to the left, so is it with the soul; the impulses of incontinent people move in contrary directions. But while in the body we see that which moves astray, in the soul we do not. No doubt, however, we must none the less suppose that in the soul too there is something contrary to the rational principle, resisting and opposing it. In what sense it is distinct from the other elements does not concern us. Now even this seems to have a share in a rational principle, as we said; at any rate in the continent man it obeys the rational principle and presumably in the temperate and brave man it is still more obedient; for in him it speaks, on all matters, with the same voice as the rational principle.

Therefore the irrational element also appears to be two-fold. For the vegetative element in no way shares in a rational principle, but the appetitive and in general the desiring element in a sense shares in it, in so far as it listens to and obeys it; this is the sense in which we speak of 'taking account' of one's father or one's friends, not that in which we speak of 'accounting for a mathematical property. That the irrational element is in some sense persuaded by a rational principle is indicated also by the giving of advice and by all reproof and exhortation. And if this element also must be said to have a rational principle, that which has a rational principle (as well as that which has not) will be two-fold, one subdivision having it in the strict sense and in itself, and the other having a tendency to obey as one does one's father.

Virtue too is distinguished into kinds in accordance with this difference; for we say that some of the virtues are intellectual and others moral, philosophic wisdom and understanding and practical wisdom being intellectual, liberality and temperance moral. For in speaking about a man's character we do not say that he is wise or has understanding but that he is good-tempered or temperate; yet we praise the wise man also with respect to his state of mind; and of states of mind we call those which merit praise virtues.

[Nicomachean Ethics. *Translated by W.D. Ross. (Oxford: Clarendon Press, 1908).]*

Nicomachean Ethics

Aristotle

(Translated by W.D. Ross and edited by Joseph R. Kirkland)

BOOK TWO

1.

Virtue, then, is of two kinds: intellectual and moral. Intellectual virtue mainly owes both its birth and its growth to teaching (for which reason it requires experience and time), while moral virtue comes about as a result of habit, whence also its name (*ethike*) is one that is formed by a slight variation from the word *ethos* (habit). From this it is also plain that none of the moral virtues arises in us by nature; for nothing that exists by nature can form a habit contrary to its nature. For instance the stone which by nature moves downwards cannot be habituated to move upwards, not even if one tries to train it by throwing it up ten thousand times; nor can fire be habituated to move downwards, nor can anything else that by nature behaves in one way be trained to behave in another. Neither by nature, then, nor contrary to nature do the virtues arise in us; rather we are adapted by nature to receive them, and are made perfect by habit.

Again, of all the things that come to us by nature we first acquire the potentiality and later exhibit the activity (this is plain in the case of the senses; for it was not by often seeing or often hearing that we got these senses, but on the contrary we had them before we used them, and did not come to have them by using them); but the virtues we get by first exercising them, as also happens in the case of the arts as well. For the things we have to learn before we can do them, we learn by doing them, e.g. men become builders by building and lyre-players by playing the lyre; so too we become just by doing just acts, temperate by doing temperate acts, brave by doing brave acts.

This is confirmed by what happens in states; for legislators make the citizens good by forming habits in them, and this is the wish of every legislator, and those who do not effect it miss their mark, and it is in this that a good constitution differs from a bad one.

Again, it is from the same causes and by the same means that every virtue is both produced and destroyed, and similarly every art; for it is from playing the lyre that both good and bad lyre-players are produced. And the corresponding statement is true of builders and of all the rest; men will be good or bad builders as a result of building well or badly. For if this were not so, there would have been no need of a teacher, but all men would have been born good or bad at their craft. This, then, is the case with the virtues also; by doing the acts that we do in our transactions with other men we become just or unjust, and by doing the acts that we do in the presence of danger, and being habituated to feel fear or confidence, we become brave or cowardly. The same is true of appetites and feelings of anger; some men become temperate and good-tempered, others self-indulgent and irascible, by behaving in one way or the other in the appropriate circumstances. Thus, in one word, states of character arise out of like activities. This is why the activities we exhibit must be of a certain kind; it is because the states of character correspond to the differences between these. It makes no small difference, then, whether we form habits of one kind or of another from our very youth; it makes a very great difference, or rather all the difference.

2.

Since, then, the present inquiry does not aim at theoretical knowledge like the others (for we are inquiring not in order to know what virtue is, but in order to become good, since otherwise our inquiry would have been of no use), we must examine the nature of actions, namely how we ought to do them; for these determine also the nature of the states of character that are produced, as we have said. Now, that we must act according to the right rule is a common principle and must be assumed-it will be discussed later, i.e. both what the right rule is, and how it is related to the other virtues. But this must be agreed upon beforehand, that the whole account of matters of conduct must be given in outline and not precisely, as we said at the very beginning that the accounts we demand must be in accordance with the subject-matter; matters concerned with conduct and questions of what is good for us have no fixity, any more than matters of health. The general account being of this nature, the account of particular cases is yet more lacking in exactness; for they do not fall under any art or precept but the agents themselves must in each case consider what is appropriate to the occasion, as happens also in the art of medicine or of navigation.

But though our present account is of this nature we must give what help we can. First, then, let us consider this, that it is the nature of such things to be destroyed by defect and excess, as we see in the case of strength and of health (for to gain light on things imperceptible we must use the evidence of sensible things); both excessive and defective exercise destroys the strength, and similarly drink or food which is above or below a certain amount destroys the health, while that which is proportionate both produces and increases and preserves it. So too is it, then, in the case of temperance and courage and the other virtues. For the man who flies from and fears everything and does not stand his ground against anything becomes a coward, and the man who fears nothing at all but goes to meet every danger becomes rash; and similarly the man who indulges in every pleasure and abstains from none becomes self-indulgent, while the man who shuns every pleasure, as boors do, becomes in a way insensible; temperance and courage, then, are destroyed by excess and defect, and preserved by the mean.

But not only are the sources and causes of their origination and growth the same as those of their destruction, but also the sphere of their actualization will be the same; for this is also true of the things which are more evident to sense, e.g. of strength; it is produced by taking much food and undergoing much exertion, and it is the strong man that will be most able to do these things. So too is it with the virtues; by abstaining from pleasures we become temperate, and it is when we have become so that we are most able to abstain from them; and similarly too in the case of courage; for by being habituated to despise things that are terrible and to stand our ground against them we become brave, and it is when we have become so that we shall be most able to stand our ground against them.

3.

We must take as a sign of states of character the pleasure or pain that ensues on acts; for the man who abstains from bodily pleasures and delights in this very fact is temperate, while the man who is annoyed at it is self-indulgent, and he who stands his ground against things that are terrible and delights in this or at least is not pained is brave, while the man who is pained is a coward. For moral excellence is concerned with pleasures and pains; it is on account of the pleasure that

we do bad things, and on account of the pain that we abstain from noble ones. Hence we ought to have been brought up in a particular way from our very youth, as Plato says, so as both to delight in and to be pained by the things that we ought; for this is the right education.

Again, if the virtues are concerned with actions and passions, and every passion and every action is accompanied by pleasure and pain, for this reason also virtue will be concerned with pleasures and pains. This is indicated also by the fact that punishment is inflicted by these means; for it is a kind of cure, and it is the nature of cures to be effected by contraries.

Again, as we said but lately, every state of soul has a nature relative to and concerned with the kind of things by which it tends to be made worse or better; but it is by reason of pleasures and pains that men become bad, by pursuing and avoiding these- either the pleasures and pains they ought not or when they ought not or as they ought not, or by going wrong in one of the other similar ways that may be distinguished. Hence men even define the virtues as certain states of impassivity and rest; not well, however, because they speak absolutely, and do not say 'as one ought' and 'as one ought not' and 'when one ought or ought not', and the other things that may be added. We assume, then, that this kind of excellence tends to do what is best with regard to pleasures and pains, and vice does the contrary.

The following facts also may show us that virtue and vice are concerned with these same things. There being three objects of choice and three of avoidance, the noble, the advantageous, the pleasant, and their contraries, the base, the injurious, the painful, about all of these the good man tends to go right and the bad man to go wrong, and especially about pleasure; for this is common to the animals, and also it accompanies all objects of choice; for even the noble and the advantageous appear pleasant.

Again, it has grown up with us all from our infancy; this is why it is difficult to rub off this passion, engrained as it is in our life. And we measure even our actions, some of us more and others less, by the rule of pleasure and pain. For this reason, then, our whole inquiry must be about these; for to feel delight and pain rightly or wrongly has no small effect on our actions.

Again, it is harder to fight with pleasure than with anger, to use Heraclitus' phrase', but both art and virtue are always concerned with what is harder; for even the good is better when it is harder. Therefore for this reason also the whole concern both of virtue and of political science is with pleasures and pains; for the man who uses these well will be good, he who uses them badly bad.

That virtue, then, is concerned with pleasures and pains, and that by the acts from which it arises it is both increased and, if they are done differently, destroyed, and that the acts from which it arose are those in which it actualizes itself- let this be taken as said.

4.

The question might be asked,; what we mean by saying that we must become just by doing just acts, and temperate by doing temperate acts; for if men do just and temperate acts, they are already just and temperate, exactly as, if they do what is in accordance with the laws of grammar and of music, they are grammarians and musicians.

Or is this not true even of the arts? It is possible to do something that is in accordance with the laws of grammar, either by chance or at the suggestion of another. A man will be a grammarian, then, only when he has both done something grammatical and done it grammatically; and this means doing it in accordance with the grammatical knowledge in himself.

Again, the case of the arts and that of the virtues are not similar; for the products of the arts have their goodness in themselves, so that it is enough that they should have a certain character, but if the acts that are in accordance with the virtues have themselves a certain character it does not follow that they are done justly or temperately. The agent also must be in a certain condition when he does them; in the first place he must have knowledge, secondly he must choose the acts, and choose them for their own sakes, and thirdly his action must proceed from a firm and unchangeable character. These are not reckoned in as conditions of the possession of the arts, except the bare knowledge; but as a condition of the possession of the virtues knowledge has little or no weight, while the other conditions count not for a little but for everything, i.e. the very conditions which result from often doing just and temperate acts.

Actions, then, are called just and temperate when they are such as the just or the temperate man would do; but it is not the man who does these that is just and temperate, but the man who also does them as just and temperate men do them. It is well said, then, that it is by doing just acts that the just man is produced, and by doing temperate acts the temperate man; without doing these no one would have even a prospect of becoming good.

But most people do not do these, but take refuge in theory and think they are being philosophers and will become good in this way, behaving somewhat like patients who listen attentively to their doctors, but do none of the things they are ordered to do. As the latter will not be made well in body by such a course of treatment, the former will not be made well in soul by such a course of philosophy.

5.

Next we must consider what virtue is. Since things that are found in the soul are of three kinds- passions, faculties, states of character, virtue must be one of these. By passions I mean appetite, anger, fear, confidence, envy, joy, friendly feeling, hatred, longing, emulation, pity, and in general the feelings that are accompanied by pleasure or pain; by faculties the things in virtue of which we are said to be capable of feeling these, e.g. of becoming angry or being pained or feeling pity; by states of character the things in virtue of which we stand well or badly with reference to the passions, e.g. with reference to anger we stand badly if we feel it violently or too weakly, and well if we feel it moderately; and similarly with reference to the other passions.

Now neither the virtues nor the vices are passions, because we are not called good or bad on the ground of our passions, but are so called on the ground of our virtues and our vices, and because we are neither praised nor blamed for our passions (for the man who feels fear or anger is not praised, nor is the man who simply feels anger blamed, but the man who feels it in a certain way), but for our virtues and our vices we are praised or blamed.

Again, we feel anger and fear without choice, but the virtues are modes of choice or involve choice. Further, in respect of the passions we are said to be moved, but in respect of the virtues and the vices we are said not to be moved but to be disposed in a particular way.

For these reasons also they are not faculties; for we are neither called good nor bad, nor praised nor blamed, for the simple capacity of feeling the passions; again, we have the faculties by nature, but we are not made good or bad by nature; we have spoken of this before. If, then, the virtues are neither passions nor faculties, all that remains is that they should be states of character.

Thus we have stated what virtue is in respect of its genus.

6.

We must, however, not only describe virtue as a state of character, but also say what sort of state it is. We may remark, then, that every virtue or excellence both brings into good condition the thing of which it is the excellence and makes the work of that thing be done well; e.g. the excellence of the eye makes both the eye and its work good; for it is by the excellence of the eye that we see well. Similarly the excellence of the horse makes a horse both good in itself and good at running and at carrying its rider and at awaiting the attack of the enemy. Therefore, if this is true in every case, the virtue of man also will be the state of character which makes a man good and which makes him do his own work well.

How this is to happen we have stated already, but it will be made plain also by the following consideration of the specific nature of virtue. In everything that is continuous and divisible it is possible to take more, less, or an equal amount, and that either in terms of the thing itself or relatively to us; and the equal is an intermediate between excess and defect. By the intermediate in the object I mean that which is equidistant from each of the extremes, which is one and the same for all men; by the intermediate relatively to us that which is neither too much nor too little- and this is not one, nor the same for all. For instance, if ten is many and two is few, six is the intermediate, taken in terms of the object; for it exceeds and is exceeded by an equal amount; this is intermediate according to arithmetical proportion. But the intermediate relatively to us is not to be taken so; if ten pounds are too much for a particular person to eat and two too little, it does not follow that the trainer will order six pounds; for this also is perhaps too much for the person who is to take it, or too little- too little for Milo, too much for the beginner in athletic exercises. The same is true of running and wrestling. Thus a master of any art avoids excess and defect, but seeks the intermediate and chooses this- the intermediate not in the object but relatively to us.

If it is thus, then, that every art does its work well- by looking to the intermediate and judging its works by this standard (so that we often say of good works of art that it is not possible either to take away or to add anything, implying that excess and defect destroy the goodness of works of art, while the mean preserves it; and good artists, as we say, look to this in their work), and if, further, virtue is more exact and better than any art, as nature also is, then virtue must have the quality of aiming at the intermediate. I mean moral virtue; for

it is this that is concerned with passions and actions, and in these there is excess, defect, and the intermediate. For instance, both fear and confidence and appetite and anger and pity and in general pleasure and pain may be felt both too much and too little, and in both cases not well; but to feel them at the right times, with reference to the right objects, towards the right people, with the right motive, and in the right way, is what is both intermediate and best, and this is characteristic of virtue. Similarly with regard to actions also there is excess, defect, and the intermediate. Now virtue is concerned with passions and actions, in which excess is a form of failure, and so is defect, while the intermediate is praised and is a form of success; and being praised and being successful are both characteristics of virtue. Therefore virtue is a kind of mean, since, as we have seen, it aims at what is intermediate.

Again, it is possible to fail in many ways (for evil belongs to the class of the unlimited, as the Pythagoreans conjectured, and good to that of the limited), while to succeed is possible only in one way (for which reason also one is easy and the other difficult- to miss the mark easy, to hit it difficult); for these reasons also, then, excess and defect are characteristic of vice, and the mean of virtue;

For men are good in but one way, but bad in many.

Virtue, then, is a state of character concerned with choice, lying in a mean, i.e. the mean relative to us, this being determined by a rational principle, and by that principle by which the man of practical wisdom would determine it. Now it is a mean between two vices, that which depends on excess and that which depends on defect; and again it is a mean because the vices respectively fall short of or exceed what is right in both passions and actions, while virtue both finds and chooses that which is intermediate. Hence in respect of its substance and the definition which states its essence virtue is a mean, with regard to what is best and right an extreme.

But not every action nor every passion admits of a mean; for some have names that already imply badness, e.g. spite, shamelessness, envy, and in the case of actions adultery, theft, murder; for all of these and suchlike things imply by their names that they are themselves bad, and not the excesses or deficiencies of them. It is not possible, then, ever to be right with regard to them; one must always be wrong. Nor does goodness or badness with regard to such things depend on committing adultery with the right woman, at the right time, and in the right way, but simply to do any of them is to go wrong. It would be equally absurd, then, to expect that in unjust, cowardly, and voluptuous action there should be a mean, an excess, and a deficiency; for at that rate there would be a mean of excess and of deficiency, an excess of excess, and a deficiency of deficiency. But as there is no excess and deficiency of temperance and courage because what is intermediate is in a sense an extreme, so too of the actions we have mentioned there is no mean nor any excess and deficiency, but however they are done they are wrong; for in general there is neither a mean of excess and deficiency, nor excess and deficiency of a mean.

7.

We must, however, not only make this general statement, but also apply it to the individual facts. For among statements about conduct those which are general apply more widely, but those which are particular are more genuine, since conduct has to do with individual cases, and our statements must harmonize with the facts in these cases. We may take these cases from our table. With regard to feelings of fear and confidence courage is the mean; of the people who exceed, he who exceeds in fearlessness has no name (many of the states have no name), while the man who exceeds in confidence is rash, and he who exceeds in fear and falls short in confidence is a coward. With regard to pleasures and pains - not all of them, and not so much with regard to the pains - the mean is temperance, the excess self-indulgence. Persons deficient with regard to the pleasures are not often found; hence such persons also have received no name. But let us call them 'insensible'.

With regard to giving and taking of money the mean is liberality, the excess and the defect prodigality and meanness. In these actions people exceed and fall short in contrary ways; the prodigal exceeds in spending and falls short in taking, while the mean man exceeds in taking and falls short in spending. (At present we are giving a mere outline or summary, and are satisfied with this; later these states will be more exactly determined.) With regard to money there are also other dispositions- a mean, magnificence (for the magnificent man differs from the liberal man; the former deals with large sums, the latter with small ones), an excess, tastelessness and vulgarity, and a deficiency, stinginess; these differ from the states opposed to liberality, and the mode of their difference will be stated later. With regard to honor and dishonor the mean is proper

pride, the excess is known as a sort of 'empty vanity', and the deficiency is undue humility; and as we said liberality was related to magnificence, differing from it by dealing with small sums, so there is a state similarly related to proper pride, being concerned with small honors while that is concerned with great. For it is possible to desire honor as one ought, and more than one ought, and less, and the man who exceeds in his desires is called ambitious, the man who falls short unambitious, while the intermediate person has no name. The dispositions also are nameless, except that that of the ambitious man is called ambition. Hence the people who are at the extremes lay claim to the middle place; and we ourselves sometimes call the intermediate person ambitious and sometimes unambitious, and sometimes praise the ambitious man and sometimes the unambitious. The reason of our doing this will be stated in what follows; but now let us speak of the remaining states according to the method which has been indicated.

With regard to anger also there is an excess, a deficiency, and a mean. Although they can scarcely be said to have names, yet since we call the intermediate person good-tempered let us call the mean good temper; of the persons at the extremes let the one who exceeds be called irascible, and his vice irascibility, and the man who falls short an inirascible sort of person, and the deficiency inirascibility.

There are also three other means, which have a certain likeness to one another, but differ from one another: for they are all concerned with intercourse in words and actions, but differ in that one is concerned with truth in this sphere, the other two with pleasantness; and of this one kind is exhibited in giving amusement, the other in all the circumstances of life. We must therefore speak of these too, that we may the better see that in all things the mean is praise-worthy, and the extremes neither praiseworthy nor right, but worthy of blame. Now most of these states also have no names, but we must try, as in the other cases, to invent names ourselves so that we may be clear and easy to follow. With regard to truth, then, the intermediate is a truthful sort of person and the mean may be called truthfulness, while the pretense which exaggerates is boastfulness and the person characterized by it a boaster, and that which understates is mock modesty and the person characterized by it mock-modest. With regard to pleasantness in the giving of amusement the intermediate person is ready-witted and the disposition ready wit, the excess is buffoonery and the person characterized by it a buffoon, while the man who falls short is a sort of boor and his state is boorishness. With regard to the remaining kind of pleasantness, that which is exhibited in life in general, the man who is pleasant in the right way is friendly and the mean is friendliness, while the man who exceeds is an obsequious person if he has no end in view, a flatterer if he is aiming at his own advantage, and the man who falls short and is unpleasant in all circumstances is a quarrelsome and surly sort of person.

There are also means in the passions and concerned with the passions; since shame is not a virtue, and yet praise is extended to the modest man. For even in these matters one man is said to be intermediate, and another to exceed, as for instance the bashful man who is ashamed of everything; while he who falls short or is not ashamed of anything at all is shameless, and the intermediate person is modest. Righteous indignation is a mean between envy and spite, and these states are concerned with the pain and pleasure that are felt at the fortunes of our neighbors; the man who is characterized by righteous indignation is pained at undeserved good fortune, the envious man, going beyond him, is pained at all good fortune, and the spiteful man falls so far short of being pained that he even rejoices. But these states there will be an opportunity of describing elsewhere; with regard to justice, since it has not one simple meaning, we shall, after describing the other states, distinguish its two kinds and say how each of them is a mean; and similarly we shall treat also of the rational virtues.

8.

There are three kinds of disposition, then, two of them vices, involving excess and deficiency respectively, and one a virtue, viz. the mean, and all are in a sense opposed to all; for the extreme states are contrary both to the intermediate state and to each other, and the intermediate to the extremes; as the equal is greater relatively to the less, less relatively to the greater, so the middle states are excessive relatively to the deficiencies, deficient relatively to the excesses, both in passions and in actions. For the brave man appears rash relatively to the coward, and cowardly relatively to the rash man; and similarly the temperate man appears self-indulgent relatively to the insensible man, insensible relatively to the self-indulgent, and the liberal man prodigal relatively to the mean man, mean relatively to the prodigal. Hence also the people at the extremes push the intermediate man each over to the other, and

the brave man is called rash by the coward, cowardly by the rash man, and correspondingly in the other cases.

These states being thus opposed to one another, the greatest contrariety is that of the extremes to each other, rather than to the intermediate; for these are further from each other than from the intermediate, as the great is further from the small and the small from the great than both are from the equal. Again, to the intermediate some extremes show a certain likeness, as that of rashness to courage and that of prodigality to liberality; but the extremes show the greatest unlikeness to each other; now contraries are defined as the things that are furthest from each other, so that things that are further apart are more contrary.

To the mean in some cases the deficiency, in some the excess is more opposed; e.g. it is not rashness, which is an excess, but cowardice, which is a deficiency, that is more opposed to courage, and not insensibility, which is a deficiency, but self-indulgence, which is an excess, that is more opposed to temperance. This happens from two reasons, one being drawn from the thing itself; for because one extreme is nearer and liker to the intermediate, we oppose not this but rather its contrary to the intermediate. E.g. since rashness is thought more like and nearer to courage, and cowardice more unlike, we oppose rather the latter to courage; for things that are further from the intermediate are thought more contrary to it. This, then, is one cause, drawn from the thing itself; another is drawn from ourselves; for the things to which we ourselves more naturally tend seem more contrary to the intermediate. For instance, we ourselves tend more naturally to pleasures, and hence are more easily carried away towards self-indulgence than towards propriety. We describe as contrary to the mean, then, rather the directions in which we more often go to great lengths; and therefore self-indulgence, which is an excess, is the more contrary to temperance.

9.

That moral virtue is a mean, then, and in what sense it is so, and that it is a mean between two vices, the one involving excess, the other deficiency, and that it is such because its character is to aim at what is intermediate in passions and in actions, has been sufficiently stated. Hence also it is no easy task to be good. For in everything it is no easy task to find the middle, e.g. to find the middle of a circle is not for everyone but for him who knows; so, too, anyone can get angry - that is easy - or give or spend money; but to do this to the right person, to the right extent, at the right time, with the right motive, and in the right way, that is not for everyone, nor is it easy; wherefore goodness is both rare and laudable and noble.

Hence he who aims at the intermediate must first depart from what is the more contrary to it, as Calypso advises:

Hold the ship out beyond that surf and spray.

For of the extremes one is more erroneous, one less so; therefore, since to hit the mean is hard in the extreme, we must as a second best, as people say, take the least of the evils; and this will be done best in the way we describe. But we must consider the things towards which we ourselves also are easily carried away; for some of us tend to one thing, some to another; and this will be recognizable from the pleasure and the pain we feel. We must drag ourselves away to the contrary extreme; for we shall get into the intermediate state by drawing well away from error, as people do in straightening sticks that are bent.

Now in everything the pleasant or pleasure is most to be guarded against; for we do not judge it impartially. We ought, then, to feel towards pleasure as the elders of the people felt towards Helen, and in all circumstances repeat their saying; for if we dismiss pleasure thus we are less likely to go astray. It is by doing this, then, (to sum the matter up) that we shall best be able to hit the mean.

But this is no doubt difficult, and especially in individual cases; for it is not easy to determine both how and with whom and on what provocation and how long one should be angry; for we too sometimes praise those who fall short and call them good-tempered, but sometimes we praise those who get angry and call them manly. The man, however, who deviates little from goodness is not blamed, whether he do so in the direction of the more or of the less, but only the man who deviates more widely; for he does not fail to be noticed. But up to what point and to what extent a man must deviate before he becomes blameworthy it is not easy to determine by reasoning, any more than anything else that is perceived by the senses; such things depend on particular facts, and the decision rests with perception. So much, then, is plain, that the intermediate state is in all things to be praised, but that we must incline sometimes towards the excess, sometimes towards the deficiency; for so shall we most easily hit the mean and what is right.

[Nicomachean Ethics. Translated by W.D. Ross. (Oxford: Clarendon Press, 1908).]

Nicomachean Ethics

Aristotle

(Translated by W. D. Ross and edited by Joseph R. Kirkland)

BOOK THREE

I.

Since virtue is concerned with passions and actions, and on voluntary passions and actions praise and blame are bestowed, on those that are involuntary pardon, and sometimes also pity, to distinguish the voluntary and the involuntary is presumably necessary for those who are studying the nature of virtue, and useful also for legislators with a view to the assigning both of honors and of punishments. Those things, then, are thought-involuntary, which take place under compulsion or owing to ignorance; and that is compulsory of which the moving principle is outside, being a principle in which nothing is contributed by the person who is acting or is feeling the passion, e.g. if he were to be carried somewhere by a wind, or by men who had him in their power.

But with regard to the things that are done from fear of greater evils or for some noble object (e.g. if a tyrant were to order one to do something base, having one's parents and children in his power, and if one did the action they were to be saved, but otherwise would be put to death), it may be debated whether such actions are involuntary or voluntary. Something of the sort happens also with regard to the throwing of goods overboard in a storm; for in the abstract no one throws goods away voluntarily, but on condition of its securing the safety of himself and his crew any sensible man does so. Such actions, then, are mixed, but are more like voluntary actions; for they are worthy of choice at the time when they are done, and the end of an action is relative to the occasion. Both the terms, then, 'voluntary' and 'involuntary', must be used with reference to the moment of action. Now the man acts voluntarily; for the principle that moves the instrumental parts of the body in such actions is in him, and the things of which the moving principle is in a man himself are in his power to do or not to do. Such actions, therefore, are voluntary, but in the abstract perhaps involuntary; for no one would choose any such act in itself.

For such actions men are sometimes even praised, when they endure something base or painful in return for great and noble objects gained; in the opposite case they are blamed, since to endure the greatest indignities for no noble end or for a trifling end is the mark of an inferior person. On some actions praise indeed is not bestowed, but pardon is, when one does what he ought not under pressure which overstrains human nature and which no one could withstand. But some acts, perhaps, we cannot be forced to do, but ought rather to face death after the most fearful sufferings; for the things that 'forced' Euripides Alcmaeon to slay his mother seem absurd. It is difficult sometimes to determine what should be chosen at what cost, and what should be endured in return for what gain, and yet more difficult to abide by our decisions; for as a rule what is expected is painful, and what we are forced to do is base, whence praise and blame are bestowed on those who have been compelled or have not.

What sort of acts, then, should be called compulsory? We answer that without qualification actions are so when the cause is in the external circumstances and the agent contributes nothing. But the things that in themselves are involuntary, but now and in return for these gains are worthy of choice, and whose moving principle is in the agent, are in themselves involuntary, but now and in return for these gains voluntary. They are more like voluntary acts; for actions are in the class of particulars, and the particular acts here are voluntary. What sort of things are to be chosen, and in return for what, it is not easy to state; for there are many differences in the particular cases.

But if someone were to say that pleasant and noble objects have a compelling power, forcing us from without, all acts would be for him compulsory; for it is for these objects that all men do everything they do. And those who act under compulsion and unwillingly act with pain, but those who do acts for their pleasantness and nobility do them with pleasure; it is absurd to make external circumstances responsible, and not oneself, as being easily caught by such attractions, and to make oneself responsible for noble acts but the pleasant objects responsible for base acts. The compulsory, then, seems to be that whose moving principle is outside, the person compelled contributing nothing.

Everything that is done by reason of ignorance is not voluntary; it is only what produces pain and repentance that is involuntary. For the man who has done something owing to ignorance, and feels not the least vexation at his action, has not acted voluntarily, since he did not know what he was doing, nor yet involuntarily, since he is not pained. Of people, then, who act by reason of ignorance he who repents is thought an involuntary agent, and the man who does not repent may, since he is different, be called a not voluntary agent; for, since he differs from the other, it is better that he should have a name of his own.

Acting by reason of ignorance seems also to be different from acting in ignorance; for the man who is drunk or in a rage is thought to act as a result not of ignorance but of one of the causes mentioned, yet not knowingly but in ignorance.

Now every wicked man is ignorant of what he ought to do and what he ought to abstain from, and it is by reason of error of this kind that men become unjust and in general bad; but the term 'involuntary' tends to be used not if a man is ignorant of what is to his advantage- for it is not mistaken purpose that causes involuntary action (it leads rather to wickedness), nor ignorance of the universal (for that men are blamed), but ignorance of particulars, i.e. of the circumstances of the action and the objects with which it is concerned. For it is on these that both pity and pardon depend, since the person who is ignorant of any of these acts involuntarily.

Perhaps it is just as well, therefore, to determine their nature and number. A man may be ignorant, then, of who he is, what he is doing, what or whom he is acting on, and sometimes also what (e.g. what instrument) he is doing it with, and to what end (e.g. he may think his act will conduce to some one's safety), and how he is doing it (e.g. whether gently or violently). Now of all of these no one could be ignorant unless he were mad, and evidently also he could not be ignorant of the agent; for how could he not know himself? But of what he is doing a man might be ignorant, as for instance people say 'it slipped out of their mouths as they were speaking', or 'they did not know it was a secret', as Aeschylus said of the mysteries, or a man might say he 'let it go off when he merely wanted to show its working', as the man did with the catapult. Again, one might think one's son was an enemy, as Merope did, or that a pointed spear had a button on it, or that a stone was pumice-stone; or one might give a man a draught to save him, and really kill him; or one might want to touch a man, as people do in sparring, and really wound him. The ignorance may relate, then, to any of these things, i.e. of the circumstances of the action, and the man who was ignorant of any of these is thought to have acted involuntarily, and especially if he was ignorant on the most important points; and these are thought to be the circumstances of the action and its end. Further, the doing of an act that is called involuntary in virtue of ignorance of this sort must be painful and involve repentance.

Since that which is done under compulsion or by reason of ignorance is involuntary, the voluntary would seem to be that of which the moving principle is in the agent himself, he being aware of the particular circumstances of the action. Presumably acts done by reason of anger or appetite are not rightly called involuntary. For in the first place, on that showing none of the other animals will act voluntarily, nor will children; and secondly, is it meant that we do not do voluntarily any of the acts that are due to appetite or anger, or that we do the noble acts voluntarily and the base acts involuntarily? Is not this absurd, when one and the same thing is the cause? But it would surely be odd to describe as involuntary the things one ought to desire; and we ought both to be angry at certain things and to have an appetite for certain things, e.g. for health and for learning. Also what is involuntary is thought to be painful, but what is in accordance with appetite is thought to be pleasant. Again, what is the difference in respect of involuntariness between errors committed upon calculation and those committed in anger? Both are to be avoided, but the irrational passions are thought not less human than reason is, and therefore also the actions which proceed from anger or appetite are the man's actions. It would be odd, then, to treat them as involuntary.

2.

Both the voluntary and the involuntary having been delimited, we must next discuss choice; for it is thought to be most closely bound up with virtue and to discriminate characters better than actions do.

Choice, then, seems to be voluntary, but not the same thing as the voluntary; the latter extends more widely. For both children and the lower animals share in voluntary action, but not in choice, and acts done on the spur of the moment we describe as voluntary, but not as chosen.

Those who say it is appetite or anger or wish or a kind of opinion do not seem to be right. For choice is not common to irrational creatures as well, but appetite and anger are. Again, the incontinent man acts with appetite, but not with choice; while the continent man on the contrary acts with choice, but not with appetite. Again, appetite is contrary to choice, but not appetite to appetite. Again, appetite relates to the pleasant and the painful, choice neither to the painful nor to the pleasant.

Still less is it anger; for acts due to anger are thought to be less than any others objects of choice.

But neither is it wish, though it seems near to it; for choice cannot relate to what is impossible, and if any one said he chose them he would be thought silly; but there may be a wish even for what is impossible, e.g. for immortality. And wish may relate to things that could in no way be brought about by one's own efforts, e.g. that a particular actor or athlete should win in a competition; but no one chooses such things, but only the things that he thinks could be brought about by his own efforts. Again, wish relates rather to the end, choice to the means; for instance, we wish to be healthy, but we choose the acts which will make us healthy, and we wish to be happy and say we do, but we cannot well say we choose to be so; for, in general, choice seems to relate to the things that are in our own power.

For this reason, too, it cannot be opinion; for opinion is thought to relate to all kinds of things, no less to eternal things and impossible things than to things in our own power; and it is distinguished by its falsity or truth, not by its badness or goodness, while choice is distinguished rather by these.

Now with opinion in general perhaps no one even says it is identical. But it is not identical even with any kind of opinion; for by choosing what is good or bad we are men of a certain character, which we are not by holding certain opinions. And we choose to get or avoid something good or bad, but we have opinions about what a thing is or whom it is good for or how it is good for him; we can hardly be said to opine to get or avoid anything. And choice is praised for being related to the right object rather than for being rightly related to it, opinion for being truly related to its object. And we choose what we best know to be good, but we opine what we do not quite know; and it is not the same people that are thought to make the best choices and to have the best opinions, but some are thought to have fairly good opinions, but by reason of vice to choose what they should not. If opinion precedes choice or accompanies it, that makes no difference; for it is not this

that we are considering, but whether it is identical with some kind of opinion.

What, then, or what kind of thing is it, since it is none of the things we have mentioned? It seems to be voluntary, but not all that is voluntary to be an object of choice. Is it, then, what has been decided on by previous deliberation? At any rate choice involves a rational principle and thought. Even the name seems to suggest that it is what is chosen before other things.

3.

Do we deliberate about everything, and is everything a possible subject of deliberation, or is deliberation impossible about some things? We ought presumably to call not what a fool or a madman would deliberate about, but what a sensible man would deliberate about, a subject of deliberation. Now about eternal things no one deliberates, e.g. about the material universe or the incommensurability of the diagonal and the side of a square. But no more do we deliberate about the things that involve movement but always happen in the same way, whether of necessity or by nature or from any other cause, e.g. the solstices and the risings of the stars; nor about things that happen now in one way, now in another, e.g. droughts and rains; nor about chance events, like the finding of treasure. But we do not deliberate even about all human affairs; for instance, no Spartan deliberates about the best constitution for the Scythians. For none of these things can be brought about by our own efforts.

We deliberate about things that are in our power and can be done; and these are in fact what is left. For nature, necessity, and chance are thought to be causes, and also reason and everything that depends on man. Now every class of men deliberates about the things that can be done by their own efforts. And in the case of exact and self-contained sciences there is no deliberation, e.g. about the letters of the alphabet (for we have no doubt how they should be written); but the things that are brought about by our own efforts, but not always in the same way, are the things about which we deliberate, e.g. questions of medical treatment or of money-making. And we do so more in the case of the art of navigation than in that of gymnastics, inasmuch as it has been less exactly worked out, and again about other things in the same ratio, and more also in the case of the arts than in that of the sciences; for we have more doubt about the former. Deliberation is concerned with things that happen in a certain way for the most part, but in which the event is obscure, and with things in which it is indeterminate. We call in others to aid us in deliberation on important questions, distrusting ourselves as not being equal to deciding.

We deliberate not about ends but about means. For a doctor does not deliberate whether he shall heal, nor an orator whether he shall persuade, nor a statesman whether he shall produce law and order, nor does anyone else deliberate about his end. They assume the end and consider how and by what means it is to be attained; and if it seems to be produced by several means they consider by which it is most easily and best produced, while if it is achieved by one only they consider how it will be achieved by this and by what means this will be achieved, till they come to the first cause, which in the order of discovery is last. For the person who deliberates seems to investigate and analyze in the way described as though he were analyzing a geometrical construction (not all investigation appears to be deliberation - for instance mathematical investigations - but all deliberation is investigation), and what is last in the order of analysis seems to be first in the order of becoming. And if we come on an impossibility, we give up the search, e.g. if we need money and this cannot be got; but if a thing appears possible we try to do it. By 'possible' things I mean things that might be brought about by our own efforts; and these in a sense include things that can be brought about by the efforts of our friends, since the moving principle is in ourselves. The subject of investigation is sometimes the instruments, sometimes the use of them; and similarly in the other cases- sometimes the means, sometimes the mode of using it or the means of bringing it about. It seems, then, as has been said, that man is a moving principle of actions; now deliberation is about the things to be done by the agent himself, and actions are for the sake of things other than themselves. For the end cannot be a subject of deliberation, but only the means; nor indeed can the particular facts be a subject of it, as whether this is bread or has been baked as it should; for these are matters of perception. If we are to be always deliberating, we shall have to go on to infinity.

The same thing is deliberated upon and is chosen, except that the object of choice is already determinate, since it is that which has been decided upon as a result of deliberation that is the object of choice. For every one ceases to inquire how he is to act when he has brought the moving principle back to himself and to the ruling part of himself; for this is what chooses. This is plain also from the ancient constitutions, which Homer represented; for the kings announced their choices to the people. The object of choice being one of the things in our own power which is desired after deliberation, choice will be deliberate desire of things in our own power; for when we have decided as a result of deliberation, we desire in accordance with our deliberation.

We may take it, then, that we have described choice in outline, and stated the nature of its objects and the fact that it is concerned with means.

4.

That wish is for the end has already been stated; some think it is for the good, others for the apparent good. Now those who say that the good is the object of wish must admit in consequence that that which the man who does not choose aright wishes for is not an object of wish (for if it is to be so, it must also be good; but it was, if it so happened, bad); while those who say the apparent good is the object of wish must admit that there is no natural object of wish, but only what seems good to each man. Now different things appear good to different people, and, if it so happens, even contrary things.

If these consequences are unpleasing, are we to say that absolutely and in truth the good is the object of wish, but for each person the apparent good; that that which is in truth an object of wish is an object of wish to the good man, while any chance thing may be so the bad man, as in the case of bodies also the things that are in truth wholesome are wholesome for bodies which are in good condition, while for those that are diseased other things are wholesome- or bitter or sweet or hot or heavy, and so on; since the good man judges each class of things rightly, and in each the truth appears to him? For each state of character has its own ideas of the noble and the pleasant, and perhaps the good man differs from others most by seeing the truth in each class of things, being as it were the norm and measure of them. In most things the error seems to be due to pleasure; for it appears a good when it is not. We therefore choose the pleasant as a good, and avoid pain as an evil.

5.

The end, then, being what we wish for, the means what we deliberate about and choose, actions concerning means must be according to choice and voluntary. Now the exercise of the virtues is concerned with means. Therefore virtue also is in our own power, and so too vice. For where it is in our power to act it is also in our power not to act, and vice versa; so that, if to act, where this is noble, is in our power, not to act, which will be base, will also be in our power, and if not to act, where this is noble, is in our power, to act, which will be base, will also be in our power. Now if it is in our power to do noble or base acts, and likewise in our power not to do them, and this was what being good or bad meant, then it is in our power to be virtuous or vicious.

The saying that 'no one is voluntarily wicked nor involuntarily happy' seems to be partly false and partly true; for no one is involuntarily happy, but wickedness is voluntary. Or else we shall have to dispute what has just been said, at any rate, and deny that man is a moving principle or begetter of his actions as of children. But if these facts are evident and we cannot refer actions to moving principles other than those in ourselves, the acts whose moving principles are in us must themselves also be in our power and voluntary.

Witness seems to be borne to this both by individuals in their private capacity and by legislators themselves; for these punish and take vengeance on those who do wicked acts (unless they have acted under compulsion or as a result of ignorance for which they are not themselves responsible), while they honor those who do noble acts, as though they meant to encourage the latter and deter the former. But no one is encouraged to do the things that are neither in our power nor voluntary; it is assumed that there is no gain in being persuaded not to be hot or in pain or hungry or the like, since we shall experience these feelings none the less. Indeed, we punish a man for his very ignorance, if he is thought responsible for the ignorance, as when penalties are doubled in the case of drunkenness; for the moving principle is in the man himself, since he had the power of not getting drunk and his getting drunk was the cause of his ignorance. And we punish those who are ignorant of anything in the laws that they ought to know and that is not difficult, and so too in the case of anything else that they are thought to be ignorant of through carelessness; we assume that it is in their power not to be ignorant, since they have the power of taking care.

But perhaps a man is the kind of man not to take care. Still they are themselves by their slack lives responsible for becoming men of that kind, and men make themselves responsible for being unjust or self-indulgent, in the one case by cheating and in the other by spending their time in drinking bouts and the like; for it is activities exercised on particular objects that make the corresponding character. This is plain from the case of people training for any contest or action; they practice the activity the whole time. Now not to know that it is from the exercise of activities on particular objects that states of character are produced is the mark of a thoroughly senseless person. Again, it is irrational to suppose that a man who acts unjustly does not wish to be unjust or a man who acts self-indulgently to be self-indulgent. But if without being ignorant a man does the things which will make him unjust, he will be unjust voluntarily. Yet it does not follow that if he wishes he will cease to be unjust and will be just. For neither does the man who is ill become well on those terms. We may suppose a case in which he is ill voluntarily, through living incontinently and disobeying his doctors. In that case it was then open to him not to be ill, but not now, when he has thrown away his chance, just as when you have let a stone go it is too late to recover it; but yet it was in your power to throw it, since the moving principle was in you. So, too, to the unjust and to the self-indulgent man it was open at the beginning not to become men of this kind, and so they are unjust and self-indulgent voluntarily; but now that they have become so it is not possible for them not to be so.

But not only are the vices of the soul voluntary, but those of the body also for some men, whom we accordingly blame; while no one blames those who are ugly by nature, we blame those who are so owing to want of exercise and care. So it is, too, with respect to weakness and infirmity; no one would reproach a man blind from birth or by disease or from a blow, but rather pity him, while everyone would blame a man who was blind from drunkenness or some other form of self-indulgence. Of vices of the body, then, those in our own power are blamed, those not in our power are not. And if this be so, in the other cases also the vices that are blamed must be in our own power.

Now some one may say that all men desire the apparent good, but have no control over the appearance, but the end appears to each man in a form answering to his character. We reply that if each man is somehow responsible for his state of mind, he will also be himself somehow responsible for the appearance; but if not, no one is responsible for his own evildoing, but everyone does evil acts through ignorance of the end, thinking that by these he will get what is best, and the aiming at the end is not self-chosen but one must be born with an eye, as it were, by which to judge rightly and choose what is truly good, and he is well endowed by nature who is well endowed with this. For it is what is greatest and most noble, and what we cannot get or learn from another, but must have just such as it was when given us at birth, and to be well and nobly endowed with this will be perfect and true excellence of natural endowment. If this is true, then, how will virtue be more voluntary than vice? To both men alike, the good and the bad, the end appears and is fixed by nature or however it may be, and it is by referring everything else to this that men do whatever they do.

Whether, then, it is not by nature that the end appears to each man such as it does appear, but something also depends on him, or the end is natural but because the good man adopts the means voluntarily virtue is voluntary, vice also will be none the less voluntary; for in the case of the bad man there is equally present that which depends on himself in his actions even if not in his end. If, then, as is asserted, the virtues are voluntary (for we are ourselves somehow partly responsible for our states of character, and it is by being persons of a certain kind that we assume the end to be so and so), the vices also will be voluntary; for the same is true of them.

With regard to the virtues in general we have stated their genus in outline, viz. that they are means and that they are states of character, and that they tend, and by their own nature, to the doing of the acts by which they are produced, and that they are in our power and voluntary, and act as the right rule prescribes. But actions and states of character are not voluntary in the same way; for we are masters of our actions from the beginning right to the end, if we know the particular facts, but though we control the beginning of our states of character the gradual progress is not obvious any more than it is in illnesses; because it was in our power, however, to act in this way or not in this way, therefore the states are voluntary.

Let us take up the several virtues, however, and say which they are and what sort of things they are concerned with and how they are concerned with them; at the same time it will become plain how many they are. And first let us speak of courage.

6.

That courage is a mean with regard to feelings of fear and confidence has already been made evident; and plainly the things we fear are terrible things, and these are, to speak without qualification, evils; for which reason people even define fear as expectation of evil. Now we fear all evils, e.g. disgrace, poverty, disease, friendlessness, death, but the brave man is not thought to be concerned with all; for to fear some things is even

right and noble, and it is base not to fear them - e.g. disgrace; he who fears this is good and modest, and he who does not is shameless. He is, however, by some people called brave, by a transference of the word to a new meaning; for he has in him something which is like the brave man, since the brave man also is a fearless person. Poverty and disease we perhaps ought not to fear, nor in general the things that do not proceed from vice and are not due to a man himself. But not even the man who is fearless of these is brave. Yet we apply the word to him also in virtue of a similarity; for some who in the dangers of war are cowards are liberal and are confident in face of the loss of money. Nor is a man a coward if he fears insult to his wife and children or envy or anything of the kind; nor brave if he is confident when he is about to be flogged. With what sort of terrible things, then, is the brave man concerned? Surely with the greatest; for no one is more likely than he to stand his ground against what is awe-inspiring. Now death is the most terrible of all things; for it is the end, and nothing is thought to be any longer either good or bad for the dead. But the brave man would not seem to be concerned even with death in all circumstances, e.g. at sea or in disease. In what circumstances, then? Surely in the noblest. Now such deaths are those in battle; for these take place in the greatest and noblest danger. And these are correspondingly honored in city-states and at the courts of monarchs. Properly, then, he will be called brave who is fearless in face of a noble death, and of all emergencies that involve death; and the emergencies of war are in the highest degree of this kind. Yet at sea also, and in disease, the brave man is fearless, but not in the same way as the seaman; for he has given up hope of safety, and is disliking the thought of death in this shape, while they are hopeful because of their experience. At the same time, we show courage in situations where there is the opportunity of showing prowess or where death is noble; but in these forms of death neither of these conditions is fulfilled.

7.

What is terrible is not the same for all men; but we say there are things terrible even beyond human strength. These, then, are terrible to every one- at least to every sensible man; but the terrible things that are not beyond human strength differ in magnitude and degree, and so too do the things that inspire confidence. Now the brave man is as dauntless as man may be. Therefore, while he will fear even the things that are not beyond human strength, he will face them as he ought and as the rule directs, for honor's sake; for this is the end of virtue. But it is possible to fear these more, or less, and again to fear things that are not terrible as if they were. Of the faults that are committed one consists in fearing what one should not, another in fearing as we should not, another in fearing when we should not, and so on; and so too with respect to the things that inspire confidence. The man, then, who faces and who fears the right things and from the right motive, in the right way and from the right time, and who feels confidence under the corresponding conditions, is brave; for the brave man feels and acts according to the merits of the case and in whatever way the rule directs. Now the end of every activity is conformity to the corresponding state of character. This is true, therefore, of the brave man as well as of others. But courage is noble. Therefore the end also is noble; for each thing is defined by its end. Therefore it is for a noble end that the brave man endures and acts as courage directs.

Of those who go to excess he who exceeds in fearlessness has no name (we have said previously that many states of character have no names), but he would be a sort of madman or insensible person if he feared nothing, neither earthquakes nor the waves, as they say the Celts do not; while the man who exceeds in confidence about what really is terrible is rash. The rash man, however, is also thought to be boastful and only a pretender to courage; at all events, as the brave man is with regard to what is terrible, so the rash man wishes to appear; and so he imitates him in situations where he can. Hence also most of them are a mixture of rashness and cowardice; for, while in these situations they display confidence, they do not hold their ground against what is really terrible. The man who exceeds in fear is a coward; for he fears both what he ought not and as he ought not, and all the similar characterizations attach to him. He is lacking also in confidence; but he is more conspicuous for his excess of fear in painful situations. The coward, then, is a despairing sort of person; for he fears everything. The brave man, on the other hand, has the opposite disposition; for confidence is the mark of a hopeful disposition. The coward, the rash man, and the brave man, then, are concerned with the same objects but are differently disposed towards them; for the first two exceed and fall short, while the third holds the middle, which is the right, position; and rash men are precipitate, and wish for dangers beforehand but draw back when they are in them, while brave men are keen in the moment of action, but quiet beforehand.

As we have said, then, courage is a mean with respect to things that inspire confidence or fear, in the circumstances that have been stated; and it chooses or endures things because it is noble to do so, or because it is base not to do so. But to die to escape from poverty or love or anything painful is not the mark of a brave man, but rather of a coward; for it is softness to fly from what is troublesome, and such a man endures death not because it is noble but to fly from evil.

8.

Courage, then, is something of this sort, but the name is also applied to five other kinds.

1. First comes the courage of the citizen-soldier; for this is most like true courage. Citizen-soldiers seem to face dangers because of the penalties imposed by the laws and the reproaches they would otherwise incur, and because of the honors they win by such action; and therefore those peoples seem to be bravest among whom cowards are held in dishonor and brave men in honor. . . .

   This kind of courage is most like to that which we described earlier, because it is due to virtue; for it is due to shame and to desire of a noble object (i.e. honor) and avoidance of disgrace, which is ignoble. One might rank in the same class even those who are compelled by their rulers; but they are inferior, inasmuch as they do what they do not from shame but from fear, and to avoid not what is disgraceful but what is painful; for their masters compel them, as Hector does:

   > But if I shall spy any dastard that cowers far from the fight,
   >
   > Vainly will such an one hope to escape from the dogs.

   And those who give them their posts, and beat them if they retreat, do the same, and so do those who draw them up with trenches or something of the sort behind them; all of these apply compulsion. But one ought to be brave not under compulsion but because it is noble to be so.

2. Experience with regard to particular facts is also thought to be courage; this is indeed the reason why Socrates thought courage was knowledge. Other people exhibit this quality in other dangers, and professional soldiers exhibit it in the dangers of war; for there seem to be many empty alarms in war, of which these have had the most comprehensive experience; therefore they seem brave, because the others do not know the nature of the facts. Again, their experience

makes them most capable in attack and in defense, since they can use their arms and have the kind that are likely to be best both for attack and for defense; therefore they fight like armed men against unarmed or like trained athletes against amateurs; for in such contests too it is not the bravest men that fight best, but those who are strongest and have their bodies in the best condition. Professional soldiers turn cowards, however, when the danger puts too great a strain on them and they are inferior in numbers and equipment; for they are the first to fly, while citizen-forces die at their posts, as in fact happened at the temple of Hermes. For to the latter flight is disgraceful and death is preferable to safety on those terms; while the former from the very beginning faced the danger on the assumption that they were stronger, and when they know the facts they fly, fearing death more than disgrace; but the brave man is not that sort of person.

3. Passion also is sometimes reckoned as courage; those who act from passion, like wild beasts rushing at those who have wounded them, are thought to be brave, because brave men also are passionate; for passion above all things is eager to rush on danger, and hence Homer's 'put strength into his passion' and 'aroused their spirit and passion and 'hard he breathed panting' and 'his blood boiled'. For all such expressions seem to indicate the stirring and onset of passion. Now brave men act for honor's sake, but passion aids them; while wild beasts act under the influence of pain; for they attack because they have been wounded or because they are afraid, since if they are in a forest they do not come near one. Thus they are not brave because, driven by pain and passion, they rush on danger without foreseeing any of the perils, since at that rate even asses would be brave when they are hungry; for blows will not drive them from their food; and lust also makes adulterers do many daring things. (Those creatures are not brave, then, which are driven on to danger by pain or passion.) The 'courage' that is due to passion seems to be the most natural, and to be courage if choice and motive be added.

Men, then, as well as beasts, suffer pain when they are angry, and are pleased when they exact their revenge; those who fight for these reasons, however, are pugnacious but not brave; for they do not act for honor's sake nor as the rule directs, but from strength of feeling; they have, however, something akin to courage.

4. Nor are sanguine people brave; for they are confident in danger only because they have conquered often and against many foes. Yet they closely resemble brave men, because both are confident; but brave men are confident for the reasons stated earlier, while these are so because they think they are the strongest and can suffer nothing. (Drunken men also behave in this way; they become sanguine). When their adventures do not succeed, however, they run away; but it was the mark of a brave man to face things that are, and seem, terrible for a man, because it is noble to do so and disgraceful not to do so. Hence also it is thought the mark of a braver man to be fearless and undisturbed in sudden alarms than to be so in those that are foreseen; for it must have proceeded more from a state of character, because less from preparation; acts that are foreseen may be chosen by calculation and rule, but sudden actions must be in accordance with one's state of character.

5. People who are ignorant of the danger also appear brave, and they are not far removed from those of a sanguine temper, but are inferior inasmuch as they have no self-reliance while these have. Hence also the sanguine hold their ground for a time; but those who have been deceived about the facts fly if they know or suspect that these are different from what they supposed, as happened to the Argives when they fell in with the Spartans and took them for Sicyonians.

We have, then, described the character both of brave men and of those who are thought to be brave.

9.

Though courage is concerned with feelings of confidence and of fear, it is not concerned with both alike, but more with the things that inspire fear; for he who is undisturbed in face of these and bears himself as he should towards these is more truly brave than the man who does so towards the things that inspire confidence. It is for facing what is painful, then, as has been said, that men are called brave. Hence also courage involves pain, and is justly praised; for it is harder to face what is painful than to abstain from what is pleasant.

Yet the end which courage sets before it would seem to be pleasant, but to be concealed by the attending circumstances, as happens also in athletic contests; for the end at which boxers aim is pleasant- the crown and the honors - but the blows they take are distressing to flesh and blood, and painful, and so is their whole exertion; and because the blows and the exertions are many the end, which is but small, appears to have nothing pleasant in it. And so, if the case of courage is similar, death and wounds will be painful to the brave man and against his will, but he will face them because it is noble to do so or because it is base not to do so. And the more he is possessed of virtue in its entirety and the happier he is, the more he will be pained at the thought of death; for life is best worth living for such a man, and he is knowingly losing the greatest goods, and this is painful. But he is none the less brave, and perhaps all the more so, because he chooses noble deeds of war at that cost. It is not the case, then, with all the virtues that the exercise of them is pleasant, except in so far as it reaches its end. But it is quite possible that the best soldiers may be not men of this sort but those who are less brave but have no other good; for these are ready to face danger, and they sell their life for trifling gains.

So much, then, for courage; it is not difficult to grasp its nature in outline, at any rate, from what has been said.

10.

After courage let us speak of temperance; for these seem to be the virtues of the irrational parts. We have said that temperance is a mean with regard to pleasures (for it is less, and not in the same way, concerned with pains); self-indulgence also is manifested in the same sphere. Now, therefore, let us determine with what sort of pleasures they are concerned. We may assume the distinction between bodily pleasures and those of the soul, such as love of honor and love of learning; for the lover of each of these delights in that of which he is a lover, the body being in no way affected, but rather the mind; but men who are concerned with such pleasures are called neither temperate nor self-indulgent. Nor, again, are those who are concerned with the other pleasures that are not bodily; for those who are fond of hearing and telling stories and who spend their days on anything that turns up are called gossips, but not self-indulgent, nor are those who are pained at the loss of money or of friends.

Temperance must be concerned with bodily pleasures, but not all even of these; for those who delight in objects of vision, such as colors and shapes and painting, are called neither temperate nor self-indulgent; yet it would seem possible to delight even in these either as one should or to excess or to a deficient degree.

And so too is it with objects of hearing; no one calls those who delight extravagantly in music or acting self-indulgent, nor those who do so as they ought temperate.

Nor do we apply these names to those who delight in odor, unless it be incidentally; we do not call those self-indulgent who delight in the odor of apples or roses or incense, but rather those who delight in the odor of unguents or of dainty dishes; for self-indulgent people delight in these because these remind them of the objects of their appetite. And one may see even other people, when they are hungry, delighting in the smell of food; but to delight in this kind of thing is the mark of the self-indulgent man; for these are objects of appetite to him.

Nor is there in animals other than man any pleasure connected with these senses, except incidentally. For dogs do not delight in the scent of hares, but in the eating of them, but the scent told them the hares were there; nor does the lion delight in the lowing of the ox, but in eating it; but he perceived by the lowing that it was near, and therefore appears to delight in the lowing; and similarly he does not delight because he sees 'a stag or a wild goat', but because he is going to make a meal of it. Temperance and self-indulgence, however, are concerned with the kind of pleasures that the other animals share in, which therefore appear slavish and brutish; these are touch and taste. But even of taste they appear to make little or no use; for the business of taste is the discriminating of flavors, which is done by wine-tasters and people who season dishes; but they hardly take pleasure in making these discriminations, or at least self-indulgent people do not, but in the actual enjoyment, which in all cases comes through touch, both in the case of food and in that of drink and in that of sexual intercourse. This is why a certain gourmand prayed that his throat might become longer than a crane's, implying that it was the contact that he took pleasure in. Thus the sense with which self-indulgence is connected is the most widely shared of the senses; and self-indulgence would seem to be justly a matter of reproach, because it attaches to us not as men but as animals. To delight in such things, then, and to love them above all others, is brutish. For even of the pleasures of touch the most liberal have been eliminated, e.g. those produced in the gymnasium by rubbing and by the consequent heat; for the contact characteristic of the self-indulgent man does not affect the whole body but only certain parts.

11.

Of the appetites some seem to be common, others to be peculiar to individuals and acquired; e.g. the appetite for food is natural, since everyone who is without it craves for food or drink, and sometimes for both, and for love also (as Homer says) if he is young and lusty; but not everyone craves for this or that kind of nourishment or love, nor for the same things. Hence such craving appears to be our very own. Yet it has of course something natural about it; for different things are pleasant to different kinds of people, and some things are more pleasant to everyone than chance objects. Now in the natural appetites few go wrong, and only in one direction, that of excess; for to eat or drink whatever offers itself till one is surfeited is to exceed the natural amount, since natural appetite is the replenishment of one's deficiency. Hence these people are called belly-gods, this implying that they fill their belly beyond what is right. It is people of entirely slavish character that become like this. But with regard to the pleasures peculiar to individuals many people go wrong and in many ways. For while the people who are 'fond of so and so' are so called because they delight either in the wrong things, or more than most people do, or in the wrong way, the self-indulgent exceed in all three ways; they both delight in some things that they ought not to delight in (since they are hateful), and if one ought to delight in some of the things they delight in, they do so more than one ought and more than most men do.

Plainly, then, excess with regard to pleasures is self-indulgence and is culpable; with regard to pains one is not, as in the case of courage, called temperate for facing them or self-indulgent for not doing so, but the self-indulgent man is so called because he is pained more than he ought at not getting pleasant things (even his pain being caused by pleasure), and the temperate man is so called because he is not pained at the absence of what is pleasant and at his abstinence from it.

The self-indulgent man, then, craves for all pleasant things or those that are most pleasant, and is led by his appetite to choose these at the cost of everything else; hence he is pained both when he fails to get them and when he is merely craving for them (for appetite involves pain); but it seems absurd to be pained for the sake of pleasure. People who fall short with regard to pleasures and delight in them less than they should are hardly found; for such insensibility is not human. Even the other animals distinguish different kinds of food and enjoy some and not others; and if there is anyone who finds nothing pleasant and nothing more attractive than anything else, he must be something quite different from a man; this sort of person has not received a name because he hardly occurs. The temperate man

occupies a middle position with regard to these objects. For he neither enjoys the things that the self-indulgent man enjoys most-but rather dislikes them-nor in general the things that he should not, nor anything of this sort to excess, nor does he feel pain or craving when they are absent, or does so only to a moderate degree, and not more than he should, nor when he should not, and so on; but the things that, being pleasant, make for health or for good condition, he will desire moderately and as he should, and also other pleasant things if they are not hindrances to these ends, or contrary to what is noble, or beyond his means. For he who neglects these conditions loves such pleasures more than they are worth, but the temperate man is not that sort of person, but the sort of person that the right rule prescribes.

12.

Self-indulgence is more like a voluntary state than cowardice. For the former is actuated by pleasure, the latter by pain, of which the one is to be chosen and the other to be avoided; and pain upsets and destroys the nature of the person who feels it, while pleasure does nothing of the sort. Therefore self-indulgence is more voluntary. Hence also it is more a matter of reproach; for it is easier to become accustomed to its objects, since there are many things of this sort in life, and the process of habituation to them is free from danger, while with terrible objects the reverse is the case. But cowardice would seem to be voluntary in a different degree from its particular manifestations; for it is itself painless, but in these we are upset by pain, so that we even throw down our arms and disgrace ourselves in other ways; hence our acts are even thought to be done under compulsion. For the self-indulgent man, on the other hand, the particular acts are voluntary (for he does them with craving and desire), but the whole state is less so; for no one craves to be self-indulgent.

The name self-indulgence is applied also to childish faults; for they bear a certain resemblance to what we have been considering. Which is called after which, makes no difference to our present purpose; plainly, however, the later is called after the earlier. The transference of the name seems not a bad one; for that which desires what is base and which develops quickly ought to be kept in a chastened condition, and these characteristics belong above all to appetite and to the child, since children in fact live at the beck and call of appetite, and it is in them that the desire for what is pleasant is strongest. If, then, it is not going to be obedient and subject to the ruling principle, it will go to great lengths; for in an irrational being the desire for pleasure is insatiable even if it tries every source of gratification, and the exercise of appetite increases its innate force, and if appetites are strong and violent they even expel the power of calculation. Hence they should be moderate and few, and should in no way oppose the rational principle-and this is what we call an obedient and chastened state-and as the child should live according to the direction of his tutor, so the appetitive element should live according to rational principle. Hence the appetitive element in a temperate man should harmonize with the rational principle; for the noble is the mark at which both aim, and the temperate man craves for the things he ought, as he ought, as when he ought; and when he ought; and this is what rational principle directs.

Here we conclude our account of temperance.

_____

[Nicomachean Ethics. *Translated by W.D. Ross. (Oxford: Clarendon Press, 1908).]*

CHAPTER FIVE

Aquinas on the Existence of God

Image © Anastazzo, 2014. Used under license from Shutterstock, Inc.

Thomas Aquinas (1225–1274)

SELECTED READINGS

▶ "The Five Ways" from *Summa Theologica*—St. Thomas Aquinas

"The Five Ways" from *Summa Theologica*

St. Thomas Aquinas
(Edited by Joseph R. Kirkland)

QUESTION 2. THE EXISTENCE OF GOD
ARTICLE 1. Whether the existence of God is self-evident?

Objection 1. It seems that the existence of God is self-evident. Now those things are said to be self-evident to us the knowledge of which is naturally implanted in us, as we can see in regard to first principles. But as Damascene says (De Fide Orth. i, 1,3), "the knowledge of God is naturally implanted in all." Therefore the existence of God is self-evident.

Objection 2. Further, those things are said to be self-evident which are known as soon as the terms are known, which the Philosopher (1 Poster. iii) says is true of the first principles of demonstration. Thus, when the nature of a whole and of a part is known, it is at once recognized that every whole is greater than its part. But as soon as the signification of the word "God" is understood, it is at once seen that God exists. For by this word is signified that thing than which nothing greater can be conceived. But that which exists actually and mentally is greater than that which exists only mentally. Therefore, since as soon as the word "God" is understood it exists mentally, it also follows that it exists actually. Therefore the proposition "God exists" is self-evident.

Objection 3. Further, the existence of truth is self-evident. For whoever denies the existence of truth grants that truth does not exist: and, if truth does not exist, then the proposition "Truth does not exist" is true: and if there is anything true, there must be truth. But God is truth itself: "I am the way, the truth, and the life" (John 14:6) Therefore "God exists" is self-evident.

On the contrary, No one can mentally admit the opposite of what is self-evident; as the Philosopher (Metaph. iv, lect. vi) states concerning the first principles of demonstration. But the opposite of the proposition "God is" can be mentally admitted: "The fool said in his heart, There is no God" (Psalm 52:1). Therefore, that God exists is not self-evident.

I answer that, A thing can be self-evident in either of two ways: on the one hand, self-evident in itself, though not to us; on the other, self-evident in itself, and to us. A proposition is self-evident because the predicate is included in the essence of the subject, as "Man is an animal," for animal is contained in the essence of man. If, therefore the essence of the predicate and subject be known to all, the proposition will be self-evident to all; as is clear with regard to the first principles of demonstration, the terms of which are common things that no one is ignorant of, such as being and non-being, whole and part, and such like. If, however, there are some to whom the essence of the predicate and subject is unknown, the proposition will be self-evident in itself, but not to those who do not know the meaning of the predicate and subject of the proposition. Therefore, it happens, as Boethius says (Hebdom., the title of which is: "Whether all that is, is good"), "that there are some mental concepts self-evident only to the learned, as that incorporeal substances are not in space." Therefore I say that this proposition, "God exists," of itself is self-evident, for the predicate is the same as the subject, because God is His own existence as will be hereafter shown (3, 4). Now because we do not know the essence of God, the proposition is not self-evident to us; but needs to be demonstrated by things that are more known to us, though less known in their nature—namely, by effects.

Reply to Objection 1. To know that God exists in a general and confused way is implanted in us by nature, inasmuch as God is man's beatitude. For man naturally desires happiness, and what is naturally desired by man must be naturally known to him. This, however, is not to know absolutely that God exists; just as to know that someone is approaching is not the same as to know that Peter is approaching, even though it is Peter who is approaching; for many there are who imagine that man's perfect good which is happiness, consists in riches, and others in pleasures, and others in something else.

Reply to Objection 2. Perhaps not everyone who hears this word "God" understands it to signify something than which nothing greater can be thought, seeing that some have believed God to be a body. Yet, granted that everyone understands that by this word "God" is signified something than which nothing greater can be thought, nevertheless, it does not therefore follow that he understands that what the word signifies exists actually, but only that it exists mentally. Nor can it be argued that it actually exists, unless it be admitted that there actually exists something than which nothing greater can be thought; and this precisely is not admitted by those who hold that God does not exist.

Reply to Objection 3. The existence of truth in general is self-evident but the existence of a Primal Truth is not self-evident to us.

ARTICLE 2. Whether it can be demonstrated that God exists?

Objection 1. It seems that the existence of God cannot be demonstrated. For it is an article of faith that God exists. But what is of faith cannot be demonstrated, because a demonstration produces scientific knowledge; whereas faith is of the unseen (Hebrews 11:1). Therefore it cannot be demonstrated that God exists.

Objection 2. Further, the essence is the middle term of demonstration. But we cannot know in what God's essence consists, but solely in what it does not consist; as Damascene says (De Fide Orth. i, 4). Therefore we cannot demonstrate that God exists.

Objection 3. Further, if the existence of God were demonstrated, this could only be from His effects. But His effects are not proportionate to Him, since He is infinite and His effects are finite; and between the finite and infinite there is no proportion. Therefore, since a cause cannot be demonstrated by an effect not proportionate to it, it seems that the existence of God cannot be demonstrated.

On the contrary, The Apostle says: "The invisible things of Him are clearly seen, being understood by the things that are made" (Romans 1:20). But this would not be unless the existence of God could be demonstrated through the things that are made; for the first thing we must know of anything is whether it exists.

I answer that, Demonstration can be made in two ways: One is through the cause, and is called "a priori," and this is to argue from what is prior absolutely. The other is through the effect, and is called a demonstration "a posteriori"; this is to argue from what is prior relatively only to us. When an effect is better known to us than its cause, from the effect we proceed to the knowledge of the cause. And from every effect the existence of its proper cause can be demonstrated, so long as its effects are better known to us; because since every effect depends upon its cause, if the effect exists, the cause must pre-exist. Hence the existence of God, in so far as it is

not self-evident to us, can be demonstrated from those of His effects which are known to us.

Reply to Objection 1. The existence of God and other like truths about God, which can be known by natural reason, are not articles of faith, but are preambles to the articles; for faith presupposes natural knowledge, even as grace presupposes nature, and perfection supposes something that can be perfected. Nevertheless, there is nothing to prevent a man, who cannot grasp a proof, accepting, as a matter of faith, something which in itself is capable of being scientifically known and demonstrated.

Reply to Objection 2. When the existence of a cause is demonstrated from an effect, this effect takes the place of the definition of the cause in proof of the cause's existence. This is especially the case in regard to God, because, in order to prove the existence of anything, it is necessary to accept as a middle term the meaning of the word, and not its essence, for the question of its essence follows on the question of its existence. Now the names given to God are derived from His effects; consequently, in demonstrating the existence of God from His effects, we may take for the middle term the meaning of the word "God".

Reply to Objection 3. From effects not proportionate to the cause no perfect knowledge of that cause can be obtained. Yet from every effect the existence of the cause can be clearly demonstrated, and so we can demonstrate the existence of God from His effects; though from them we cannot perfectly know God as He is in His essence.

ARTICLE 3. Whether God exists?

Objection 1. It seems that God does not exist; because if one of two contraries be infinite, the other would be altogether destroyed. But the word "God" means that He is infinite goodness. If, therefore, God existed, there would be no evil discoverable; but there is evil in the world. Therefore God does not exist.

Objection 2. Further, it is superfluous to suppose that what can be accounted for by a few principles has been produced by many. But it seems that everything we see in the world can be accounted for by other principles, supposing God did not exist. For all natural things can be reduced to one principle which is nature; and all voluntary things can be reduced to one principle which is human reason, or will. Therefore there is no need to suppose God's existence.

On the contrary, It is said in the person of God: "I am Who am." (Exodus 3:14)

I answer that, The existence of God can be proved in five ways.

The first and more manifest way is the argument from motion. It is certain, and evident to our senses, that in the world some things are in motion. Now whatever is in motion is put in motion by another, for nothing can be in motion except it is in potentiality to that towards which it is in motion; whereas a thing moves inasmuch as it is in act. For motion is nothing else than the reduction of something from potentiality to actuality. But nothing can be reduced from potentiality to actuality, except by something in a state of actuality. Thus that which is actually hot, as fire, makes wood, which is potentially hot, to be actually hot, and thereby moves and changes it. Now it is not possible that the same thing should be at once in actuality and potentiality in the same respect, but only in different respects. For what is actually hot cannot simultaneously be potentially hot; but it is simultaneously potentially cold. It is therefore impossible that in the same respect and in the same way a thing should be both mover and moved, i.e. that it should move itself. Therefore, whatever is in motion must be put in motion by another. If that by which it is put in motion be itself put in motion, then this also must needs be put in motion by another, and that by another again. But this cannot go on to infinity, because then there would be no first mover, and, consequently, no other mover; seeing that subsequent movers move only inasmuch as they are put in motion by the first mover; as the staff moves only because it is put in motion by the hand. Therefore it is necessary to arrive at a first mover, put in motion by no other; and this everyone understands to be God.

The second way is from the nature of the efficient cause. In the world of sense we find there is an order of efficient causes. There is no case known (neither is it, indeed, possible) in which a thing is found to be the efficient cause of itself; for so it would be prior to itself, which is impossible. Now in efficient causes it is not possible to go on to infinity, because in all efficient causes following in order, the first is the cause of the intermediate cause, and the intermediate is the cause of the ultimate cause, whether the intermediate cause be several, or only one. Now to take away the cause is to take away the effect. Therefore, if there be no first cause among efficient causes, there will be no ultimate, nor any intermediate cause. But if in efficient causes it is possible to go on to infinity, there will be no first efficient cause,

neither will there be an ultimate effect, nor any intermediate efficient causes; all of which is plainly false. Therefore it is necessary to admit a first efficient cause, to which everyone gives the name of God.

The third way is taken from possibility and necessity, and runs thus. We find in nature things that are possible to be and not to be, since they are found to be generated, and to corrupt, and consequently, they are possible to be and not to be. But it is impossible for these always to exist, for that which is possible not to be at some time is not. Therefore, if everything is possible not to be, then at one time there could have been nothing in existence. Now if this were true, even now there would be nothing in existence, because that which does not exist only begins to exist by something already existing. Therefore, if at one time nothing was in existence, it would have been impossible for anything to have begun to exist; and thus even now nothing would be in existence—which is absurd. Therefore, not all beings are merely possible, but there must exist something the existence of which is necessary. But every necessary thing either has its necessity caused by another, or not. Now it is impossible to go on to infinity in necessary things which have their necessity caused by another, as has been already proved in regard to efficient causes. Therefore we cannot but postulate the existence of some being having of itself its own necessity, and not receiving it from another, but rather causing in others their necessity. This all men speak of as God.

The fourth way is taken from the gradation to be found in things. Among beings there are some more and some less good, true, noble and the like. But "more" and "less" are predicated of different things, according as they resemble in their different ways something which is the maximum, as a thing is said to be hotter according as it more nearly resembles that which is hottest; so that there is something which is truest, something best, something noblest and, consequently, something which is uttermost being; for those things that are greatest in truth are greatest in being, as it is written in Metaph. ii. Now the maximum in any genus is the cause of all in that genus; as fire, which is the maximum heat, is the cause of all hot things. Therefore there must also be something which is to all beings the cause of their being, goodness, and every other perfection; and this we call God.

The fifth way is taken from the governance of the world. We see that things which lack intelligence, such as natural bodies, act for an end, and this is evident from their acting always, or nearly always, in the same way, so as to obtain the best result. Hence it is plain that not fortuitously, but designedly, do they achieve their end. Now whatever lacks intelligence cannot move towards an end, unless it be directed by some being endowed with knowledge and intelligence; as the arrow is shot to its mark by the archer. Therefore some intelligent being exists by whom all natural things are directed to their end; and this being we call God.

Reply to Objection 1. As Augustine says (Enchiridion xi): "Since God is the highest good, He would not allow any evil to exist in His works, unless His omnipotence and goodness were such as to bring good even out of evil." This is part of the infinite goodness of God, that He should allow evil to exist, and out of it produce good.

Reply to Objection 2. Since nature works for a determinate end under the direction of a higher agent, whatever is done by nature must needs be traced back to God, as to its first cause. So also whatever is done voluntarily must also be traced back to some higher cause other than human reason or will, since these can change or fail; for all things that are changeable and capable of defect must be traced back to an immovable and self-necessary first principle, as was shown in the body of the Article.

[from The Summa Theologica of St. Thomas Aquina. Second and Revised Edition, 1920. Literally translated by Fathers of the English Dominican Province.]

CHAPTER SIX

Descartes on Certainty and the Self

Image © Georgios Kollidas, 2014. Used under license from Shutterstock, Inc.

Rene Descartes (1596–1650)

SELECTED READINGS

▶ *Meditations on First Philosophy*—Rene Descartes

Meditations on First Philosophy

Rene Descartes

(Translated by Donald A. Cress and edited by Joseph R. Kirkland)

MEDITATION ONE: CONCERNING THOSE THINGS THAT CAN BE CALLED INTO DOUBT

Several years have now passed since I first realized how numerous were the false opinions that in my youth I had taken to be true, and thus how doubtful were all those that I had subsequently built upon them. And thus I realized that once in my life I had to raze everything to the ground and begin again from the original foundations, if I wanted to establish anything firm and lasting in the sciences. But the task seemed enormous, and I was waiting until I reached a point in my life that was so timely that no more suitable time for undertaking these plans of action would come to pass. For this reason, I procrastinated for so long that I would henceforth be at fault, were I to waste the time that remains for carrying out the project by brooding over it. Accordingly, I have today suitably freed my mind of all cares, secured for myself a period of leisurely tranquility, and am withdrawing into solitude. At last I will apply myself earnestly and unreservedly to this general demolition of my opinions.

Yet to bring this about I will not need to show that all my opinions are false, which is perhaps something I could never accomplish. But reason now persuades me that I should withhold my assent no less carefully from opinions that are not completely certain and indubitable than I would from those that are patently false. For this reason, it will suffice for the rejection of all of these opinions, if I find in each of them some reason for doubt. Nor therefore need I survey each opinion individually, a task that would be endless. Rather, because undermining the foundations will cause whatever has been built upon them to crumble of its own accord, I will attack straightaway those principles which supported everything I once believed.

Surely whatever I had admitted until now as most true I received either from the senses or through the senses. However, I have noticed that the senses are sometimes deceptive; and it is a mark of prudence never to place our complete trust in those who have deceived us even once.

But perhaps, even though the senses do sometimes deceive us when it is a question of very small and distant things, still there are many other matters concerning which one simply cannot doubt, even though they are derived from the very same senses: for example, that I am sitting here next to the fire, wearing my winter dressing gown, that I am holding this sheet of paper in my hands, and the like. But on what grounds could one deny that these hands and this entire body are mine? Unless perhaps I were to liken myself to the insane, whose brains are impaired by such an unrelenting vapor of black bile that they steadfastly insist that they are kings when they are utter paupers, or that they are arrayed in purple robes when they are naked, or that they have heads made or clay, or that they are gourds, or that they are made of glass. But such people are mad, and I would appear no less mad, were I to take their behavior as an example for myself.

This would all be well and good, were I not a man who is accustomed to sleeping at night, and to experiencing in my dreams the very same things, or now and then even less plausible ones, as these insane people do when they are awake. How often does my evening slumber persuade me of such ordinary things as these: that I am here, clothed in my dressing gown, seated next to the fireplace – when in fact I am lying undressed in bed! But right now my eyes are certainly wide awake when I gaze upon this sheet of paper. This head which I am shaking is not heavy with sleep. I extend this hand consciously and deliberately, and I feel it. Such things would not be so distinct for someone who is asleep. As if I did not recall having been deceived on other occasions even by similar thoughts in my dreams! As I consider these matters more carefully, I see so plainly that there are no definitive signs by which to distinguish being awake from being asleep. As a result, I am becoming quite dizzy, and this dizziness nearly convinces me that I am asleep.

Let us assume then, for the sake of argument, that we are dreaming and that such particulars as these are not true: that we are opening our eyes, moving our head, and extending our hands. Perhaps we do not even have such hands, or any such body at all. Nevertheless, it surely must be admitted that the things seen during slumber are, as it were, like painted images, which could only have been produced in the likeness of true things, and that therefore at least these general things – eyes, head, hands, and the whole body – are not imaginary things, but are true and exist. For indeed when painters themselves wish to represent sirens and satyrs by means of especially bizarre forms, they surely cannot assign to them utterly new natures. Rather, they simply fuse together the members of various animals. Or if perhaps they concoct something so utterly novel that nothing like it has ever been seen before (and thus is something utterly fictitious and false), yet certainly at the very least the colors from which they fashion it ought to be true. And by the same token, although even these general things – eyes, head, hands and the like – could be imaginary, still one has to admit that at least certain other things that are even more simple and universal are true. It is from these components, as if from true colors, that all those images of things that are in our thought are fashioned, be they true or false.

This class of things appears to include corporeal nature in general, together with its extension; the shape of extended things; their quantity, that is, their size and number; as well as the place where they exist; the time through which they endure, and the like.

Thus it is not improper to conclude from this that physics, astronomy, medicine, and all the other disciplines that are dependent upon the consideration of composite things are doubtful, and that, on the other hand, arithmetic, geometry, and other such disciplines, which treat of nothing but the simplest and most general things and which are indifferent as to whether these things do or do not in fact exist, contain something certain and indubitable. For whether I am awake or asleep, two plus three make five, and a square does not have more than four sides. It does not seem possible that such obvious truths should be subject to the suspicion of being false.

Be that as it may, there is fixed in my mind a certain opinion of long standing, namely that there exists a God who is able to do anything and by whom I, such as I am, have been created. How do I know that he did not bring it about that there is no earth at all, no heavens, no extended thing, no shape, no size, no place, and yet bringing it about that all these things appear to me to exist precisely as they do now? Moreover, since I judge that others sometimes make mistakes in matters that they believe they know most perfectly, may I not, in like fashion, be deceived every time I add two and three or count the sides of a square, or perform an even simpler operation, if that can be imagined? But perhaps God has not willed that I be deceived in this way, for he is said to be supremely good. Nonetheless, if it were repugnant to his goodness to have created me such that I be deceived all the time, it would also seem foreign to that same goodness to permit me to be deceived even occasionally. But we cannot make this last assertion.

Perhaps there are some who would rather deny so a powerful a God than believe that everything else is uncertain. Let us not oppose them; rather, let us grant that everything said here about God is fictitious. Now they suppose that I came to be what I am either by fate, or by chance, or by a connected chain of events, or by some other way. But because being deceived and being mistaken appear to be a certain imperfection, the less powerful they take the author of my origin to be, the more probable it will be that I am so imperfect that I am always deceived. I have nothing to say in response to these arguments. But eventually I am forced to admit that there is nothing among the things I once believed to be true which it is not permissible to doubt – and not out of frivolity or lack of forethought, but for valid and considered reasons. Thus I must be no less careful to withhold assent henceforth even from these beliefs than I would from those that are patently false, if I wish to find anything certain.

But it is not enough simply to have realized these things; I must take steps to keep myself mindful of them. For long-standing opinions keep returning, and, almost against my will, they take advantage of my credulity, as if it were bound over to them by long use and the claims of intimacy. Nor will I ever get out of the habit of assenting to them and believing in them, so long as I take them to be exactly what they are, namely, in some respects doubtful, as has just now been shown, but nevertheless highly probable, so that it is much more consonant with reason to believe them than to deny them. Hence, it seems to me I would do well to deceive myself by turning my will in completely the opposite direction and pretend for a time that these opinions are wholly false and imaginary, until finally, as if with prejudices weighing down each side equally, no bad habit should turn my judgment any further from the correct perception of things. For indeed I know that meanwhile there is no danger or error in following this procedure, and that it is impossible for me to indulge in too much distrust, since I am now concentrating only on knowledge, not on action.

Accordingly, I will suppose not a supremely good God, the source of truth, but rather an evil genius, supremely powerful and clever, who has directed his entire effort at deceiving me. I will regard the heavens, the air, the earth, colors, shapes, sounds, and all external things as nothing but the bedeviling hoaxes of my dreams, with which he lays snares for my credulity. I will regard myself as not having hands, or eyes, or flesh, or blood, or any senses, but as nevertheless falsely believing that I possess all these things. I will remain resolute and steadfast in this meditation, and even if it is not within my power to know anything true, it certainly is within my power to take care resolutely to withhold my assent to what is false, lest this deceiver, however powerful, however clever he may be, have any effect on me. But this undertaking is arduous, and a certain laziness brings me back to my customary way of living. I am not unlike a prisoner who enjoyed an imaginary freedom during his sleep, but, when he later begins to suspect that he is dreaming, fears being awakened and nonchalantly conspires with these pleasant illusions. In just the same way, I fall back of my own accord into my old opinions, and dread being awakened, lest the toilsome wakefulness which follows upon a peaceful rest must be spent thenceforward not in the light but among the inextricable shadows of the difficulties now brought forward.

MEDITATION TWO: CONCERNING THE NATURE OF THE HUMAN MIND – THAT IT IS BETTER KNOWN THAN THE BODY

Yesterday's meditation has thrown me into such doubts that I can no longer ignore them, yet I fail to see how they are to be resolved. It is as if I had suddenly fallen into a deep whirlpool; I am so tossed about that I can neither touch bottom with my foot, nor swim up to the top. Nevertheless I will work my way up and will once again attempt the same path I entered upon yesterday. I will accomplish this by putting aside everything that admits of the least doubt, as if I had discovered it to be completely false. I will stay on this course until I know something certain, or, if nothing else, until I at least know for certain that nothing is certain. Archimedes sought but one firm and immovable point in order to move the entire earth from one place to another. Just so, great things are also to be hoped for if I succeed in finding just one thing, however slight, that is certain and unshaken.

Therefore I suppose that everything I see is false. I believe that none of what my deceitful memory represents ever existed. I have no senses whatever. Body,

shape, extension, movement, and place are all chimeras. What then will be true? Perhaps just the single fact that nothing is certain.

But how do I know there is not something else, over and above all those things that I have just reviewed, concerning which there is not even the slightest occasion for doubt? Is there not some God, or by whatever name I might call him, who instills these very thoughts in me? But why would I think that, since I myself could perhaps be the author of these thoughts? Am I not then at least something? But I have already denied that I have any senses and any body. Still I hesitate; for what follows from this? Am I so tied to a body and to the senses that I cannot exist without them? But I have persuaded myself that there is absolutely nothing in the world: no sky, no earth, no minds, no bodies. Is it then the case that I too do not exist? But doubtless I did exist, if I persuaded myself of something. But there is some deceiver or other who is supremely powerful and supremely sly and who is always deliberately deceiving me. Then too there is no doubt that I exist, if he is deceiving me. And let him do his best at deception, he will never bring it about that I am nothing so long as I shall think that I am something. Thus, after everything has been most carefully weighed, it must finally be established that this pronouncement "I am, I exist" is necessarily true every time I utter it or conceive it in my mind.

But I do not yet understand sufficiently what I am – I, who now necessarily exist. And so from this point on, I must be careful lest I unwittingly mistake something else for myself, and thus err in that very item of knowledge that I claim to be the most certain and evident of all. Thus, I will meditate once more on what I once believed myself to be, prior to embarking upon these thoughts. For this reason, then, I will set aside whatever can be weakened even to the slightest degree by the arguments brought forward, so that eventually all that remains is precisely nothing but what is certain and unshaken.

What then did I use to think I was? A man, of course. But what is a man? Might I not say a "rational animal"? No, because then I would have to inquire what "animal" and "rational" mean. And thus from one question I would slide into many more difficult ones. Nor do I now have enough free time that I want to waste it on subtleties of this sort. Instead, permit me to focus here on what came spontaneously and naturally into my thinking whenever I pondered what I was. Now it occurred to me first that

I had a face, hands, arms, and this entire mechanism of bodily members: the very same as are discerned in a corpse, and which I referred to by the name "body." It next occurred to me that I took in food, that I walked about, and that I sensed and thought various things; these actions I used to attribute to the soul. But as to what this soul might be, I either did not think about it or else I imagined it a rarified I-know-not-what, like a wind, or a fire, or ether, which had been infused into my coarser parts. But as to the body I was not in any doubt. On the contrary, I was under the impression that I knew its nature distinctly. Were I perhaps tempted to describe this nature such as I conceived it in my mind, I would have described it thus: by "body," I understand all that is capable of being bounded by some shape, of being enclosed in a place, and of filling up a space in such a way as to exclude any other body from it; of being perceived by touch, sight, hearing, taste, or smell; of being moved in several ways, not, of course, by itself, but by whatever else impinges upon it. For it was my view that the power of self-motion, and likewise of sensing or of thinking, in no way belonged to the nature of the body. Indeed I used rather to marvel that such faculties were to be found in certain bodies.

But now what am I, when I suppose that there is some supremely powerful and, if I may be permitted to say so, malicious deceiver who deliberately tries to fool me in any way he can? Can I not affirm that I possess at least a small measure of all those things which I have already said belong to the nature of the body? I focus my attention on them, I think about them, I review them again, but nothing comes to mind. I am tired of repeating this to no purpose. But what about those things I ascribed to the soul? What about being nourished or moving about? Since I now do not have a body, these are surely nothing but fictions. What about sensing? Surely this too does not take place without a body; and I seemed to have sensed in my dreams many things that I later realized I did not sense. What about thinking? Here I make my discovery: thought exists; it alone cannot be separated from me. I am; I exist – this is certain. But for how long? For as long as I am thinking; for perhaps it could also come to pass that if I were to cease all thinking I would then utterly cease to exist. At this time I admit nothing that is not necessarily true. I am therefore precisely nothing but a thinking thing; that is, a mind, or intellect, or understanding, or reason – words of whose meanings I was previously ignorant. Yet I am a true thing and am truly existing; but what kind of thing? I have said it already: a thinking thing.

What else am I? I will set my imagination in motion. I am not that concatenation of members we call the human body. Neither am I even some subtle air infused into these members, nor a wind, nor a fire, nor a vapor, nor a breath, nor anything I devise for myself. For I have supposed these things to be nothing. The assumption still stands; yet nevertheless I am something. But is it perhaps the case that these very things which I take to be nothing, because they are unknown to me, nevertheless are in fact no different from that "me" that I know? This I do not know, and I will not quarrel about it now. I can make a judgment only about things that are known to me. I know that I exist; I ask now who is this "I" whom I know? Most certainly, in the strict sense the knowledge of this "I" does not depend upon things of whose existence I do not yet have knowledge. Therefore it is not dependent upon any of those things that I simulate in my imagination. But this word "simulate" warns me of my error. For I would indeed be simulating were I to "imagine" that I was something, because imagining is merely the contemplating of the shape or image of a corporeal thing. But I now know with certainty that I am and also that all these images – and, generally, everything belonging to the nature of the body – could turn out to be nothing but dreams. Once I have realized this, I would seem to be speaking no less foolishly were I to say: "I will use my imagination in order to recognize more distinctly who I am," than were I to say: "Now I surely am awake, and I see something true; but since I do not yet see it clearly enough, I will deliberately fall asleep so that my dreams might represent it to me more truly and more clearly." Thus I realize that none of what I can grasp by means of the imagination pertains to this knowledge that I have of myself. Moreover, I realize that I must be most diligent about withdrawing my mind from these things so that it can perceive its nature as distinctly as possible.

But what then am I? A thing that thinks. What is that? A thing that doubts, understands, affirms, denies, wills, refuses, and that also imagines and senses.

Indeed it is no small matter if all of these things belong to me. But why should they not belong to me? Is it not the very same "I" who now doubts almost everything, who nevertheless understands something, who affirms that this one thing is true, who denies other things, who desires to know more, who wishes not to be deceived, who imagines many things even against my will, who also notices many things which appear to come from the senses? What is there in all of this that is not every bit as true as the fact that I exist – even if I am always asleep or even if my creator makes every effort to mislead me? Which of these things is distinct from my thought? Which of them can be said to be separate from myself? For it is so obvious that it is I who doubt, I who understand, and I who will, that there is nothing by which it could be explained more clearly. But indeed it is also the same "I" who imagines; for although perhaps, as I supposed before, absolutely nothing that I imagined is true, still the very power of imagining really does exist, and constitutes a part of my thought. Finally, it is this same "I" who senses or who is cognizant of bodily things as if through the senses. For example, I now see a light, I hear a noise, I feel heat. These things are false, since I am asleep. Yet I certainly do seem to see, hear, and feel warmth. This cannot be false. Properly speaking, this is what in me is called "sensing." But this, precisely so taken, is nothing other than thinking.

From these considerations I am beginning to know a little better what I am. But it still seems (and I cannot resist believing) that corporeal things – whose images are formed by thought, and which the senses themselves examine – are much more distinctly known than this mysterious "I" which does not fall within the imagination. And yet it would be strange indeed were I to grasp the very things I consider to be doubtful, unknown, and foreign to me more distinctly than what is true, what is known - than, in short, myself. But I see what is happening: my mind loves to wander and does not yet permit itself to be restricted within the confines of truth. So be it then; let us just this once allow it completely free rein, so that, a little while later, when the time has come to pull in the reins, the mind may more readily permit itself to be controlled.

Let us consider those things which are commonly believed to be the most distinctly grasped of all: namely the bodies we touch and see. Not bodies in general, mind you, for these general perceptions are apt to be somewhat more confused, but one body in particular. Let us take, for instance, this piece of wax. It has been taken quite recently from the honeycomb; it has not yet lost all the honey flavor. It retains some of the scent of the flowers from which it was collected. Its color, shape, and size are manifest. It is hard and cold; it is easy to touch. If you rap on it with your knuckle it will emit a sound. In short, everything is present in it that appears needed to enable a body to be known as distinctly as possible. But notice that, as I am speaking, I am bringing it close to the fire. The remaining traces of the honey flavor are disappearing;

the scent is vanishing; the color is changing; the original shape is disappearing. Its size is increasing; it is becoming liquid and hot; you can hardly touch it. And now, when you rap on it, it no longer emits any sound. Does the same wax still remain? I must confess that it does; no one denies it; no one thinks otherwise. So what was there in the wax that was so distinctly grasped? Certainly none of the aspects that I reached by means of the senses. For whatever came under the senses of taste, smell, sight, touch or hearing has now changed; and yet the wax remains.

Perhaps the wax was what I now think it is: namely that the wax itself never really was the sweetness of the honey, nor the fragrance of the flowers, nor the whiteness, nor the shape, nor the sound, but instead was a body that a short time ago manifested itself to me in these ways, and now does so in other ways. But just what precisely is this thing that I thus imagine? Let us focus our attention on this and see what remains after we have removed everything that does not belong to the wax: only that it is something extended, flexible, and mutable. But what is it to be flexible and mutable? Is it what my imagination shows it to be: namely, that this piece of wax can change from a round to a square shape, or from the latter to a triangular shape? Not at all; for I grasp that the wax is capable of innumerable changes of this sort, even though I am incapable of running through these innumerable changes by using my imagination. Therefore this insight is not achieved by the faculty of imagination. What is it to be extended? Is this thing's extension also unknown? For it becomes greater in wax that is beginning to melt, greater in boiling wax, and greater still as the heat is increased. And I would not judge correctly what the wax is if I did not believe that it takes on an even greater variety of dimensions than I could ever grasp with the imagination. It remains then for me to concede that I do not grasp what this wax is through the imagination; rather, I perceive it through the mind alone. The point I am making refers to this particular piece of wax, for the case of wax in general is clearer still. But what is this piece of wax which is perceived only by the mind? Surely it is the same piece of wax that I see, touch, and imagine; in short it is the same piece of wax I took it to be from the very beginning. But I need to realize that the perception of the wax is neither a seeing, nor a touching, nor an imagining. Nor has it ever been, even though it previously seemed so; rather it is an inspection on the part of the mind alone. This inspection can be imperfect and confused, as it was before, or clear and distinct, as it is now, depending on how closely I pay attention to the things in which the piece of wax consists.

But meanwhile I marvel at how prone my mind is to errors. For although I am considering these things within myself silently and without words, nevertheless I seize upon words themselves and I am nearly deceived by the ways in which people commonly speak. For we say that we see the wax itself, if it is present, and not that we judge it to be present from its color or shape. Whence I might conclude straightaway that I know the wax through the vision had by the eye, and not through an inspection on the part of the mind alone. But then were I perchance to look out my window and observe men crossing the square, I would ordinarily say I see the men themselves just as I say I see the wax. But what do I see aside from hats and clothes, which could conceal automata? Yet I judge them to be men. Thus what I thought I had seen with my eyes, I actually grasped solely with the faculty of judgment, which is in my mind.

But a person who seeks to know more than the common crowd ought to be ashamed of himself for looking for doubt in common ways of speaking. Let us then go forward and inquire when it was that I perceived more perfectly and evidently what the piece of wax was. Was it when I first saw it and believed I knew it by the external sense, or at least by the so-called common sense, that is, the power of imagination? Or do I have more perfect knowledge now, when I have diligently examined both what the wax is and how it is known? Surely it is absurd to be in doubt about this matter. For what was there in my initial perception that was distinct? What was there that any animal seemed incapable of possessing? But indeed when I distinguish the wax from its external forms, as if stripping it of its clothing, and look at the wax in its nakedness, then, even though there can be still an error in my judgment, nevertheless I cannot perceive it thus without a human mind.

But what am I to say about this mind, that is, about myself? For as yet I admit nothing else to be in me over and above the mind. What, I ask, am I who seem to perceive this wax so distinctly? Do I not know myself not only much more truly and with greater certainty, but also much more distinctly and evidently? For if I judge that the wax exists from the fact that I see it, certainly from this same fact that I see the wax it follows much more evidently that I myself exist. For it could happen that what I see is not truly wax. It could happen that I have no eyes with which to see anything.

But it is utterly impossible that, while I see or think I see (I do not now distinguish these two), I who think am not something. Likewise, if I judge that the wax exists from the fact that I touch it, the same outcome will again obtain, namely that I exist. If I judge that the wax exists from the fact that I imagine it, or for any other reason, plainly the same thing follows. But what I note regarding the wax applies to everything else that is external to me. Furthermore, if my perception of the wax seemed more distinct after it became known to me not only on account of sight or touch, but on account of many reasons, one has to admit how much more distinctly I am now known to myself. For there is not a single consideration that can aid in my perception of the wax or of any other body that fails to make even more manifest the nature of my mind. But there are still so many other things in the mind itself on the basis of which my knowledge of it can be rendered more distinct that it hardly seems worth enumerating those things which emanate to it from the body.

But lo and behold, I have returned on my own to where I wanted to be. For since I now know that even bodies are not, properly speaking, perceived by the senses or by the faculty of imagination, but by the intellect alone, and that they are not perceived through their being touched or seen, but only through their being understood, I manifestly know that nothing can be perceived more easily and more evidently than my own mind. But since the tendency to hang on to long-held beliefs cannot be put aside so quickly, I want to stop here, so that by the length of my meditation this new knowledge may be more deeply impressed upon my memory.

MEDITATION THREE: CONCERNING GOD, THAT HE EXISTS

I will now shut my eyes, stop up my ears, and withdraw all my senses. I will also blot out from my thoughts all images of corporeal things, or rather, since the latter is hardly possible, I will regard these images as empty, false and worthless. And as I converse with myself alone and look more deeply into myself, I will attempt to render myself gradually better known and more familiar to myself. I am a thing that thinks, that is to say, a thing that doubts, affirms, denies, understands a few things, is ignorant of many things, wills, refrains from willing, and also imagines and senses. For as I observed earlier, even though these things that I sense or imagine may perhaps be nothing at all outside me, nevertheless I am certain that these modes of thinking, which are cases of what I call sensing and imagining, insofar as they are merely modes of thinking, do exist within me.

In these few words, I have reviewed everything I truly know, or at least what so far I have noticed that I know. Now I will ponder more carefully to see whether perhaps there may be other things belonging to me that up until now I have failed to notice. I am certain that I am a thinking thing. But do I not therefore also know what is required for me to be certain of anything? Surely in this first instance of knowledge, there is nothing but a certain clear and distinct perception of what I affirm. Yet this would hardly be enough to render me certain of the truth of a thing, if it could ever happen that something that I perceived so clearly and distinctly were false. And thus I now seem able to posit as a general rule that everything I very clearly and distinctly perceive is true.

Be that as it may, I have previously admitted many things as wholly certain and evident that nevertheless I later discovered to be doubtful. What sort of things were these? Why, the earth, the sky, the stars, and all the other things I perceived by means of the senses. But what was it about these things that I clearly perceived? Surely the fact that the ideas or thoughts of these things were hovering before my mind. But even now I do not deny that these ideas are in me. Yet there was something else I used to affirm, which, owing to my habitual tendency to believe it, I used to think was something I clearly perceived, even though I actually did not perceive it at all: namely, that certain things existed outside me, things from which those ideas proceeded and which those ideas completely resembled. But on this point I was mistaken; or rather, if my judgment was a true one, it was not the result of the force of my perception.

But what about when I considered something very simple and easy in the areas of arithmetic or geometry, for example that two plus three make five, and the like? Did I not intuit them at least clearly enough so as to affirm them as true? To be sure, I did decide later on that I must doubt these things, but that was only because it occurred to me that some God could perhaps have given me a nature such that I might be deceived even about matters that seemed most evident. But whenever this preconceived opinion about the supreme power of God occurs to me, I cannot help admitting that, were he to wish it, it would be easy for him to cause me to err even in those matters that I think I intuit as clearly as possible with the eyes of the mind. On the other hand, whenever I turn my attention to those very things that I think I perceive with such great clarity, I am so completely persuaded by them that I spontaneously blurt out these words: "let anyone who can do so deceive me; so long as I think that I am something, he will never bring it about that I am nothing. Nor will he one day make it true that I never existed, for it is true now that I do exist. Nor will he even bring it about that perhaps two plus three might equal more or less than five, or similar items in which I recognize an obvious contradiction." And certainly, because I have no reason for thinking that there is a God who is a deceiver (and of course I do not yet sufficiently know whether there even is a God), the basis for doubting, depending as it does merely on the above hypothesis, is very tenuous and, so to speak, metaphysical. But in order to remove even this basis for doubt, I should at the first opportunity inquire whether there is a God, and, if there is, whether or not he can be a deceiver. For if I am ignorant of this, it appears I am never capable of being completely certain about anything else.

However, at this stage good order seems to demand that I first group all my thoughts into certain classes, and ask in which of them truth or falsity properly resides. Some of these thoughts are like images of things; to these alone does the word "idea" properly apply, as when I think of a man, or a chimera, or the sky, or an angel, or God. Again there are other thoughts that take different forms: for example, when I will, or fear, or affirm, or deny, there is always something that I grasp as the subject of my thought, yet I embrace in my thought something more than the likeness of that thing. Some of these thoughts are called volitions or affects, while others are called judgments.

Now as far as ideas are concerned, if they are considered alone and in their own right, without being referred to something else, they cannot, properly speaking, be false. For whether it is a she-goat or a chimera that I am imagining, it is no less true that I imagine the one than the other. Moreover, we need not fear that there is falsity in the will itself or in the affects, for although I can choose evil things or even things that are utterly non-existent, I cannot conclude from this that it is untrue that I do choose these things. Thus there remain only judgments in which I must take care not to be mistaken. Now the principal and most frequent error to be found in judgments consists in the fact that I judge that the ideas which are in me are similar to or in conformity with certain things outside me. Obviously, if I were to consider these ideas merely as certain modes of my thought, and were not to refer them to anything else, they could hardly give me any subject matter for error.

Among these ideas, some appear to me to be innate, some adventitious, and some produced by me. For I understand what a thing is, what truth is, what thought is, and I appear to have derived this exclusively from my very own nature. But say I am now hearing a noise, or looking at the sun, or feeling the fire; up until now I judged that these things proceeded from certain things outside me, and finally, that sirens, hippogriffs, and the like are made by me. Or perhaps I can even think of all these ideas as being adventitious, or as being innate, or as fabrications, for I have not yet clearly ascertained their true origin.

But here I must inquire particularly into those ideas that I believe to be derived from things existing outside me. Just what reason do I have for believing that these ideas resemble those things? Well, I do seem to have been so taught by nature. Moreover, I do know from experience that these ideas do not depend upon my will, nor consequently upon myself, for I often notice them even against my will. Now, for example, whether or not I will it, I feel heat. It is for this reason that I believe this feeling or idea of heat comes to me from something other than myself, namely from the heat of the fire by which I am sitting. Nothing is more obvious than the judgment that this thing is sending its likeness rather than something else into me.

I will now see whether these reasons are powerful enough. When I say here "I have been so taught by nature," all I have in mind is that I am driven by a spontaneous impulse to believe this, and not that some light of nature is showing me that it is true. These are two very different things. For whatever is shown me by this light of nature, for example, that from the fact that I doubt, it follows that I am, and the like, cannot in any way be doubtful. This is owing to the fact that there can be no other faculty that I can trust as much as this light and which could teach that these things are not true. But as far as natural impulses are concerned, in the past I have often judged myself to have been driven by them to make the poorer choice when it was a question of choosing a good; and I fail to see why I should place any greater faith in them than in other matters.

Again, although these ideas do not depend upon my will, it does not follow that they necessarily proceed from things existing outside me. For just as these impulses about which I spoke just now seem to be different from my will, even though they are in me, so

too perhaps there is also in me some other faculty, one not yet sufficiently known to me, which produces these ideas, just as it has always seemed up to now that ideas are formed in me without any help from external things when I am asleep.

And finally, even if these ideas did proceed from things other than myself, it does not therefore follow that they must resemble those things. Indeed it seems I have frequently noticed a vast difference in many respects. For example, I find within myself two distinct ideas of the sun. One idea is drawn, as it were, from the senses. Now it is this idea which, of all those that I take to be derived from outside me, is most in need of examination. By means of this idea the sun appears to me to be quite small. But there is another idea, one derived from astronomical reasoning, that is, it is elicited from certain notions that are innate in me, or else is fashioned by me in some other way. Through this idea the sun is shown to be several times larger than the earth. Both ideas surely cannot resemble the same sun existing outside me; and reason convinces me that the idea that seems to have emanated from the sun itself from so close is the very one that least resembles the sun.

All these points demonstrate sufficiently that up to this point it was not a well-founded judgment but only a blind impulse that formed the basis of my belief that things existing outside me send ideas or images of themselves to me through the sense organs or by some other means.

But still another way occurs to me for inquiring whether some of the things of which there are ideas in me do exist outside me: insofar as these ideas are merely modes of thought, I see no inequality among them; they all seem to proceed from me in the same manner. But insofar as one idea represents one thing and another idea another thing, it is obvious that they do differ very greatly from one another. Unquestionably, those ideas that display substances to me are something more and, if I may say so, contain within themselves more objective reality than those which represent only modes or accidents. Again, the idea that enables me to understand a supreme deity, eternal, infinite, omniscient, omnipotent, and creator of all things other than himself, clearly has more objective reality within it than do those ideas through which finite substances are displayed.

Now it is indeed evident by the light of nature that there must be at least as much [reality] in the efficient and total cause as there is in the effect of that same cause. For whence, I ask, could an effect get its reality, if not from its cause? And how could the cause give that reality to the effect, unless it also possessed that reality? Hence it follows that something cannot come into being out of nothing, and also that what is more perfect (that is, what contains in itself more reality) cannot come into being from what is less perfect. But this is manifestly true not merely for those effects whose reality is actual or formal, but also for ideas in which only objective reality is considered. For example, not only can a stone which did not exist previously not now begin to exist unless it is produced by something in which there is, either formally or eminently, everything that is in the stone; nor heat be introduced into a subject which was not already hot unless it is done by something that is of at least as perfect an order as heat – and the same for the rest – but it is also true that there can be in me no idea of heat, or of a stone, unless it is placed in me by some cause that has at least as much reality as I conceive to be in the heat or in the stone. For although this cause conveys none of its actual or formal reality to my idea, it should not be thought for that reason that it must be less real. Rather, the very nature of an idea is such that of itself it needs no formal reality other than what it borrows from my thought, of which it is a mode. But that a particular idea contains this as opposed to that objective reality is surely owing to some cause in which there is at least as much formal reality as there is objective reality contained in the idea. For if we assume that something is found in the idea that was not in its cause, then the idea gets that something from nothing. Yet as imperfect a mode of being as this is by which a thing exists in the intellect objectively through an idea, nevertheless it is plainly not nothing; hence it cannot get its being from nothing.

Moreover, even though the reality that I am considering in my ideas is merely objective reality, I ought not on that account to suspect that , there is no need for the same reality to be formally in the causes of these ideas, but that it suffices for it to be in them objectively. For just as the objective mode of being belongs to ideas by their very nature, so the formal mode of being belongs to the causes of ideas, at least to the first and preeminent ones, by their very nature. And although one idea can perhaps issue from another, nevertheless no infinite regress is permitted here; eventually some first idea must be reached whose cause is a sort of archetype that contains formally all the reality that is in the idea merely objectively. Thus it is clear to me by the light of nature that the ideas that are in me are like images that can easily fail to match the perfection of the things from which they have been drawn, but which can contain nothing greater or more perfect.

And the longer and more attentively I examine all these points, the more clearly and distinctly I know they are true. But what am I ultimately to conclude? If the objective reality of any of my ideas is found to be so great that I am certain that the same reality was not in me, either formally or eminently, and that therefore I myself cannot be the cause of the idea, then it necessarily follows that I am not alone in the world, but that something else, which is the cause of this idea, also exists. But if no such idea is found in me, I will have no argument whatsoever to make me certain of the existence of anything other than myself, for I have conscientiously reviewed all these arguments, and so far I have been unable to find any other.

Among my ideas, in addition to the one that displays me to myself (about which there can be no difficulty at this point), are others that represent God, corporeal and inanimate things, angels, animals, and finally other men like myself.

As to the ideas that display other men, or animals, or angels, I easily understand that they could be fashioned from the ideas that I have of myself, of corporeal things, and of God – even if no men (except myself), no animals, and no angels existed in the world.

As to the ideas of corporeal things, there is nothing in them that is so great that it seems incapable of having originated from me. For if I investigate them thoroughly and examine each one individually in the way I examined the idea of wax yesterday, I notice that there are only a very few things in them that I perceive clearly and distinctly: namely, size, or extension in length, breadth, and depth; shape, which arises from the limits of this extension; position, which various things possessing shape have in relation to one another; and motion, or alteration in position. To these can be added substance, duration, and number. But as for the remaining items, such as light and colors, sounds, odors, tastes, heat and cold and other tactile qualities, I think of these only in a very confused and obscure manner, to the extent that I do not even know whether they are true or false, that is, whether the ideas I have of them are ideas of things or ideas of non-things. For although a short time ago I noted that falsity properly so called (or "formal" falsity) is to be found only in judgments, nevertheless there is another kind of falsity (called "material" falsity) which is found in ideas whenever they represent a non-thing as if it were a thing. For example, the ideas I have of heat and cold fall so far short of being clear and distinct that I cannot tell from them whether cold is merely the privation of heat or whether heat is the privation of cold, or whether both are real qualities, or whether neither is. And because ideas can only be, as it were, of things, if it is true that cold is merely the absence of heat, then an idea that represents cold to me as something real and positive will not inappropriately be called false. The same holds for other similar ideas.

Assuredly I need not assign to these ideas an author distinct from myself. For if they were false, that is, if they were to represent non- things, I know by the light of nature that they proceed from nothing; that is, they are in me for no other reason than that something is lacking in my nature, and that my nature is not entirely perfect. If, on the other hand, these ideas are true, then because they exhibit so little reality to me that I cannot distinguish it from a non-thing, I see no reason why they cannot get their being from me.

As for what is clear and distinct in the ideas of corporeal things, it appears I could have borrowed some of these from the idea of myself: namely, substance, duration, number, and whatever else there may be of this type. For instance, I think that a stone is a substance, that is to say, a thing that is suitable for existing in itself; and likewise I think that I too am a substance. Despite the fact that I conceive myself to be a thinking thing and not an extended thing, whereas I conceive of a stone as an extended thing and not a thinking thing, and hence there is the greatest diversity between these two concepts, nevertheless they seem to agree with one another when considered under the rubric of substance. Furthermore, I perceive that I now exist and recall that I have previously existed for some time. And I have various thoughts and know how many of them there are. It is in doing these things that I acquire the ideas of duration and number, which I can then apply to other things. However, none of the other components out of which the ideas of corporeal things are fashioned (namely extension, shape, position, and motion) are contained in me formally, since I am merely a thinking thing. But since these are only certain modes of a substance, whereas I am a substance, it seems possible that they are contained in me eminently.

Thus there remains only the idea of God. I must consider whether there is anything in this idea that could not have originated from me. I understand by the name "God" a certain substance that is infinite, independent, supremely intelligent and supremely powerful, and that created me along with everything else that exists – if anything else exists. Indeed all these are such that, the more carefully I focus my attention on them, the less possible it seems they could have arisen from myself alone. Thus, from what has been said, I must conclude that God necessarily exists.

For although the idea of substance is in me by virtue of the fact that I am a substance, that fact is not sufficient to explain my having the idea of an infinite substance, since I am finite, unless this idea proceeded from some substance which really was infinite.

Nor should I think that I do not perceive the infinite by means of a true idea, but only through a negation of the finite, just as I perceive rest and darkness by means of a negation of motion and light. On the contrary, I clearly understand that there is more reality in an infinite substance than there is in a finite one. Thus the perception of the infinite is somehow prior in me to the perception of the finite, that is, my perception of God is prior to my perception of myself. For how would I understand that I doubt and that I desire, that is, that I lack something and that I am not wholly perfect, unless there were some idea in me of a more perfect being, by comparison with which I might recognize my defects?

Nor can it be said that this idea of God is perhaps materially false and thus can originate from nothing, as I remarked just now about the ideas of heat and cold, and the like. On the contrary, because it is the most clear and distinct and because it contains more objective reality than any other idea, no idea is in and of itself truer and has less of a basis for being suspected of falsehood. I maintain that this idea of a being that is supremely perfect and infinite is true in the highest degree. For although I could perhaps pretend that such a being does not exist, nevertheless I could not pretend that the idea of such a being discloses to me nothing real, as was the case with the idea of cold which I referred to earlier. It is indeed an idea that is utterly clear and distinct; for whatever I clearly and distinctly perceive to be real and true and to involve some perfection is wholly contained in that idea. It is no objection that I do not comprehend the infinite or that there are countless other things in God that I can in no way either comprehend or perhaps even touch with my thought. For the nature of the infinite is such that it is not comprehended by a being such as I, who am finite. And it is sufficient that I understand this very point and judge that all those things that I clearly perceive and that I know to contain some perfection – and perhaps even countless other things of which I am ignorant –are in God either formally or eminently. The result is that, of all the ideas that are in me, the idea that I have of God is the most true, the most clear and distinct.

But perhaps I am something greater than I myself understand. Perhaps all these perfections that I am attributing to God are somehow in me potentially, although they do no yet assert themselves and are not yet actualized. For I now observe that my knowledge is gradually being increased, and I see nothing standing in the way of its being increased more and more to infinity. Moreover, I see no reason why, with my knowledge thus increased, I could not acquire all the remaining perfections of God. And, finally, if the potential for these perfections is in me already, I see no reason why this potential would not suffice to produce the idea of these perfections.

Yet none of these things can be the case. First, while it is true that my knowledge is gradually being increased and that there are many things in me potentially that are not yet actual, nevertheless, none of these pertains to the idea of God, in which there is nothing whatever that is potential. Indeed this gradual increase is itself a most certain proof of imperfection. Moreover, although my knowledge may always increase more and more, nevertheless I understand that this knowledge will never by this means be actually infinite, because it will never reach a point where it is incapable of greater increase. On the contrary, I judge God to be actually infinite, so that nothing can be added to his perfection. Finally, I perceive that the objective being of an idea cannot be produced by a merely potential being (which, strictly speaking, is nothing), but only by an actual or formal being,

Indeed there is nothing in all these things that is not manifest by the light of nature to one who is conscientious and attentive. But when I am less attentive, and the images of sensible things blind the mind's eye, I do not so easily recall why the idea of a being more perfect than me necessarily proceeds from a being that really is more perfect. This being the case, it is appropriate to ask further whether I myself who have this idea could exist, if such a being did not exist.

From what source, then, do I derive my existence? Why, from myself, or from my parents, or from whatever other things there are that are less perfect than God. For nothing more perfect than God, or even as perfect as God, can be thought or imagined.

But if I got my being from myself, I would not doubt, nor would I desire, nor would I lack anything at all. For I would have given myself all the perfections of which I have some idea; in so doing, I myself would be God! I must not think that the things I lack could perhaps be more difficult to acquire than the ones I have now. On the contrary, it is obvious that it would have been much more difficult for me (that is, a thing or substance that thinks) to emerge out of nothing than it would be to acquire the knowledge of many things about which I am ignorant (these items of knowledge being merely accidents of that substance). Certainly, if I got this greater thing from myself, I would not have denied myself at least those things that can be had more easily. Nor would I have denied myself any of those other things that I perceive to be contained in the idea of God, for surely none of them seem to me more difficult to bring about. But if any of them were more difficult to bring about, they would certainly also seem more difficult to me, even if the remaining ones that I possess I got from myself, since it would be on account of them that I would experience that my power is limited.

Nor am I avoiding the force of these arguments, if I suppose that perhaps I have always existed as I do now, as if it then followed that no author of my existence need be sought. For because the entire span of one's life can be divided into countless parts, each one wholly independent of the rest, it does not follow from the fact that I existed a short time ago that I must exist now, unless some cause, as it were, creates me all over again at this moment, that is to say, which preserves me. For it is obvious to one who pays close attention to the nature of time that plainly the same force and action are needed to preserve anything at each individual moment that it lasts as would be required to create that same thing anew, were it not yet in existence. Thus conservation differs from creation solely by virtue of a distinction of reason; this too is one of those things that are manifest by the light of nature.

Therefore I must now ask myself whether I possess some power by which I can bring it about that I myself, who now exist, will also exist a little later on. For since I am nothing but a thinking thing – or at least since I am now dealing simply and precisely with that part of me which is a thinking thing – if such a power were in me, then I would certainly be aware of it. But I observe that there is no such power; and from this very fact I know most clearly that I depend upon some being other than myself.

But perhaps this being is not God, and I have been produced either by my parents or by some other causes less perfect than God. On the contrary, as I said before, it is obvious that there must be at least as much in the cause as there is in the effect. Thus, regardless of what it is that eventually is assigned as my cause, because I am a thinking thing and have within me a certain idea of God, it must be granted that what caused me is also a thinking thing and it too has an idea of all the perfections which I attribute to God. And I can again inquire of this cause whether it got its existence from itself or from another cause. For if it got its existence from itself, it is evident from what has been said that it is itself God, because, having the power of existing in and of itself, it unquestionably also has the power of actually possessing all the perfections of which it has in itself an idea – that is, all the perfections that I conceive to be in God. However, if it got its existence from another cause, I will once again inquire in similar fashion about this other cause: whether it got its existence from itself or from another cause, until finally I arrive at the ultimate cause, which will be God. For it is apparent enough that there can be no infinite regress here, especially since I am not dealing here merely with the cause that once produced me, but also and most especially with the cause that preserves me at the present time.

Nor can one fancy that perhaps several partial causes have concurred in bringing me into being, and that I have taken the ideas of the various perfections I attribute to God from a variety of causes, so that all of these perfections are found somewhere in the universe, but not all joined together in a single being – God. On the contrary, the unity, the simplicity, that is, the inseparability of all those features that are in God is one of the chief perfections that I understand to be in him. Certainly the idea of the unity of all his perfections could not have been placed in me by any cause from which I did not also get the ideas of the other perfections; for neither could some cause have made me understand them joined together and inseparable from one another, unless it also caused me to recognize what they were.

Finally, as to my parents, even if everything that I ever believed about them were true, still it is certainly not they who preserve me; nor is it they who in any way brought me into being, insofar as I am a thinking thing. Rather, they merely placed certain dispositions in the matter which I judged to contain me, that is, a mind, which now is the only thing I take myself to be. And thus there can be no difficulty here concerning my parents. Indeed I have no choice but to conclude that the mere fact of my existing and of there being in me an idea of a most perfect being, that is, God, demonstrates most evidently that God too exists.

All that remains for me is to ask how I received this idea of God. For I did not draw it from the senses; it never came upon me unexpectedly, as is usually the case with the ideas of sensible things when these things present themselves (or seem to present themselves) to the external sense organs. Nor was it made by me, for I plainly can neither subtract anything from it nor add anything to it. Thus the only option remaining is that this idea is innate in me, just as the idea of myself is innate in me.

To be sure, it is not astonishing that in creating me, God should have endowed me with this idea, so that it would be like the mark of the craftsman impressed upon his work, although this mark need not be something distinct from the work itself. But the mere fact that God created me makes it highly plausible that I have somehow been made in his image and likeness, and that I perceive this likeness, in which the idea of God is contained, by means of the same faculty by which I perceive myself. That is, when I turn the mind's eye toward myself, I understand not only that I am something incomplete and dependent upon another, something aspiring indefinitely for greater and greater or better things, but also that the being on whom I depend has in himself all those greater things – not merely indefinitely and potentially, but infinitely and actually, and thus that he is God. The whole force of the argument rests on the fact that I recognize that it would be impossible for me to exist, being of such a nature as I am (namely, having in me the idea of God), unless God did in fact exist. God, I say, that same being the idea of whom is in me: a being having all those perfections that I cannot comprehend, but can somehow touch with my thought, and a being subject to no defects whatever. From these considerations it is quite obvious that he cannot be a deceiver, for it is manifest by the light of nature that all fraud and deception depend on some defect. . . .

[Meditations on First Philosophy. Translated by Donald A. Cress, 3rd ed., Hackett Publishing Company, 1993). pp. 12-59.]

CHAPTER SEVEN

Locke and Berkeley on Experience and Knowledge

Image © Georgios Kollidas, 2014. Used under license from Shutterstock, Inc.

John Locke (1632–1704)

SELECTED READINGS

▶ *Essay Concerning Human Understanding*—John Locke
▶ *Treatise Concerning the Principles of Human Knowledge*—George Berkeley

Essay Concerning Human Understanding
John Locke
(Edited by Joseph R. Kirkland)

BOOK II: OF SIMPLE IDEAS

...

CHAPTER VIII: SOME FURTHER CONSIDERATIONS CONCERNING OUR SIMPLE IDEAS OF SENSATION

1.

Positive ideas from privative causes. Concerning the simple ideas of Sensation, it is to be considered,- that whatsoever is so constituted in nature as to be able, by affecting our senses, to cause any perception in the mind, doth thereby produce in the understanding a simple idea; which, whatever be the external cause of it, when it comes to be taken notice of by our discerning faculty, it is by the mind looked on and considered there to be a real positive idea in the understanding, as much as any other whatsoever; though, perhaps, the cause of it be but a privation of the subject.

2.

Ideas in the mind distinguished from that in things which gives rise to them. Thus the ideas of heat and cold, light and darkness, white and black, motion and rest, are equally clear and positive ideas in the mind; though, perhaps, some of the causes which produce them are barely privations, in those subjects from whence our senses derive those ideas. These the understanding, in its view of them, considers all as distinct positive ideas, without taking notice of the causes that produce them: which is an inquiry not belonging to the idea, as it is in the understanding, but to the nature of the things existing without us. These are two very different things, and carefully to be distinguished; it being one thing to perceive and know the idea of white or black, and quite another to examine what kind of particles they must be, and how ranged in the superficies, to make any object appear white or black.

3.

We may have the ideas when we are ignorant of their physical causes. A painter or dyer who never inquired into their causes hath the ideas of white and black, and other colors, as clearly, perfectly, and distinctly in his understanding, and perhaps more distinctly, than the philosopher who hath busied himself in considering their natures, and thinks he knows how far either of them is, in its cause, positive or privative; and the idea of black is no less positive in his mind than that of white, however the cause of that color in the external object may be only a privation.

4.

Why a privative cause in nature may occasion a positive idea. If it were the design of my present undertaking to inquire into the natural causes and manner of perception, I should offer this as a reason why a privative cause might, in some cases at least, produce a positive idea; viz. that all sensation being produced in us only by different degrees and modes of motion in our animal spirits, variously agitated by external objects, the abatement of any former motion must as necessarily produce a new sensation as the variation or increase of it; and so introduce a new idea, which depends only on a different motion of the animal spirits in that organ.

5.

Negative names need not be meaningless. But whether this be so or not I will not here determine, but appeal to every one's own experience, whether the shadow of a man, though it consists of nothing but the absence of light (and the more the absence of light is, the more discernible is the shadow) does not, when a man looks on it, cause as clear and positive idea in his mind as a man himself, though covered over with clear sunshine? And the picture of a shadow is a positive thing. Indeed, we have negative names, which stand not directly for positive ideas, but for their absence, such as insipid, silence, nihil, etc.; which words denote positive ideas, v.g., taste, sound, being, with a signification of their absence.

6.

Whether any ideas are due to causes really privative. And thus one may truly be said to see darkness. For, supposing a hole perfectly dark, from whence no light is reflected, it is certain one may see the figure of it, or it may be painted; or whether the ink I write with makes any other idea, is a question. The privative causes I have here assigned of positive ideas are according to the common opinion; but, in truth, it will be hard to determine whether there be really any ideas from a privative cause, till it be determined, whether rest be any more a privation than motion.

7.

Ideas in the mind, qualities in bodies. To discover the nature of our ideas the better, and to discourse of them intelligibly, it will be convenient to distinguish them as they are ideas or perceptions in our minds; and as they are modifications of matter in the bodies that cause such perceptions in us: that so we may not think (as perhaps usually is done) that they are exactly the images and resemblances of something inherent in the subject; most of those of sensation being in the mind no more the likeness of something existing without us, than the names that stand for them are the likeness of our ideas, which yet upon hearing they are apt to excite in us.

8.

Our ideas and the qualities of bodies. Whatsoever the mind perceives in itself, or is the immediate object of perception, thought, or understanding, that I call idea; and the power to produce any idea in our mind, I call quality of the subject wherein that power is. Thus a snowball having the power to produce in us the ideas of white, cold, and round, - the power to produce those ideas in us, as they are in the snowball, I call qualities; and as they are sensations or perceptions in our understandings, I call them ideas; which ideas, if I speak of sometimes as in the things themselves, I would be understood to mean those qualities in the objects which produce them in us.

9.

Primary qualities of bodies. Qualities thus considered in bodies are, first, such as are utterly inseparable from the body, in what state soever it be; and such as in all the alterations and changes it suffers, all the force can be used upon it, it constantly keeps; and such as sense constantly finds in every particle of matter which has bulk enough to be perceived; and the mind finds inseparable from every particle of matter, though less than to make itself singly be perceived by our senses: v.g. Take a grain of wheat, divide it into two parts; each part has still solidity, extension, figure, and mobility: divide it again, and it retains still the same qualities; and so divide it on, till the parts become insensible; they must

retain still each of them all those qualities. For division (which is all that a mill, or pestle, or any other body, does upon another, in reducing it to insensible parts) can never take away either solidity, extension, figure, or mobility from any body, but only makes two or more distinct separate masses of matter, of that which was but one before; all which distinct masses, reckoned as so many distinct bodies, after division, make a certain number. These I call original or primary qualities of body, which I think we may observe to produce simple ideas in us, viz. solidity, extension, figure, motion or rest, and number.

10.

Secondary qualities of bodies. Secondly, such qualities which in truth are nothing in the objects themselves but power to produce various sensations in us by their primary qualities, i.e. by the bulk, figure, texture, and motion of their insensible parts, as colors, sounds, tastes, etc. These I call secondary qualities. To these might be added a third sort, which are allowed to be barely powers; though they are as much real qualities in the subject as those which I, to comply with the common way of speaking, call qualities, but for distinction, secondary qualities. For the power in fire to produce a new color, or consistency, in wax or clay, - by its primary qualities, is as much a quality in fire, as the power it has to produce in me a new idea or sensation of warmth or burning, which I felt not before, - by the same primary qualities, viz. the bulk, texture, and motion of its insensible parts.

11.

How bodies produce ideas in us. The next thing to be considered is, how bodies produce ideas in us; and that is manifestly by impulse, the only way which we can conceive bodies to operate in.

12.

By motions, external, and in our organism. If then external objects be not united to our minds when they produce ideas therein; and yet we perceive these original qualities in such of them as singly fall under our senses, it is evident that some motion must be thence continued by our nerves, or animal spirits, by some parts of our bodies, to the brains or the seat of sensation, there to produce in our minds the particular ideas we have of them. And since the extension, figure, number, and motion of bodies of an observable bigness, may be perceived at a distance by the sight, it is evident some singly imperceptible bodies must come from them to the eyes, and thereby convey to the brain some motion; which produces these ideas which we have of them in us.

13.

How secondary qualities produce their ideas. After the same manner, that the ideas of these original qualities are produced in us, we may conceive that the ideas of secondary qualities are also produced, viz. by the operation of insensible particles on our senses. For, it being manifest that there are bodies and good store of bodies, each whereof are so small, that we cannot by any of our senses discover either their bulk, figure, or motion,- as is evident in the particles of the air and water, and others extremely smaller than those; perhaps as much smaller than the particles of air and water, as the particles of air and water are smaller than peas or hailstones;- let us suppose at present that the different motions and figures, bulk and number, of such particles, affecting the several organs of our senses, produce in us those different sensations which we have from the colors and smells of bodies; v.g. that a violet, by the impulse of such insensible particles of matter, of peculiar figures and bulks, and in different degrees and modifications of their motions, causes the ideas of the blue color, and sweet scent of that flower to be produced in our minds. It being no more impossible to conceive that God should annex such ideas to such motions, with which they have no similitude, than that he should annex the idea of pain to the motion of a piece of steel dividing our flesh, with which that idea hath no resemblance.

14.

They depend on the primary qualities. What I have said concerning colors and smells may be understood also of tastes and sounds, and other the like sensible qualities; which, whatever reality we by mistake attribute to them, are in truth nothing in the objects themselves, but powers to produce various sensations in us; and depend on those primary qualities, viz. bulk, figure, texture, and motion of parts as I have said.

15.

Ideas of primary qualities are resemblances; of secondary, not. From whence I think it easy to draw this observation, - that the ideas of primary qualities of bodies are resemblances of them, and their patterns do really exist in the bodies themselves, but the ideas produced in us by these secondary qualities have no resemblance of them at all. There is nothing like our

ideas, existing in the bodies themselves. They are, in the bodies we denominate from them, only a power to produce those sensations in us: and what is sweet, blue, or warm in idea, is but the certain bulk, figure, and motion of the insensible parts, in the bodies themselves, which we call so.

16.

Examples. Flame is denominated hot and light; snow, white and cold; and manna, white and sweet, from the ideas they produce in us. Which qualities are commonly thought to be the same in those bodies that those ideas are in us, the one the perfect resemblance of the other, as they are in a mirror, and it would by most men be judged very extravagant if one should say otherwise. And yet he that will consider that the same fire that, at one distance produces in us the sensation of warmth, does, at a nearer approach, produce in us the far different sensation of pain, ought to bethink himself what reason he has to say that this idea of warmth, which was produced in him by the fire, is actually in the fire; and his idea of pain, which the same fire produced in him the same way, is not in the fire. Why are whiteness and coldness in snow, and pain not, when it produces the one and the other idea in us; and can do neither, but by the bulk, figure, number, and motion of its solid parts?

17.

The ideas of the primary alone really exist. The particular bulk, number, figure, and motion of the parts of fire or snow are really in them, - whether any one's senses perceive them or no: and therefore they may be called real qualities, because they really exist in those bodies. But light, heat, whiteness, or coldness, are no more really in them than sickness or pain is in manna. Take away the sensation of them; let not the eyes see light or colors, nor the ears hear sounds; let the palate not taste, nor the nose smell, and all colors, tastes, odors, and sounds, as they are such particular ideas, vanish and cease, and are reduced to their causes, i.e. bulk, figure, and motion of parts.

18.

The secondary exist in things only as modes of the primary. A piece of manna of a sensible bulk is able to produce in us the idea of a round or square figure; and by being removed from one place to another, the idea of motion. This idea of motion represents it as it really is in manna moving: a circle or square are the same, whether in idea or existence, in the mind or in the manna. And this, both motion and figure, are really in the manna, whether we take notice of them or no: this everybody is ready to agree to. Besides, manna, by tie bulk, figure, texture, and motion of its parts, has a power to produce the sensations of sickness, and sometimes of acute pains or gripings in us. That these ideas of sickness and pain are not in the manna, but effects of its operations on us, and are nowhere when we feel them not; this also every one readily agrees to. And yet men are hardly to be brought to think that sweetness and whiteness are not really in manna; which are but the effects of the operations of manna, by the motion, size, and figure of its particles, on the eyes and palate: as the pain and sickness caused by manna are confessedly nothing but the effects of its operations on the stomach and guts, by the size, motion, and figure of its insensible parts, (for by nothing else can a body operate, as has been proved): as if it could not operate on the eyes and palate, and thereby produce in the mind particular distinct ideas, which in itself it has not, as well as we allow it can operate on the guts and stomach, and thereby produce distinct ideas, which in itself it has not. These ideas, being all effects of the operations of manna on several parts of our bodies, by the size, figure number, and motion of its parts;- why those produced by the eyes and palate should rather be thought to be really in the manna, than those produced by the stomach and guts; or why the pain and sickness, ideas that are the effect of manna, should be thought to be nowhere when they are not felt; and yet the sweetness and whiteness, effects of the same manna on other parts of the body, by ways equally as unknown, should be thought to exist in the manna, when they are not seen or tasted, would need some reason to explain.

19.

Examples. Let us consider the red and white colors in porphyry. Hinder light from striking on it, and its colors vanish; it no longer produces any such ideas in us: upon the return of light it produces these appearances on us again. Can anyone think any real alterations are made in the porphyry by the presence or absence of light; and that those ideas of whiteness and redness are really in porphyry in. the light, when it is plain it has no color in the dark? It has, indeed, such a configuration of particles, both night and day, as are apt, by the rays of light rebounding from some parts of that hard stone, to produce in us the idea of redness, and from others the idea of whiteness; but whiteness or redness are not in it at any time, but such a texture that hath the power to produce such a sensation in us.

20.

Pound an almond, and the clear white color will be altered into a dirty one, and the sweet taste into an oily one. What real alteration can the beating of the pestle make in any body, but an alteration of the texture of it?

21.

Explains how water felt as cold by one hand may be warm to the other. Ideas being thus distinguished and understood, we may be able to give an account how the same water, at the same time, may produce the idea of cold by one hand and of heat by the other: whereas it is impossible that the same water, if those ideas were really in it, should at the same time be both hot and cold. For, if we imagine warmth, as it is in our hands, to be nothing but a certain sort and degree of motion in the minute particles of our nerves or animal spirits, we may understand how it is possible that the same water may, at the same time, produce the sensations of heat in one hand and cold in the other; which yet figure never does, that never producing- the idea of a square by one hand which has produced the idea of a globe by another. But if the sensation of heat and cold be nothing but the increase or diminution of the motion of the minute parts of our bodies, caused by the corpuscles of any other body, it is easy to be understood, that if that motion be greater in one hand than in the other; if a body be applied to the two hands, which has in its minute particles a greater motion than in those of one of the hands, and a less than in those of the other, it will increase the motion of the one hand and lessen it in the other; and so cause the different sensations of heat and cold that depend thereon.

22.

An excursion into natural philosophy. I have in what just goes before been engaged in physical inquiries a little further than perhaps I intended. But, it being necessary to make the nature of sensation a little understood; and to make the difference between the qualities in bodies, and the ideas produced by them in the mind, to be distinctly conceived, without which it were impossible to discourse intelligibly of them;- I hope I shall be pardoned this little excursion into natural philosophy; it being necessary in our present inquiry to distinguish the primary and real qualities of bodies, which are always in them (viz. solidity, extension, figure, number, and motion, or rest, and are sometimes perceived by us, viz. when the bodies they are in are big enough singly to be discerned), from those secondary and imputed qualities, which are but the powers of several combinations of those primary ones, when they operate without being distinctly discerned;- whereby we may also come to know what ideas are, and what are not, resemblances of something really existing in the bodies we denominate from them.

23.

Three sorts of qualities in bodies. The qualities, then, that are in bodies, rightly considered, are of three sorts:

First, the bulk, figure, number, situation, and motion or rest of their solid parts. Those are in them, whether we perceive them or not; and when they are of that size that we can discover them, we have by these an idea of the thing as it is in itself; as is plain in artificial things. These I call primary qualities.

Secondly, the power that is in any body, by reason of its insensible primary qualities, to operate after a peculiar manner on any of our senses, and thereby produce in us the different ideas of several colors, sounds, smells, tastes, etc. These are usually called sensible qualities.

Thirdly, the power that is in any body, by reason of the particular constitution of its primary qualities, to make such a change in the bulk, figure, texture, and motion of another body, as to make it operate on our senses differently from what it did before. Thus the sun has a power to make wax white, and fire to make lead fluid. These are usually called powers.

The first of these, as has been said, I think may be properly called real, original, or primary qualities; because they are in the things themselves, whether they are perceived or not: and upon their different modifications it is that the secondary qualities depend.

The other two are only powers to act differently upon other things: which powers result from the different modifications of those primary qualities.

24.

The first are resemblances; the second thought to be resemblances, but are not; the third neither are nor are thought so. But, though the two latter sorts of qualities are powers barely, and nothing but powers, relating to several other bodies, and resulting from the different modifications of the original qualities, yet they are generally otherwise thought of. For the second sort,

viz, the powers to produce several ideas in us, by our senses, are looked upon as real qualities in the things thus affecting us: but the third sort are called and esteemed barely powers. v.g. The idea of heat or light, which we receive by our eyes, or touch, from the sun, are commonly thought real qualities existing in the sun, and something more than mere powers in it. But when we consider the sun in reference to wax, which it melts or blanches, we look on the whiteness and softness produced in the wax, not as qualities in the sun, but effects produced by powers in it. Whereas, if rightly considered, these qualities of light and warmth, which are perceptions in me when I am warmed or enlightened by the sun, are no otherwise in the sun, than the changes made in the wax, when it is blanched or melted, are in the sun. They are all of them equally powers in the sun, depending on its primary qualities; whereby it is able, in the one case, so to alter the bulk, figure, texture, or motion of some of the insensible parts of my eyes or hands, as thereby to produce in me the idea of light or heat; and in the other, it is able so to alter the bulk, figure, texture, or motion of the insensible parts of the wax, as to make them fit to produce in me the distinct ideas of white and fluid.

25.

Why the secondary are ordinarily taken for real qualities, and not for bare powers. The reason why the one are ordinarily taken for real qualities, and the other only for bare powers, seems to be, because the ideas we have of distinct colors, sounds, etc., containing nothing at all in them of bulk, figure, or motion, we are not apt to think them the effects of these primary qualities; which appear not, to our senses, to operate in their production, and with which they have not any apparent congruity or conceivable connection. Hence it is that we are so forward to imagine, that those ideas are the resemblances of something really existing in the objects themselves: since sensation discovers nothing of bulk, figure, or motion of parts in their production; nor can reason show how bodies, by their bulk, figure, and motion, should produce in the mind the ideas of blue or yellow, etc. But, in the other case, in the operations of bodies changing the qualities one of another, we plainly discover that the quality produced hath commonly no resemblance with anything in the thing producing it; wherefore we look on it as a bare effect of power. For, through receiving the idea of heat or light from the sun, we are apt to think it is a perception and resemblance of such a quality in the sun; yet when we see wax, or a fair face, receive change of color from the sun, we cannot imagine that to be the reception or resemblance of anything in the sun, because we find not those different colors in the sun itself. For, our senses being able to observe a likeness or unlikeness of sensible qualities in two different external objects, we forwardly enough conclude the production of any sensible quality in any subject to be an effect of bare power, and not the communication of any quality which was really in the efficient, when we find no such sensible quality in the thing that produced it. But our senses, not being able to discover any unlikeness between the idea produced in us, and the quality of the object producing it, we are apt to imagine that our ideas are resemblances of something in the objects, and not the effects of certain powers placed in the modification of their primary qualities, with which primary qualities the ideas produced in us have no resemblance.

26.

Secondary qualities twofold; first, immediately perceivable; secondly, mediately perceivable. To conclude: besides those before-mentioned primary qualities in bodies, viz. bulk, figure, extension, number, and motion of their solid parts; all the rest, whereby we take notice of bodies, and distinguish them one from another, are nothing else but several powers in them, depending on those primary qualities; whereby they are fitted, either by immediately operating on our bodies to produce several different ideas in us; or else, by operating on other bodies, so to change their primary qualities as to render them capable of producing ideas in us different from what before they did. The former of these, I think, may be called secondary qualities immediately perceivable: the latter, secondary qualities, mediately perceivable. . . .

CHAPTER XXIII: OF OUR COMPLEX IDEAS OF SUBSTANCES

1.

Ideas of particular substances, how made. The mind being, as I have declared, furnished with a great number of the simple ideas, conveyed in by the senses as they are found in exterior things, or by reflection on its own operations, takes notice also that a certain number of these simple ideas go constantly together; which being presumed to belong to one thing, and words being suited to common apprehensions, and made use of for quick dispatch, are called, so united in one subject, by one name; which, by inadvertency, we are apt afterward to talk of and consider as one simple idea, which

indeed is a complication of many ideas together: because, as I have said, not imagining how these simple ideas can subsist by themselves, we accustom ourselves to suppose some substratum wherein they do subsist, and from which they do result, which therefore we call substance.

2.

Our obscure idea of substance in general. So that if anyone will examine himself concerning his notion of pure substance in general, he will find he has no other idea of it at all, but only a supposition of he knows not what support of such qualities which are capable of producing simple ideas in us; which qualities are commonly called accidents. If anyone should be asked, what is the subject wherein color or weight inheres, he would have nothing to say, but the solid extended parts; and if he were demanded, what is it that solidity and extension adhere in, he would not be in a much better case than the Indian before mentioned who, saying that the world was supported by a great elephant, was asked what the elephant rested on; to which his answer was a great tortoise: but being again pressed to know what gave support to the broad-backed tortoise, replied something, he knew not what. And thus here, as in all other cases where we use words without having clear and distinct ideas, we talk like children: who, being questioned what such a thing is, which they know not, readily give this satisfactory answer, that it is something: which in truth signifies no more, when so used, either by children or men, but that they know not what; and that the thing they pretend to know, and talk of, is what they have no distinct idea of at all, and so are perfectly ignorant of it, and in the dark. The idea then we have, to which we give the general name substance, being nothing but the supposed, but unknown, support of those qualities we find existing, which we imagine cannot subsist *sine re substante*, without something to support them, we call that support *substantia*; which, according to the true import of the word, is, in plain English, "standing under" or "upholding."

3.

Of the sorts of substances. An obscure and relative idea of substance in general being thus made we come to have the ideas of particular sorts of substances, by collecting such combinations of simple ideas as are, by experience and observation of men's senses, taken notice of to exist together; and are therefore supposed to flow from the particular internal constitution, or unknown essence of that substance. Thus we come to have the ideas of a man, horse, gold, water, &c.; of which substances, whether any one has any other clear idea, further than of certain simple ideas co-existent together, I appeal to every one's own experience. It is the ordinary qualities observable in iron, or a diamond, put together, that make the true complex idea of those substances, which a smith or a jeweler commonly knows better than a philosopher; who, whatever substantial forms he may talk of, has no other idea of those substances, than what is framed by a collection of those simple ideas which are to be found in them: only we must take notice, that our complex ideas of substances, besides all those simple ideas they are made up of, have always the confused idea of something to which they belong, and in which they subsist: and therefore when we speak of any sort of substance, we say it is a thing having such or such qualities; as body is a thing that is extended, figured, and capable of motion; spirit, a thing capable of thinking; and so hardness, friability, and power to draw iron, we say, are qualities to be found in a loadstone. These, and the like fashions of speaking, intimate that the substance is supposed always something besides the extension, figure, solidity, motion, thinking, or other observable ideas, though we know not what it is.

4.

No clear or distinct idea of substance in general. Hence, when we talk or think of any particular sort of corporeal substances, as horse, stone, etc., though the idea we have of either of them be but the complication or collection of those several simple ideas of sensible qualities, which we used to find united in the thing called horse or stone; yet, because we cannot conceive how they should subsist alone, nor one in another, we suppose them existing in and supported by some common subject; which support we denote by the name substance, though it be certain we have no clear or distinct idea of that thing we suppose a support.

5.

As clear an idea of spiritual substance as of corporeal substance. The same thing happens concerning the operations of the mind, viz. thinking, reasoning, fearing, etc., which we concluding not to subsist of themselves, nor apprehending how they can belong to body, or be produced by it, we are apt to think these the actions of some other substance, which we call spirit; whereby yet it is evident that, having no other idea or notion of matter, but something wherein those many sensible qualities which affect our senses do subsist; by supposing a substance wherein thinking, knowing, doubting,

and a power of moving, etc., do subsist, we have as clear a notion of the substance of spirit, as we have of body; the one being supposed to be (without knowing what it is) the substratum to those simple ideas we have from without; and the other supposed (with a like ignorance of what it is) to be the substratum to those operations we experiment in ourselves within. It is plain then, that the idea of corporeal substance in matter is as remote from our conceptions and apprehensions, as that of spiritual substance, or spirit: and therefore, from our not having any notion of the substance of spirit, we can no more conclude its non-existence, than we can, for the same reason, deny the existence of body; it being as rational to affirm there is no body, because we have no clear and distinct idea of the substance of matter, as to say there is no spirit, because we have no clear and distinct idea of the substance of a spirit.

6.

Our ideas of particular sorts of substances. Whatever therefore be the secret abstract nature of substance in general, all the ideas we have of particular distinct sorts of substances are nothing but several combinations of simple ideas, coexisting in such, though unknown, cause of their union, as makes the whole subsist of itself It is by such combinations of simple ideas, and nothing else, that we represent particular sorts of substances to ourselves; such are the ideas we have of their several species in our minds; and such only do we, by their specific names, signify to others, v.g. man, horse, sun, water, iron: upon hearing which words, everyone who understands the language, frames in his mind a combination of those several simple ideas which he has usually observed, or fancied to exist together under that denomination; all which he supposes to rest in and be, as it were, adherent to that unknown common subject, which inheres not in anything else. Though, in the meantime, it be manifest, and every one, upon inquiry into his own thoughts, will find, that he has no other idea of any substance, v.g. let it be gold, horse, iron, man, vitriol, bread, but what he has barely of those sensible qualities, which he supposes to inhere; with a supposition of such a substratum as gives, as it were, a support to those qualities or simple ideas, which he has observed to exist united together. Thus, the idea of the sun,- what is it but an aggregate of those several simple ideas, bright, hot, roundish, having a constant regular motion, at a certain distance from us, and perhaps some other: as he who thinks and discourses of the sun has been more or less accurate in observing those sensible qualities, ideas, or properties, which are in that thing which he calls the sun. . . .

BOOK IV: OF KNOWLEDGE AND PROBABILITY

...

CHAPTER XI: OF OUR KNOWLEDGE OF THE EXISTENCE OF OTHER THINGS

1.

Knowledge of the existence of other finite beings is to be had only by actual sensation. The knowledge of our own being we have by intuition. The existence of a God, reason clearly makes known to us, as has been shown.

The knowledge of the existence of any other thing we can have only by sensation: for there being no necessary connection of real existence with any idea a man hath in his memory; nor of any other existence but that of God with the existence of any particular man: no particular man can know the existence of any other being, but only when, by actual operating upon him, it makes itself perceived by him. For, the having the idea of anything in our mind, no more proves the existence of that thing, than the picture of a man evidences his being in the world, or the visions of a dream make thereby a true history.

2.

Instance: whiteness of this paper. It is therefore the actual receiving of ideas from without that gives us notice of the existence of other things, and makes us know, that something doth exist at that time without us, which causes that idea in us; though perhaps we neither know nor consider how it does it. For it takes not from the certainty of our senses, and the ideas we receive by them, that we know not the manner wherein they are produced: v.g. whilst I write this, I have, by the paper affecting my eyes, that idea produced in my mind, which, whatever object causes, I call white; by which I know that that quality or accident (i.e. whose appearance before my eyes always causes that idea) doth really exist, and hath a being without me. And of this, the greatest assurance I can possibly have, and to which my faculties can attain, is the testimony of my eyes, which are the proper and sole judges of this thing; whose testimony I have reason to rely on as so certain, that I can no more doubt, whilst I write this, that I see white and black, and that something really exists that causes that sensation in me, than that I write or move my hand; which is a certainty as great as human nature is capable of, concerning the existence of anything, but a man's self alone, and of God.

3.

This notice by our senses, though not so certain as demonstration, yet may be called knowledge, and proves the existence of things without us. The notice we have by our senses of the existing of things without us, though it be not altogether so certain as our intuitive knowledge, or the deductions of our reason employed about the clear abstract ideas of our own minds; yet it is an assurance that deserves the name of knowledge. If we persuade ourselves that our faculties act and inform us right concerning the existence of those objects that affect them, it cannot pass for an ill-grounded confidence: for I think nobody can, in earnest, be so skeptical as to be uncertain of the existence of those things which he sees and feels. At least, he that can doubt so far, (whatever he may have with his own thoughts,) will never have any controversy with me; since he can never be sure I say anything contrary to his own opinion. As to myself, I think God has given me assurance enough of the existence of things without me: since, by their different application, I can produce in myself both pleasure and pain, which is one great concernment of my present state. This is certain: the confidence that our faculties do not herein deceive us, is the greatest assurance we are capable of concerning the existence of material beings. For we cannot act anything but by our faculties; nor talk of knowledge itself, but by the help of those faculties which are fitted to apprehend even what knowledge is.

But besides the assurance we have from our senses themselves, that they do not err in the information they give us of the existence of things without us, when they are affected by them, we are further confirmed in this assurance by other concurrent reasons:

4.

Confirmed by concurrent reasons: *First, because we cannot have ideas of sensation but by the inlet of the senses.* It is plain those perceptions are produced in us by exterior causes affecting our senses: because those that want the organs of any sense, never can have the ideas belonging to that sense produced in their minds. This is too evident to be doubted: and therefore we cannot but be assured that they come in by the organs of that sense, and no other way. The organs themselves, it is plain, do not produce them: for then the eyes of a man in the dark would produce colors, and his nose smell roses in the winter: but we see nobody gets the relish of a pineapple, till he goes to the Indies, where it is, and tastes it.

5.

Secondly, because we find that an idea from actual sensation, and another from memory, are very distinct perceptions. Because sometimes I find that I cannot avoid the having those ideas produced in my mind. For though, when my eyes are shut, or windows fast, I can at pleasure recall to my mind the ideas of light, or the sun, which former sensations had lodged in my memory; so I can at pleasure lay by that idea, and take into my view that of the smell of a rose, or taste of sugar. But, if I turn my eyes at noon towards the sun, I cannot avoid the ideas which the light or sun then produces in me. So that there is a manifest difference between the ideas laid up in my memory, (over which, if they were there only, I should have constantly the same power to dispose of them, and lay them by at pleasure,) and those which force themselves upon me, and I cannot avoid having. And therefore it must needs be some exterior cause, and the brisk acting of some objects without me, whose efficacy I cannot resist, that produces those ideas in my mind, whether I will or no. Besides, there is nobody who doth not perceive the difference in himself between contemplating the sun, as he hath the idea of it in his memory, and actually looking upon it: of which two, his perception is so distinct, that few of his ideas are more distinguishable one from another. And therefore he hath certain knowledge that they are not both memory, or the actions of his mind, and fancies only within him; but that actual seeing hath a cause without.

6.

Thirdly, because pleasure or pain, which accompanies actual sensation, accompanies not the returning of those ideas without the external objects. Add to this, that many of those ideas are produced in us with pain, which afterwards we remember without the least offence. Thus, the pain of heat or cold, when the idea of it is revived in our minds, gives us no disturbance; which, when felt, was very troublesome; and is again, when actually repeated: which is occasioned by the disorder the external object causes in our bodies when applied to them: and we remember the pains of hunger, thirst, or the headache, without any pain at all; which would either never disturb us, or else constantly do it, as often as we thought of it, were there nothing more but ideas floating in our minds, and appearances entertaining our fancies, without the real existence of things affecting us from abroad. The same may be said of pleasure, accompanying several actual sensations. And though mathematical demonstration depends not upon sense,

yet the examining them by diagrams gives great credit to the evidence of our sight, and seems to give it a certainty approaching to that of demonstration itself. For, it would be very strange, that a man should allow it for an undeniable truth, that two angles of a figure, which he measures by lines and angles of a diagram, should be bigger one than the other, and yet doubt of the existence of those lines and angles, which by looking on he makes use of to measure that by.

7.

Fourthly, because our senses assist one another's testimony of the existence of outward things, and enable us to predict. Our senses in many cases bear witness to the truth of each other's report, concerning the existence of sensible things without us. He that sees a fire, may, if he doubt whether it be anything more than a bare fancy, feel it too; and be convinced, by putting his hand in it. Which certainly could never be put into such exquisite pain by a bare idea or phantom, unless that the pain be a fancy too: which yet he cannot, when the burn is well, by raising the idea of it, bring upon himself again.

Thus I see, whilst I write this, I can change the appearance of the paper; and by designing the letters, tell beforehand what new idea it shall exhibit the very next moment, by barely drawing my pen over it: which will neither appear (let me fancy as much as I will) if my hands stand still; or though I move my pen, if my eyes be shut: nor, when those characters are once made on the paper, can I choose afterwards but see them as they are; that is, have the ideas of such letters as I have made. Whence it is manifest, that they are not barely the sport and play of my own imagination, when I find that the characters that were made at the pleasure of my own thoughts, do not obey them; nor yet cease to be, whenever I shall fancy it, but continue to affect my senses constantly and regularly, according to the figures I made them. To which if we will add, that the sight of those shall, from another man, draw such sounds as I beforehand design they shall stand for, there will be little reason left to doubt that those words I write do really exist without me, when they cause a long series of regular sounds to affect my ears, which could not be the effect of my imagination, nor could my memory retain them in that order.

8.

This certainty is as great as our condition needs. But yet, if after all this any one will be so skeptical as to distrust his senses, and to affirm that all we see and hear, feel and taste, think and do, during our whole being, is but the series and deluding appearances of a long dream, whereof there is no reality; and therefore will question the existence of all things, or our knowledge of anything: I must desire him to consider, that, if all be a dream, then he doth but dream that he makes the question, and so it is not much matter that a waking man should answer him. But yet, if he pleases, he may dream that I make him this answer: that the certainty of things existing *in rerum natura* when we have the testimony of our senses for it is not only as great as our frame can attain to, but as our condition needs. For, our faculties being suited not to the full extent of being, nor to a perfect, clear, comprehensive knowledge of things free from all doubt and scruple; but to the preservation of us, in whom they are; and accommodated to the use of life: they serve to our purpose wen enough, if they will but give us certain notice of those things, which are convenient or inconvenient to us. For he that sees a candle burning, and hath experimented the force of its flame by putting his finger in it, will little doubt that this is something existing without him, which does him harm, and puts him to great pain; which is assurance enough, when no man requires greater certainty to govern his actions by than what is as certain as his actions themselves. And if our dreamer pleases to try whether the glowing heat of a glass furnace be barely a wandering imagination in a drowsy man's fancy, by putting his hand into it, he may perhaps be wakened into a certainty greater than he could wish, that it is something more than bare imagination. So that this evidence is as great as we can desire, being as certain to us as our pleasure or pain, i.e. happiness or misery; beyond which we have no concernment, either of knowing or being. Such an assurance of the existence of things without us is sufficient to direct us in the attaining the good and avoiding the evil which is caused by them, which is the important concernment we have of being made acquainted with them.

9.

But reaches no further than actual sensation. In fine, then, when our senses do actually convey into our understandings any idea, we cannot but be satisfied that there doth something at that time really exist without us, which doth affect our senses, and by them give notice of itself to our apprehensive faculties, and actually produce that idea which we then perceive: and we cannot so far distrust their testimony, as to doubt that such collections of simple ideas as we have observed by our senses to be united together, do really exist together.

But this knowledge extends as far as the present testimony of our senses, employed about particular objects that do then affect them, and no further. For if I saw such a collection of simple ideas as is wont to be called man, existing together one minute since, and am now alone, I cannot be certain that the same man exists now, since there is no necessary connection of his existence a minute since with his existence now: by a thousand ways he may cease to be, since I had the testimony of my senses for his existence. And if I cannot be certain that the man I saw last to-day is now in being, I can less be certain that he is so who hath been longer removed from my senses, and I have not seen since yesterday, or since the last year: and much less can I be certain of the existence of men that I never saw. And, therefore, though it be highly probable that millions of men do now exist, yet, whilst I am alone, writing this, I have not that certainty of it which we strictly call knowledge; though the great likelihood of it puts me past doubt, and it be reasonable for me to do several things upon the confidence that there are men (and men also of my acquaintance, with whom I have to do) now in the world: but this is but probability, not knowledge.

10.

Folly to expect demonstration in everything. Whereby yet we may observe how foolish and vain a thing it is for a man of a narrow knowledge, who having reason given him to judge of the different evidence and probability of things, and to be swayed accordingly; how vain, I say, it is to expect demonstration and certainty in things not capable of it; and refuse assent to very rational propositions, and act contrary to very plain and clear truths, because they cannot be made out so evident, as to surmount every the least (I will not say reason, but) pretense of doubting. He that, in the ordinary affairs of life, would admit of nothing but direct plain demonstration, would be sure of nothing in this world, but of perishing quickly. The wholesomeness of his meat or drink would not give him reason to venture on it: and I would fain know what it is he could do upon such grounds as are capable of no doubt, no objection.

11.

Past existence of other things is known by memory. As when our senses are actually employed about any object, we do know that it does exist; so by our memory we may be assured, that heretofore things that affected our senses have existed. And thus we have knowledge of the past existence of several things, whereof our senses having informed us, our memories still retain the ideas; and of this we are past all doubt, so long as we remember well. But this knowledge also reaches no further than our senses have formerly assured us. Thus, seeing water at this instant, it is an unquestionable truth to me that water doth exist: and remembering that I saw it yesterday, it will also be always true, and as long as my memory retains it always an undoubted proposition to me, that water did exist the 10th of July, 1688; as it will also be equally true that a certain number of very fine colors did exist, which at the same time I saw upon a bubble of that water: but, being now quite out of sight both of the water and bubbles too, it is no more certainly known to me that the water doth now exist, than that the bubbles or colors therein do so: it being no more necessary that water should exist to-day, because it existed yesterday, than that the colors or bubbles exist to-day, because they existed yesterday, though it be exceedingly much more probable; because water hath been observed to continue long in existence, but bubbles, and the colors on them, quickly cease to be.

12.

The existence of other finite spirits not knowable, and rests on faith. What ideas we have of spirits, and how we come by them, I have already shown. But though we have those ideas in our minds, and know we have them there, the having the ideas of spirits does not make us know that any such things do exist without us, or that there are any finite spirits, or any other spiritual beings, but the Eternal God. We have ground from revelation, and several other reasons, to believe with assurance that there are such creatures: but our senses not being able to discover them, we want the means of knowing their particular existences. For we can no more know that there are finite spirits really existing, by the idea we have of such beings in our minds, than by the ideas any one has of fairies or centaurs, he can come to know that things answering those ideas do really exist.

And therefore concerning the existence of finite spirits, as well as several other things, we must content ourselves with the evidence of faith; but universal, certain propositions concerning this matter are beyond our reach. For however true it may be, v.g., that all the intelligent spirits that God ever created do still exist, yet it can never make a part of our certain knowledge. These and the like propositions we may assent to, as highly probable, but are not, I fear, in this state capable of knowing. We are not, then, to put others upon demonstrating, nor ourselves upon search of universal certainty in all those matters; wherein we are not capable

of any other knowledge, but what our senses give us in this or that particular.

13.

Only particular propositions concerning concrete existences are knowable. By which it appears that there are two sorts of propositions:

1. There is one sort of propositions concerning the existence of anything answerable to such an idea: as having the idea of an elephant, phoenix, motion, or an angel, in my mind, the first and natural inquiry is, Whether such a thing does anywhere exist? And this knowledge is only of particulars. No existence of anything without us, but only of God, can certainly be known further than our senses inform us.

2. There is another sort of propositions, wherein is expressed the agreement or disagreement of our abstract ideas, and their dependence on one another. Such propositions may be universal and certain. So, having the idea of God and myself, of fear and obedience, I cannot but be sure that God is to be feared and obeyed by me: and this proposition will be certain, concerning man in general, if I have made an abstract idea of such a species, whereof I am one particular. But yet this proposition, how certain so ever, that "men ought to fear and obey God" proves not to me the existence of men in the world; but will be true of all such creatures, whenever they do exist: which certainty of such general propositions depends on the agreement or disagreement to be discovered in those abstract ideas.

14.

And all general propositions that are known to be true concern abstract ideas. In the former case, our knowledge is the consequence of the existence of things, producing ideas in our minds by our senses: in the latter, knowledge is the consequence of the ideas (be they what they will) that are in our minds, producing there general certain propositions. Many of these are called *aeternae veritates*, and all of them indeed are so; not from being written, all or any of them, in the minds of all men; or that they were any of them propositions in any one's mind, till he, having got the abstract ideas, joined or separated them by affirmation or negation. But wheresoever we can suppose such a creature as man is, endowed with such faculties, and thereby furnished with such ideas as we have, we must conclude, he must needs, when he applies his thoughts to the consideration of his ideas, know the truth of certain propositions that will arise from the agreement or disagreement which he will perceive in his own ideas. Such propositions are therefore called eternal truths, not because they are eternal propositions actually formed, and antecedent to the understanding that at any time makes them; nor because they are imprinted on the mind from any patterns that are anywhere out of the mind, and existed before: but because, being once made about abstract ideas, so as to be true, they will, whenever they can be supposed to be made again at any time, past or to come, by a mind having those ideas, always actually be true. For names being supposed to stand perpetually for the same ideas, and the same ideas having immutably the same habitudes one to another, propositions concerning any abstract ideas that are once true must needs be eternal verities.

[Essay Concerning Human Understanding. (London: J.F. Dove, 1828).*]*

Treatise Concerning the Principles of Human Knowledge

George Berkeley
(Edited by Joseph R. Kirkland)

1.

OBJECTS OF HUMAN KNOWLEDGE. It is evident to an one who takes a survey of the objects of human knowledge, that they are either *ideas* actually imprinted on the senses; or else such as are perceived by attending to the passions and operations of the mind; or lastly, ideas formed by help of memory and imagination—either compounding, dividing, or barely representing those originally perceived in the aforesaid ways. By sight I have the ideas of light and colors, with their several degrees and variations. By touch I perceive hard and soft, heat and cold, motion and resistance, and of all these more and less either as to quantity or degree. Smelling furnishes me with odors; the palate with tastes; and hearing conveys sounds to the mind in all their variety of tone and composition. And as several of these are observed to accompany each other, they come to be marked by one name, and so to be reputed as one thing. Thus, for example a certain color, taste, smell, figure and consistence having been observed to go together, are accounted one distinct thing, signified by the name "apple." Other collections of ideas constitute a stone, a tree, a book, and the like sensible things—which as they are pleasing or disagreeable excite the passions of love, hatred, joy, grief, and so forth.

2.

MIND—SPIRIT—SOUL. But, besides all that endless variety of ideas or objects of knowledge, there is likewise something which knows or perceives them, and exercises divers operations, as willing, imagining, remembering, about them. This perceiving, active being is what I call "mind," "spirit," "soul," or "myself." By which words I do not denote any one of my ideas, but a thing entirely distinct from them, *wherein they exist*, or, which is the same thing, whereby they are perceived—for the existence of an idea consists in being perceived.

3.

HOW FAR THE ASSENT OF THE VULGAR CONCEDED. That neither our thoughts, nor passions, nor ideas formed by the imagination, exist *without* the mind, is what *everybody will allow*. And it seems no less evident that the various sensations or ideas imprinted on the sense, however blended or combined together (that is, whatever objects they compose), cannot exist otherwise than *in* a mind perceiving them. I think an intuitive knowledge may be obtained of this by any one that shall attend to *what is meant by* the term "exist," when applied to sensible things. The table I write on I say exists, that is, I see and feel it; and if I were out of my study I should say it existed—meaning thereby that if I was in my study I might perceive it, or that some other spirit actually does perceive it. There was an odor, that is, it was smelt; there was a sound, that is, it was heard; a color or figure, and it was perceived by sight or touch. This is all that I can understand by these and the like expressions. For as to what is said of the absolute existence of unthinking things without any relation to their being perceived, that seems perfectly unintelligible. Their *esse* is *percipi*, nor is it possible they should have any existence out of the minds or thinking things which perceive them.

4.

THE VULGAR OPINION INVOLVES A CONTRADICTION. It is indeed an opinion *strangely* prevailing amongst men, that houses, mountains, rivers, and in a word all sensible objects, have an existence, natural or real, distinct from their being perceived by the understanding. But, with how great an assurance and acquiescence soever this principle may be entertained in the world, yet whoever shall find in his heart to call it in question may, if I mistake not, perceive it to involve a manifest contradiction. For, what are the fore-mentioned objects but the things we perceive by sense? And what do we perceive *besides our own ideas or sensations*? And is it not plainly repugnant that any one of these, or any combination of them, should exist unperceived? . . .

17.

PHILOSOPHICAL MEANING OF "MATERIAL SUBSTANCE" DIVISIBLE INTO TWO PARTS. If we inquire into what the most accurate philosophers declare themselves to mean by "material substance," we shall find them acknowledge they have no other meaning annexed to those sounds but the idea of *being in general*, together with the relative notion of its supporting accidents. The general idea of Being appears to me the most abstract and incomprehensible of all other; and as for its supporting accidents, this, as we have just now observed, cannot be understood in the common sense of those words; it must therefore be taken in some other sense, but what that is they do not explain. So that when I consider the two parts or branches which make the signification of the words "material substance," I am convinced there is no distinct meaning annexed to them. But why should we trouble ourselves any farther, in discussing this material substratum or support of figure and motion, and other sensible qualities? Does it not suppose they have an existence without the mind? And is not this a direct repugnancy, and altogether inconceivable?

18.

THE EXISTENCE OF EXTERNAL BODIES WANTS PROOF. But, though it were possible that solid, figured, movable substances may exist without the mind, corresponding to the ideas we have of bodies, yet *how is it possible for us to know this*? Either we must know it by sense or by reason. As for our senses, by them we have the knowledge *only of our sensations*, ideas, or those things that are immediately perceived by sense, call them what you will: but they do not inform us that things exist without the mind, or unperceived, like to those which are perceived. This the materialists themselves acknowledge. It remains therefore that if we have any knowledge at all of external things, it must be by *reason*, inferring their existence from what is immediately perceived by sense. But what reason can induce us to believe the existence of bodies without the mind, from what we perceive, since the very patrons of Matter themselves do not pretend there is *any necessary connection betwixt them and our ideas*? I say it is granted on all hands (and what happens in dreams, frenzies, and the like, puts it beyond dispute) that *it is possible we might be affected with all the ideas we have now, though there were no bodies existing without resembling them.* Hence, it is evident the supposition of external bodies is not necessary for the producing our ideas; since it is granted they are produced sometimes, and might possibly be produced always in the same order, we see them in at present, without their concurrence.

19.

THE EXISTENCE OF EXTERNAL BODIES AFFORDS NO EXPLICATION OF THE MANNER IN WHICH OUR IDEAS ARE PRODUCED. But, though we might possibly have all our sensations without them, yet perhaps it may be thought *easier* to conceive and explain the *manner* of their production, by supposing external bodies in their likeness rather than otherwise; and so it might be at least probable there are such things as bodies that excite their ideas in our minds. But neither can this be said; for, though we give the materialists their external bodies, they by their own confession are never the nearer knowing how our ideas are produced; since they own themselves unable to comprehend in what manner *body can act upon spirit*, or how it is possible it should imprint any idea in the mind. Hence it is evident the production of ideas or sensations in our minds can be no reason why we should suppose Matter or corporeal substances, *since that is acknowledged to remain equally inexplicable with or without this supposition.* If therefore it were possible for bodies to exist without the mind, yet to hold they do so, must needs be a very precarious opinion; since it is to suppose, without any reason at all, that God has created innumerable beings *that are entirely useless, and serve to no manner of purpose.*

20.

DILEMMA. In short, if there were external bodies, it is impossible we should ever come to know it; and if there were not, we might have the very same reasons to think there were that we have now. Suppose--what no one can deny possible--an intelligence without the help of external bodies, to be affected with the same train of sensations or ideas that you are, imprinted in the same order and with like vividness in his mind. I ask whether that intelligence has not all the reason to believe the existence of corporeal substances, represented by his ideas, and exciting them in his mind, that you can possibly have for believing the same thing? Of this there can be no question--which one consideration were enough to make any reasonable person suspect the strength of whatever arguments be may think himself to have, for the existence of bodies without the mind.

21.

Were it necessary to add any further proof against the existence of matter after what has been said, I could instance several of those errors and difficulties (not to mention impieties) which have sprung from that tenet.

It has occasioned numberless controversies and disputes in philosophy, and not a few of far greater moment in religion. But I shall not enter into the detail of them in this place, as well because I think arguments *a posteriori* are unnecessary for confirming what has been, if I mistake not, sufficiently demonstrated *a priori*, as because I shall hereafter find occasion to speak somewhat of them.

22.

I am afraid I have given cause to think I am needlessly prolix in handling this subject. For, to what purpose is it to dilate on that which may be demonstrated with the utmost evidence in a line or two, to any one that is capable of the least reflection? It is but looking into your own thoughts, and so trying whether you can conceive it possible for a sound, or figure, or motion, or color to exist without the mind or unperceived. This easy trial may perhaps make you see that what you contend for is a downright contradiction. Insomuch that I am content to put the whole upon this issue: If you can but *conceive* it possible for one extended movable substance, or, in general, for any one idea, or anything like an idea, to exist otherwise than in a mind perceiving it, I shall readily give up the cause. And, as for all that compages of external bodies you contend for, I shall grant you its existence, though: (1.) *you cannot either give me any reason why you believe it* exists, or (2.) *assign any use to it when it is supposed to exist.* I say, the bare possibility of your opinions being true shall pass for an argument that it is so.

23.

But, say you, surely there is nothing easier than for me to imagine trees, for instance, in a park, or books existing in a closet, and nobody by to perceive them. I answer, you may so, there is no difficulty in it; but what is all this, I beseech you, more than framing in your mind certain ideas which you call "books" and "trees," and the same time omitting to frame the idea of any one that may perceive them? *But do not you yourself perceive or think of them all the while?* This therefore is nothing to the purpose; it only shows you have the power of imagining or forming ideas in your mind: but it does not show that you can conceive it possible the objects of your thought may exist without the mind. To make out this, *it is necessary that you conceive them existing unconceived or unthought of, which is a manifest repugnancy.* When we do our utmost to conceive the existence of external bodies, we are all the while only contemplating our own ideas. But the mind taking no notice of itself, is deluded to think it can and does conceive bodies existing unthought of or without the mind, though at the same time they are apprehended by or exist in itself. A little attention will discover to any one the truth and evidence of what is here said, and make it unnecessary to insist on any other proofs against the existence of material substance.

24.

THE ABSOLUTE EXISTENCE OF UNTHINKING THINGS ARE WORDS WITHOUT A MEANING.
It is very obvious, upon the least inquiry into our thoughts, to know whether it is possible for us to understand what is meant by the absolute existence of sensible objects in themselves, or without the mind. To me it is evident those words mark out either a direct contradiction, or else nothing at all. And to convince others of this, I know no readier or fairer way than to entreat they would calmly attend to their own thoughts; and if by this attention the emptiness or repugnancy of those expressions does appear, surely nothing more is requisite for the conviction. It is on this therefore that I insist, to wit, that the *absolute* existence of unthinking things are words without a meaning, or which include a contradiction. This is what I repeat and inculcate, and earnestly recommend to the attentive thoughts of the reader.

[Treatise Concerning the Principles of Human Knowledge *(1710).]*

CHAPTER EIGHT

Hume on the Limits of Human Knowledge and the Argument from Design

David Hume (1711–1776)

SELECTED READINGS

▶ "Of Personal Identity" from *A Treatise of Human Nature*—David Hume

▶ *An Enquiry Concerning Human Understanding*—David Hume

▶ "The Watch and the Watch-Maker" from *Natural Theology*—William Paley

▶ *Dialogues Concerning Natural Religion*—David Hume

"Of Personal Identity" from *A Treatise of Human Nature*

David Hume
(Edited by Joseph R. Kirkland)

BOOK ONE: OF THE UNDERSTANDING

. . .

PART IV: OF THE SKEPTICAL AND OTHER SYSTEMS OF PHILOSOPHY

. . .

SECTION VI: OF PERSONAL IDENTITY

There are some philosophers who imagine we are every moment intimately conscious of what we call our "self"; that we feel its existence and its continuance in existence and are certain, beyond the evidence of a demonstration, both of its perfect identity and simplicity. The strongest sensation, the most violent passion, say they, instead of distracting us from this view, only fix it the more intensely, and make us consider their influence on self either by their pain or pleasure. To attempt a farther proof of this were to weaken its evidence; since no proof can be derived from any fact, of which we are so intimately conscious; nor is there anything, of which we can be certain, if we doubt of this.

Unluckily all these positive assertions are contrary to that very experience which is pleaded for them, nor have we any idea of self, after the manner it is here explained. For from what impression could this idea be derived? This question is impossible to answer without a manifest contradiction and absurdity; and yet it is a question which must necessarily be answered if we would have the idea of "self" pass for clear and intelligible. It must be some one impression that gives rise to every real idea. But "self" or "person" is not any one impression, but that to which our several impressions and ideas are supposed to have a reference. If any impression gives rise to the idea of "self," that impression must continue invariably the same through the whole course of our lives, since "self" is supposed to exist after that manner. But there is no impression constant and invariable. Pain and pleasure, grief and joy, passions and sensations succeed each other, and never all exist at the same time. It cannot, therefore, be from any of these impressions, or from any other, that the idea of self is derived; and consequently there is no such idea.

But farther, what must become of all our particular perceptions upon this hypothesis? All these are different, and distinguishable, and separable from each other, and may be separately considered, and may exist separately, and have no Deed of tiny thing to support their existence. After what manner, therefore, do they belong to self; and how are they connected with it? For my part, when I enter most intimately into what I call myself, I always stumble on some particular perception or other, of heat or cold, light or shade, love or hatred, pain or pleasure. I never can catch myself at any time without a perception, and never can observe anything but the perception. When my perceptions are removed for any time, as by sound sleep; so long am I insensible of myself, and may truly be said not to exist. And were all my perceptions removed by death, and could I neither think, nor feel, nor see, nor love, nor hate after the dissolution of my body, I should be entirely annihilated, nor do I conceive what is farther requisite to make me a perfect non-entity. If anyone, upon serious and unprejudiced reflection thinks he has a different notion of himself, I must confess I can reason no longer with him. All I can allow him is that he may be in the right as well as I, and that we are essentially different in this particular. He may, perhaps, perceive something simple and continued which he calls himself, though I am certain there is no such principle in me.

But setting aside some metaphysicians of this kind, I may venture to affirm of the rest of mankind, that they are nothing but a bundle or collection of different perceptions, which succeed each other with an inconceivable rapidity, and are in a perpetual flux and movement. Our eyes cannot turn in their sockets without varying our perceptions. Our thought is still more variable than our sight; and all our other senses and faculties contribute to this change; nor is there any single power of the soul, which remains unalterably the same, perhaps for one moment. The mind is a kind of theatre, where several perceptions successively make their appearance; pass, re-pass, glide away, and mingle in an infinite variety of postures and situations. There is properly no simplicity in it at one time, nor identity in different; whatever natural tendency we may have to imagine that simplicity and identity. The comparison of the theatre must not mislead us. They are the successive perceptions only, that constitute the mind; nor have we the most distant notion of the place, where these scenes are represented, or of the materials, of which it is composed.

What then gives us so great a tendency to ascribe an identity to these successive perceptions, and to suppose ourselves possessed of an invariable and uninterrupted existence through the whole course of our lives? In order to answer this question, we must distinguish betwixt personal identity, as it regards our thought or imagination, and as it regards our passions or the concern we take in ourselves. The first is our present subject; and to explain it perfectly we must take the matter pretty deep, and account for that identity, which we attribute to plants and animals; there being a great analogy betwixt it, and the identity of a self or person.

We have a distinct idea of an object, that remains invariable and uninterrupted through a supposed variation of time; and this idea we call that of identity or sameness. We have also a distinct idea of several different objects existing in succession, and connected together by a close relation; and this to an accurate view affords as perfect a notion of diversity, as if there was no manner of relation among the objects. But though these two ideas of identity, and a succession of related objects be in themselves perfectly distinct, and even contrary, yet it is certain, that in our common way of thinking they are generally confounded with each other. That action of the imagination, by which we consider the uninterrupted and invariable object, and that by which we reflect on the succession of related objects, are almost the same to the feeling, nor is there much more effort of thought required in the latter case than in the former. The relation facilitates the transition of the mind from one object to another, and renders its passage as smooth as if it contemplated one continued object. This resemblance is the cause of the confusion and mistake, and makes us substitute the notion of identity, instead of that of related objects. However at one instant we may consider the related succession as variable or interrupted, we are sure the next to ascribe to it a perfect identity, and regard it as enviable and uninterrupted. Our propensity to this mistake is so great from the resemblance above-mentioned, that we fall into it before we are aware; and though we incessantly correct ourselves by reflection, and return to a more accurate method of thinking, yet we cannot long sustain our philosophy, or take off this bias from the imagination. Our last resource is to yield to it, and boldly assert that these different related objects are in effect the same, however interrupted and variable. In order to justify to ourselves this absurdity, we often feign some new and unintelligible principle that connects the objects together, and prevents their interruption or variation. Thus we feign the continued existence of the perceptions of our senses, to remove the interruption: and run into the notion of a soul, and self, and substance, to disguise the variation. But we may farther observe, that where we do not give rise to such a fiction, our tendency to confound identity with relation is so great, that we are apt to imagine something unknown and mysterious, connecting the parts, beside their relation; and this I take to be the case with regard to the identity we ascribe to plants and vegetables. And even when this does not take place, we still feel a propensity to confound these ideas, though we are not able fully to satisfy ourselves in that particular, nor find anything invariable and uninterrupted to justify our notion of identity.

Thus the controversy concerning identity is not merely a dispute of words. For when we attribute identity, in an improper sense, to variable or interrupted objects, our mistake is not confined to the expression, but is commonly attended with a fiction, either of something invariable and uninterrupted, or of something mysterious and inexplicable, or at least with a propensity to such fictions. What will suffice to prove this hypothesis to the satisfaction of every fair enquirer, is to show from daily experience and observation, that the objects, which are variable or interrupted, and yet are supposed to continue the same, are such only as consist of a succession of parts, connected together by resemblance, contiguity, or causation. For as such a succession answers evidently to our notion of diversity, it can only be by mistake we ascribe to it an identity; and as the relation of parts, which leads us into this mistake, is really nothing but a quality, which produces an association of ideas, and an easy transition of the imagination from one to another, it can only be from the resemblance, which this act of the mind bears to that, by which we contemplate one continued object, that the error arises. Our chief business, then, must be to prove, that all objects, to which we ascribe identity, without observing their invariableness and uninterruptedness, are such as consist of a succession of related objects.

In order to this, suppose any mass of matter, of which the parts are contiguous and connected, to be placed before us; it is plain we must attribute a perfect identity to this mass, provided all the parts continue uninterruptedly and invariably the same, whatever motion or change of place we may observe either in the whole or in any of the parts. But supposing some very small or inconsiderable part to be added to the mass, or subtracted from it; though this absolutely destroys the identity of the whole, strictly speaking; yet as we seldom think so accurately, we scruple not to pronounce a mass of matter the same, where we find so trivial an alteration. The passage of the thought from the object before the change to the object after it, is so smooth and easy, that we scarce perceive the transition, and are apt to imagine, that it is nothing but a continued survey of the same object.

There is a very remarkable circumstance, that attends this experiment; which is, that though the change of any considerable part in a mass of matter destroys the identity of the whole, let we must measure the greatness of the part, not absolutely, but by its proportion to the whole. The addition or diminution of a mountain would not be sufficient to produce a diversity in a planet: though the change of a very few inches would be able to destroy the identity of some bodies. It will be impossible to account for this, but by reflecting that objects operate upon the mind, and break or interrupt the continuity of its actions not according to their real greatness, but according to their proportion to each other: And therefore, since this interruption makes an object cease to appear the same, it must be the uninterrupted progress of the thought which constitutes the imperfect identity.

This may be confirmed by another phenomenon. A change in any considerable part of a body destroys its identity; but it is remarkable, that where the change is produced gradually and insensibly we are less apt to ascribe to it the same effect. The reason can plainly be no other, than that the mind, in following the successive changes of the body, feels an easy passage from the surveying its condition in one moment to the viewing of it in another, and at no particular time perceives any interruption in its actions. From which continued perception, it ascribes a continued existence and identity to the object.

But whatever precaution we may use in introducing the changes gradually, and making them proportional to the whole, it is certain, that where the changes are at last observed to become considerable, we make a scruple of ascribing identity to such different objects. There is, however, another artifice, by which we may induce the imagination to advance a step

farther; and that is, by producing a reference of the parts to each other, and a combination to some common end or purpose. A ship, of which a considerable part has been changed by frequent reparations, is still considered as the same; nor does the difference of the materials hinder us from ascribing an identity to it. The common end, in which the parts conspire, is the same under all their variations, and affords an easy transition of the imagination from one situation of the body to another.

But this is still more remarkable, when we add a sympathy of parts to their common end, and suppose that they bear to each other, the reciprocal relation of cause and effect in all their actions and operations. This is the case with all animals and vegetables; where not only the several parts have a reference to some general purpose, but also a mutual dependence on, and connection with each other. The effect of so strong a relation is, that though everyone must allow, that in a very few years both vegetables and animals endure a total change, yet we still attribute identity to them, while their form, size, and substance are entirely altered. An oak, that grows from a small plant to a large tree is still the same oak; though there be not one particle of matter, or figure of its parts the same. An infant becomes a man-, and is sometimes fat, sometimes lean, without any change in his identity.

We may also consider the two following phenomena, which are remarkable in their kind. The first is, that though we commonly be able to distinguish pretty exactly betwixt numerical and specific identity, yet it sometimes happens, that we confound them, and in our thinking and reasoning employ the one for the other. Thus a man, who bears a noise, that is frequently interrupted and renewed, says, it is still the same noise; though it is evident the sounds have only a specific identity or resemblance, and there is nothing numerically the same, but the cause, which produced them. In like manner it may be said without breach of the propriety of language, that such a church, which was formerly of brick, fell to ruin, and that the parish rebuilt the same church of free-stone, and according to modern architecture. Here neither the form nor materials are the same, nor is there anything common to the two objects, but their relation to the inhabitants of the parish; and yet this alone is sufficient to make us denominate them the same. But we must observe, that in these cases the first object is in a manner annihilated before the second comes into existence; by which means, we are never presented in any one point of time with the idea of difference and multiplicity: and for that reason are less scrupulous in calling them the same.

Secondly, we may remark, that though in a succession of related objects, it be in a manner requisite, that the change of parts be not sudden nor entire, in order to preserve the identity, yet where the objects are in their nature changeable and inconstant, we admit of a more sudden transition, than would otherwise be consistent with that relation. Thus as the nature of a river consists in the motion and change of parts; though in less than four and twenty hours these be totally altered; this hinders not the river from continuing the same during several ages. What is natural and essential to any thing is, in a manner, expected; and what is expected makes less impression, and appears of less moment, than what is unusual and extraordinary. A considerable change of the former kind seems really less to the imagination, than the most trivial alteration of the latter; and by breaking less the continuity of the thought, has less influence in destroying the identity.

We now proceed to explain the nature of personal identity, which has become so great a question ill philosophy, especially of late years in England, where all the more abstruse sciences are studied with a peculiar ardor and application. And here it is evident, the same method of reasoning must be continued which has so successfully explained the identity of plants, and animals, and ships, and houses, and of all the compounded and changeable productions either of art or nature. The identity, which we ascribe to the mind of man, is only a fictitious one, and of a like kind with that which we ascribe to vegetables and animal bodies. It cannot, therefore, have a different origin, but must proceed from a like operation of the imagination upon like objects.

But lest this argument should not convince the reader; though in my opinion perfectly decisive; let him weigh the following reasoning, which is still closer and more immediate. It is evident, that the identity, which we attribute to the human mind, however perfect we may imagine it to be, is not able to run the several different perceptions into one, and make them lose their characters of distinction and difference, which are essential to them. It is still true, that every distinct perception, which enters into the composition of the mind, is a distinct existence, and is different, and distinguishable, and separable from every other perception, either contemporary or successive. But, as, notwithstanding this distinction and separability, we suppose the whole train of perceptions to be united by identity, a question naturally

arises concerning this relation of identity; whether it be something that really binds our several perceptions together, or only associates their ideas in the imagination. That is, in other words, whether in pronouncing concerning the identity of a person, we observe some real bond among his perceptions, or only feel one among the ideas we form of them. This question we might easily decide, if we would recollect what has been already proud at large, that the understanding never observes any real connection among objects, and that even the union of cause and effect, when strictly examined, resolves itself into a customary association of ideas. For from thence it evidently follows, that identity is nothing really belonging to these different perceptions, and uniting them together; but is merely a quality, which we attribute to them, because of the union of their ideas in the imagination, when we reflect upon them. Now the only qualities, which can give ideas a union in the imagination, are these three relations above-mentioned. There are the uniting principles in the ideal world, and without them every distinct object is separable by the mind, and may be separately considered, and appears not to have any more connection with any other object, than if disjoined by the greatest difference and remoteness. It is, therefore, on some of these three relations of resemblance, contiguity and causation, that identity depends; and as the very essence of these relations consists in their producing an easy transition of ideas; it follows, that our notions of personal identity, proceed entirely from the smooth and uninterrupted progress of the thought along a train of connected ideas, according to the principles above-explained.

The only question, therefore, which remains, is, by what relations this uninterrupted progress of our thought is produced, when we consider the successive existence of a mind or thinking person. And here it is evident we must confine ourselves to resemblance and causation, and must drop contiguity, which has little or no influence in the present case.

To begin with resemblance; suppose we could see clearly into the breast of another, and observe that succession of perceptions, which constitutes his mind or thinking principle, and suppose that he always preserves the memory of a considerable part of past perceptions; it is evident that nothing could more contribute to the bestowing a relation on this succession amidst all its variations. For what is the memory but a faculty, by which we raise up the images of past perceptions? And as an image necessarily resembles its object, must not. The frequent placing of these resembling perceptions in the chain of thought, convey the imagination more easily from one link to another, and make the whole seem like the continuance of one object? In this particular, then, the memory not only discovers the identity, but also contributes to its production, by producing the relation of resemblance among the perceptions. The case is the same whether we consider ourselves or others.

As to causation; we may observe, that the true idea of the human mind, is to consider it as a system of different perceptions or different existences, which are linked together by the relation of cause and effect, and mutually produce, destroy, influence, and modify each other. Our impressions give rise to their correspondent ideas; said these ideas in their turn produce other impressions. One thought chases another, and draws after it a third, by which it is expelled in its turn. In this respect, I cannot compare the soul more properly to anything than to a republic or commonwealth, in which the several members are united by the reciprocal ties of government and subordination, and give rise to other persons, who propagate the same republic in the incessant changes of its parts. And as the same individual republic may not only change its members, but also its laws and constitutions; in like manner the same person may vary his character and disposition, as well as his impressions and ideas, without losing his identity. Whatever changes he endures, his several parts are still connected by the relation of causation. And in this view our identity with regard to the passions serves to corroborate that with regard to the imagination, by the making our distant perceptions influence each other, and by giving us a present concern for our past or future pains or pleasures.

As a memory alone acquaints us with the continuance and extent of this succession of perceptions, it is to be considered, upon that account chiefly, as the source of personal identity. Had we no memory, we never should have any notion of causation, nor consequently of that chain of causes and effects, which constitute our self or person. But having once acquired this notion of causation from the memory, we can extend the same chain of causes, and consequently the identity of car persons beyond our memory, and can comprehend times, and circumstances, and actions, which we have entirely forgot, but suppose in general to have existed. For how few of our past actions are there, of which we have any memory? Who can tell me, for instance, what were his thoughts and actions on the 1st of January 1715, the 11th of March 1719, and the 3rd of August 1733? Or will he affirm, because he has entirely forgot the incidents of

these days, that the present self is not the same person with the self of that time; and by that means overturn all the most established notions of personal identity? In this view, therefore, memory does not so much produce as discover personal identity, by showing us the relation of cause and effect among our different perceptions. It will be incumbent on those, who affirm that memory produces entirely our personal identity, to give a reason why we cm thus extend our identity beyond our memory.

The whole of this doctrine leads us to a conclusion, which is of great importance in the present affair, *viz.* that all the nice and subtle questions concerning personal identity can never possibly be decided, and are to be regarded as grammatical rather than as philosophical difficulties. Identity depends on the relations of ideas; and these relations produce identity, by means of that easy transition they occasion. But as the relations, and the easiness of the transition may diminish by insensible degrees, we have no just standard, by which we can decide any dispute concerning the time, when they acquire or lose a title to the name of identity. All the disputes concerning the identity of connected objects are merely verbal, except so fax as the relation of parts gives rise to some fiction or imaginary principle of union, as we have already observed.

What I have said concerning the first origin and uncertainty of our notion of identity, as applied to the human mind, may be extended with little or no variation to that of simplicity. An object, whose different co-existent parts are bound together by a close relation, operates upon the imagination after much the same manner as one perfectly simple and indivisible and requires not a much greater stretch of thought in order to its conception. From this similarity of operation we attribute a simplicity to it, and feign a principle of union as the support of this simplicity, and the center of all the different parts and qualities of the object.

. . .

SECTION VII. CONCLUSION OF THIS BOOK

But before I launch out into those immense depths of philosophy, which lie before me, I find myself inclined to stop a moment in my present station, and to ponder that voyage, which I have undertaken, and which undoubtedly requires the utmost art and industry to be brought to a happy conclusion. Methinks I am like a man, who having struck on many shoals, and having narrowly escaped shipwreck in passing a small safe landing, has yet the temerity to put out to sea in the same leaky weather-beaten vessel, and even carries his ambition so far as to think of compassing the globe under these disadvantageous circumstances. My memory of past errors and perplexities, makes me diffident for the future. The wretched condition, weakness, and disorder of the faculties, I must employ in my enquiries, increase my apprehensions. And the impossibility of amending or correcting these faculties, reduces me almost to despair, and makes me resolve to perish on the barren rock, on which I am at present, rather than venture myself upon that boundless ocean, which runs out into immensity. This sudden view of my danger strikes me with melancholy; and as it is usual for that passion, above all others, to indulge itself; I cannot forbear feeding my despair, with all those desponding reflections, which the present subject furnishes me with in such abundance.

I am first affrighted and confounded with that forlorn solitude, in which I am placed in my philosophy, and fancy myself some strange uncouth monster, who not being able to mingle and unite in society, has been expelled all human commerce, and left utterly abandoned and disconsolate. Fain would I run into the crowd for shelter and warmth; but cannot prevail with myself to mix with such deformity. I call upon others to join me, in order to make a company apart; but no one will hearken to me. Everyone keeps at a distance, and dreads that storm, which beats upon me from every side. I have exposed myself to the enmity of all metaphysicians, logicians, mathematicians, and even theologians; and can I wonder at the insults I must suffer? I have declared my disapprobation of their systems; and can I be surprised, if they should express a hatred of mine and of my person? When I look abroad, I foresee on every side, dispute, contradiction, anger, calumny and detraction. When I turn my eye inward, I find nothing but doubt and ignorance. All the world conspires to oppose and contradict me; though such is my weakness, that I feel all my opinions loosen and fall of themselves, when unsupported by the approbation of others. Every step I take is with hesitation, and every new reflection makes me dread an error and absurdity in my reasoning.

For with what confidence can I venture upon such bold enterprises, when beside those numberless infirmities peculiar to myself, I find so many which are common to human nature? Can I be sure, that in leaving all established opinions I am following truth; and by what criterion shall I distinguish her, even if fortune should at last guide me on her foot-steps? After the

most accurate and exact of my reasonings, I can give no reason why I should assent to it; and feel nothing but a strong propensity to consider objects strongly in that view, under which they appear to me. Experience is a principle, which instructs me in the several conjunctions of objects for the past. Habit is another principle, which determines me to expect the same for the future; and both of them conspiring to operate upon the imagination, make me form certain ideas in a more intense and lively manner, than others, which are not attended with the same advantages. Without this quality, by which the mind enlivens some ideas beyond others (which seemingly is so trivial, and so little founded on reason) we could never assent to any argument, nor carry our view beyond those few objects, which are present to our senses. Nay, even to these objects we could never attribute any existence, but what was dependent on the senses; and must comprehend them entirely in that succession of perceptions, which constitutes our self or person. Nay farther, even with relation to that succession, we could only admit of those perceptions, which are immediately present to our consciousness, nor could those lively images, with which the memory presents us, be ever received as true pictures of past perceptions. The memory, senses, and understanding are, therefore, all of them founded on the imagination, or the vivacity of our ideas.

No wonder a principle so inconstant and fallacious should lead us into errors, when implicitly followed (as it must be) in all its variations. It is this principle, which makes us reason from causes and effects; and it is the same principle, which convinces us of the continued existence of external objects, when absent from the senses. But though these two operations be equally natural and necessary in the human mind, yet in some circumstances they are directly contrary, nor is it possible for us to reason justly and regularly from causes and effects, and at the same time believe the continued existence of matter. How then shall we adjust those principles together? Which of them shall we prefer? Or in case we prefer neither of them, but successively assent to both, as is usual among philosophers, with what confidence can we afterwards usurp that glorious title, when we thus knowingly embrace a manifest contradiction?

This contradiction would be more excusable, were it compensated by any degree of solidity and satisfaction in the other parts of our reasoning. But the case is quite contrary. When we trace up the human understanding to its first principles, we find it to lead us into such sentiments, as seem to turn into ridicule all our past pains and industry, and to discourage us from future enquiries. Nothing is more curiously enquired after by the mind of man, than the causes of every phenomenon; nor are we content with knowing the immediate causes, but push on our enquiries, till we arrive at the original and ultimate principle. We would not willingly stop before we are acquainted with that energy in the cause, by which it operates on its effect; that tie, which connects them together; and that efficacious quality, on which the tie depends. This is our aim in all our studies and reflections: And how must we be disappointed, when we learn, that this connection, tie, or energy lies merely in ourselves, and is nothing but that determination of the mind, which is acquired by custom, and causes us to make a transition from an object to its usual attendant, and from the impression of one to the lively idea of the other? Such a discovery not only cuts off all hope of ever attaining satisfaction, but even prevents our very wishes; since it appears, that when we say we desire to know the ultimate and operating principle, as something, which resides in the external object, we either contradict ourselves, or talk without a meaning.

This deficiency in our ideas is not, indeed, perceived in common life, nor are we sensible, that in the most usual conjunctions of cause and effect we are as ignorant of the ultimate principle, which binds them together, as in the most unusual and extraordinary. But this proceeds merely from an illusion of the imagination; and the question is, how far we ought to yield to these illusions. This question is very difficult, and reduces us to a very dangerous dilemma, whichever way we answer it. For if we assent to every trivial suggestion of the fancy; beside that these suggestions are often contrary to each other; they lead us into such errors, absurdities, and obscurities, that we must at last become ashamed of our credulity. Nothing is more dangerous to reason than the flights of the imagination, and nothing has been the occasion of more mistakes among philosophers. Men of bright fancies may in this respect be compared to those angels, whom the scripture represents as covering their eyes with their wings. This has already appeared in so many instances, that we may spare ourselves the trouble of enlarging upon it any farther.

But on the other hand, if the consideration of these instances makes us take a resolution to reject all the trivial suggestions of the fancy, and adhere to the understanding, that is, to the general and more established properties of the imagination; even this resolution, if steadily executed, would be dangerous, and attended with the most fatal consequences. For I have already shown, that the understanding, when it acts alone, and according to its most general principles, entirely subverts itself, and leaves not the lowest degree of evidence in any proposition, either in philosophy or common life. We save ourselves from this total skepticism only by means of that singular and seemingly trivial property of the fancy, by which we enter with difficulty into remote views of things, and are not able to accompany them with so sensible an impression, as we do those, which are more easy and natural. Shall we, then, establish it for a general maxim, that no refined or elaborate reasoning is ever to be received? Consider well the consequences of such a principle. By this means you cut off entirely all science and philosophy: You proceed upon one singular quality of the imagination, and by a parity of reason must embrace all of them: And you expressly contradict yourself; since this maxim must be built on the preceding reasoning, which will be allowed to be sufficiently refined and metaphysical. What party, then, shall we choose among these difficulties? If we embrace this principle, and condemn all refined reasoning, we run into the most manifest absurdities. If we reject it in favor of these reasonings, we subvert entirely the human understanding. We have, therefore, no choice left but betwixt a false reason and none at all. For my part, know not what ought to be done in the present case. I can only observe what is commonly done; which is, that this difficulty is seldom or never thought of; and even where it has once been present to the mind, is quickly forgot, and leaves but a small impression behind it. Very refined reflections have little or no influence upon us; and yet we do not, and cannot establish it for a rule, that they ought not to have any influence; which implies a manifest contradiction.

But what have I here said, that reflections very refined and metaphysical have little or no influence upon us? This opinion I can scarce forbear retracting, and condemning from my present feeling and experience. The intense view of these manifold contradictions and imperfections in human reason has so wrought upon me, and heated my brain, that I am ready to reject all belief and reasoning, and can look upon no opinion even as more probable or likely than another. Where am I, or what? From what causes do I derive my existence, and to what condition shall I return? Whose favor shall I court, and whose anger must I dread? What beings surround me? and on whom have, I any influence, or who have any influence on me? I am confounded with all these questions, and begin to fancy myself in the most deplorable condition imaginable, environed with the deepest darkness, and utterly deprived of the use of every member and faculty.

Most fortunately it happens, that since reason is incapable of dispelling these clouds, nature herself suffices to that purpose, and cures me of this philosophical melancholy and delirium, either by relaxing this bent of mind, or by some avocation, and lively impression of my senses, which obliterate all these chimeras. I dine, I play a game of backgammon, I converse, and am merry with my friends; and when after three or four hours' amusement, I would return to these speculations, they appear so cold, and strained, and ridiculous, that I cannot find in my heart to enter into them any farther.

Here then I find myself absolutely and necessarily determined to live, and talk, and act like other people in the common affairs of life. But notwithstanding that my natural propensity, and the course of my animal spirits and passions reduce me to this indolent belief in the general maxims of the world, I still feel such remains of my former disposition, that I am ready to throw all my books and papers into the fire, and resolve never more to renounce the pleasures of life for the sake of reasoning and philosophy. For those are my sentiments in that splenetic humor, which governs me at present. I may, nay I must yield to the current of nature, in submitting to my senses and understanding; and in this blind submission I show most perfectly my skeptical disposition and principles. But does it follow, that I must strive against the current of nature, which leads me to indolence and pleasure; that I must seclude myself, in some measure, from the commerce and society of men, which is so agreeable; and that I must torture my brains with subtleties and sophistries, at the very time that I cannot satisfy myself concerning the reasonableness of so painful an application, nor have any tolerable prospect of arriving by its means at truth and certainty. Under what obligation do I lie of making such an abuse of time? And to what end can it serve either for the service of mankind, or for my own private interest? No: If I must be a fool, as all those who reason or believe anything certainly are, my follies shall at least be natural and agreeable. Where I strive against my inclination, I shall have a good reason for my resistance; and will no more be led a wandering into such dreary solitudes, and rough passages, as I have hitherto met with.

These are the sentiments of my spleen and indolence; and indeed I must confess, that philosophy has nothing to oppose to them, and expects a victory more from the returns of a serious good-humored disposition, than from the force of reason and conviction. In all the incidents of life we ought still to preserve our skepticism. If we believe, that fire warms, or water refreshes, it is only because it costs us too much pains to think otherwise. Nay if we are philosophers, it ought only to be upon skeptical principles, and from an inclination, which we feel to the employing ourselves after that manner. Where reason is lively, and mixes itself with some propensity, it ought to be assented to. Where it does not, it never can have any title to operate upon us.

At the time, therefore, that I am tired with amusement and company, and have indulged a reverie in my chamber, or in a solitary walk by a riverside, I feel my mind all collected within itself, and am naturally inclined to carry my view into all those subjects, about which I have met with so many disputes in the course of my reading and conversation. I cannot forbear having a curiosity to be acquainted with the principles of moral good and evil, the nature and foundation of government, and the cause of those several passions and inclinations, which actuate and govern me. I am uneasy to think I approve of one object, and disapprove of another; call one thing beautiful, and another deformed; decide concerning truth and falsehood, reason and folly, without knowing upon what principles I proceed. I am concerned for the condition of the learned world, which lies under such t deplorable ignorance in all these particulars. I feel an ambition to arise in me of contributing to the instruction of mankind, and of acquiring a name by my inventions and discoveries. These sentiments spring up naturally in my present disposition; and should I endeavor to banish them, by attaching myself to any other business or diversion, I feel I should be a loser in point of pleasure; and this is the origin of my philosophy.

But even suppose this curiosity and ambition should not transport me into speculations without the sphere of common life, it would necessarily happen, that from my very weakness I must be led into such enquiries. It is certain, that superstition is much more bold in its systems and hypotheses than philosophy; and while the latter contents itself with assigning new causes and principles to the phenomena, which appear in the visible world, the former opens a world of its own, and presents us with scenes, and beings, and objects, which are altogether new. Since therefore it is almost impossible for the mind of man to rest, like those of beasts, in that narrow circle of objects, which are the subject of daily conversation and action, we ought only to deliberate concerning the choice of our guide, and ought to prefer that which is safest and most agreeable. And in this respect I make bold to recommend philosophy, and shall not scruple to give it the preference to superstition of every kind or denomination. For as superstition arises naturally and easily from the popular opinions of mankind, it seizes more strongly on the mind, and is often able to disturb us in the conduct of our lives and actions. Philosophy on the contrary, if just, can present us only with mild and moderate sentiments; and if false and extravagant, its opinions are merely the objects of a cold and general speculation, and seldom go so far as to interrupt the course of our natural propensities. The CYNICS are an extraordinary instance of philosophers, who from reasonings purely philosophical ran into as great extravagancies of conduct as any monk or dervish that ever was in the world. Generally speaking, the errors in religion are dangerous; those in philosophy only ridiculous.

I am sensible, that these two cases of the strength and weakness of the mind will not comprehend all mankind, and that there are in England, in particular, many honest gentlemen, who being always employed in their domestic affairs, or amusing themselves in common recreations, have carried their thoughts very little beyond those objects, which are every day exposed to their senses. And indeed, of such as these I pretend not to make philosophers, nor do I expect them either to be associates in these researches or auditors of these discoveries. They do well to keep themselves in their present situation; and instead of refining them into philosophers, I wish we could communicate to our founders of systems, a share of this gross earthy mixture, as an ingredient, which they commonly stand much in need of, and which would serve to temper those fiery particles, of which they are composed. While a warm imagination is allowed to enter into philosophy, and hypotheses embraced merely for being specious and agreeable, we can never have any steady principles, nor any sentiments, which will suit with common practice and experience. But were these hypotheses once removed, we might hope to establish a system or set of opinions, which if not true (for that, perhaps, is too much to be hoped for) might at least be satisfactory to the human mind, and

might stand the test of the most critical examination. Nor should we despair of attaining this end, because of the many chimerical systems, which have successively arisen and decayed away among men, would we consider the shortness of that period, wherein these questions have been the subjects of enquiry and reasoning. Two thousand years with such long interruptions, and under such mighty discouragements are a small space of time to give any tolerable perfection to the sciences; and perhaps we are still in too early an age of the world to discover any principles, which will bear the examination of the latest posterity. For my part, my only hope is, that I may contribute a little to the advancement of knowledge, by giving in some particulars a different turn to the speculations of philosophers, and pointing out to them more distinctly those subjects, where alone they can expect assurance and conviction. Human Nature is the only science of man; and yet has been hitherto the most neglected. It will be sufficient for me, if I can bring it a little more into fashion; and the hope of this serves to compose my temper from that spleen, and invigorate it from that indolence, which sometimes prevail upon me. If the reader finds himself in the same easy disposition, let him follow me in my future speculations. If not, let him follow his inclination, and wait the returns of application and good humor. The conduct of a man, who studies philosophy in this careless manner, is more truly skeptical than that of one, who feeling in himself an inclination to it, is yet so overwhelmed with doubts and scruples, as totally to reject it. A true sceptic will be diffident of his philosophical doubts, as well as of his philosophical conviction; and will never refuse any innocent satisfaction, which offers itself, upon account of either of them.

Nor is it only proper we should in general indulge our inclination in the most elaborate philosophical researches, notwithstanding our skeptical principles, but also that we should yield to that propensity, which inclines us to be positive and certain in particular points, according to the light, in which we survey them in any particular instant. It is easier to forbear all examination and enquiry, than to check ourselves in so natural a propensity, and guard against that assurance, which always arises from an exact and full survey of an object. On such an occasion we are apt not only to forget our skepticism, but even our modesty too; and make use of such terms as these, it is evident, it is certain, it is undeniable; which a due deference to the public ought, perhaps, to prevent. I may have fallen into this fault after the example of others; but I here enter a caveat against any Objections, which may be offered on that head; and declare that such expressions were extorted from me by the present view of the object, and imply no dogmatic spirit, nor conceited idea of my own judgment, which are sentiments that I am sensible can become no body, and a skeptic still less than any other.

[A Treatise of Human Nature. (Chicago: Open Court Pub. Co., 1921).*]*

An Enquiry Concerning Human Understanding

David Hume

(Edited by Joseph R. Kirkland)

SECTION II: OF THE ORIGIN OF IDEAS

…

11.

Everyone will readily allow that there is a considerable difference between the perceptions of the mind, [as] when a man feels the pain of excessive heat or the pleasure of moderate warmth, and when he afterwards recalls to his memory this sensation, or anticipates it by his imagination. These faculties may mimic or copy the perceptions of the senses, but they never can entirely reach the force and vivacity of the original sentiment. The utmost we say of them, even when they operate with greatest vigor, is, that they represent their object in so lively a manner, that we could *almost* say we feel or see it: But, except the mind be disordered by disease or madness, they never can arrive at such a pitch of vivacity, as to render these perceptions altogether undistinguishable. All the colors of poetry, however splendid, can never paint natural objects in such a manner as to make the description be taken for a real landscape. The most lively thought is still inferior to the dullest sensation.

We may observe a like distinction to run through all the other perceptions of the mind. A man in a fit of anger is actuated in a very different manner from one who only thinks of that emotion. If you tell me, that any person is in love, I easily understand your meaning, and form a just conception of his situation; but never can mistake that conception for the real disorders and agitations of the passion. When we reflect on our past sentiments and affections, our thought is a faithful mirror, and copies its objects truly; but the colors which it employs are faint and dull, in comparison of those in which our original perceptions were clothed. It requires no nice discernment or metaphysical head to mark the distinction between them.

12.

Here therefore we may divide all the perceptions of the mind into two classes or species, which are distinguished by their different degrees of force and vivacity. The less forcible and lively are commonly denominated *Thoughts* or *Ideas*. The other species want a name in our language, and in most others; I suppose, because it was not requisite for any, but philosophical purposes, to rank them under a general term or appellation. Let us, therefore, use a little freedom, and call them *Impressions*; employing that word in a sense somewhat different from the usual. By the term *impression*, then, I mean all our more lively perceptions, when we hear, or see, or feel, or love, or hate, or desire, or will. And impressions are distinguished from ideas, which are the less lively perceptions, of which we are conscious, when we reflect on any of those sensations or movements above mentioned.

13.

Nothing, at first view, may seem more unbounded than the thought of man, which not only escapes all human power and authority, but is not even restrained within the limits of nature and reality. To form monsters, and join incongruous shapes and appearances, costs the imagination no more trouble than to conceive the most natural and familiar objects. And while the body is confined to one planet, along which it creeps with pain and difficulty; the thought can in an instant transport us into the most distant regions of the universe; or even beyond the universe, into the unbounded chaos, where nature is supposed to lie in total confusion. What never was seen, or heard of, may yet be conceived; nor is anything beyond the power of thought, except what implies an absolute contradiction.

But though our thought seems to possess this unbounded liberty, we shall find, upon a nearer examination, that it is really confined within very narrow limits, and that all this creative power of the mind amounts to no more than the faculty of compounding, transposing, augmenting, or diminishing the materials afforded us by the senses and experience. When we think of a golden mountain, we only join two consistent ideas, *gold*, and *mountain*, with which we were formerly acquainted. A virtuous horse we can conceive; because, from our own feeling, we can conceive virtue; and this we may unite to the figure and shape of a horse, which is an animal familiar to us. In short, all the materials of thinking are derived either from our outward or inward sentiment: the mixture and composition of these belongs alone to the mind and will. Or, to express myself in philosophical language, all our ideas or more feeble perceptions are copies of our impressions or more lively ones.

14.

To prove this, the . . . following [argument] will, I hope, be sufficient. First, when we analyze our thoughts or ideas, however compounded or sublime, we always find that they resolve themselves into such simple ideas as were copied from a precedent feeling or sentiment. Even those ideas, which, at first view, seem the most wide of this origin, are found, upon a nearer scrutiny, to be derived from it. The idea of God, as meaning an infinitely intelligent, wise, and good Being, arises from reflecting on the operations of our own mind, and augmenting, without limit, those qualities of goodness and wisdom. We may prosecute this enquiry to what length we please; where we shall always find, that every idea which we examine is copied from a similar impression. Those who would assert that this position is not universally true nor without exception, have only one, and that an easy method of refuting it; by producing that idea, which, in their opinion, is not derived from this source. It will then be incumbent on us, if we would maintain our doctrine, to produce the impression, or lively perception, which corresponds to it. . . .

17.

Here, therefore, is a proposition, which not only seems, in itself, simple and intelligible; but, if a proper use were made of it, might render every dispute equally intelligible and banish all that jargon which has so long taken possession of metaphysical reasonings, and drawn disgrace upon them. All ideas, especially abstract ones, are naturally faint and obscure: the mind has but a slender hold of them: they are apt to be confounded with other resembling ideas; and when we have often employed any term, though without a distinct meaning, we are apt to imagine it has a determinate idea annexed to it. On the contrary, all impressions, that is, all sensations, either outward or inward, are strong and vivid: the limits between them are more exactly determined: nor is it easy to fall into any error or mistake with regard to them. When we entertain, therefore, any suspicion that a philosophical term is employed without any meaning or idea (as is but too frequent), we need but enquire, *from what impression is that supposed idea*

derived? And if it be impossible to assign any, this will serve to confirm our suspicion. By bringing ideas into so clear a light we may reasonably hope to remove all dispute which may arise concerning their nature and reality.

SECTION III: OF THE ASSOCIATION OF IDEAS

18.

It is evident that there is a principle of connection between the different thoughts or ideas of the mind, and that, in their appearance to the memory or imagination, they introduce each other with a certain degree of method and regularity. In our more serious thinking or discourse this is so observable that any particular thought, which breaks in upon the regular tract or chain of ideas, is immediately remarked and rejected. And even in our wildest and most wandering reveries, nay in our very dreams, we shall find, if we reflect, that the imagination ran not altogether at adventures, but that there was still a connection upheld among the different ideas, which succeeded each other. Were the loosest and freest conversation to be transcribed, there would immediately be observed something which connected it in all its transitions. Or where this is wanting, the person who broke the thread of discourse might still inform you, that there had secretly revolved in his mind a succession of thought, which had gradually led him from the subject of conversation. Among different languages, even where we cannot suspect the least connection or communication, it is found, that the words, expressive of ideas, the most compounded, do yet nearly correspond to each other: a certain proof that the simple ideas, comprehended in the compound ones, were bound together by some universal principle, which had an equal influence on all mankind.

19.

Though it be too obvious to escape observation, that different ideas are connected together; I do not find that any philosopher has attempted to enumerate or class all the principles of association; a subject, however, that seems worthy of curiosity. To me, there appear to be only three principles of connection among ideas, namely, *Resemblance*, *Contiguity* in time or place, and *Cause or Effect*.

That these principles serve to connect ideas will not, I believe, be much doubted. A picture naturally leads our thoughts to the original (i.e., resemblance); the mention of one apartment in a building naturally introduces an enquiry or discourse concerning the others (i.e., contiguity); and if we think of a wound, we can scarcely forbear reflecting on the pain which follows it (i.e., cause or effect). But that this enumeration is complete, and that there are no other principles of association except these, may be difficult to prove to the satisfaction of the reader, or even to a man's own satisfaction. All we can do, in such cases, is to run over several instances, and examine carefully the principle which binds the different thoughts to each other, never stopping till we render the principle as general as possible. The more instances we examine, and the more care we employ, the more assurance shall we acquire, that the enumeration, which we form from the whole, is complete and entire. . . .

SECTION IV: SKEPTICAL DOUBTS CONCERNING THE OPERATIONS OF THE UNDERSTANDING

20.

All the objects of human reason or enquiry may naturally be divided into two kinds, to wit, *Relations of Ideas*, and *Matters of Fact*. Of the first kind are the sciences of Geometry, Algebra, and Arithmetic; and in short, every affirmation which is either intuitively or demonstratively certain. That the square of the hypotenuse is equal to the square of the two sides, is a proposition which expresses a relation between these figures. That three times five is equal to the half of thirty, expresses a relation between these numbers.

Propositions of this kind are discoverable by the mere operation of thought, without dependence on what is anywhere existent in the universe. Though there never were a circle or triangle in nature, the truths demonstrated by Euclid would forever retain their certainty and evidence.

21.

Matters of fact, which are the second objects of human reason, are not ascertained in the same manner; nor is our evidence of their truth, however great, of a like nature with the foregoing. The contrary of every matter of fact is still possible; because it can never imply a contradiction, and is conceived by the mind with the same facility and distinctness, as if ever so conformable to reality. That the sun will not rise tomorrow is no less intelligible a proposition, and implies no more

contradiction than the affirmation, that it will rise. We should in vain, therefore, attempt to demonstrate its falsehood. Were it demonstratively false, it would imply a contradiction, and could never be distinctly conceived by the mind.

It may, therefore, be a subject worthy of curiosity, to enquire what is the nature of that evidence which assures us of any real existence and matter of fact, beyond the present testimony of our senses, or the records of our memory. This part of philosophy, it is observable, has been little cultivated, either by the ancients or moderns; and therefore our doubts and errors, in the prosecution of so important an enquiry, may be the more excusable; while we march through such difficult paths without any guide or direction. They may even prove useful, by exciting curiosity, and destroying that implicit faith and security, which is the bane of all reasoning and free enquiry. The discovery of defects in the common philosophy, if any such there be, will not, I presume, be a discouragement, but rather an incitement, as is usual, to attempt something more full and satisfactory than has yet been proposed to the public.

22.

All reasonings concerning matter of fact seem to be founded on the relation of Cause and Effect. By means of that relation alone we can go beyond the evidence of our memory and senses. If you were to ask a man, why he believes any matter of fact, which is absent; for instance, that his friend is in the country, or in France; he would give you a reason; and this reason would be some other fact; as a letter received from him, or the knowledge of his former resolutions and promises. A man finding a watch or any other machine in a desert island, would conclude that there had once been men in that island. All our reasonings concerning fact are of the same nature. And here it is constantly supposed that there is a connection between the present fact and that which is inferred from it. Were there nothing to bind them together, the inference would be entirely precarious. The hearing of an articulate voice and rational discourse in the dark assures us of the presence of some person: Why? Because these are the effects of the human make and fabric, and closely connected with it. If we anatomize all the other reasonings of this nature, we shall find that they are founded on the relation of cause and effect, and that this relation is either near or remote, direct or collateral. Heat and light are collateral effects of fire, and the one effect may justly be inferred from the other.

23.

If we would satisfy ourselves, therefore, concerning the nature of that evidence, which assures us of matters of fact, we must enquire how we arrive at the knowledge of cause and effect. I shall venture to affirm, as a general proposition, which admits of no exception, that the knowledge of this relation is not, in any instance, attained by reasonings *a priori*; but arises entirely from experience, when we find that any particular objects are constantly conjoined with each other. Let an object be presented to a man of ever so strong natural reason and abilities; if that object be entirely new to him, he will not be able, by the most accurate examination of its sensible qualities, to discover any of its causes or effects. Adam, though his rational faculties be supposed, at the very first, entirely perfect, could not have inferred from the fluidity and transparency of water that it would suffocate him, or from the light and warmth of fire that it would consume him. No object ever discovers, by the qualities which appear to the senses, either the causes which produced it, or the effects which will arise from it; nor can our reason, unassisted by experience, ever draw any inference concerning real existence and matter of fact.

24.

This proposition that causes and effects are discoverable, not by reason but by experience, will readily be admitted with regard to such objects, as we remember to have once been altogether unknown to us; since we must be conscious of the utter inability, which we then lay under, of foretelling what would arise from them. Present two smooth pieces of marble to a man who has no tincture of natural philosophy; he will never discover that they will adhere together in such a manner as to require great force to separate them in a direct line, while they make so small a resistance to a lateral pressure. Such events, as bear little analogy to the common course of nature, are also readily confessed to be known only by experience; nor does any man imagine that the explosion of gunpowder, or the attraction of a loadstone, could ever be discovered by arguments *a priori*. In like manner, when an effect is supposed to depend upon an intricate machinery or secret structure of parts, we make no difficulty in attributing all our knowledge of it to experience. Who will assert that he can give the ultimate reason, why milk or bread is proper nourishment for a man, not for a lion or a tiger?

But the same truth may not appear, at first sight, to have the same evidence with regard to events, which have become familiar to us from our first appearance in the world, which bear a close analogy to the whole course of nature, and which are supposed to depend on the simple qualities of objects, without any secret structure of parts. We are apt to imagine that we could discover these effects by the mere operation of our reason, without experience. We fancy, that were we brought on a sudden into this world, we could at first have inferred that one billiard-ball would communicate motion to another upon impulse; and that we needed not to have waited for the event, in order to pronounce with certainty concerning it. Such is the influence of custom, that, where it is strongest, it not only covers our natural ignorance, but even conceals itself, and seems not to take place, merely because it is found in the highest degree.

25.

But to convince us that all the laws of nature, and all the operations of bodies without exception, are known only by experience, the following reflections may, perhaps, suffice. Were any object presented to us, and were we required to pronounce concerning the effect, which will result from it, without consulting past observation; after what manner, I beseech you, must the mind proceed in this operation? It must invent or imagine some event, which it ascribes to the object as its effect; and it is plain that this invention must be entirely arbitrary. The mind can never possibly find the effect in the supposed cause, by the most accurate scrutiny and examination. For the effect is totally different from the cause, and consequently can never be discovered in it. Motion in the second Billiard-ball is a quite distinct event from motion in the first; nor is there anything in the one to suggest the smallest hint of the other. A stone or piece of metal raised into the air, and left without any support, immediately falls: but to consider the matter _a priori_, is there anything we discover in this situation which can beget the idea of a downward, rather than an upward, or any other motion, in the stone or metal? And as the first imagination or invention of a particular effect, in all natural operations, is arbitrary, where we consult not experience; so must we also esteem the supposed tie or connection between the cause and effect, which binds them together, and renders it impossible that any other effect could result from the operation of that cause. When I see, for instance, a Billiard-ball moving in a straight line towards another; even suppose motion in the second ball should by accident be suggested to me, as the result of their contact or impulse; may I not conceive, that a hundred different events might as well follow from that cause?

May not both these balls remain at absolute rest? May not the first ball return in a straight line, or leap off from the second in any line or direction? All these suppositions are consistent and conceivable. Why then should we give the preference to one, which is no more consistent or conceivable than the rest? All our reasonings *a priori* will never be able to show us any foundation for this preference.

In a word, then, every effect is a distinct event from its cause. It could not, therefore, be discovered in the cause, and the first invention or conception of it, *a priori*, must be entirely arbitrary.

And even after it is suggested, the conjunction of it with the cause must appear equally arbitrary; since there are always many other effects, which, to reason, must seem fully as consistent and natural. In vain, therefore, should we pretend to determine any single event, or infer any cause or effect, without the assistance of observation and experience.

26.

Hence we may discover the reason why no philosopher, who is rational and modest, has ever pretended to assign the ultimate cause of any natural operation, or to show distinctly the action of that power, which produces any single effect in the universe. It is confessed, that the utmost effort of human reason is to reduce the principles, productive of natural phenomena, to a greater simplicity, and to resolve the many particular effects into a few general causes, by means of reasonings from analogy, experience, and observation. But as to the causes of these general causes, we should in vain attempt their discovery; nor shall we ever be able to satisfy ourselves, by any particular explication of them. These ultimate springs and principles are totally shut up from human curiosity and enquiry. Elasticity, gravity, cohesion of parts, communication of motion by impulse; these are probably the ultimate causes and principles which we shall ever discover in nature; and we may esteem ourselves sufficiently happy, if, by accurate enquiry and reasoning, we can trace up the particular phenomena to, or near to, these general principles. The most perfect philosophy of the natural kind only staves off our ignorance a little longer: as perhaps the most perfect philosophy of the moral or metaphysical kind serves only to discover larger portions of it. Thus the observation of human blindness and weakness is the result of all philosophy, and meets us at every turn, in spite of our endeavors to elude or avoid it.

27.

Nor is geometry, when taken into the assistance of natural philosophy, ever able to remedy this defect, or lead us into the knowledge of ultimate causes, by all that accuracy of reasoning for which it is so justly celebrated. Every part of mixed mathematics proceeds upon the supposition that certain laws are established by nature in her operations; and abstract reasonings are employed, either to assist experience in the discovery of these laws, or to determine their influence in particular instances, where it depends upon any precise degree of distance and quantity. Thus, it is a law of motion, discovered by experience, that the moment or force of any body in motion is in the compound ratio or proportion of its solid contents and its velocity; and consequently, that a small force may remove the greatest obstacle or raise the greatest weight, if, by any contrivance or machinery, we can increase the velocity of that force, so as to make it an overmatch for its antagonist. Geometry assists us in the application of this law, by giving us the just dimensions of all the parts and figures which can enter into any species of machine; but still the discovery of the law itself is owing merely to experience, and all the abstract reasonings in the world could never lead us one step towards the knowledge of it. When we reason *a priori*, and consider merely any object or cause, as it appears to the mind, independent of all observation, it never could suggest to us the notion of any distinct object, such as its effect; much less, show us the inseparable and inviolable connection between them. A man must be very sagacious who could discover by reasoning that crystal is the effect of heat, and ice of cold, without being previously acquainted with the operation of these qualities.

28.

But we have not yet attained any tolerable satisfaction with regard to the question first proposed. Each solution still gives rise to a new question as difficult as the foregoing, and leads us on to farther inquiries. When it is asked: "What is the nature of all our reasonings concerning matter of fact?" the proper answer seems to be, that they are founded on the relation of cause and effect. When again it is asked: "What is the foundation of all our reasonings and conclusions concerning that relation?" it may be replied in one word, Experience. But if we still carry on our sifting humor, and ask: "What is the foundation of all conclusions from experience?" this implies a new question, which may be of more difficult solution and explication. Philosophers, that give themselves airs of superior wisdom and sufficiency, have a hard task when they encounter persons of inquisitive dispositions, who push them from every corner to which they retreat, and who are sure at last to bring them to some dangerous dilemma. The best expedient to prevent this confusion, is to be modest in our pretensions; and even to discover the difficulty ourselves before it is objected to us. By this means, we may make a kind of merit of our very ignorance.

I shall content myself, in this section, with an easy task, and shall pretend only to give a negative answer to the question here proposed. I say then, that, even after we have experience of the operations of cause and effect, our conclusions from that experience are *not* founded on reasoning, or any process of the understanding. This answer we must endeavor both to explain and to defend.

29.

It must certainly be allowed, that nature has kept us at a great distance from all her secrets, and has afforded us only the knowledge of a few superficial qualities of objects; while she conceals from us those powers and principles on which the influence of those objects entirely depends. Our senses inform us of the color, weight, and consistence of bread; but neither sense nor reason can ever inform us of those qualities which fit it for the nourishment and support of a human body.

Sight or feeling conveys an idea of the actual motion of bodies; but as to that wonderful force or power, which would carry on a moving body forever in a continued change of place, and which bodies never lose but by communicating it to others; of this we cannot form the most distant conception. But notwithstanding this ignorance of natural powers and principles, we always presume, when we see like sensible qualities, that they have like secret powers, and expect that effects, similar to those which we have experienced, will follow from them. If a body of like color and consistence with that bread, which we have formerly eat, be presented to us, we make no scruple of repeating the experiment, and foresee, with certainty, like nourishment and support. Now this is a process of the mind or thought, of which I would willingly know the foundation. It is allowed on all hands that there is no known connection between the sensible qualities and the secret powers; and consequently, that the mind is not led to form such a conclusion concerning their constant and regular conjunction, by anything which

it knows of their nature. As to past *experience*, it can be allowed to give *direct* and *certain* information of those precise objects only, and that precise period of time, which fell under its cognizance: but why this experience should be extended to future times, and to other objects, which for aught we know, may be only in appearance similar; this is the main question on which I would insist. The bread, which I formerly eat, nourished me; that is, a body of such sensible qualities was, at that time, endued with such secret powers: but does it follow, that other bread must also nourish me at another time, and that like sensible qualities must always be attended with like secret powers? The consequence seems nowise necessary. At least, it must be acknowledged that there is here a consequence drawn by the mind; that there is a certain step taken; a process of thought, and an inference, which wants to be explained. These two propositions are far from being the same: "I have found that such an object has always been attended with such an effect," and "I foresee, that other objects, which are, in appearance, similar, will be attended with similar effects." I shall allow, if you please, that the one proposition may justly be inferred from the other: I know, in fact, that it always is inferred. But if you insist that the inference is made by a chain of reasoning, I desire you to produce that reasoning. The connection between these propositions is not intuitive.

There is required a medium, which may enable the mind to draw such an inference, if indeed it be drawn by reasoning and argument. What that medium is, I must confess, passes my comprehension; and it is incumbent on those to produce it, who assert that it really exists, and is the origin of all our conclusions concerning matter of fact.

30.

This negative argument must certainly, in process of time, become altogether convincing, if many penetrating and able philosophers shall turn their enquiries this way and no one be ever able to discover any connecting proposition or intermediate step, which supports the understanding in this conclusion. But as the question is yet new, every reader may not trust so far to his own penetration, as to conclude, because an argument escapes his enquiry, that therefore it does not really exist. For this reason it may be requisite to venture upon a more difficult task; and enumerating all the branches of human knowledge, endeavor to show that none of them can afford such an argument.

All reasonings may be divided into two kinds, namely, demonstrative reasoning, or that concerning relations of ideas, and moral reasoning, or that concerning matter of fact and existence. That there are no demonstrative arguments in the case seems evident; since it implies no contradiction that the course of nature may change, and that an object, seemingly like those which we have experienced, may be attended with different or contrary effects. May I not clearly and distinctly conceive that a body, falling from the clouds, and which, in all other respects, resembles snow, has yet the taste of salt or feeling of fire? Is there any more intelligible proposition than to affirm, that all the trees will flourish in December and January, and decay in May and June? Now whatever is intelligible, and can be distinctly conceived, implies no contradiction, and can never be proved false by any demonstrative argument or abstract reasoning *a priori*.

If we be, therefore, engaged by arguments to put trust in past experience, and make it the standard of our future judgment, these arguments must be probable only, or such as regard matter of fact and real existence, according to the division above mentioned. But that there is no argument of this kind, must appear, if our explication of that species of reasoning be admitted as solid and satisfactory. We have said that all arguments concerning existence are founded on the relation of cause and effect; that our knowledge of that relation is derived entirely from experience; and that all our experimental conclusions proceed upon the supposition that the future will be conformable to the past. To endeavor, therefore, the proof of this last supposition by probable arguments, or arguments regarding existence, must be evidently going in a circle, and taking that for granted, which is the very point in question.

31.

In reality, all arguments from experience are founded on the similarity which we discover among natural objects, and by which we are induced to expect effects similar to those which we have found to follow from such objects. And though none but a fool or madman will ever pretend to dispute the authority of experience, or to reject that great guide of human life, it may surely be allowed a philosopher to have so much curiosity at least as to examine the principle of human nature, which gives this mighty authority to experience, and makes us draw advantage from that similarity which nature has placed among different objects. From causes which appear *similar* we expect similar effects.

This is the sum of all our experimental conclusions. Now it seems evident that, if this conclusion were formed by reason, it would be as perfect at first, and upon one instance, as after ever so long a course of experience. But the case is far otherwise. Nothing so like as eggs; yet no one, on account of this appearing similarity, expects the same taste and relish in all of them. It is only after a long course of uniform experiments in any kind, that we attain a firm reliance and security with regard to a particular event. Now where is that process of reasoning which, from one instance, draws a conclusion, so different from that which it infers from a hundred instances that are nowise different from that single one? This question I propose as much for the sake of information, as with an intention of raising difficulties. I cannot find, I cannot imagine any such reasoning. But I keep my mind still open to instruction, if any one will vouchsafe to bestow it on me.

32.

Should it be said that, from a number of uniform experiments, we *infer* a connection between the sensible qualities and the secret powers; this, I must confess, seems the same difficulty, couched in different terms. The question still recurs, on what process of argument this *inference* is founded? Where is the medium, the interposing ideas, which join propositions so very wide of each other? It is confessed that the color, consistence, and other sensible qualities of bread appear not, of themselves, to have any connection with the secret powers of nourishment and support. For otherwise we could infer these secret powers from the first appearance of these sensible qualities, without the aid of experience; contrary to the sentiment of all philosophers, and contrary to plain matter of fact. Here, then, is our natural state of ignorance with regard to the powers and influence of all objects. How is this remedied by experience? It only shows us a number of uniform effects, resulting from certain objects, and teaches us that those particular objects, at that particular time, were endowed with such powers and forces. When a new object, endowed with similar sensible qualities, is produced, we expect similar powers and forces, and look for a like effect. From a body of like color and consistence with bread we expect like nourishment and support. But this surely is a step or progress of the mind, which wants to be explained. When a man says: "I have found, in all past instances, such sensible qualities conjoined with such secret powers," and when he says: "Similar sensible qualities will always be conjoined with similar secret powers," he is not guilty of a tautology, nor are these propositions in any respect the same. You say that the one proposition is an inference from the other. But you must confess that the inference is not intuitive; neither is it demonstrative: Of what nature is it, then? To say it is experimental, is begging the question. For all inferences from experience suppose, as their foundation, that the future will resemble the past, and that similar powers will be conjoined with similar sensible qualities. If there be any suspicion that the course of nature may change, and that the past may be no rule for the future, all experience becomes useless, and can give rise to no inference or conclusion. It is impossible, therefore, that any arguments from experience can prove this resemblance of the past to the future; since all these arguments are founded on the supposition of that resemblance. Let the course of things be allowed hitherto ever so regular; that alone, without some new argument or inference, proves not that, for the future, it will continue so. In vain do you pretend to have learned the nature of bodies from your past experience. Their secret nature, and consequently all their effects and influence, may change, without any change in their sensible qualities.

This happens sometimes, and with regard to some objects: Why may it not happen always, and with regard to all objects? What logic, what process of argument secures you against this supposition? My practice, you say, refutes my doubts. But you mistake the purport of my question. As an agent, I am quite satisfied in the point; but as a philosopher, who has some share of curiosity, I will not say skepticism, I want to learn the foundation of this inference. No reading, no enquiry has yet been able to remove my difficulty, or give me satisfaction in a matter of such importance. Can I do better than propose the difficulty to the public, even though, perhaps, I have small hopes of obtaining a solution? We shall at least, by this means, be sensible of our ignorance, if we do not augment our knowledge.

33.

I must confess that a man is guilty of unpardonable arrogance who concludes, because an argument has escaped his own investigation, that therefore it does not really exist. I must also confess that, though all the learned, for several ages, should have employed themselves in fruitless search upon any subject, it may still, perhaps, be rash to conclude positively that the subject must, therefore, pass all human comprehension. Even

though we examine all the sources of our knowledge, and conclude them unfit for such a subject, there may still remain a suspicion, that the enumeration is not complete, or the examination not accurate. But with regard to the present subject, there are some considerations which seem to remove all this accusation of arrogance or suspicion of mistake.

It is certain that the most ignorant and stupid peasants—nay infants, nay even brute beasts—improve by experience, and learn the qualities of natural objects, by observing the effects which result from them. When a child has felt the sensation of pain from touching the flame of a candle, he will be careful not to put his hand near any candle; but will expect a similar effect from a cause which is similar in its sensible qualities and appearance. If you assert, therefore, that the understanding of the child is led into this conclusion by any process of argument or ratiocination, I may justly require you to produce that argument; nor have you any pretense to refuse so equitable a demand. You cannot say that the argument is abstruse, and may possibly escape your enquiry; since you confess that it is obvious to the capacity of a mere infant. If you hesitate, therefore, a moment, or if, after reflection, you produce any intricate or profound argument, you, in a manner, give up the question, and confess that it is not reasoning which engages us to suppose the past resembling the future, and to expect similar effects from causes which are, to appearance, similar. This is the proposition which I intended to enforce in the present section. If I be right, I pretend not to have made any mighty discovery. And if I be wrong, I must acknowledge myself to be indeed a very backward scholar; since I cannot now discover an argument which, it seems, was perfectly familiar to me long before I was out of my cradle.

SECTION V: SKEPTICAL SOLUTION OF THESE DOUBTS

34.

The passion for philosophy, like that for religion, seems liable to this inconvenience, that, though it aims at the correction of our manners, and extirpation of our vices, it may only serve, by imprudent management, to foster a predominant inclination, and push the mind, with more determined resolution, towards that side which already draws too much, by the bias and propensity of the natural temper. It is certain that, while we aspire to the magnanimous firmness of the philosophic sage, and endeavor to confine our pleasures altogether within our own minds, we may, at last, render our philosophy like that of Epictetus, and other Stoics, only a more refined system of selfishness, and reason ourselves out of all virtue as well as social enjoyment. While we study with attention the vanity of human life, and turn all our thoughts towards the empty and transitory nature of riches and honors, we are, perhaps, all the while flattering our natural indolence, which, hating the bustle of the world, and drudgery of business, seeks a pretense of reason to give itself a full and uncontrolled indulgence. There is, however, one species of philosophy which seems little liable to this inconvenience, and that because it strikes in with no disorderly passion of the human mind, nor can mingle itself with any natural affection or propensity; and that is the Academic or Skeptical philosophy. The academics always talk of doubt and suspense of judgment, of danger in hasty determinations, of confining to very narrow bounds the enquiries of the understanding, and of renouncing all speculations which lie not within the limits of common life and practice. Nothing, therefore, can be more contrary than such a philosophy to the supine indolence of the mind, its rash arrogance, its lofty pretensions, and its superstitious credulity. Every passion is mortified by it, except the love of truth; and that passion never is, nor can be, carried to too high a degree. It is surprising, therefore, that this philosophy, which, in almost every instance, must be harmless and innocent, should be the subject of so much groundless reproach and obloquy. But, perhaps, the very circumstance which renders it so innocent is what chiefly exposes it to the public hatred and resentment. By flattering no irregular passion, it gains few partisans: By opposing so many vices and follies, it raises to itself abundance of enemies, who stigmatize it as libertine profane, and irreligious.

Nor need we fear that this philosophy, while it endeavors to limit our enquiries to common life, should ever undermine the reasonings of common life, and carry its doubts so far as to destroy all action, as well as speculation. Nature will always maintain her rights, and prevail in the end over any abstract reasoning whatsoever. Though we should conclude, for instance, as in the foregoing section, that, in all reasonings from experience, there is a step taken by the mind which is not supported by any argument or process of the understanding; there is no danger that these reasonings, on which almost all knowledge depends, will ever be affected by such a discovery. If the mind be not engaged by argument to make this step, it must be induced by some other principle of equal weight and authority; and that principle will preserve its influence as long as human nature remains the same. What that principle is may well be worth the pains of enquiry.

35.

Suppose a person, though endowed with the strongest faculties of reason and reflection, to be brought on a sudden into this world; he would, indeed, immediately observe a continual succession of objects, and one event following another; but he would not be able to discover anything farther. He would not, at first, by any reasoning, be able to reach the idea of cause and effect; since the particular powers, by which all natural operations are performed, never appear to the senses; nor is it reasonable to conclude, merely because one event, in one instance, precedes another, that therefore the one is the cause, the other the effect. Their conjunction may be arbitrary and casual. There may be no reason to infer the existence of one from the appearance of the other. And in a word, such a person, without more experience, could never employ his conjecture or reasoning concerning any matter of fact, or be assured of anything beyond what was immediately present to his memory and senses.

Suppose, again, that he has acquired more experience, and has lived so long in the world as to have observed familiar objects or events to be constantly conjoined together; what is the consequence of this experience? He immediately infers the existence of one object from the appearance of the other. Yet he has not, by all his experience, acquired any idea or knowledge of the secret power by which the one object produces the other; nor is it, by any process of reasoning, he is engaged to draw this inference. But still he finds himself determined to draw it: And though he should be convinced that his understanding has no part in the operation, he would nevertheless continue in the same course of thinking. There is some other principle which determines him to form such a conclusion.

36.

This principle is *Custom* or *Habit*. For wherever the repetition of any particular act or operation produces a propensity to renew the same act or operation, without being impelled by any reasoning or process of the understanding, we always say, that this propensity is the effect of Custom. By employing that word, we pretend not to have given the ultimate reason of such a propensity. We only point out a principle of human nature, which is universally acknowledged, and which is well known by its effects. Perhaps we can push our enquiries no farther, or pretend to give the cause of this cause; but must rest contented with it as the ultimate principle, which we can assign, of all our conclusions from experience. It is sufficient satisfaction, that we can go so far, without repining at the narrowness of our faculties because they will carry us no farther. And it is certain we here advance a very intelligible proposition at least, if not a true one, when we assert that, after the constant conjunction of two objects—heat and flame, for instance, weight and solidity—we are determined by custom alone to expect the one from the appearance of the other. This hypothesis seems even the only one which explains the difficulty, why we draw, from a thousand instances, an inference which we are not able to draw from one instance, that is, in no respect, different from them. Reason is incapable of any such variation. The conclusions which it draws from considering one circle are the same which it would form upon surveying all the circles in the universe. But no man, having seen only one body move after being impelled by another, could infer that every other body will move after a like impulse. All inferences from experience, therefore, are effects of custom, not of reasoning.

Custom, then, is the great guide of human life. It is that principle alone which renders our experience useful to us, and makes us expect, for the future, a similar train of events with those which have appeared in the past.

Without the influence of custom, we should be entirely ignorant of every matter of fact beyond what is immediately present to the memory and senses. We should never know how to adjust means to ends, or to employ our natural powers in the production of any effect. There would be an end at once of all action, as well as of the chief part of speculation.

37.

But here it may be proper to remark, that though our conclusions from experience carry us beyond our memory and senses, and assure us of matters of fact which happened in the most distant places and most remote ages, yet some fact must always be present to the senses or memory, from which we may first proceed in drawing these conclusions. A man, who should find in a desert country the remains of pompous buildings, would conclude that the country had, in ancient times, been cultivated by civilized inhabitants; but did nothing of this nature occur to him, he could never form

such an inference. We learn the events of former ages from history; but then we must peruse the volumes in which this instruction is contained, and thence carry up our inferences from one testimony to another, till we arrive at the eyewitnesses and spectators of these distant events. In a word, if we proceed not upon some fact, present to the memory or senses, our reasonings would be merely hypothetical; and however the particular links might be connected with each other, the whole chain of inferences would have nothing to support it, nor could we ever, by its means, arrive at the knowledge of any real existence. If I ask why you believe any particular matter of fact, which you relate, you must tell me some reason; and this reason will be some other fact, connected with it. But as you cannot proceed after this manner, in infinitum, you must at last terminate in some fact, which is present to your memory or senses; or must allow that your belief is entirely without foundation.

38.

What, then, is the conclusion of the whole matter? A simple one; though, it must be confessed, pretty remote from the common theories of philosophy. All belief of matter of fact or real existence is derived merely from some object, present to the memory or senses, and a customary conjunction between that and some other object. Or in other words; having found, in many instances, that any two kinds of objects—flame and heat, snow and cold—have always been conjoined together; if flame or snow be presented anew to the senses, the mind is carried by custom to expect heat or cold, and to believe that such a quality does exist, and will discover itself upon a nearer approach. This belief is the necessary result of placing the mind in such circumstances. It is an operation of the soul, when we are so situated, as unavoidable as to feel the passion of love, when we receive benefits; or hatred, when we meet with injuries. All these operations are a species of natural instincts, which no reasoning or process of the thought and understanding is able either to produce or to prevent.

At this point, it would be very allowable for us to stop our philosophical researches. In most questions we can never make a single step farther; and in all questions we must terminate here at last, after our most restless and curious enquiries. But still our curiosity will be pardonable, perhaps commendable, if it carry us on to still farther researches, and make us examine more accurately the nature of this belief, and of the customary conjunction, whence it is derived. By this means we may meet with some explications and analogies that will give satisfaction; at least to such as love the abstract sciences, and can be entertained with speculations, which, however accurate, may still retain a degree of doubt and uncertainty. As to readers of a different taste; the remaining part of this section is not calculated for them, and the following enquiries may well be understood, though it be neglected.

39.

Nothing is more free than the imagination of man; and though it cannot exceed that original stock of ideas furnished by the internal and external senses, it has unlimited power of mixing, compounding, separating, and dividing these ideas, in all the varieties of fiction and vision. It can feign a train of events, with all the appearance of reality, ascribe to them a particular time and place, conceive them as existent, and paint them out to itself with every circumstance, that belongs to any historical fact, which it believes with the greatest certainty. Wherein, therefore, consists the difference between such a fiction and belief? It lies not merely in any peculiar idea, which is annexed to such a conception as commands our assent, and which is wanting to every known fiction. For as the mind has authority over all its ideas, it could voluntarily annex this particular idea to any fiction, and consequently be able to believe whatever it pleases; contrary to what we find by daily experience. We can, in our conception, join the head of a man to the body of a horse; but it is not in our power to believe that such an animal has ever really existed.

It follows, therefore, that the difference between fiction and belief lies in some sentiment or feeling, which is annexed to the latter, not to the former, and which depends not on the will, nor can be commanded at pleasure. It must be excited by nature, like all other sentiments; and must arise from the particular situation, in which the mind is placed at any particular juncture. Whenever any object is presented to the memory or senses, it immediately, by the force of custom, carries the imagination to conceive that object, which is usually conjoined to it; and this conception is attended with a feeling or sentiment, different from the loose reveries of the fancy. In this consists the whole nature of belief. For as there is no matter of fact which we believe so firmly that we cannot conceive the contrary, there would be no difference between the conception assented to and that which is rejected, were it not for some sentiment which distinguishes the one from the other. If I see a billiard-ball moving towards another,

on a smooth table, I can easily conceive it to stop upon contact. This conception implies no contradiction; but still it feels very differently from that conception by which I represent to myself the impulse and the communication of motion from one ball to another.

40.

Were we to attempt a definition of this sentiment, we should, perhaps, find it a very difficult, if not an impossible task; in the same manner as if we should endeavor to define the feeling of cold or passion of anger, to a creature who never had any experience of these sentiments. Belief is the true and proper name of this feeling; and no one is ever at a loss to know the meaning of that term; because every man is every moment conscious of the sentiment represented by it. It may not, however, be improper to attempt a description of this sentiment; in hopes we may, by that means, arrive at some analogies, which may afford a more perfect explication of it. I say, then, that belief is nothing but a more vivid, lively, forcible, firm, steady conception of an object, than what the imagination alone is ever able to attain. This variety of terms, which may seem so unphilosophical, is intended only to express that act of the mind, which renders realities, or what is taken for such, more present to us than fictions, causes them to weigh more in the thought, and gives them a superior influence on the passions and imagination. Provided we agree about the thing, it is needless to dispute about the terms. The imagination has the command over all its ideas, and can join and mix and vary them, in all the ways possible. It may conceive fictitious objects with all the circumstances of place and time. It may set them, in a manner, before our eyes, in their true colors, just as they might have existed. But as it is impossible that this faculty of imagination can ever, of itself, reach belief, it is evident that belief consists not in the peculiar nature or order of ideas, but in the manner of their conception, and in their feeling to the mind. I confess, that it is impossible perfectly to explain this feeling or manner of conception. We may make use of words which express something near it. But its true and proper name, as we observed before, is belief; which is a term that everyone sufficiently understands in common life. And in philosophy, we can go no farther than assert, that belief is something felt by the mind, which distinguishes the ideas of the judgment from the fictions of the imagination. It gives them more weight and influence; makes them appear of greater importance; enforces them in the mind; and renders them the governing principle of our actions. I hear at present, for instance, a person's voice, with whom I am acquainted; and the sound comes as from the next room. This impression of my senses immediately conveys my thought to the person, together with all the surrounding objects. I paint them out to myself as existing at present, with the same qualities and relations, of which I formerly knew them possessed. These ideas take faster hold of my mind than ideas of an enchanted castle. They are very different to the feeling, and have a much greater influence of every kind, either to give pleasure or pain, joy or sorrow.

Let us, then, take in the whole compass of this doctrine, and allow, that the sentiment of belief is nothing but a conception more intense and steady than what attends the mere fictions of the imagination, and that this manner of conception arises from a customary conjunction of the object with something present to the memory or senses: I believe that it will not be difficult, upon these suppositions, to find other operations of the mind analogous to it, and to trace up these phenomena to principles still more general.

41.

We have already observed that nature has established connections among particular ideas, and that no sooner one idea occurs to our thoughts than it introduces its correlative, and carries our attention towards it, by a gentle and insensible movement. These principles of connection or association we have reduced to three, namely, *Resemblance*, *Contiguity* and *Causation*; which are the only bonds that unite our thoughts together, and beget that regular train of reflection or discourse, which, in a greater or less degree, takes place among all mankind. Now here arises a question, on which the solution of the present difficulty will depend. Does it happen, in all these relations, that, when one of the objects is presented to the senses or memory, the mind is not only carried to the conception of the correlative, but reaches a steadier and stronger conception of it than what otherwise it would have been able to attain? This seems to be the case with that belief which arises from the relation of cause and effect. And if the case be the same with the other relations or principles of associations, this may be established as a general law, which takes place in all the operations of the mind.

We may, therefore, observe, as the first experiment to our present purpose, that, upon the appearance of the picture of an absent friend, our idea of him is evidently enlivened by the resemblance, and that every passion, which that idea occasions, whether of joy or sorrow,

acquires new force and vigor. In producing this effect, there concur both a relation and a present impression. Where the picture bears him no resemblance, at least was not intended for him, it never so much as conveys our thought to him: And where it is absent, as well as the person, though the mind may pass from the thought of the one to that of the other, it feels its idea to be rather weakened than enlivened by that transition. We take a pleasure in viewing the picture of a friend, when it is set before us; but when it is removed, rather choose to consider him directly than by reflection in an image, which is equally distant and obscure.

The ceremonies of the Roman Catholic religion may be considered as instances of the same nature. The devotees of that superstition usually plead in excuse for the mummeries, with which they are upbraided, that they feel the good effect of those external motions, and postures, and actions, in enlivening their devotion and quickening their fervor, which otherwise would decay, if directed entirely to distant and immaterial objects. We shadow out the objects of our faith, say they, in sensible types and images, and render them more present to us by the immediate presence of these types, than it is possible for us to do merely by an intellectual view and contemplation. Sensible objects have always a greater influence on the fancy than any other; and this influence they readily convey to those ideas to which they are related, and which they resemble. I shall only infer from these practices, and this reasoning, that the effect of resemblance in enlivening the ideas is very common; and as in every case a resemblance and a present impression must concur, we are abundantly supplied with experiments to prove the reality of the foregoing principle.

42.

We may add force to these experiments by others of a different kind, in considering the effects of contiguity as well as of resemblance. It is certain that distance diminishes the force of every idea, and that, upon our approach to any object; though it does not discover itself to our senses; it operates upon the mind with an influence, which imitates an immediate impression. The thinking on any object readily transports the mind to what is contiguous; but it is only the actual presence of an object, that transports it with a superior vivacity. When I am a few miles from home, whatever relates to it touches me more nearly than when I am two hundred leagues distant; though even at that distance the reflecting on anything in the neighborhood of my friends or family naturally produces an idea of them. But as in this latter case, both the objects of the mind are ideas; notwithstanding there is an easy transition between them; that transition alone is not able to give a superior vivacity to any of the ideas, for want of some immediate impression8.

43.

No one can doubt but causation has the same influence as the other two relations of resemblance and contiguity. Superstitious people are fond of the relics of saints and holy men, for the same reason, that they seek after types or images, in order to enliven their devotion, and give them a more intimate and strong conception of those exemplary lives, which they desire to imitate. Now it is evident, that one of the best relics, which a devotee could procure, would be the handiwork of a saint; and if his clothes and furniture are ever to be considered in this light, it is because they were once at his disposal, and were moved and affected by him; in which respect they are to be considered as imperfect effects, and as connected with him by a shorter chain of consequences than any of those, by which we learn the reality of his existence.

Suppose, that the son of a friend, who had been long dead or absent, were presented to us; it is evident, that this object would instantly revive its correlative idea, and recall to our thoughts all past intimacies and familiarities, in more lively colors than they would otherwise have appeared to us. This is another phenomenon, which seems to prove the principle above mentioned.

44.

We may observe, that, in these phenomena, the belief of the correlative object is always presupposed; without which the relation could have no effect. The influence of the picture supposes, that we believe our friend to have once existed. Contiguity to home can never excite our ideas of home, unless we believe that it really exists. Now I assert, that this belief, where it reaches beyond the memory or senses, is of a similar nature, and arises from similar causes, with the transition of thought and vivacity of conception here explained. When I throw a piece of dry wood into a fire, my mind is immediately carried to conceive, that it augments, not extinguishes the flame. This transition of thought from the cause to the effect proceeds not from reason. It derives its origin altogether from custom and experience. And as it first begins from an object, present to the senses, it renders the idea or conception of flame

more strong and lively than any loose, floating reverie of the imagination. That idea arises immediately. The thought moves instantly towards it, and conveys to it all that force of conception, which is derived from the impression present to the senses. When a sword is levelled at my breast, does not the idea of wound and pain strike me more strongly, than when a glass of wine is presented to me, even though by accident this idea should occur after the appearance of the latter object? But what is there in this whole matter to cause such a strong conception, except only a present object and a customary transition to the idea of another object, which we have been accustomed to conjoin with the former? This is the whole operation of the mind, in all our conclusions concerning matter of fact and existence; and it is a satisfaction to find some analogies, by which it may be explained. The transition from a present object does in all cases give strength and solidity to the related idea.

Here, then, is a kind of pre-established harmony between the course of nature and the succession of our ideas; and though the powers and forces, by which the former is governed, be wholly unknown to us; yet our thoughts and conceptions have still, we find, gone on in the same train with the other works of nature. Custom is that principle, by which this correspondence has been effected; so necessary to the subsistence of our species, and the regulation of our conduct, in every circumstance and occurrence of human life. Had not the presence of an object, instantly excited the idea of those objects, commonly conjoined with it, all our knowledge must have been limited to the narrow sphere of our memory and senses; and we should never have been able to adjust means to ends, or employ our natural powers, either to the producing of good, or avoiding of evil. Those, who delight in the discovery and contemplation of final causes, have here ample subject to employ their wonder and admiration.

45.

I shall add, for a further confirmation of the foregoing theory, that, as this operation of the mind, by which we infer like effects from like causes, and vice versa, is so essential to the subsistence of all human creatures, it is not probable, that it could be trusted to the fallacious deductions of our reason, which is slow in its operations; appears not, in any degree, during the first years of infancy; and at best is, in every age and period of human life, extremely liable to error and mistake. It is more conformable to the ordinary wisdom of nature to secure so necessary an act of the mind, by some instinct or mechanical tendency, which may be infallible in its operations, may discover itself at the first appearance of life and thought, and may be independent of all the labored deductions of the understanding. As nature has taught us the use of our limbs, without giving us the knowledge of the muscles and nerves, by which they are actuated; so has she implanted in us an instinct, which carries forward the thought in a correspondent course to that which she has established among external objects; though we are ignorant of those powers and forces, on which this regular course and succession of objects totally depends.

[An Enquiry Concerning Human Understanding. 1777. (Chicago: Open Court Pub. Co., 1921).*]*

"The Watch and the Watch-Maker"
from *Natural Theology*

William Paley
(Edited by Joseph R. Kirkland)

CHAPTER 1: STATE OF THE ARGUMENT

In crossing a heath, suppose I pitched my foot against a stone, and were asked how the stone came to be there, I might possibly answer, that, for any thing I knew to the contrary, it had lain there forever ; nor would it, perhaps, be very easy to show the absurdity of this answer.

But suppose I had found a watch upon the ground, and it should be inquired how the watch happened to be in that place, I should hardly think of the answer which I had before given, that, for any thing I knew, the watch might have always been there. Yet why should not this answer serve for the watch as well as for the stone? Why is it not as admissible in the second case as in the first? For this reason, and for no other, viz. that, when we come to inspect the watch, we perceive (what we could not discover in the stone) that its several parts are framed and put together for a purpose, e. g., that they are so formed and adjusted as to produce motion, and that motion so regulated as to point out the hour of the day ; that, if the different parts had been differently shaped from what they are, of a different size from what they are, or placed after any other manner, or in any other order than that in which they are placed, either no motion at all would have been carried on in the machine, or none which would have answered the use that is now served by it. To reckon tip a few of the plainest of these parts, and of their offices, all tending to one result: We see a cylindrical box containing a coiled, elastic spring, which, by its endeavor to relax itself, turns round the box. We next observe a flexible chain (artificially wrought for the sake of flexure) communicating the action of the spring from the box to the fusee. We then find a series of wheels, the teeth of which catch in, and apply to, each other, conducting the motion from the fusee to the balance, and from the balance to the pointer, and, at the same time, by the size and shape of those wheels, so regulating that motion as to terminate in causing an index, by an equable and measured progression, to pass over a given space in a, given time. We take notice that the wheels are made of brass' in order to keep them from rust; the springs of steel, no other metal being so elastic; that

over the face of the watch there is placed a glass, a material employed in no other part of the work, but in the room of which, if there had been any other than a transparent substance, the hour could not be seen without opening the case. This mechanism being observed, (it requires indeed an examination of the instrument, and perhaps some previous knowledge of the subject, to perceive and understand it; but being once, as we have said, observed and understood,) the inference, we think, is inevitable, that the watch must have had a maker : that there must have existed, at some time, and at some place or other, an artificers who formed it for the purpose which we find it actually to answer; who comprehended its construction, and designed its use.

I.

Nor would it, I apprehend, weaken the conclusion, that we had never known an artist capable of making one; that we were altogether incapable of executing such a piece of workmanship ourselves, or of understanding in what is true of some exquisite remains of ancient art, of some lost arts, and, to the generality of mankind, of the more curious productions of modern manufacture. Does one man in a million know how oval frames are turned? Ignorance of this kind exalts our opinion of the unseen and unknown but raises no doubt in our minds of the existence and agency of such an artist, at some former time, and in some place or other. Nor can I perceive that it varies at all the inference, whether the question arise concerning a human agent, or concerning an agent of a different species, or an agent possessing, in some respects, a different nature.

II.

Neither, secondly, would it invalidate our conclusion, that the watch sometimes went wrong, or that it seldom went exactly right. The purpose of the machinery, the design, and the designer, might be evident, and, in the case supposed, would be evident, in whatever way we accounted for the irregularity of the movement, or whether we could account for it or not. It is not necessary that a machine be perfect, in order to show with what design it was made: still less necessary, where the only question is whether it were made with any design at all.

III.

Nor, thirdly, would it bring any uncertainty into the argument , if there were a few parts of the watch, concerning which we could not discover, or had not yet discovered, in what manner they conduced to the general effect ; or even some parts, concerning which we could not ascertain whether they conduced to that effect in any manner whatever. For, as to the first branch of the case, if by the loss, or disorder, or decay of the parts in question, the movement of the watch were found in fact to be stopped, or disturbed, or retarded, no doubt would remain in our minds as to the utility or intention of these parts, although we should be unable to investigate the manner according to which, or the connection by which, the ultimate effect depended upon their action or assistance; and the more complex is the machine, the more likely is this obscurity to arise. Then, as to the second thing supposed, namely, that there were parts he might be spared without prejudice to the movement to the watch, and that we bad proved this by experiment, these superfluous parts, even if we were completely assured that they were such, would not vacate the reasoning which we bad instituted concerning other parts. The indication of contrivance remained, with respect to them, nearly as it was before.

IV.

Nor, fourthly, would any man in his senses think the existence of the watch, with its various machinery, accounted for, by being told that it was one out of many possible combinations of material forms; that whatever he had found in the place where lie found the watch, must have contained some internal configuration or other; and that this configuration might be the structure now exhibited, viz., of the works of a watch, as well as a different structure.

V.

Nor, fifthly, would it yield his inquiry more satisfaction, to be answered, that there existed in things a principle of order, which had disposed the parts of the watch into their present form and situation. He never knew a watch made by the principle of order; nor can he even form to himself an idea of what is meant by a principle of order, distinct from the intelligence of the watchmaker.

VI.

Sixthly, be would be surprised to hear that the mechanism of the watch was no proof of contrivance, only a motive to induce the mind to think so:

VII.

And not less surprised to be informed, that the watch in his band was nothing more than the result of the laws of metallic nature. It is a perversion of language to assign any law as the efficient, operative cause of any thing. A law presupposes an agent; for it is only the mode according to which an agent proceeds: it implies a power; for it is the order according to which that power acts. Without this agent, without this power, which are both distinct from itself, the law does nothing, is nothing. The expression, "the law of metallic nature," may sound strange and harsh to a philosophic ear; but it seems quite as justifiable as some others which are more familiar to him, such as "the law of vegetable nature," "the law of animal nature," or, indeed, as "the law of nature" in general, when assigned as the cause of phenomena, in exclusion of agency and power, or when it is substituted into the place of these.

VIII.

Neither, lastly, would our observer be driven out of his conclusion, or from his confidence in its truth, by being told that he knew nothing at all about the matter. He knows enough for his argument: he knows the utility of the end; he knows the subserviency and adaptation of the means to the end. These points being known, his ignorance of other points, his doubts concerning other points, affect not the certainty of his reasoning. The consciousness of knowing little need not beget a distrust of that which he does know. . . .

CHAPTER III: APPLICATION OF THE ARGUMENT

. . . for every indication of contrivance, every manifestation of design which existed in the watch, exists in the works of nature, with the difference on the side of nature of being greater and more, and that in a degree which exceeds all computation. I mean, that the contrivances of nature surpass the contrivances of art, in the complexity, subtlety, and curiosity of the mechanism; and still more, if possible, do they go beyond them in number and variety; yet, in a multitude of cases, are not less evidently mechanical, not less evidently contrivances, not less evidently accommodated to their end or suited to their office, than are the most perfect productions of human ingenuity.

I know no better method of introducing so large a subject, than that of comparing a single thing with a single thing: an eye, for example, with a telescope. As far as the examination of the instrument goes, there is precisely the same proof that the eye was made for vision, as there is that the telescope was made for assisting it. They are made upon the same principles; both being adjusted to the laws by which the transmission and refraction of rays of light are regulated. I speak not of the origin of the laws themselves; but such laws being fixed, the construction in both cases is adapted to them. For instance, these laws require, in order to produce the same effect, that the rays of light, in passing from water into the eye, should be refracted by a more convex surface than when it passes out of air into the eye. Accordingly we find that the eye of a fish, in that part of it called the crystalline lens, is much rounder than the eye of terrestrial animals. What plainer manifestation of design can there be than this difference? What could a mathematical instrument maker have done more to show his knowledge of his principle, his application of that knowledge, his suiting of his means to his end— I will not say to display the compass or excellence of his skill and art, for in these all comparison is indecorous, but to testify counsel, choice, consideration, purpose?

[*"The Watch and the Watch-Maker" from Ch. 1 & 3 of Paley's Natural Theology*. (Marsh, Capen, Lyon and Webb, 1839).]

Dialogues Concerning Natural Religion

David Hume
(Edited by Joseph R. Kirkland)

. . .

PART II

DEMEA: I must admit, Cleanthes, that nothing can more surprise me than the light in which you have all along put this argument. By the whole tenor of your discourse, one would imagine that you were maintaining the being of a God against the cavils of atheists and infidels, and were required to become a champion for that fundamental principle of all religion. But this, I hope, is not by any means a question among us. No man, no man at least of common sense, I am persuaded, ever entertained a serious doubt with regard to a truth so certain and self-evident. The question is not concerning the being, but the nature of God. This, I affirm, from the infirmities of human understanding, to be altogether incomprehensible and unknown to us. The essence of that supreme Mind, his attributes, the manner of his existence, the very nature of his duration; these, and every particular which regards so divine a Being, are mysterious to men. Finite, weak, and blind creatures, we ought to humble ourselves in his august presence; and, conscious of our frailties, adore in silence his infinite perfections, which eye hath not seen, ear hath not heard, neither hath it entered into the heart of man to conceive. They are covered in a deep cloud from human curiosity. It is profaneness to attempt penetrating through these sacred obscurities. And, next to the impiety of denying his existence, is the temerity of prying into his nature and essence, decrees and attributes.

But lest you should think that my piety has here got the better of my philosophy, I shall support my opinion, if it needs any support, by a very great authority. I might cite all the divines, almost, from the foundation of Christianity, who have ever treated of this or any other theological subject: But I shall confine myself, at present, to one equally celebrated for piety and philosophy. It is Father Malebranche, who, I remember, thus expresses himself: "One ought not so much," says he, "to call God a spirit, in order to express positively what he is, as in order to signify that he is not matter. He is a Being infinitely perfect: Of this we cannot doubt. But in the same manner as we ought not to imagine, even supposing him corporeal, that he is clothed with a human body, as the Anthropomorphites asserted, under color that that figure was the most perfect of any; so, neither ought we to imagine that the spirit of God has human ideas, or bears any resemblance to our spirit, under color that we know nothing more perfect than a human mind. We ought rather to believe, that as he comprehends the perfections of matter without being material. . . . he comprehends also the perfections of created spirits without being spirit, in the manner we conceive spirit: That his true name is, He that is; or, in other words, Being without restriction, All Being, the Being infinite and universal."

PHILO: After so great an authority, Demea, as that which you have produced, and a thousand more which you might produce, it would appear ridiculous in me to add my sentiment or express my approval of your doctrine. But surely, where reasonable men treat these subjects, the question can never be concerning the Being, but only the Nature, of the Deity. The former truth, as you well observe, is unquestionable and self-evident. Nothing exists without a cause; and the original cause of this universe (whatever it be) we call God; and piously ascribe to him every species of perfection. Whoever doubts this fundamental truth, deserves every punishment which can be inflicted among philosophers, to wit, the greatest ridicule, contempt, and disapproval. But as all perfection is entirely relative, we ought never to imagine that we comprehend the attributes of this divine Being, or to suppose that his perfections have any analogy or likeness to the perfections of a human creature. Wisdom, Thought, Design, Knowledge: these we justly ascribe to him because these words are honorable among men, and we have no other language or other conceptions by which we can express our adoration of him. But let us beware, lest we think that our ideas anywise correspond to his perfections, or that his attributes have any resemblance to these qualities among men. He is infinitely superior to our limited view and comprehension; and is more the object of worship in the temple than of disputation in the schools.

In reality, Cleanthes, there is no need of having recourse to that affected skepticism so displeasing to you, in order to come at this determination. Our ideas reach no further than our experience. We have no experience of divine attributes and operations. I need not conclude my syllogism. You can draw the inference yourself. And it is a pleasure to me (and I hope to you too) that just reasoning and sound piety here concur in the same conclusion, and both of them establish the adorably mysterious and incomprehensible nature of the Supreme Being.

CLEANTHES: [addressing Demea] Not to lose any time in circumlocutions much less in replying to the pious declamations of Philo, I shall briefly explain how I conceive this matter. Look round the world: contemplate the whole and every part of it. You will find it to be nothing but one great machine, subdivided into an infinite number of lesser machines, which again admit of subdivisions to a degree beyond what human senses and faculties can trace and explain. All these various machines, and even their most minute parts, are adjusted to each other with an accuracy which ravishes into admiration all men who have ever contemplated them. The curious adapting of means to ends, throughout all nature, resembles exactly, though it much exceeds, the productions of human contrivance; of human designs, thought, wisdom, and intelligence. Since, therefore, the effects resemble each other, we are led to infer by all the rules of analogy that the causes also resemble; and to infer that the Author of Nature is somewhat similar to the mind of man, though possessed of much larger faculties, proportioned to the grandeur of the work which he has executed. By this argument *a posteriori*, and by this argument alone, do we prove at once the existence of a Deity, and his similarity to human mind and intelligence.

DEMEA: I shall be so free, Cleanthes, as to tell you that from the beginning, I could not approve of your conclusion concerning the similarity of the Deity to men; still less can I approve of the mediums by which you endeavor to establish it. What!? No demonstration of the Being of God! No abstract arguments! No proofs *a priori*! Are these, which have hitherto been so much insisted on by philosophers, all fallacy, all sophism? Can we reach no further in this subject than experience and probability? I will not say that this is betraying the cause of a Deity: But surely, by this affected candor, you give advantages to atheists, which they never could obtain by the mere dint of argument and reasoning.

PHILO: What I chiefly doubt in this subject is not so much that all religious arguments are by Cleanthes

reduced to experience, as that they appear not to be even the most certain and irrefragable of that inferior kind. That a stone will fall, that fire will burn, that the earth has solidity, we have observed a thousand and a thousand times; and when any new instance of this nature is presented, we draw without hesitation the accustomed inference. The exact similarity of the cases gives us a perfect assurance of a similar event, and a stronger evidence is never desired nor sought after. But wherever you depart, in the least, from the similarity of the cases, you diminish proportionately the evidence; and may at last bring it to a very weak analogy, which is confessedly liable to error and uncertainty. After having experienced the circulation of the blood in human creatures, we make no doubt that it takes place in Titius and Maevius. But from its circulation in frogs and fishes, it is only a presumption, though a strong one, from analogy, that it takes place in men and other animals. The analogical reasoning is much weaker, when we infer the circulation of the sap in vegetables from our experience that the blood circulates in animals; and those, who hastily followed that imperfect analogy, are found, by more accurate experiments, to have been mistaken.

If we see a house, Cleanthes, we conclude with the greatest certainty that it had an architect or builder, because this is precisely that species of effect which we have experienced to proceed from that species of cause. But surely you will not affirm that the universe bears such a resemblance to a house that we can, with the same certainty, infer a similar cause, or that the analogy is here entire and perfect. The dissimilitude is so striking, that the utmost you can here pretend to is a guess, a conjecture, a presumption concerning a similar cause; and how that pretension will be received in the world, I leave you to consider.

CLEANTHES: It would surely be very ill received, and I should be deservedly blamed and detested did I allow that the proofs of a Deity amounted to no more than a guess or conjecture. But is the whole adjustment of means to ends in a house and in the universe so slight a resemblance? The economy of final causes? The order, proportion, and arrangement of every part? Steps of a stair are plainly contrived that human legs may use them in mounting, and this inference is certain and infallible. Human legs are also contrived for walking and mounting, and this inference, I allow, is not altogether so certain because of the dissimilarity which you remark. But does it, therefore, deserve the name only of presumption or conjecture?

DEMEA: [*interrupting Cleanthes*] Good God! Where are we? Zealous defenders of religion allow that the proofs of a Deity fall short of perfect evidence! And you, Philo, on whose assistance I depended in proving the adorable mysteriousness of the Divine Nature, do you assent to all these extravagant opinions of Cleanthes? For what other name can I give them? Or, why spare my censure when such principles are advanced, supported by such an authority before so young a man as Pamphilus?

PHILO: You seem not to apprehend that I argue with Cleanthes in his own way; and, by showing him the dangerous consequences of his tenets, hope at last to reduce him to our opinion. But what sticks most with you, I observe, is the representation which Cleanthes has made of the argument *a posteriori*; and finding that that argument is likely to escape your hold and vanish into air, you think it so disguised, that you can scarcely believe it to be set in its true light. Now, however much I may dissent, in other respects, from the dangerous principles of Cleanthes, I must allow that he has fairly represented that argument; and I shall endeavor so to state the matter to you, that you will entertain no further scruples with regard to it.

Were a man to abstract from everything which he knows or has seen, he would be altogether incapable, merely from his own ideas, to determine what kind of scene the universe must be, or to give the preference to one state or situation of things above another. For as nothing which he clearly conceives could be esteemed impossible or implying a contradiction, every chimera of his fancy would be upon an equal footing; nor could he assign any just reason why he adheres to one idea or system, and rejects the others which are equally possible.

Again; after he opens his eyes, and contemplates the world as it really is, it would be impossible for him at first to assign the cause of any one event, much less of the whole of things, or of the universe. He might set his fancy a rambling; and she might bring him in an infinite variety of reports and representations. These would all be possible; but being all equally possible, he would never of himself give a satisfactory account for his preferring one of them to the rest. Experience alone can point out to him the true cause of any phenomenon.

Now, according to this method of reasoning, Demea, it follows, (and is, indeed, tacitly allowed by Cleanthes himself,) that order, arrangement, or the adjustment of final causes, is not of itself any proof of design; but

only so far as it has been experienced to proceed from that principle. For aught we can know a priori, matter may contain the source or spring of order originally within itself, as well as mind does; and there is no more difficulty in conceiving, that the several elements, from an internal unknown cause, may fall into the most exquisite arrangement, than to conceive that their ideas, in the great universal mind, from a like internal unknown cause, fall into that arrangement. The equal possibility of both these suppositions is allowed. But, by experience, we find, (according to Cleanthes), that there is a difference between them. Throw several pieces of steel together, without shape or form; they will never arrange themselves so as to compose a watch. Stone, and mortar, and wood, without an architect, never erect a house. But the ideas in a human mind, we see, by an unknown, inexplicable economy, arrange themselves so as to form the plan of a watch or house. Experience, therefore, proves, that there is an original principle of order in mind, not in matter. From similar effects we infer similar causes. The adjustment of means to ends is alike in the universe, as in a machine of human contrivance. The causes, therefore, must be resembling.

I was from the beginning scandalized, I must own, with this resemblance, which is asserted, between the Deity and human creatures; and must conceive it to imply such a degradation of the Supreme Being as no sound Theist could endure. With your assistance, therefore, Demea, I shall endeavor to defend what you justly call the adorable mysteriousness of the Divine Nature, and shall refute this reasoning of Cleanthes, provided he allows that I have made a fair representation of it.

[Cleanthes assents. After a short pause, Philo proceeds.]

PHILO: That all inferences, Cleanthes, concerning fact, are founded on experience; and that all experimental reasonings are founded on the supposition that similar causes prove similar effects, and similar effects similar causes; I shall not at present much dispute with you. But observe, I entreat you, with what extreme caution all just reasoners proceed in the transferring of experiments to similar cases. Unless the cases be exactly similar, they repose no perfect confidence in applying their past observation to any particular phenomenon. Every alteration of circumstances occasions a doubt concerning the event; and it requires new experiments to prove certainly, that the new circumstances are of no moment or importance. A change in bulk, situation, arrangement, age, disposition of the air, or surrounding bodies; any of these particulars may be attended with the most unexpected consequences: And unless the objects be quite familiar to us, it is the highest temerity to expect with assurance, after any of these changes, an event similar to that which before fell under our observation. The slow and deliberate steps of philosophers here, if anywhere, are distinguished from the precipitate march of the vulgar, who, hurried on by the smallest similitude, are incapable of all discernment or consideration.

But can you think, Cleanthes, that your usual phlegm and philosophy have been preserved in so wide a step as you have taken, when you compared to the universe houses, ships, furniture, machines, and, from their similarity in some circumstances, inferred a similarity in their causes? Thought, design, intelligence, such as we discover in men and other animals, is no more than one of the springs and principles of the universe, as well as heat or cold, attraction or repulsion, and a hundred others, which fall under daily observation. It is an active cause, by which some particular parts of nature, we find, produce alterations on other parts. But can a conclusion, with any propriety, be transferred from parts to the whole? Does not the great disproportion bar all comparison and inference? From observing the growth of a hair, can we learn anything concerning the generation of a man? Would the manner of a leaf's blowing, even though perfectly known, afford us any instruction concerning the vegetation of a tree?

But, allowing that we were to take the operations of one part of nature upon another, for the foundation of our judgment concerning the origin of the whole, (which never can be admitted,) yet why select so minute, so weak, so bounded a principle, as the reason and design of animals is found to be upon this planet? What peculiar privilege has this little agitation of the brain which we call thought, that we must thus make it the model of the whole universe? Our partiality in our own favor does indeed present it on all occasions; but sound philosophy ought carefully to guard against so natural an illusion.

So far from admitting, continued Philo, that the operations of a part can afford us any just conclusion concerning the origin of the whole, I will not allow any one part to form a rule for another part, if the latter be very remote from the former. Is there any reasonable ground to conclude, that the inhabitants of other planets possess thought, intelligence, reason, or anything similar to these faculties in men? When nature has so extremely diversified her manner of operation in this small globe, can we imagine that she incessantly copies herself throughout so immense a universe? And if thought, as we may well suppose, be confined merely to this narrow corner, and has even there so limited a sphere of action, with what propriety can we assign it for the original cause of all things? The narrow views of a peasant, who makes his domestic economy the rule for the government of kingdoms, is in comparison a pardonable sophism.

But were we ever so much assured, that a thought and reason, resembling the human, were to be found throughout the whole universe, and were its activity elsewhere vastly greater and more commanding than it appears in this globe; yet I cannot see, why the operations of a world constituted, arranged, adjusted, can with any propriety be extended to a world which is in its embryo state, and is advancing towards that constitution and arrangement. By observation, we know somewhat of the economy, action, and nourishment of a finished animal; but we must transfer with great caution that observation to the growth of a fetus in the womb, and still more to the formation of an animalcule in the loins of its male parent. Nature, we find, even from our limited experience, possesses an infinite number of springs and principles, which incessantly discover themselves on every change of her position and situation. And what new and unknown principles would actuate her in so new and unknown a situation as that of the formation of a universe, we cannot, without the utmost temerity, pretend to determine.

A very small part of this great system, during a very short time, is very imperfectly discovered to us; and do we thence pronounce decisively concerning the origin of the whole?

Admirable conclusion! Stone, wood, brick, iron, brass, have not, at this time, in this minute globe of earth, an order or arrangement without human art and contrivance; therefore the universe could not originally attain its order and arrangement, without something similar to human art. But is a part of nature a rule for another part very wide of the former? Is it a rule for the whole? Is a very small part a rule for the universe? Is nature in one situation, a certain rule for nature in another situation vastly different from the former?

And can you blame me, Cleanthes, if I here imitate the prudent reserve of Simonides, who, according to the noted story, being asked by Hiero, What God was? desired a day to think of it, and then two days more;

and after that manner continually prolonged the term, without ever bringing in his definition or description? Could you even blame me, if I had answered at first, that I did not know, and was sensible that this subject lay vastly beyond the reach of my faculties? You might cry out skeptic and railler, as much as you pleased: but having found, in so many other subjects much more familiar, the imperfections and even contradictions of human reason, I never should expect any success from its feeble conjectures, in a subject so sublime, and so remote from the sphere of our observation. When two species of objects have always been observed to be conjoined together, I can infer, by custom, the existence of one wherever I see the existence of the other; and this I call an argument from experience. But how this argument can have place, where the objects, as in the present case, are single, individual, without parallel, or specific resemblance, may be difficult to explain. And will any man tell me with a serious countenance, that an orderly universe must arise from some thought and art like the human, because we have experience of it? To ascertain this reasoning, it were requisite that we had experience of the origin of worlds; and it is not sufficient, surely, that we have seen ships and cities arise from human art and contrivance . . .

[Philo was proceeding in this vehement manner, somewhat between jest and earnest, as it appeared to me, when he observed some signs of impatience in Cleanthes, and then immediately stopped short.]

CLEANTHES: What I had to suggest, is only that you would not abuse terms, or make use of popular expressions to subvert philosophical reasonings. You know, that the vulgar often distinguish reason from experience, even where the question relates only to matter of fact and existence; though it is found, where that reason is properly analyzed, that it is nothing but a species of experience. To prove by experience the origin of the universe from mind, is not more contrary to common speech, than to prove the motion of the earth from the same principle. And a caviller might raise all the same objections to the Copernican system, which you have urged against my reasonings. Have you other earths, might he say, which you have seen to move? Have . . .

PHILO: Yes! We have other earths. Is not the moon another earth, which we see to turn round its center? Is not Venus another earth, where we observe the same phenomenon? Are not the revolutions of the sun also a confirmation, from analogy, of the same theory? All the planets, are they not earths, which revolve about the sun? Are not the satellites moons, which move round Jupiter and Saturn, and along with these primary planets round the sun? These analogies and resemblances, with others which I have not mentioned, are the sole proofs of the Copernican system; and to you it belongs to consider, whether you have any analogies of the same kind to support your theory.

In reality, Cleanthes, continued he, the modern system of astronomy is now so much received by all inquirers, and has become so essential a part even of our earliest education, that we are not commonly very scrupulous in examining the reasons upon which it is founded. It is now become a matter of mere curiosity to study the first writers on that subject, who had the full force of prejudice to encounter, and were obliged to turn their arguments on every side in order to render them popular and convincing. But if we peruse Galileo's famous *Dialogues* concerning the system of the world, we shall find, that that great genius, one of the most sublime who ever existed, first bent all his endeavors to prove that there was no foundation for the distinction commonly made between elementary and celestial substances. The schools, proceeding from the illusions of sense, had carried this distinction very far; and had established the latter substances to be ingenerable, incorruptible, unalterable, impassable; and had assigned all the opposite qualities to the former. But Galileo, beginning with the moon, proved its similarity in every particular to the earth; its convex figure, its natural darkness when not illuminated, its density, its distinction into solid and liquid, the variations of its phases, the mutual illuminations of the earth and moon, their mutual eclipses, the inequalities of the lunar surface, etc. After many instances of this kind, with regard to all the planets, men plainly saw that these bodies became proper objects of experience; and that the similarity of their nature enabled us to extend the same arguments and phenomena from one to the other.

In this cautious proceeding of the astronomers, you may read your own condemnation, Cleanthes; or rather may see, that the subject in which you are engaged exceeds all human reason and inquiry. Can you pretend to show any such similarity between the fabric of a house, and the generation of a universe? Have you ever seen nature in any such situation as resembles the first arrangement of the elements? Have worlds ever been formed under your eye; and have you had leisure to observe the whole progress of the phenomenon, from the first appearance of order to its final consummation? If you have, then cite your experience, and deliver your theory.

PART III

CLEANTHES: How the most absurd argument in the hands of a man of ingenuity and invention, may acquire an air of probability! Are you not aware, Philo, that it became necessary for Copernicus and his first disciples to prove the similarity of the terrestrial and celestial matter; because several philosophers, blinded by old systems, and supported by some sensible appearances, had denied this similarity? but that it is by no means necessary, that Theists should prove the similarity of the works of Nature to those of Art; because this similarity is self-evident and undeniable? The same matter, a like form; what more is requisite to show an analogy between their causes, and to ascertain the origin of all things from a divine purpose and intention? Your objections, I must freely tell you, are no better than the abstruse cavils of those philosophers who denied motion; and ought to be refuted in the same manner, by illustrations, examples, and instances, rather than by serious argument and philosophy.

Suppose, therefore, that an articulate voice were heard in the clouds, much louder and more melodious than any which human art could ever reach: Suppose, that this voice were extended in the same instant over all nations, and spoke to each nation in its own language and dialect: Suppose, that the words delivered not only contain a just sense and meaning, but convey some instruction altogether worthy of a benevolent Being, superior to mankind: Could you possibly hesitate a moment concerning the cause of this voice? and must you not instantly ascribe it to some design or purpose? Yet I cannot see but all the same objections (if they merit that appellation) which lie against the system of Theism, may also be produced against this inference.

Might you not say, that all conclusions concerning fact were founded on experience: that when we hear an articulate voice in the dark, and thence infer a man, it is only the resemblance of the effects which leads us to conclude that there is a like resemblance in the cause: but that this extraordinary voice, by its loudness, extent, and flexibility to all languages, bears so little analogy to any human voice, that we have no reason to suppose any analogy in their causes: and consequently, that a rational, wise, coherent speech proceeded, you know not whence, from some accidental whistling of the winds, not from any divine reason or intelligence? You see clearly your own objections in these cavils, and I hope too you see clearly, that they cannot possibly have more force in the one case than in the other.

But to bring the case still nearer the present one of the universe, I shall make two suppositions, which imply not any absurdity or impossibility. Suppose that there is a natural, universal, invariable language, common to every individual of human race; and that books are natural productions, which perpetuate themselves in the same manner with animals and vegetables, by descent and propagation. Several expressions of our passions contain a universal language: all brute animals have a natural speech, which, however limited, is very intelligible to their own species. And as there are infinitely fewer parts and less contrivance in the finest composition of eloquence, than in the coarsest organized body, the propagation of an Iliad or Aeneid is an easier supposition than that of any plant or animal.

Suppose, therefore, that you enter into your library, thus peopled by natural volumes, containing the most refined reason and most exquisite beauty; could you possibly open one of them, and doubt, that its original cause bore the strongest analogy to mind and intelligence? When it reasons and discourses; when it expostulates, argues, and enforces its views and topics; when it applies sometimes to the pure intellect, sometimes to the affections; when it collects, disposes, and adorns every consideration suited to the subject; could you persist in asserting, that all this, at the bottom, had really no meaning; and that the first formation of this volume in the loins of its original parent proceeded not from thought and design? Your obstinacy, I know, reaches not that degree of firmness: even your skeptical play and wantonness would be abashed at so glaring an absurdity.

But if there be any difference, Philo, between this supposed case and the real one of the universe, it is all to the advantage of the latter. The anatomy of an animal affords many stronger instances of design than the perusal of Livy or Tacitus; and any objection which you start in the former case, by carrying me back to so unusual and extraordinary a scene as the first formation of worlds, the same objection has place on the supposition of our vegetating library. Choose, then, your party, Philo, without ambiguity or evasion; assert either that a rational volume is no proof of a rational cause, or admit of a similar cause to all the works of nature.

Let me here observe too, that this religious argument, instead of being weakened by that skepticism so much affected by you, rather acquires force from it, and becomes more firm and undisputed. To exclude all argument or reasoning of every kind, is either affectation or madness. The declared profession of every reasonable skeptic is only to reject abstruse, remote, and refined arguments; to adhere to common sense and the plain instincts of nature; and to assent, wherever any reasons strike him with so full a force that he cannot, without the greatest violence, prevent it. Now the arguments for Natural Religion are plainly of this kind; and nothing but the most perverse, obstinate metaphysics can reject them. Consider, anatomize the eye; survey its structure and contrivance; and tell me, from your own feeling, if the idea of a contriver does not immediately flow in upon you with a force like that of sensation. The most obvious conclusion, surely, is in favor of design; and it requires time, reflection, and study, to summon up those frivolous, though abstruse objections, which can support Infidelity. Who can behold the male and female of each species, the correspondence of their parts and instincts, their passions, and whole course of life before and after generation, but must be sensible, that the propagation of the species is intended by Nature? Millions and millions of such instances present themselves through every part of the universe; and no language can convey a more intelligible irresistible meaning, than the curious adjustment of final causes. To what degree, therefore, of blind dogmatism must one have attained, to reject such natural and such convincing arguments?

Some beauties in writing we may meet with, which seem contrary to rules, and which gain the affections, and animate the imagination, in opposition to all the precepts of criticism, and to the authority of the established masters of art. And if the argument for Theism be, as you pretend, contradictory to the principles of logic; its universal, its irresistible influence proves clearly, that there may be arguments of a like irregular nature. Whatever cavils may be urged, an orderly world, as well as a coherent, articulate speech, will still be received as an incontestable proof of design and intention.

It sometimes happens, I own, that the religious arguments have not their due influence on an ignorant savage and barbarian; not because they are obscure and difficult, but because he never asks himself any question with regard to them. Whence arises the curious structure of an animal? From the copulation of its parents. And these whence? From their parents? A few removes set the objects at such a distance, that to him they are lost in darkness and confusion; nor is he actuated by any curiosity to trace them further. But this is neither dogmatism nor skepticism, but stupidity: a state of mind very different from your sifting, inquisitive disposition, my ingenious friend. You can trace causes from effects: You can compare the most distant and remote objects: and your greatest errors proceed not from barrenness of thought and invention, but from too luxuriant a fertility, which suppresses your natural good sense, by a profusion of unnecessary scruples and objections.

[Here I could observe, Hermippus, that Philo was a little embarrassed and confounded: But while he hesitated in delivering an answer, luckily for him, Demea broke in upon the discourse, and saved his countenance.]

DEMEA: Your instance, Cleanthes, drawn from books and language, being familiar, has, I confess, so much more force on that account: but is there not some danger too in this very circumstance; and may it not render us presumptuous, by making us imagine we comprehend the Deity, and have some adequate idea of his nature and attributes? When I read a volume, I enter into the mind and intention of the author: I become him, in a manner, for the instant; and have an immediate feeling and conception of those ideas which revolved in his imagination while employed in that composition. But so near an approach we never surely can make to the Deity. His ways are not our ways. His attributes are perfect, but incomprehensible. And this volume of nature contains a great and inexplicable riddle, more than any intelligible discourse or reasoning.

The ancient Platonists, you know, were the most religious and devout of all the Pagan philosophers; yet many of them, particularly Plotinus, expressly declare, that intellect or understanding is not to be ascribed to the Deity; and that our most perfect worship of him consists, not in acts of veneration, reverence, gratitude, or love; but in a certain mysterious self-annihilation, or total extinction of all our faculties. These ideas are, perhaps, too far stretched; but still it must be acknowledged, that, by representing the Deity as so intelligible and comprehensible, and so similar to a human mind, we are guilty of the grossest and most narrow partiality, and make ourselves the model of the whole universe.

All the sentiments of the human mind, gratitude, resentment, love, friendship, approbation, blame, pity, emulation, envy, have a plain reference to the state and situation of man, and are calculated for preserving the existence and promoting the activity of such a being in such circumstances. It seems, therefore, unreasonable to transfer such sentiments to a supreme existence, or to suppose him actuated by them; and the phenomena besides of the universe will not support us in such a theory. All our ideas, derived from the senses, are confessedly false and illusive; and cannot therefore be supposed to have place in a supreme intelligence: And as the ideas of internal sentiment, added to those of the external senses, compose the whole furniture of human understanding, we may conclude, that none of the materials of thought are in any respect similar in the human and in the divine intelligence. Now, as to the manner of thinking; how can we make any comparison between them, or suppose them any wise resembling? Our thought is fluctuating, uncertain, fleeting, successive, and compounded; and were we to remove these circumstances, we absolutely annihilate its essence, and it would in such a case be an abuse of terms to apply to it the name of thought or reason. At least if it appear more pious and respectful (as it really is) still to retain these terms, when we mention the Supreme Being, we ought to acknowledge, that their meaning, in that case, is totally incomprehensible; and that the infirmities of our nature do not permit us to reach any ideas which in the least correspond to the ineffable sublimity of the Divine attributes.

PART IV

CLEANTHES: It seems strange to me that you, Demea, who are so sincere in the cause of religion, should still maintain the mysterious, incomprehensible nature of the Deity, and should insist so strenuously that he has no manner of likeness or resemblance to human creatures. The Deity, I can readily allow, possesses many powers and attributes of which we can have no comprehension: But if our ideas, so far as they go, be not just, and adequate, and correspondent to his real nature, I know not what there is in this subject worth insisting on. Is the name, without any meaning, of such mighty importance? Or how do you mystics, who maintain the absolute incomprehensibility of the Deity, differ from skeptics or atheists, who assert, that the first cause of all is unknown and unintelligible? Their temerity must be very great, if, after rejecting the production by a mind, I mean a mind resembling the human, (for I know of no other,) they pretend to assign, with certainty, any other specific intelligible cause: And their conscience must be very scrupulous indeed, if they refuse to call the universal unknown cause a God or Deity; and to bestow on him as many sublime eulogies and unmeaning epithets as you shall please to require of them.

DEMEA: Who could imagine, that Cleanthes, the calm philosophical Cleanthes, would attempt to refute his antagonists by affixing a nickname to them; and, like the common bigots and inquisitors of the age, have recourse to invective and declamation, instead of reasoning? Or does he not perceive, that these topics are easily retorted, and that Anthropomorphite is an appellation as invidious, and implies as dangerous consequences, as the epithet of Mystic, with which he has honored us? In reality, Cleanthes, consider what it is you assert when you represent the Deity as similar to a human mind and understanding. What is the soul of man? A composition of various faculties, passions, sentiments, ideas; united, indeed, into one self or person, but still distinct from each other. When it reasons, the ideas, which are the parts of its discourse, arrange themselves in a certain form or order; which is not preserved entire for a moment, but immediately gives place to another arrangement. New opinions, new passions, new affections, new feelings arise, which continually diversify the mental scene, and produce in it the greatest variety and most rapid succession imaginable. How is this compatible with that perfect immutability and simplicity which all true Theists ascribe to the Deity? By the same act, say they, he sees past, present, and future: His love and hatred, his mercy and justice, are one individual operation: He is entire in every point of space; and complete in every instant of duration. No succession, no change, no acquisition, no diminution. What he is implies not in it any shadow of distinction or diversity. And what he is this moment he ever has been, and ever will be, without any new judgment, sentiment, or operation. He stands fixed in one simple, perfect state: nor can you ever say, with any propriety, that this act of his is different from that other; or that this judgment or idea has been lately formed, and will give place, by succession, to any different judgment or idea.

CLEANTHES: I can readily allow that those who maintain the perfect simplicity of the Supreme Being, to the extent in which you have explained it, are complete Mystics, and chargeable with all the consequences which I have drawn from their opinion. They are, in a word, Atheists, without knowing it. For though it be allowed, that the Deity possesses attributes of which we have no comprehension, yet ought we never to ascribe to him any attributes which are absolutely incompatible with that intelligent nature essential to him. A mind, whose acts and sentiments and ideas are not distinct and successive; one, that is wholly simple, and totally immutable, is a mind which has no thought, no reason, no will, no sentiment, no love, no hatred; or, in a word, is no mind at all. It is an abuse of terms to give it that appellation; and we may as well speak of limited extension without figure, or of number without composition.

PHILO: Pray consider whom you are at present inveighing against. You are honoring with the appellation of Atheist all the sound, orthodox divines, almost, who have treated of this subject; and you will at last be, yourself, found, according to your reckoning, the only sound Theist in the world. But if idolaters be Atheists, as, I think, may justly be asserted, and Christian Theologians the same, what becomes of the argument, so much celebrated, derived from the universal consent of mankind?

But because I know you are not much swayed by names and authorities, I shall endeavor to show you, a little more distinctly, the inconveniences of that Anthropomorphism, which you have embraced; and shall prove, that there is no ground to suppose a plan of the world to be formed in the Divine mind, consisting of distinct ideas, differently arranged, in the same manner as an architect forms in his head the plan of a house which he intends to execute.

It is not easy, I own, to see what is gained by this supposition, whether we judge of the matter by Reason or by Experience. We are still obliged to mount higher, in order to find the cause of this cause, which you had assigned as satisfactory and conclusive.

If Reason (I mean abstract reason, derived from inquiries *a priori*) be not alike mute with regard to all questions concerning cause and effect, this sentence at least it will venture to pronounce, That a mental world, or universe of ideas, requires a cause as much, as does a material world, or universe of objects; and, if similar in its arrangement, must require a similar cause. For what is there in this subject, which should occasion a different conclusion or inference? In an abstract view, they are entirely alike; and no difficulty attends the one supposition, which is not common to both of them.

Again, when we will needs force Experience to pronounce some sentence, even on these subjects which lie beyond her sphere, neither can she perceive any material difference in this particular, between these two kinds of worlds; but finds them to be governed by similar principles, and to depend upon an equal variety of causes in their operations. We have specimens in miniature of both of them. Our own mind resembles the one; a vegetable or animal body the other. Let experience, therefore, judge from these samples. Nothing seems more delicate, with regard to its causes, than thought; and as these causes never operate in two persons after the same manner, so we never find two persons who think exactly alike. Nor indeed does the same person think exactly alike at any two different periods of time. A difference of age, of the disposition of his body, of weather, of food, of company, of books, of passions; any of these particulars, or others more minute, are sufficient to alter the curious machinery of thought, and communicate to it very different movements and operations. As far as we can judge, vegetables and animal bodies are not more delicate in their motions, nor depend upon a greater variety or more curious adjustment of springs and principles.

How, therefore, shall we satisfy ourselves concerning the cause of that Being whom you suppose the Author of Nature, or, according to your system of Anthropomorphism, the ideal world, into which you trace the material? Have we not the same reason to trace that ideal world into another ideal world, or new intelligent principle? But if we stop, and go no further; why go so far? why not stop at the material world? How can we satisfy ourselves without going on in infinitum? And, after all, what satisfaction is there in that infinite progression? Let us remember the story of the Indian philosopher and his elephant. It was never more applicable than to the present subject. If the material world rests upon a similar ideal world, this ideal world must rest upon some other; and so on, without end. It were better, therefore, never to look beyond the present material world. By supposing it to contain the principle of its order within itself, we really assert it to be God; and the sooner we arrive at that Divine Being, so much the better. When you go one step beyond the mundane system, you only excite an inquisitive humor which it is impossible ever to satisfy.

To say, that the different ideas which compose the reason of the Supreme Being, fall into order of themselves, and by their own nature, is really to talk without any precise meaning. If it has a meaning, I would fain know, why it is not as good sense to say, that the parts of the material world fall into order of themselves and by their own nature. Can the one opinion be intelligible, while the other is not so?

We have, indeed, experience of ideas which fall into order of themselves, and without any known cause. But, I am sure, we have a much larger experience of matter which does the same; as, in all instances of generation and vegetation, where the accurate analysis of the cause exceeds all human comprehension. We have also experience of particular systems of thought and of matter which have no order; of the first in madness, of the second in corruption. Why, then, should we think, that order is more essential to one than the other? And if it requires a cause in both, what do we gain by your system, in tracing the universe of objects into a similar universe of ideas? The first step which we make leads us on for ever. It were, therefore, wise in us to limit all our inquiries to the present world, without looking further. No satisfaction can ever be attained by these speculations, which so far exceed the narrow bounds of human understanding.

It was usual with the Peripatetics, you know, Cleanthes, when the cause of any phenomenon was demanded, to have recourse to their faculties or occult qualities; and to say, for instance, that bread nourished by its nutritive faculty, and senna purged by its purgative. But it has been discovered, that this subterfuge was nothing but the disguise of ignorance; and that these philosophers, though less ingenuous, really said the same thing with the skeptics or the vulgar, who fairly confessed that they knew not the cause of these phenomena. In like manner, when it is asked, what cause produces order in the ideas of the Supreme Being; can any other reason be assigned by you, Anthropomorphites, than that it is a rational faculty, and that such is the nature of the Deity? But why a similar answer will not be equally satisfactory in accounting for the order of the world, without having recourse to any such intelligent creator as you insist on, may be difficult to determine. It is only to say, that such is the nature of material objects, and that they are all originally possessed of a faculty of order and proportion. These are only more learned and elaborate ways of confessing our ignorance; nor has the one hypothesis any real advantage above the other, except in its greater conformity to vulgar prejudices.

CLEANTHES: You have displayed this argument with great emphasis: You seem not sensible how easy it is to answer it. Even in common life, if I assign a cause for any event, is it any objection, Philo, that I cannot assign the cause of that cause, and answer every new question which may incessantly be started? And what philosophers could possibly submit to so rigid a rule? philosophers, who confess ultimate causes to be totally unknown; and are sensible, that the most refined principles into which they trace the phenomena, are still to them as inexplicable as these phenomena themselves are to the vulgar. The order and arrangement of nature, the curious adjustment of final causes, the plain use

and intention of every part and organ; all these bespeak in the clearest language an intelligent cause or author. The heavens and the earth join in the same testimony: The whole chorus of Nature raises one hymn to the praises of its Creator. You alone, or almost alone, disturb this general harmony. You start abstruse doubts, cavils, and objections: You ask me, what is the cause of this cause? I know not; I care not; that concerns not me. I have found a Deity; and here I stop my inquiry. Let those go further, who are wiser or more enterprising.

PHILO: I pretend to be neither: And for that very reason, I should never perhaps have attempted to go so far; especially when I am sensible, that I must at last be contented to sit down with the same answer, which, without further trouble, might have satisfied me from the beginning. If I am still to remain in utter ignorance of causes, and can absolutely give an explication of nothing, I shall never esteem it any advantage to shove off for a moment a difficulty, which, you acknowledge, must immediately, in its full force, recur upon me. Naturalists indeed very justly explain particular effects by more general causes, though these general causes themselves should remain in the end totally inexplicable; but they never surely thought it satisfactory to explain a particular effect by a particular cause, which was no more to be accounted for than the effect itself. An ideal system, arranged of itself, without a precedent design, is not a whit more explicable than a material one, which attains its order in a like manner; nor is there any more difficulty in the latter supposition than in the former.

PART V

PHILO: But to show you still more inconveniences in your Anthropomorphism, please to take a new survey of your principles. Like effects prove like causes. This is the experimental argument; and this, you say too, is the sole theological argument. Now, it is certain, that the liker the effects are which are seen, and the liker the causes which are inferred, the stronger is the argument. Every departure on either side diminishes the probability, and renders the experiment less conclusive. You cannot doubt of the principle; neither ought you to reject its consequences.

All the new discoveries in astronomy, which prove the immense grandeur and magnificence of the works of Nature, are so many additional arguments for a Deity, according to the true system of Theism; but, according to your hypothesis of experimental Theism, they become so many objections, by removing the effect still further from all resemblance to the effects of human art and contrivance. . . .

If this argument, I say, had any force in former ages, how much greater must it have at present, when the bounds of Nature are so infinitely enlarged, and such a magnificent scene is opened to us? It is still more unreasonable to form our idea of so unlimited a cause from our experience of the narrow productions of human design and invention.

The discoveries by microscopes, as they open a new universe in miniature, are still objections, according to you, arguments, according to me. The further we push our researches of this kind, we are still led to infer the universal cause of all to be vastly different from mankind, or from any object of human experience and observation.

CLEANTHES: And what say you to the discoveries in anatomy, chemistry, botany? These surely are no objections; they only discover new instances of art and contrivance. It is still the image of mind reflected on us from innumerable objects.

PHILO: Add, a mind like the human.

CLEANTHES: I know of no other.

PHILO: And the liker the better.

CLEANTHES: To be sure.

PHILO: Now, Cleanthes, mark the consequences. First, by this method of reasoning, you renounce all claim to infinity in any of the attributes of the Deity. For, as the cause ought only to be proportioned to the effect, and the effect, so far as it falls under our cognizance, is not infinite; what pretensions have we, upon your suppositions, to ascribe that attribute to the Divine Being? You will still insist, that, by removing him so much from all similarity to human creatures, we give in to the most arbitrary hypothesis, and at the same time weaken all proofs of his existence.

Secondly, you have no reason, on your theory, for ascribing perfection to the Deity, even in his finite capacity, or for supposing him free from every error, mistake, or incoherence, in his undertakings. There are many inexplicable difficulties in the works of Nature, which, if we allow a perfect author to be proved a priori, are easily solved, and become only seeming difficulties, from the narrow capacity of man, who cannot trace infinite relations. But according to your method of reasoning, these difficulties become all real; and perhaps will be

insisted on, as new instances of likeness to human art and contrivance. At least, you must acknowledge, that it is impossible for us to tell, from our limited views, whether this system contains any great faults, or deserves any considerable praise, if compared to other possible, and even real systems. Could a peasant, if the Aeneid were read to him, pronounce that poem to be absolutely faultless, or even assign to it its proper rank among the productions of human wit, he, who had never seen any other production?

But were this world ever so perfect a production, it must still remain uncertain, whether all the excellences of the work can justly be ascribed to the workman. If we survey a ship, what an exalted idea must we form of the ingenuity of the carpenter who framed so complicated, useful, and beautiful a machine? And what surprise must we feel, when we find him a stupid mechanic, who imitated others, and copied an art, which, through a long succession of ages, after multiplied trials, mistakes, corrections, deliberations, and controversies, had been gradually improving? Many worlds might have been botched and bungled, throughout an eternity, ere this system was struck out; much labor lost, many fruitless trials made; and a slow, but continued improvement carried on during infinite ages in the art of world-making. In such subjects, who can determine, where the truth; nay, who can conjecture where the probability lies, amidst a great number of hypotheses which may be proposed, and a still greater which may be imagined?

And what shadow of an argument can you produce, from your hypothesis, to prove the unity of the Deity? A great number of men join in building a house or ship, in rearing a city, in framing a commonwealth; why may not several deities combine in contriving and framing a world? This is only so much greater similarity to human affairs. By sharing the work among several, we may so much further limit the attributes of each, and get rid of that extensive power and knowledge, which must be supposed in one deity, and which, according to you, can only serve to weaken the proof of his existence. And if such foolish, such vicious creatures as man, can yet often unite in framing and executing one plan, how much more those deities or demons, whom we may suppose several degrees more perfect!

To multiply causes without necessity, is indeed contrary to true philosophy: but this principle applies not to the present case. Were one deity antecedently proved by your theory, who were possessed of every attribute requisite to the production of the universe; it would be needless, I own, (though not absurd,) to suppose any other deity existent. But while it is still a question, Whether all these attributes are united in one subject, or dispersed among several independent beings, by what phenomena in nature can we pretend to decide the controversy? Where we see a body raised in a scale, we are sure that there is in the opposite scale, however concealed from sight, some counterpoising weight equal to it; but it is still allowed to doubt, whether that weight be an aggregate of several distinct bodies, or one uniform united mass. And if the weight requisite very much exceeds any thing which we have ever seen conjoined in any single body, the former supposition becomes still more probable and natural. An intelligent being of such vast power and capacity as is necessary to produce the universe, or, to speak in the language of ancient philosophy, so prodigious an animal exceeds all analogy, and even comprehension.

But further, Cleanthes: men are mortal, and renew their species by generation; and this is common to all living creatures. The two great sexes of male and female, says Milton, animate the world. Why must this circumstance, so universal, so essential, be excluded from those numerous and limited deities? Behold, then, the theogony of ancient times brought back upon us.

And why not become a perfect Anthropomorphite? Why not assert the deity or deities to be corporeal, and to have eyes, a nose, mouth, ears, etc.? Epicurus maintained, that no man had ever seen reason but in a human figure; therefore the gods must have a human figure. And this argument, which is deservedly so much ridiculed by Cicero, becomes, according to you, solid and philosophical.

In a word, Cleanthes, a man who follows your hypothesis is able perhaps to assert, or conjecture, that the universe, sometime, arose from something like design: but beyond that position he cannot ascertain one single circumstance; and is left afterwards to fix every point of his theology by the utmost license of fancy and hypothesis. This world, for aught he knows, is very faulty and imperfect, compared to a superior standard; and was only the first rude essay of some infant deity, who afterwards abandoned it, ashamed of his lame performance: it is the work only of some dependent, inferior deity; and is the object of derision to his superiors: it is the production of old age and dotage in some superannuated deity; and ever since his death, has run on at adventures, from the first impulse and active force which

it received from him. You justly give signs of horror, Demea, at these strange suppositions; but these, and a thousand more of the same kind, are Cleanthes's suppositions, not mine. From the moment the attributes of the Deity are supposed finite, all these have place. And I cannot, for my part, think that so wild and unsettled a system of theology is, in any respect, preferable to none at all.

CLEANTHES: These suppositions I absolutely disown. They strike me, however, with no horror, especially when proposed in that rambling way in which they drop from you. On the contrary, they give me pleasure, when I see, that, by the utmost indulgence of your imagination, you never get rid of the hypothesis of design in the universe, but are obliged at every turn to have recourse to it. To this concession I adhere steadily; and this I regard as a sufficient foundation for religion. . . .

PART VII

PHILO: But here, in examining the ancient system of the soul of the world, there strikes me, all on a sudden, a new idea, which, if just, must go near to subvert all your reasoning, and destroy even your first inferences, on which you repose such confidence. If the universe bears a greater likeness to animal bodies and to vegetables, than to the works of human art, it is more probable that its cause resembles the cause of the former than that of the latter, and its origin ought rather to be ascribed to generation or vegetation, than to reason or design. Your conclusion, even according to your own principles, is therefore lame and defective.

DEMEA: Pray open up this argument a little further, for I do not rightly apprehend it in that concise manner in which you have expressed it.

PHILO: Our friend Cleanthes, as you have heard, asserts that since no question of fact can be proved otherwise than by experience, the existence of a Deity admits not of proof from any other medium. The world, says he, resembles the works of human contrivance; therefore its cause must also resemble that of the other. Here we may remark, that the operation of one very small part of nature, to wit man, upon another very small part, to wit that inanimate matter lying within his reach, is the rule by which Cleanthes judges of the origin of the whole; and he measures objects, so widely disproportioned, by the same individual standard. But to waive all objections drawn from this topic, I affirm, that there are other parts of the universe (besides the machines of human invention) which bear still a greater resemblance to the fabric of the world, and which, therefore, afford a better conjecture concerning the universal origin of this system. These parts are animals and vegetables. The world plainly resembles more an animal or a vegetable, than it does a watch or a knitting-loom. Its cause, therefore, it is more probable, resembles the cause of the former. The cause of the former is generation or vegetation. The cause, therefore, of the world, we may infer to be something similar or analogous to generation or vegetation.

DEMEA: But how is it conceivable that the world can arise from anything similar to vegetation or generation?

PHILO: Very easily. In like manner as a tree sheds its seed into the neighboring fields, and produces other trees; so the great vegetable, the world, or this planetary system, produces within itself certain seeds, which, being scattered into the surrounding chaos, vegetate into new worlds. A comet, for instance, is the seed of a world; and after it has been fully ripened, by passing from sun to sun, and star to star, it is at last tossed into the unformed elements which everywhere surround this universe, and immediately sprouts up into a new system.

Or if, for the sake of variety (for I see no other advantage), we should suppose this world to be an animal; a comet is the egg of this animal: and in like manner as an ostrich lays its egg in the sand, which, without any further care, hatches the egg, and produces a new animal; so . . .

DEMEA: I understand you: But what wild, arbitrary suppositions are these! What data have you for such extraordinary conclusions? And is the slight, imaginary resemblance of the world to a vegetable or an animal sufficient to establish the same inference with regard to both? Objects, which are in general so widely different, ought they to be a standard for each other?

PHILO: Right! This is the topic on which I have all along insisted. I have still asserted, that we have no data to establish any system of cosmogony. Our experience, so imperfect in itself, and so limited both in extent and duration, can afford us no probable conjecture concerning the whole of things. But if we must needs fix on some hypothesis; by what rule, pray, ought we to determine our choice? Is there any other rule than the greater similarity of the objects compared? And does not a plant or an animal, which springs from vegetation or generation, bear a stronger resemblance to the

world, than does any artificial machine, which arises from reason and design?

DEMEA: But what is this vegetation and generation of which you talk? Can you explain their operations, and anatomize that fine internal structure on which they depend?

PHILO: As much, at least, as Cleanthes can explain the operations of reason, or anatomize that internal structure on which it depends. But without any such elaborate disquisitions, when I see an animal, I infer, that it sprang from generation; and that with as great certainty as you conclude a house to have been reared by design. These words, generation, reason, mark only certain powers and energies in nature, whose effects are known, but whose essence is incomprehensible; and one of these principles, more than the other, has no privilege for being made a standard to the whole of nature.

In reality, Demea, it may reasonably be expected, that the larger the views are which we take of things, the better will they conduct us in our conclusions concerning such extraordinary and such magnificent subjects. In this little corner of the world alone, there are four principles, reason, instinct, generation, vegetation, which are similar to each other, and are the causes of similar effects. What a number of other principles may we naturally suppose in the immense extent and variety of the universe, could we travel from planet to planet, and from system to system, in order to examine each part of this mighty fabric? Any one of these four principles above mentioned, (and a hundred others which lie open to our conjecture,) may afford us a theory by which to judge of the origin of the world; and it is a palpable and egregious partiality to confine our view entirely to that principle by which our own minds operate. Were this principle more intelligible on that account, such a partiality might be somewhat excusable: But reason, in its internal fabric and structure, is really as little known to us as instinct or vegetation; and, perhaps, even that vague, indeterminate word, Nature, to which the vulgar refer everything, is not at the bottom more inexplicable. The effects of these principles are all known to us from experience; but the principles themselves, and their manner of operation, are totally unknown; nor is it less intelligible, or less conformable to experience, to say, that the world arose by vegetation, from a seed shed by another world, than to say that it arose from a divine reason or contrivance, according to the sense in which Cleanthes understands it.

DEMEA: But methinks, if the world had a vegetative quality, and could sow the seeds of new worlds into the infinite chaos, this power would be still an additional argument for design in its author. For whence could arise so wonderful a faculty but from design? Or how can order spring from anything which perceives not that order which it bestows?

PHILO: You need only look around you to satisfy yourself with regard to this question. A tree bestows order and organization on that tree which springs from it, without knowing the order; an animal in the same manner on its offspring; a bird on its nest; and instances of this kind are even more frequent in the world than those of order, which arise from reason and contrivance. To say, that all this order in animals and vegetables proceeds ultimately from design, is begging the question; nor can that great point be ascertained otherwise than by proving, a priori, both that order is, from its nature, inseparably attached to thought; and that it can never of itself, or from original unknown principles, belong to matter.

But further, Demea; this objection which you urge can never be made use of by Cleanthes, without renouncing a defense which he has already made against one of my objections. When I inquired concerning the cause of that supreme reason and intelligence into which he resolves everything; he told me, that the impossibility of satisfying such inquiries could never be admitted as an objection in any species of philosophy. "We must stop somewhere", says he; "nor is it ever within the reach of human capacity to explain ultimate causes, or show the last connections of any objects. It is sufficient, if any steps, so far as we go, are supported by experience and observation." Now, that vegetation and generation, as well as reason, are experienced to be principles of order in nature, is undeniable. If I rest my system of cosmogony on the former, preferably to the latter, it is at my choice. The matter seems entirely arbitrary. And when Cleanthes asks me what is the cause of my great vegetative or generative faculty, I am equally entitled to ask him the cause of his great reasoning principle. These questions we have agreed to forbear on both sides; and it is chiefly his interest on the present occasion to stick to this agreement. Judging by our limited and imperfect experience, generation has some privileges above reason: for we see every day the latter arise from the former, never the former from the latter.

Compare, I beseech you, the consequences on both sides. The world, say I, resembles an animal; therefore it is an animal, therefore it arose from generation. The steps, I confess, are wide; yet there is some small appearance of analogy in each step. The world, says Cleanthes, resembles a machine; therefore it is a machine, therefore it arose from design. The steps are here equally wide, and the analogy less striking. And if he pretends to carry on my hypothesis a step further, and to infer design or reason from the great principle of generation, on which I insist; I may, with better authority, use the same freedom to push further his hypothesis, and infer a divine generation or theogony from his principle of reason. I have at least some faint shadow of experience, which is the utmost that can ever be attained in the present subject. Reason, in innumerable instances, is observed to arise from the principle of generation, and never to arise from any other principle.

Hesiod, and all the ancient mythologists, were so struck with this analogy, that they universally explained the origin of nature from an animal birth, and copulation. Plato too, so far as he is intelligible, seems to have adopted some such notion in his *Timaeus.*

The Brahmins assert, that the world arose from an infinite spider, who spun this whole complicated mass from his bowels, and annihilates afterwards the whole or any part of it, by absorbing it again, and resolving it into his own essence. Here is a species of cosmogony, which appears to us ridiculous; because a spider is a little contemptible animal, whose operations we are never likely to take for a model of the whole universe. But still here is a new species of analogy, even in our globe. And were there a planet wholly inhabited by spiders, (which is very possible,) this inference would there appear as natural and irrefragable as that which in our planet ascribes the origin of all things to design and intelligence, as explained by Cleanthes. Why an orderly system may not be spun from the belly as well as from the brain, it will be difficult for him to give a satisfactory reason.

CLEANTHES: I must confess, Philo, that of all men living, the task which you have undertaken, of raising doubts and objections, suits you best, and seems, in a manner, natural and unavoidable to you. So great is your fertility of invention, that I am not ashamed to acknowledge myself unable, on a sudden, to solve regularly such out-of-the-way difficulties as you incessantly start upon me: though I clearly see, in general, their fallacy and error. And I question not, but you are yourself, at present, in the same case, and have not the solution so ready as the objection: while you must be sensible, that common sense and reason are entirely against you; and that such whimsies as you have delivered, may puzzle, but never can convince us.

PART VIII

PHILO: What you ascribe to the fertility of my invention is entirely owing to the nature of the subject. In subjects adapted to the narrow compass of human reason, there is commonly but one determination, which carries probability or conviction with it; and to a man of sound judgment, all other suppositions, but that one, appear entirely absurd and chimerical. But in such questions as the present, a hundred contradictory views may preserve a kind of imperfect analogy; and invention has here full scope to exert itself. Without any great effort of thought, I believe that I could, in an instant, propose other systems of cosmogony, which would have some faint appearance of truth, though it is a thousand, a million to one, if either yours or any one of mine be the true system.

For instance, what if I should revive the old Epicurean hypothesis? This is commonly, and I believe justly, esteemed the most absurd system that has yet been proposed; yet I know not whether, with a few alterations, it might not be brought to bear a faint appearance of probability. Instead of supposing matter infinite, as Epicurus did, let us suppose it finite. A finite number of particles is only susceptible of finite transpositions: and it must happen, in an eternal duration, that every possible order or position must be tried an infinite number of times. This world, therefore, with all its events, even the most minute, has before been produced and destroyed, and will again be produced and destroyed, without any bounds and limitations. No one, who has a conception of the powers of infinite, in comparison of finite, will ever scruple this determination.

DEMEA: But this supposes that matter can acquire motion, without any voluntary agent or first mover.

PHILO: And where is the difficulty of that supposition? Every event, before experience, is equally difficult and incomprehensible; and every event, after experience, is equally easy and intelligible. Motion, in many instances, from gravity, from elasticity, from electricity, begins in matter, without any known voluntary agent: and to suppose always, in these cases, an unknown voluntary agent, is mere hypothesis; and hypothesis attended with no advantages. The beginning of motion in matter itself is as conceivable a priori as its communication from mind and intelligence.

Besides, why may not motion have been propagated by impulse through all eternity, and the same stock of it, or nearly the same, be still upheld in the universe? As much is lost by the composition of motion, as much is gained by its resolution. And whatever the causes are, the fact is certain, that matter is, and always has been, in continual agitation, as far as human experience or tradition reaches. There is not probably, at present, in the whole universe, one particle of matter at absolute rest.

And this very consideration too, which we have stumbled on in the course of the argument, suggests a new hypothesis of cosmogony, that is not absolutely absurd and improbable. Is there a system, an order, an economy of things, by which matter can preserve that perpetual agitation which seems essential to it, and yet maintain a constancy in the forms which it produces? There certainly is such an economy; for this is actually the case with the present world. The continual motion of matter, therefore, in less than infinite transpositions, must produce this economy or order; and by its very nature, that order, when once established, supports itself, for many ages, if not to eternity. But wherever matter is so poised, arranged, and adjusted, as to continue in perpetual motion, and yet preserve a constancy in the forms, its situation must, of necessity, have all the same appearance of art and contrivance which we observe at present. All the parts of each form must have a relation to each other, and to the whole; and the whole itself must have a relation to the other parts of the universe; to the element in which the form subsists; to the materials with which it repairs its waste and decay; and to every other form which is hostile or friendly. A defect in any of these particulars destroys the form; and the matter of which it is composed is again set loose, and is thrown into irregular motions and fermentations, till it unite itself to some other regular form. If no such form be prepared to receive it, and if there be a great quantity of this corrupted matter in the universe, the universe itself is entirely disordered; whether it be the feeble embryo of a world in its first beginnings that is thus destroyed, or the rotten carcass of one languishing in old age and infirmity. In either case, a chaos ensues; till finite, though innumerable revolutions produce at last some forms, whose parts and organs are so adjusted as to support the forms amidst a continued succession of matter.

Suppose (for we shall endeavor to vary the expression), that matter were thrown into any position, by a blind, unguided force; it is evident that this first position must, in all probability, be the most confused and most disorderly imaginable, without any resemblance to those works of human contrivance, which, along with a symmetry of parts, discover an adjustment of means to ends, and a tendency to self-preservation. If the actuating force cease after this operation, matter must remain forever in disorder, and continue an immense chaos, without any proportion or activity. But suppose that the actuating force, whatever it be, still continues in matter, this first position will immediately give place to a second, which will likewise in all probability be as disorderly as the first, and so on through many successions of changes and revolutions. No particular order or position ever continues a moment unaltered. The original force, still remaining in activity, gives a perpetual restlessness to matter. Every possible situation is produced, and instantly destroyed. If a glimpse or dawn of order appears for a moment, it is instantly hurried away, and confounded, by that never-ceasing force which actuates every part of matter.

Thus the universe goes on for many ages in a continued succession of chaos and disorder. But is it not possible that it may settle at last, so as not to lose its motion and active force (for that we have supposed inherent in it), yet so as to preserve a uniformity of appearance, amidst the continual motion and fluctuation of its parts? This we find to be the case with the universe at present. Every individual is perpetually changing, and every part of every individual; and yet the whole remains, in appearance, the same. May we not hope for such a position, or rather be assured of it, from the eternal revolutions of unguided matter; and may not this account for all the appearing wisdom and contrivance which is in the universe? Let us contemplate the subject a little, and we shall find, that this adjustment, if attained by matter of a seeming stability in the forms, with a real and perpetual revolution or motion of parts, affords a plausible, if not a true solution of the difficulty.

It is in vain, therefore, to insist upon the uses of the parts in animals or vegetables, and their curious adjustment to each other. I would fain know, how an animal could subsist, unless its parts were so adjusted? Do we not find, that it immediately perishes whenever this adjustment ceases, and that its matter corrupting tries some new form? It happens indeed, that the parts of the world are so well adjusted, that some regular form immediately lays claim to this corrupted matter: and if it were not so, could the world subsist? Must it not dissolve as well as the animal, and pass through new

positions and situations, till in great, but finite succession, it falls at last into the present or some such order?

CLEANTHES: It is well, you told us, that this hypothesis was suggested on a sudden, in the course of the argument. Had you had leisure to examine it, you would soon have perceived the insuperable objections to which it is exposed. No form, you say, can subsist, unless it possess those powers and organs requisite for its subsistence: some new order or economy must be tried, and so on, without intermission; till at last some order, which can support and maintain itself, is fallen upon. But according to this hypothesis, whence arise the many conveniences and advantages which men and all animals possess? Two eyes, two ears, are not absolutely necessary for the subsistence of the species. Human race might have been propagated and preserved, without horses, dogs, cows, sheep, and those innumerable fruits and products which serve to our satisfaction and enjoyment. If no camels had been created for the use of man in the sandy deserts of AFRICA and ARABIA, would the world have been dissolved? If no lodestone had been framed to give that wonderful and useful direction to the needle, would human society and the human kind have been immediately extinguished? Though the maxims of Nature be in general very frugal, yet instances of this kind are far from being rare; and any one of them is a sufficient proof of design, and of a benevolent design, which gave rise to the order and arrangement of the universe.

PHILO: At least, you may safely infer that the foregoing hypothesis is so far incomplete and imperfect, which I shall not scruple to allow. But can we ever reasonably expect greater success in any attempts of this nature? Or can we ever hope to erect a system of cosmogony, that will be liable to no exceptions, and will contain no circumstance repugnant to our limited and imperfect experience of the analogy of Nature? Your theory itself cannot surely pretend to any such advantage, even though you have run into Anthropomorphism, the better to preserve a conformity to common experience. Let us once more put it to trial. In all instances which we have ever seen, ideas are copied from real objects, and are ectypal, not archetypal, to express myself in learned terms: You reverse this order, and give thought the precedence. In all instances which we have ever seen, thought has no influence upon matter, except where that matter is so conjoined with it as to have an equal reciprocal influence upon it. No animal can move immediately anything but the members of its own body; and indeed, the equality of action and reaction seems to be an universal law of nature: But your theory implies a contradiction to this experience. These instances, with many more, which it were easy to collect, (particularly the supposition of a mind or system of thought that is eternal, or, in other words, an animal ingenerable and immortal); these instances, I say, may teach all of us sobriety in condemning each other, and let us see, that as no system of this kind ought ever to be received from a slight analogy, so neither ought any to be rejected on account of a small incongruity. For that is an inconvenience from which we can justly pronounce no one to be exempted.

All religious systems, it is confessed, are subject to great and insuperable difficulties. Each disputant triumphs in his turn; while he carries on an offensive war, and exposes the absurdities, barbarities, and pernicious tenets of his antagonist. But all of them, on the whole, prepare a complete triumph for the Skeptic; who tells them, that no system ought ever to be embraced with regard to such subjects: For this plain reason, that no absurdity ought ever to be assented to with regard to any subject. A total suspense of judgment is here our only reasonable resource. And if every attack, as is commonly observed, and no defense, among Theologians, is successful; how complete must be his victory, who remains always, with all mankind, on the offensive, and has himself no fixed station or abiding city, which he is ever, on any occasion, obliged to defend?

PART IX

DEMEA: But if so many difficulties attend the argument a posteriori had we not better adhere to that simple and sublime argument a priori, which, by offering to us infallible demonstration, cuts off at once all doubt and difficulty? By this argument, too, we may prove the infinity of the Divine attributes, which, I am afraid, can never be ascertained with certainty from any other topic. For how can an effect, which either is finite, or, for aught we know, may be so; how can such an effect, I say, prove an infinite cause? The unity too of the Divine Nature, it is very difficult, if not absolutely impossible, to deduce merely from contemplating the works of nature; nor will the uniformity alone of the plan, even were it allowed, give us any assurance of that attribute. Whereas the argument a priori . . .

CLEANTHES: You seem to reason, Demea, as if those advantages and conveniences in the abstract argument were full proofs of its solidity. But it is first proper, in my opinion, to determine what argument of

this nature you choose to insist on; and we shall afterwards, from itself, better than from its useful consequences, endeavor to determine what value we ought to put upon it.

DEMEA: The argument which I would insist on, is the common one. Whatever exists must have a cause or reason of its existence; it being absolutely impossible for anything to produce itself, or be the cause of its own existence. In mounting up, therefore, from effects to causes, we must either go on in tracing an infinite succession, without any ultimate cause at all; or must at last have recourse to some ultimate cause, that is necessarily existent: Now, that the first supposition is absurd, may be thus proved. In the infinite chain or succession of causes and effects, each single effect is determined to exist by the power and efficacy of that cause which immediately preceded; but the whole eternal chain or succession, taken together, is not determined or caused by anything; and yet it is evident that it requires a cause or reason, as much as any particular object which begins to exist in time. The question is still reasonable, why this particular succession of causes existed from eternity, and not any other succession, or no succession at all. If there be no necessarily existent being, any supposition which can be formed is equally possible; nor is there any more absurdity in Nothing's having existed from eternity, than there is in that succession of causes which constitutes the universe. What was it, then, which determined Something to exist rather than Nothing, and bestowed being on a particular possibility, exclusive of the rest? External causes, there are supposed to be none. Chance is a word without a meaning. Was it Nothing? But that can never produce any thing. We must, therefore, have recourse to a necessarily existent Being, who carries the Reason of his existence in himself, and who cannot be supposed not to exist, without an express contradiction. There is, consequently, such a Being; that is, there is a Deity.

CLEANTHES: I shall not leave it to Philo, though I know that the starting objections is his chief delight, to point out the weakness of this metaphysical reasoning. It seems to me so obviously ill-grounded, and at the same time of so little consequence to the cause of true piety and religion, that I shall myself venture to show the fallacy of it.

I shall begin with observing, that there is an evident absurdity in pretending to demonstrate a matter of fact, or to prove it by any arguments a priori. Nothing is demonstrable, unless the contrary implies a contradiction. Nothing, that is distinctly conceivable, implies a contradiction. Whatever we conceive as existent, we can also conceive as non-existent. There is no being, therefore, whose non-existence implies a contradiction. Consequently there is no being, whose existence is demonstrable. I propose this argument as entirely decisive, and am willing to rest the whole controversy upon it.

It is pretended that the Deity is a necessarily existent being; and this necessity of his existence is attempted to be explained by asserting, that if we knew his whole essence or nature, we should perceive it to be as impossible for him not to exist, as for twice two not to be four. But it is evident that this can never happen, while our faculties remain the same as at present. It will still be possible for us, at any time, to conceive the non-existence of what we formerly conceived to exist; nor can the mind ever lie under a necessity of supposing any object to remain always in being; in the same manner as we lie under a necessity of always conceiving twice two to be four. The words, therefore, necessary existence, have no meaning; or, which is the same thing, none that is consistent.

But further, why may not the material universe be the necessarily existent Being, according to this pretended explication of necessity? We dare not affirm that we know all the qualities of matter; and for aught we can determine, it may contain some qualities, which, were they known, would make its non-existence appear as great a contradiction as that twice two is five. I find only one argument employed to prove, that the material world is not the necessarily existent Being: and this argument is derived from the contingency both of the matter and the form of the world. "Any particle of matter," it is said Dr. Clarke, "may be conceived to be annihilated; and any form may be conceived to be altered. Such an annihilation or alteration, therefore, is not impossible." But it seems a great partiality not to perceive, that the same argument extends equally to the Deity, so far as we have any conception of him; and that the mind can at least imagine him to be non-existent, or his attributes to be altered. It must be some unknown, inconceivable qualities, which can make his non-existence appear impossible, or his attributes unalterable: And no reason can be assigned, why these qualities may not belong to matter. As they are altogether unknown and inconceivable, they can never be proved incompatible with it.

Add to this, that in tracing an eternal succession of objects, it seems absurd to inquire for a general cause or first author. How can anything, that exists from eternity, have a cause, since that relation implies a priority in time, and a beginning of existence?

In such a chain, too, or succession of objects, each part is caused by that which preceded it, and causes that which succeeds it. Where then is the difficulty? But the whole, you say, wants a cause. I answer, that the uniting of these parts into a whole, like the uniting of several distinct countries into one kingdom, or several distinct members into one body, is performed merely by an arbitrary act of the mind, and has no influence on the nature of things. Did I show you the particular causes of each individual in a collection of twenty particles of matter, I should think it very unreasonable, should you afterwards ask me, what was the cause of the whole twenty. This is sufficiently explained in explaining the cause of the parts.

PHILO: Though the reasonings which you have urged, Cleanthes, may well excuse me from starting any further difficulties, yet I cannot forbear insisting still upon another topic. It is observed by arithmeticians, that the products of 9, compose always either 9, or some lesser product of 9, if you add together all the characters of which any of the former products is composed. Thus, of 18, 27, 36, which are products of 9, you make 9 by adding 1 to 8, 2 to 7, 3 to 6. Thus, 369 is a product also of 9; and if you add 3, 6, and 9, you make 18, a lesser product of 9. To a superficial observer, so wonderful a regularity may be admired as the effect either of chance or design: but a skilful algebraist immediately concludes it to be the work of necessity, and demonstrates, that it must for ever result from the nature of these numbers. Is it not probable, I ask, that the whole economy of the universe is conducted by a like necessity, though no human algebra can furnish a key which solves the difficulty? And instead of admiring the order of natural beings, may it not happen, that, could we penetrate into the intimate nature of bodies, we should clearly see why it was absolutely impossible they could ever admit of any other disposition? So dangerous is it to introduce this idea of necessity into the present question! and so naturally does it afford an inference directly opposite to the religious hypothesis!

But dropping all these abstractions and confining ourselves to more familiar topics, I shall venture to add an observation, that the argument a priori has seldom been found very convincing, except to people of a metaphysical head, who have accustomed themselves to abstract reasoning, and who, finding from mathematics, that the understanding frequently leads to truth through obscurity, and, contrary to first appearances, have transferred the same habit of thinking to subjects where it ought not to have place. Other people, even of good sense and the best inclined to religion, feel always some deficiency in such arguments, though they are not perhaps able to explain distinctly where it lies; a certain proof that men ever did, and ever will derive their religion from other sources than from this species of reasoning.

PART X

DEMEA: It is my opinion, I own, that each man feels, in a manner, the truth of religion within his own breast, and, from a consciousness of his imbecility and misery, rather than from any reasoning, is led to seek protection from that Being, on whom he and all nature is dependent. So anxious or so tedious are even the best scenes of life, that futurity is still the object of all our hopes and fears. We incessantly look forward, and endeavor, by prayers, adoration, and sacrifice, to appease those unknown powers, whom we find, by experience, so able to afflict and oppress us. Wretched creatures that we are! what resource for us amidst the innumerable ills of life, did not religion suggest some methods of atonement, and appease those terrors with which we are incessantly agitated and tormented?

PHILO: I am indeed persuaded that the best, and indeed the only method of bringing everyone to a due sense of religion, is by just representations of the misery and wickedness of men. And for that purpose a talent of eloquence and strong imagery is more requisite than that of reasoning and argument. For is it necessary to prove what everyone feels within himself? It is only necessary to make us feel it, if possible, more intimately and sensibly.

DEMEA: The people, indeed, are sufficiently convinced of this great and melancholy truth. The miseries of life; the unhappiness of man; the general corruptions of our nature; the unsatisfactory enjoyment of pleasures, riches, honors; these phrases have become almost proverbial in all languages. And who can doubt of what all men declare from their own immediate feeling and experience?

PHILO: In this point the learned are perfectly agreed with the vulgar; and in all letters, sacred and profane, the topic of human misery has been insisted on with the most pathetic eloquence that sorrow and melancholy could inspire. The poets, who speak from sentiment, without a system, and whose testimony has therefore the more authority, abound in images of this nature. From Homer down to Dr. Young, the whole inspired tribe have ever been sensible, that no other representation of things would suit the feeling and observation of each individual.

DEMEA: As to authorities, you need not seek them. Look round this library of Cleanthes. I shall venture to affirm, that, except authors of particular sciences, such as chemistry or botany, who have no occasion to treat of human life, there is scarce one of those innumerable writers, from whom the sense of human misery has not, in some passage or other, extorted a complaint and confession of it. At least, the chance is entirely on that side; and no one author has ever, so far as I can recollect, been so extravagant as to deny it.

PHILO: There you must excuse me: Leibniz has denied it; and is perhaps the first who ventured upon so bold and paradoxical an opinion; at least, the first who made it essential to his philosophical system.

DEMEA: And by being the first, might he not have been sensible of his error? For is this a subject in which philosophers can propose to make discoveries especially in so late an age? And can any man hope by a simple denial (for the subject scarcely admits of reasoning), to bear down the united testimony of mankind, founded on sense and consciousness?

And why should man, added he, pretend to an exemption from the lot of all other animals? The whole earth, believe me, Philo, is cursed and polluted. A perpetual war is kindled amongst all living creatures. Necessity, hunger, want, stimulate the strong and courageous: Fear, anxiety, terror, agitate the weak and infirm. The first entrance into life gives anguish to the new-born infant and to its wretched parent: Weakness, impotence, distress, attend each stage of that life: and it is at last finished in agony and horror.

PHILO: Observe, too, the curious artifices of Nature, in order to embitter the life of every living being. The stronger prey upon the weaker, and keep them in perpetual terror and anxiety. The weaker too, in their turn, often prey upon the stronger, and vex and molest them without relaxation. Consider that innumerable race of insects, which either are bred on the body of each animal, or, flying about, infix their stings in him. These insects have others still less than themselves, which torment them. And thus on each hand, before and behind, above and below, every animal is surrounded with enemies, which incessantly seek his misery and destruction.

DEMEA: Man alone seems to be, in part, an exception to this rule. For by combination in society, he can easily master lions, tigers, and bears, whose greater strength and agility naturally enable them to prey upon him.

PHILO: On the contrary! It is here chiefly that the uniform and equal maxims of Nature are most apparent. Man, it is true, can, by combination, surmount all his real enemies, and become master of the whole animal creation: but does he not immediately raise up to himself imaginary enemies, the demons of his fancy, who haunt him with superstitious terrors, and blast every enjoyment of life? His pleasure, as he imagines, becomes, in their eyes, a crime: his food and repose give them umbrage and offence: his very sleep and dreams furnish new materials to anxious fear: and even death, his refuge from every other ill, presents only the dread of endless and innumerable woes. Nor does the wolf molest more the timid flock, than superstition does the anxious breast of wretched mortals.

Besides, consider, Demea: This very society, by which we surmount those wild beasts, our natural enemies; what new enemies does it not raise to us? What woe and misery does it not occasion? Man is the greatest enemy of man. Oppression, injustice, contempt, contumely, violence, sedition, war, calumny, treachery, fraud; by these they mutually torment each other; and they would soon dissolve that society which they had formed, were it not for the dread of still greater ills, which must attend their separation.

DEMEA: But though these external insults from animals, from men, from all the elements, which assault us, form a frightful catalogue of woes, they are nothing in comparison of those which arise within ourselves, from the distempered condition of our mind and body. How many lie under the lingering torment of diseases? Hear the pathetic enumeration of the great poet:

Intestine stone and ulcer, colic-pangs,

Demoniac frenzy, moping melancholy,

And moon-struck madness, pining atrophy,

Marasmus, and wide-wasting pestilence.

Dire was the tossing, deep the groans: despair

Tended the sick, busiest from couch to couch.

And over them triumphant death his dart

Shook: but delay'd to strike, though oft invok'd

With vows, as their chief good and final hope.

DEMEA: The disorders of the mind, though more secret, are not perhaps less dismal and vexatious. Remorse, shame, anguish, rage, disappointment, anxiety, fear, dejection, despair; who has ever passed through life without cruel inroads from these tormentors? How many have scarcely ever felt any better sensations? Labor and poverty, so abhorred by everyone, are the certain lot of the far greater number; and those few privileged persons, who enjoy ease and opulence, never reach contentment or true felicity. All the goods of life united would not make a very happy man; but all the ills united would make a wretch indeed; and any one of them almost (and who can be free from every one?) nay often the absence of one good (and who can possess all?) is sufficient to render life ineligible.

Were a stranger to drop on a sudden into this world, I would show him, as a specimen of its ills, a hospital full of diseases, a prison crowded with malefactors and debtors, a field of battle strewed with carcasses, a fleet foundering in the ocean, a nation languishing under tyranny, famine, or pestilence. To turn the gay side of life to him, and give him a notion of its pleasures; whither should I conduct him? to a ball, to an opera, to court? He might justly think, that I was only showing him a diversity of distress and sorrow.

PHILO: There is no evading such striking instances but by apologies, which still further aggravate the charge. Why have all men, I ask, in all ages, complained incessantly of the miseries of life? . . . They have no just reason, says one: these complaints proceed only from their discontented, repining, anxious disposition . . . And can there possibly, I reply, be a more certain foundation of misery, than such a wretched temper?

But if they were really as unhappy as they pretend, says my antagonist, why do they remain in life? . . .

Not satisfied with life, afraid of death.

This is the secret chain, say I, that holds us. We are terrified, not bribed to the continuance of our existence.

It is only a false delicacy, he may insist, which a few refined spirits indulge, and which has spread these complaints among the whole race of mankind. . . . And what is this delicacy, I ask, which you blame? Is it anything but a greater sensibility to all the pleasures and pains of life? and if the man of a delicate, refined temper, by being so much more alive than the rest of the world, is only so much more unhappy, what judgment must we form in general of human life?

Let men remain at rest, says our adversary, and they will be easy. They are willing artificers of their own misery. . . . No! reply I: an anxious languor follows their repose; disappointment, vexation, trouble, their activity and ambition.

CLEANTHES: I can observe something like what you mention in some others: but I confess I feel little or nothing of it in myself, and hope that it is not so common as you represent it.

DEMEA: If you feel not human misery yourself, I congratulate you on so happy a singularity. Others, seemingly the most prosperous, have not been ashamed to vent their complaints in the most melancholy strains. Let us attend to the great, the fortunate emperor, Charles V, when, tired with human grandeur, he resigned all his extensive dominions into the hands of his son. In the last harangue which he made on that memorable occasion, he publicly avowed, that the greatest prosperities which he had ever enjoyed, had been mixed with so many adversities, that he might truly say he had never enjoyed any satisfaction or contentment. But did the retired life, in which he sought for shelter, afford him any greater happiness? If we may credit his son's account, his repentance commenced the very day of his resignation.

Cicero's fortune, from small beginnings, rose to the greatest luster and renown; yet what pathetic complaints of the ills of life do his familiar letters, as well as philosophical discourses, contain? And suitably to his own experience, he introduces Cato, the great, the fortunate Cato, protesting in his old age, that had he a new life in his offer, he would reject the present.

Ask yourself, ask any of your acquaintance, whether they would live over again the last ten or twenty years of their life. No! but the next twenty, they say, will be better:

And from the dregs of life, hope to receive

What the first sprightly running could not give.

Thus at last they find (such is the greatness of human misery, it reconciles even contradictions), that they complain at once of the shortness of life, and of its vanity and sorrow.

PHILO: And is it possible, Cleanthes, that after all these reflections, and infinitely more, which might be suggested, you can still persevere in your Anthropomorphism, and assert the moral attributes of the Deity, his justice, benevolence, mercy, and rectitude, to be of the same nature with these virtues in human creatures? His power we allow is infinite: whatever he wills is executed: but neither man nor any other animal is happy: therefore he does not will their happiness. His wisdom is infinite: He is never mistaken in choosing the means to any end: But the course of Nature tends not to human or animal felicity: therefore it is not established for that purpose. Through the whole compass of human knowledge, there are no inferences more certain and infallible than these. In what respect, then, do his benevolence and mercy resemble the benevolence and mercy of men?

Epicurus's old questions are yet unanswered. Is he willing to prevent evil, but not able? then is he impotent. Is he able, but not willing? then is he malevolent. Is he both able and willing? whence then is evil?

You ascribe, Cleanthes (and I believe justly), a purpose and intention to Nature. But what, I beseech you, is the object of that curious artifice and machinery, which she has displayed in all animals? The preservation alone of individuals, and propagation of the species. It seems enough for her purpose, if such a rank be barely upheld in the universe, without any care or concern for the happiness of the members that compose it. No resource for this purpose: no machinery, in order merely to give pleasure or ease: no fund of pure joy and contentment: no indulgence, without some want or necessity accompanying it. At least, the few phenomena of this nature are overbalanced by opposite phenomena of still greater importance.

Our sense of music, harmony, and indeed beauty of all kinds, gives satisfaction, without being absolutely necessary to the preservation and propagation of the species. But what racking pains, on the other hand, arise from gouts, gravels, megrims, toothaches, rheumatisms, where the injury to the animal machinery is either small or incurable? Mirth, laughter, play, frolic, seem gratuitous satisfactions, which have no further tendency: spleen, melancholy, discontent, superstition, are pains of the same nature. How then does the Divine benevolence display itself, in the sense of you Anthropomorphites? None but we Mystics, as you were pleased to call us, can account for this strange mixture of phenomena, by deriving it from attributes, infinitely perfect, but incomprehensible.

CLEANTHES: [smiling] And have you at last betrayed your intentions, Philo? Your long agreement with Demea did indeed a little surprise me; but I find you were all the while erecting a concealed battery against me. And I must confess, that you have now fallen upon a subject worthy of your noble spirit of opposition and controversy. If you can make out the present point, and prove mankind to be unhappy or corrupted, there is an end at once of all religion. For to what purpose establish the natural attributes of the Deity, while the moral are still doubtful and uncertain?

DEMEA: You take umbrage very easily at opinions the most innocent, and the most generally received, even amongst the religious and devout themselves: and nothing can be more surprising than to find a topic like this, concerning the wickedness and misery of man, charged with no less than Atheism and profaneness. Have not all pious divines and preachers, who have indulged their rhetoric on so fertile a subject; have they not easily, I say, given a solution of any difficulties which may attend it? This world is but a point in comparison of the universe; this life but a moment in comparison of eternity. The present evil phenomena, therefore, are rectified in other regions, and in some future period of existence. And the eyes of men, being then opened to larger views of things, see the whole connection of general laws; and trace with adoration, the benevolence and rectitude of the Deity, through all the mazes and intricacies of his providence.

CLEANTHES: No! No! These arbitrary suppositions can never be admitted, contrary to matter of fact, visible and uncontroverted. Whence can any cause be known but from its known effects? Whence can any hypothesis be proved but from the apparent phenomena? To establish one hypothesis upon another, is building entirely in the air; and the utmost we ever attain, by these conjectures and fictions, is to ascertain the bare possibility of our opinion; but never can we, upon such terms, establish its reality.

The only method of supporting Divine benevolence, and it is what I willingly embrace, is to deny absolutely the misery and wickedness of man. Your representations are exaggerated; your melancholy views mostly fictitious; your inferences contrary to fact and experience. Health is more common than sickness; pleasure than pain; happiness than misery. And for one vexation which we meet with, we attain, upon computation, a hundred enjoyments.

Admitting your position, replied Philo, which yet is extremely doubtful, you must at the same time allow, that if pain be less frequent than pleasure, it is infinitely more violent and durable. One hour of it is often able to outweigh a day, a week, a month of our common insipid enjoyments; and how many days, weeks, and months, are passed by several in the most acute torments? Pleasure, scarcely in one instance, is ever able to reach ecstasy and rapture; and in no one instance can it continue for any time at its highest pitch and altitude. The spirits evaporate, the nerves relax, the fabric is disordered, and the enjoyment quickly degenerates into fatigue and uneasiness. But pain often, good God, how often! rises to torture and agony; and the longer it continues, it becomes still more genuine agony and torture. Patience is exhausted, courage languishes, melancholy seizes us, and nothing terminates our misery but the removal of its cause, or another event, which is the sole cure of all evil, but which, from our natural folly, we regard with still greater horror and consternation.

PHILO: But not to insist upon these topics though most obvious, certain, and important; I must use the freedom to admonish you, Cleanthes, that you have put the controversy upon a most dangerous issue, and are unawares introducing a total skepticism into the most essential articles of natural and revealed theology. What! no method of fixing a just foundation for religion, unless we allow the happiness of human life, and maintain a continued existence even in this world, with all our present pains, infirmities, vexations, and follies, to be eligible and desirable! But this is contrary to every one's feeling and experience: It is contrary to an authority so established as nothing can subvert. No decisive proofs can ever be produced against this authority; nor is it possible for you to compute, estimate, and compare, all the pains and all the pleasures in the lives of all men and of all animals: And thus, by your resting the whole system of religion on a point, which, from its very nature, must forever be uncertain, you tacitly confess, that that system is equally uncertain.

But allowing you what never will be believed, at least what you never possibly can prove, that animal, or at least human happiness, in this life, exceeds its misery, you have yet done nothing: For this is not, by any means, what we expect from infinite power, infinite wisdom, and infinite goodness. Why is there any misery at all in the world? Not by chance surely. From some cause then. Is it from the intention of the Deity? But he is perfectly benevolent. Is it contrary to his intention? But he is almighty. Nothing can shake the solidity of this reasoning, so short, so clear, so decisive; except we assert, that these subjects exceed all human capacity, and that our common measures of truth and falsehood are not applicable to them; a topic which I have all along insisted on, but which you have, from the beginning, rejected with scorn and indignation.

But I will be contented to retire still from this entrenchment, for I deny that you can ever force me in it. I will allow, that pain or misery in man is compatible with infinite power and goodness in the Deity, even in your sense of these attributes: What are you advanced by all these concessions? A mere possible compatibility is not sufficient. You must prove these pure, unmixed, and uncontrollable attributes from the present mixed and confused phenomena, and from these alone. A hopeful undertaking! Were the phenomena ever so pure and unmixed, yet being finite, they would be insufficient for that purpose. How much more, where they are also so jarring and discordant!

Here, Cleanthes, I find myself at ease in my argument. Here I triumph. Formerly, when we argued concerning the natural attributes of intelligence and design, I needed all my skeptical and metaphysical subtlety to elude your grasp. In many views of the universe, and of its parts, particularly the latter, the beauty and fitness of final causes strike us with such irresistible force, that all objections appear (what I believe they really are) mere cavils and sophisms; nor can we then imagine how it was ever possible for us to repose any weight on them. But there is no view of human life, or of the condition of mankind, from which, without the greatest violence, we can infer the moral attributes, or learn that infinite benevolence, conjoined with infinite power and infinite wisdom, which we must discover by the eyes of faith alone. It is your turn now to tug the laboring oar, and to support your philosophical subtleties against the dictates of plain reason and experience.

PART XI

CLEANTHES: I scruple not to allow that I have been apt to suspect the frequent repetition of the word infinite, which we meet with in all theological writers, to savor more of panegyric than of philosophy; and that any purposes of reasoning, and even of religion, would be better served, were we to rest contented with more accurate and more moderate expressions. The terms, admirable, excellent, superlatively great, wise, and holy; these sufficiently fill the imaginations of men; and anything beyond, besides that it leads into absurdities, has no influence on the affections or sentiments.

Thus, in the present subject, if we abandon all human analogy, as seems your intention, Demea, I am afraid we abandon all religion, and retain no conception of the great object of our adoration. If we preserve human analogy, we must for ever find it impossible to reconcile any mixture of evil in the universe with infinite attributes; much less can we ever prove the latter from the former. But supposing the Author of Nature to be finitely perfect, though far exceeding mankind, a satisfactory account may then be given of natural and moral evil, and every untoward phenomenon be explained and adjusted. A less evil may then be chosen, in order to avoid a greater; inconveniences be submitted to, in order to reach a desirable end; and in a word, benevolence, regulated by wisdom, and limited by necessity, may produce just such a world as the present. You, Philo, who are so prompt at starting views, and reflections, and analogies, I would gladly hear, at length, without interruption, your opinion of this new theory; and if it deserve our attention, we may afterwards, at more leisure, reduce it into form.

PHILO: My sentiments are not worth being made a mystery of; and therefore, without any ceremony, I shall deliver what occurs to me with regard to the present subject. It must, I think, be allowed, that if a very limited intelligence, whom we shall suppose utterly unacquainted with the universe, were assured, that it were the production of a very good, wise, and powerful Being, however finite, he would, from his conjectures, form beforehand a different notion of it from what we find it to be by experience; nor would he ever imagine, merely from these attributes of the cause, of which he is informed, that the effect could be so full of vice and misery and disorder, as it appears in this life. Supposing now, that this person were brought into the world, still assured that it was the workmanship of such a sublime and benevolent Being; he might, perhaps, be surprised at the disappointment; but would never retract his former belief, if founded on any very solid argument; since such a limited intelligence must be sensible of his own blindness and ignorance, and must allow, that there may be many solutions of those phenomena, which will forever escape his comprehension. But supposing, which is the real case with regard to man, that this creature is not antecedently convinced of a supreme intelligence, benevolent, and powerful, but is left to gather such a belief from the appearances of things; this entirely alters the case, nor will he ever find any reason for such a conclusion. He may be fully convinced of the narrow limits of his understanding;

but this will not help him in forming an inference concerning the goodness of superior powers, since he must form that inference from what he knows, not from what he is ignorant of. The more you exaggerate his weakness and ignorance, the more diffident you render him, and give him the greater suspicion that such subjects are beyond the reach of his faculties. You are obliged, therefore, to reason with him merely from the known phenomena, and to drop every arbitrary supposition or conjecture.

Did I show you a house or palace, where there was not one apartment convenient or agreeable; where the windows, doors, fires, passages, stairs, and the whole economy of the building, were the source of noise, confusion, fatigue, darkness, and the extremes of heat and cold; you would certainly blame the contrivance, without any further examination. The architect would in vain display his subtlety, and prove to you, that if this door or that window were altered, greater ills would ensue. What he says may be strictly true: The alteration of one particular, while the other parts of the building remain, may only augment the inconveniences. But still you would assert in general, that, if the architect had had skill and good intentions, he might have formed such a plan of the whole, and might have adjusted the parts in such a manner, as would have remedied all or most of these inconveniences. His ignorance, or even your own ignorance of such a plan, will never convince you of the impossibility of it. If you find any inconveniences and deformities in the building, you will always, without entering into any detail, condemn the architect.

In short, I repeat the question: Is the world, considered in general, and as it appears to us in this life, different from what a man, or such a limited being, would, beforehand, expect from a very powerful, wise, and benevolent Deity? It must be strange prejudice to assert the contrary. And from thence I conclude, that however consistent the world may be, allowing certain suppositions and conjectures, with the idea of such a Deity, it can never afford us an inference concerning his existence. The consistence is not absolutely denied, only the inference. Conjectures, especially where infinity is excluded from the Divine attributes, may perhaps be sufficient to prove a consistence, but can never be foundations for any inference.

There seem to be four circumstances, on which depend all, or the greatest part of the ills, that molest sensible creatures; and it is not impossible but all these circumstances may be necessary and unavoidable. We know so little beyond common life, or even of common life, that, with regard to the economy of a universe, there is no conjecture, however wild, which may not be just; nor any one, however plausible, which may not be erroneous. All that belongs to human understanding, in this deep ignorance and obscurity, is to be skeptical, or at least cautious, and not to admit of any hypothesis whatever, much less of any which is supported by no appearance of probability. Now, this I assert to be the case with regard to all the causes of evil, and the circumstances on which it depends. None of them appear to human reason in the least degree necessary or unavoidable; nor can we suppose them such, without the utmost license of imagination.

The first circumstance which introduces evil, is that contrivance or economy of the animal creation, by which pains, as well as pleasures, are employed to excite all creatures to action, and make them vigilant in the great work of self-preservation. Now pleasure alone, in its various degrees, seems to human understanding sufficient for this purpose. All animals might be constantly in a state of enjoyment: but when urged by any of the necessities of nature, such as thirst, hunger, weariness; instead of pain, they might feel a diminution of pleasure, by which they might be prompted to seek that object which is necessary to their subsistence. Men pursue pleasure as eagerly as they avoid pain; at least they might have been so constituted. It seems, therefore, plainly possible to carry on the business of life without any pain. Why then is any animal ever rendered susceptible of such a sensation? If animals can be free from it an hour, they might enjoy a perpetual exemption from it; and it required as particular a contrivance of their organs to produce that feeling, as to endow them with sight, hearing, or any of the senses. Shall we conjecture, that such a contrivance was necessary, without any appearance of reason? And shall we build on that conjecture as on the most certain truth?

But a capacity of pain would not alone produce pain, were it not for the second circumstance, viz. the conducting of the world by general laws; and this seems nowise necessary to a very perfect Being. It is true, if everything were conducted by particular volitions, the course of nature would be perpetually broken, and no man could employ his reason in the conduct of life. But might not other particular volitions remedy this inconvenience? In short, might not the Deity exterminate all ill, wherever it were to be found; and produce all good, without any preparation, or long progress of causes and effects?

Besides, we must consider, that, according to the present economy of the world, the course of nature, though supposed exactly regular, yet to us appears not so, and many events are uncertain, and many disappoint our expectations. Health and sickness, calm and tempest, with an infinite number of other accidents, whose causes are unknown and variable, have a great influence both on the fortunes of particular persons and on the prosperity of public societies; and indeed all human life, in a manner, depends on such accidents. A being, therefore, who knows the secret springs of the universe, might easily, by particular volitions, turn all these accidents to the good of mankind, and render the whole world happy, without discovering himself in any operation. A fleet, whose purposes were salutary to society, might always meet with a fair wind. Good princes enjoy sound health and long life. Persons born to power and authority, be framed with good tempers and virtuous dispositions. A few such events as these, regularly and wisely conducted, would change the face of the world; and yet would no more seem to disturb the course of nature, or confound human conduct, than the present economy of things, where the causes are secret, and variable, and compounded. Some small touches given to CALIGULA's brain in his infancy, might have converted him into a TRAJAN. One wave, a little higher than the rest, by burying CAESAR and his fortune in the bottom of the ocean, might have restored liberty to a considerable part of mankind. There may, for aught we know, be good reasons why Providence interposes not in this manner; but they are unknown to us; and though the mere supposition, that such reasons exist, may be sufficient to save the conclusion concerning the Divine attributes, yet surely it can never be sufficient to establish that conclusion.

If everything in the universe be conducted by general laws, and if animals be rendered susceptible of pain, it scarcely seems possible but some ill must arise in the various shocks of matter, and the various concurrence and opposition of general laws; but this ill would be very rare, were it not for the third circumstance, which I proposed to mention, viz. the great frugality with which all powers and faculties are distributed to every particular being. So well-adjusted are the organs and capacities of all animals, and so well fitted to their preservation, that, as far as history or tradition reaches, there appears not to be any single species which has yet been extinguished in the universe. Every animal has the requisite endowments; but these endowments are bestowed with so scrupulous an economy, that any considerable diminution must entirely destroy the creature. Wherever one power is increased, there is a proportional abatement in the others. Animals which excel in swiftness are commonly defective in force. Those which possess both are either imperfect in some of their senses, or are oppressed with the most craving wants. The human species, whose chief excellence is reason and sagacity, is of all others the most necessitous, and the most deficient in bodily advantages; without clothes, without arms, without food, without lodging, without any convenience of life, except what they owe to their own skill and industry. In short, nature seems to have formed an exact calculation of the necessities of her creatures; and, like a rigid master, has afforded them little more powers or endowments than what are strictly sufficient to supply those necessities. An indulgent parent would have bestowed a large stock, in order to guard against accidents, and secure the happiness and welfare of the creature in the most unfortunate concurrence of circumstances. Every course of life would not have been so surrounded with precipices, that the least departure from the true path, by mistake or necessity, must involve us in misery and ruin. Some reserve, some fund, would have been provided to ensure happiness; nor would the powers and the necessities have been adjusted with so rigid an economy. The Author of Nature is inconceivably powerful: his force is supposed great, if not altogether inexhaustible: nor is there any reason, as far as we can judge, to make him observe this strict frugality in his dealings with his creatures. It would have been better, were his power extremely limited, to have created fewer animals, and to have endowed these with more faculties for their happiness and preservation. A builder is never esteemed prudent, who undertakes a plan beyond what his stock will enable him to finish.

In order to cure most of the ills of human life, I require not that man should have the wings of the eagle, the swiftness of the stag, the force of the ox, the arms of the lion, the scales of the crocodile or rhinoceros; much less do I demand the sagacity of an angel or cherubim. I am contented to take an increase in one single power or faculty of his soul. Let him be endowed with a greater propensity to industry and labor; a more vigorous spring and activity of mind; a more constant bent to business and application. Let the whole species possess naturally an equal diligence with that which many individuals are able to attain by habit and reflection; and the most beneficial consequences, without any allay of ill, is the immediate and necessary result of this endowment. Almost all the moral, as well as natural evils of human life, arise from idleness; and were our species, by the original constitution of their frame, exempt from this vice or infirmity, the perfect cultivation of land, the improvement of arts and manufactures, the exact execution of every office and duty, immediately follow; and men at once may fully reach that state of society, which is so imperfectly attained by the best regulated government. But as industry is a power, and the most valuable of any, Nature seems determined, suitably to her usual maxims, to bestow it on men with a very sparing hand; and rather to punish him severely for his deficiency in it, than to reward him for his attainments. She has so contrived his frame, that nothing but the most violent necessity can oblige him to labor; and she employs all his other wants to overcome, at least in part, the want of diligence, and to endow him with some share of a faculty of which she has thought fit naturally to bereave him. Here our demands may be allowed very humble, and therefore the more reasonable. If we required the endowments of superior penetration and judgment, of a more delicate taste of beauty, of a nicer sensibility to benevolence and friendship; we might be told, that we impiously pretend to break the order of Nature; that we want to exalt ourselves into a higher rank of being; that the presents which we require, not being suitable to our state and condition, would only be pernicious to us. But it is hard; I dare to repeat it, it is hard, that being placed in a world so full of wants and necessities, where almost every being and element is either our foe or refuses its assistance . . . we should also have our own temper to struggle with, and should be deprived of that faculty which can alone fence against these multiplied evils.

The fourth circumstance, whence arises the misery and ill of the universe, is the inaccurate workmanship of all the springs and principles of the great machine of nature. It must be acknowledged, that there are few parts of the universe, which seem not to serve some purpose, and whose removal would not produce a visible defect and disorder in the whole. The parts hang all together; nor can one be touched without affecting the rest, in a greater or less degree. But at the same time, it must be observed, that none of these parts or principles, however useful, are so accurately adjusted, as to keep precisely within those bounds in which their utility consists; but they are, all of them, apt, on every occasion, to run into the one extreme or the other. One would imagine, that this grand production had not received the last hand of the maker; so little finished is

every part, and so coarse are the strokes with which it is executed. Thus, the winds are requisite to convey the vapors along the surface of the globe, and to assist men in navigation: but how oft, rising up to tempests and hurricanes, do they become pernicious? Rains are necessary to nourish all the plants and animals of the earth: but how often are they defective? How often excessive? Heat is requisite to all life and vegetation; but is not always found in the due proportion. On the mixture and secretion of the humors and juices of the body depend the health and prosperity of the animal: but the parts perform not regularly their proper function. What more useful than all the passions of the mind, ambition, vanity, love, anger? But how oft do they break their bounds, and cause the greatest convulsions in society? There is nothing so advantageous in the universe, but what frequently becomes pernicious, by its excess or defect; nor has Nature guarded, with the requisite accuracy, against all disorder or confusion. The irregularity is never perhaps so great as to destroy any species; but is often sufficient to involve the individuals in ruin and misery.

On the concurrence, then, of these four circumstances, does all or the greatest part of natural evil depend. Were all living creatures incapable of pain, or were the world administered by particular volitions, evil never could have found access into the universe: and were animals endowed with a large stock of powers and faculties, beyond what strict necessity requires; or were the several springs and principles of the universe so accurately framed as to preserve always the just temperament and medium; there must have been very little ill in comparison of what we feel at present. What then shall we pronounce on this occasion? Shall we say that these circumstances are not necessary, and that they might easily have been altered in the contrivance of the universe? This decision seems too presumptuous for creatures so blind and ignorant. Let us be more modest in our conclusions. Let us allow, that, if the goodness of the Deity (I mean a goodness like the human) could be established on any tolerable reasons a priori, these phenomena, however untoward, would not be sufficient to subvert that principle; but might easily, in some unknown manner, be reconcilable to it. But let us still assert, that as this goodness is not antecedently established, but must be inferred from the phenomena, there can be no grounds for such an inference, while there are so many ills in the universe, and while these ills might so easily have been remedied, as far as human understanding can be allowed to judge on such a subject.

I am Skeptic enough to allow, that the bad appearances, notwithstanding all my reasonings, may be compatible with such attributes as you suppose; but surely they can never prove these attributes. Such a conclusion cannot result from Skepticism, but must arise from the phenomena, and from our confidence in the reasonings which we deduce from these phenomena.

Look round this universe. What an immense profusion of beings, animated and organized, sensible and active! You admire this prodigious variety and fecundity. But inspect a little more narrowly these living existences, the only beings worth regarding. How hostile and destructive to each other! How insufficient all of them for their own happiness! How contemptible or odious to the spectator! The whole presents nothing but the idea of a blind Nature, impregnated by a great vivifying principle, and pouring forth from her lap, without discernment or parental care, her maimed and abortive children!

Here the Manichean system occurs as a proper hypothesis to solve the difficulty: and no doubt, in some respects, it is very specious, and has more probability than the common hypothesis, by giving a plausible account of the strange mixture of good and ill which appears in life. But if we consider, on the other hand, the perfect uniformity and agreement of the parts of the universe, we shall not discover in it any marks of the combat of a malevolent with a benevolent being. There is indeed an opposition of pains and pleasures in the feelings of sensible creatures: but are not all the operations of Nature carried on by an opposition of principles, of hot and cold, moist and dry, light and heavy? The true conclusion is, that the original Source of all things is entirely indifferent to all these principles; and has no more regard to good above ill, than to heat above cold, or to drought above moisture, or to light above heavy.

There may four hypotheses be framed concerning the first causes of the universe: that they are endowed with perfect goodness; that they have perfect malice; that they are opposite, and have both goodness and malice; that they have neither goodness nor malice. Mixed phenomena can never prove the two former unmixed principles; and the uniformity and steadiness of general laws seem to oppose the third. The fourth, therefore, seems by far the most probable.

What I have said concerning natural evil will apply to moral, with little or no variation; and we have no more reason to infer, that the rectitude of the Supreme Being resembles human rectitude, than that his benevolence resembles the human. Nay, it will be thought, that we have still greater cause to exclude from him moral sentiments, such as we feel them; since moral evil, in the opinion of many, is much more predominant above moral good than natural evil above natural good.

But even though this should not be allowed, and though the virtue which is in mankind should be acknowledged much superior to the vice, yet so long as there is any vice at all in the universe, it will very much puzzle you Anthropomorphites, how to account for it. You must assign a cause for it, without having recourse to the first cause. But as every effect must have a cause, and that cause another, you must either carry on the progression in infinitum, or rest on that original principle, who is the ultimate cause of all things . . .

DEMEA: Hold! Hold! Does your imagination hurry you? I joined in alliance with you, in order to prove the incomprehensible nature of the Divine Being, and refute the principles of Cleanthes, who would measure everything by human rule and standard. But I now find you running into all the topics of the greatest libertines and infidels, and betraying that holy cause which you seemingly espoused. Are you secretly, then, a more dangerous enemy than Cleanthes himself?

CLEANTHES: And are you so late in perceiving it? Believe me, Demea, your friend Philo, from the beginning, has been amusing himself at both our expense; and it must be confessed, that the injudicious reasoning of our vulgar theology has given him but too just a handle of ridicule. The total infirmity of human reason, the absolute incomprehensibility of the Divine Nature, the great and universal misery, and still greater wickedness of men; these are strange topics, surely, to be so fondly cherished by orthodox divines and doctors. In ages of stupidity and ignorance, indeed, these principles may safely be espoused; and perhaps no views of things are more proper to promote superstition, than such as encourage the blind amazement, the diffidence, and melancholy of mankind. But at presents . . .

PHILO: Blame not so much the ignorance of these reverend gentlemen. They know how to change their style with the times. Formerly it was a most popular theological topic to maintain, that human life was vanity and misery, and to exaggerate all the ills and pains which are incident to men. But of late years, divines, we find, begin to retract this position; and maintain, though still with some hesitation, that there are more goods than evils, more pleasures than pains, even in this life. When religion stood entirely upon temper and education, it was thought proper to encourage melancholy; as indeed mankind never have recourse to superior powers so readily as in that disposition. But as men have now learned to form principles, and to draw consequences, it is necessary to change the batteries, and to make use of such arguments as will endure at least some scrutiny and examination. This variation is the same (and from the same causes) with that which I formerly remarked with regard to Skepticism.

[Thus Philo continued to the last his spirit of opposition, and his censure of established opinions. But I could observe that Demea did not at all relish the latter part of the discourse; and he took occasion soon after, on some pretense or other, to leave the company.]

[Dialogues Concerning Natural Religion (1779).]

CHAPTER NINE

Kant on Duty and the Categorical Imperative

Image © Nicku, 2014. Used under license from Shutterstock, Inc.

Immanuel Kant.

Immanuel Kant (1724–1804)

SELECTED READINGS

▶ *Groundwork of the Metaphysics of Morals*—Immanuel Kant

Groundwork of the Metaphysics of Morals

Immanuel Kant

(Translated by Mary Gregor and edited by Joseph R. Kirkland)

SECTION I: TRANSITION FROM COMMON RATIONAL TO PHILOSOPHIC MORAL COGNITION

It is impossible to think of anything at all in the world, or indeed even beyond it, that could be considered good without limitation except a **good will**. Understanding, wit, judgment and the like, whatever such *talents* of mind may be called, or courage, resolution, and perseverance in one's plans, as qualities of *temperament*, are undoubtedly good and desirable for many purposes, but they can also be extremely evil and harmful if the will which is to make use of these gifts of nature, and whose distinctive constitution is therefore called *character*, is not good. It is the same with *gifts of fortune*. Power, riches, honor, even health and that complete wellbeing and satisfaction with one's condition called *happiness*, produce boldness and thereby often arrogance as well unless a good will is present which corrects the influence of these on the mind and, in so doing, also corrects the whole principle of action and brings it into conformity with universal ends—not to mention that an impartial rational spectator can take no delight in seeing the uninterrupted prosperity of a being graced with no feature of a pure and good will, so that a good will seems to constitute the indispensable condition even of worthiness to be happy.

Some qualities are even conducive to this good will itself and can make its work much easier; despite this, however, they have no inner unconditional worth but always presuppose a good will, which limits the esteem one otherwise rightly has for them and does not permit their being taken as absolutely good. Moderation in affects and passions, self-control, and calm reflection are not only good for all sorts of purposes but even seem to constitute a part of the *inner* worth of a person; but they lack much that would be required to declare them good without limitation (however unconditionally they were praised by the ancients); for, without the basic principles of a good will they can become extremely evil, and the coolness of a scoundrel makes him not only far more dangerous but also immediately more abominable in our eyes than we would have taken him to be without it.

A good will is not good because of what it effects or accomplishes, because of its fitness to attain some proposed end, but only because of its volition, that is, it is good in itself and, regarded for itself, is to be valued incomparably higher than all that could merely be brought about by it in favor of some inclination and indeed, if you will, of the sum of all inclinations. Even if, by a special disfavor of fortune or by the [miserly] provision of a step-motherly nature, this will should wholly lack the capacity to carry out its purpose—if with its greatest efforts it should yet achieve nothing and only the good will were left (not, of course, as a mere wish but as the summoning of all means insofar as they are in our control)—then, like a jewel, it would still shine by itself, as something that has its full worth in itself. Usefulness or fruitlessness can neither add anything to this worth nor take anything away from it. Its usefulness would be, as it were, only the setting to enable us to handle it more conveniently in ordinary commerce or to attract to it the attention of those who are not yet expert enough, but not to recommend it to experts or to determine its worth.

There is, however, something so strange in this idea of the absolute worth of a mere will, in the estimation of which no allowance is made for any usefulness, that, despite all the agreement even of common understanding with this idea, a suspicion must yet arise that its covert basis is perhaps mere high-flown fantasy and that we may have misunderstood the purpose of nature in assigning reason to our will as its governor. Hence we shall put this idea to the test from this point of view.

In the natural constitution of an organized being, that is, one constituted purposively for life, we assume as a principle that there will be found in it no instrument for some end other than what is also most appropriate to that end and best adapted to it. Now in a being that has reason and a will, if the proper end of nature were its *preservation*, its *welfare*, in a word its *happiness*, then nature would have hit upon a very bad arrangement in selecting the reason of the creature to carry out this purpose. For all the actions that the creature has to perform for this purpose, and the whole rule of its conduct, would be marked out for it far more accurately by instinct, and that end would have thereby been attained much more surely than it ever can be by reason; and if reason should have been given, over and above, to this favored creature, it must have served it only to contemplate the fortunate constitution of its nature, to admire this, to delight in it, and to be grateful for it to the beneficent cause, but not to submit its faculty of desire to that weak and deceptive guidance and meddle with nature's purpose. In a word, nature would have taken care that reason should not break forth into *practical use* and have the presumption, with its weak insight, to think out for itself a plan for happiness and for the means of attaining it. Nature would have taken upon itself the choice not only of ends but also of means and, with wise foresight, would have entrusted them both simply to instinct.

And, in fact, we find that the more a cultivated reason purposely occupies itself with the enjoyment of life and with happiness, so much the further does one get away from true satisfaction; and from this there arises in many, and indeed in those who have experimented most with this use of reason, if only they are candid enough to admit it, a certain degree of *misology*, that is, hatred of reason; for, after calculating all the advantages they draw—do not say from the invention of all the arts of common luxury, but even from the sciences (which seem to them to be, at bottom, only a luxury of the understanding)—they find that they have in fact only brought more trouble upon themselves instead of gaining in happiness; and because of this they finally envy rather than despise the more common run of people, who are closer to the guidance of mere natural instinct and do not allow their reason much influence on their behavior. And to this extent we must admit that the judgment of those who greatly moderate, and even reduce below zero, eulogies extolling the advantages that reason is supposed to procure for us with regard to the happiness and satisfaction of life is by no means surly or ungrateful to the goodness of the government of the world; we must admit, instead, that these judgments have as their covert basis the idea of another and far worthier purpose of one's existence, to which therefore, and not to happiness, reason is properly destined, and to which, as supreme condition, the private purpose of the human being must for the most part defer.

Since reason is not sufficiently competent to guide the will surely with regard to its objects and the satisfaction of all our needs (which it to some extent even multiplies)—an end to which an implanted natural instinct would have led much more certainly; and since reason

is nevertheless given to us as a practical faculty, that is, as one that is to influence the *will*; then, where nature has everywhere else gone to work purposively in distributing its capacities, the true vocation of reason must be to produce a will that is good, not perhaps *as a means* to other purposes, but *good in itself*, for which reason was absolutely necessary. This will need not, because of this, be the sole and complete good, but it must still be the highest good and the condition of every other, even of all demands for happiness. In this case it is entirely consistent with the wisdom of nature if we perceive that the cultivation of reason, which is requisite to the first and unconditional purpose, limits in many ways—at least in this life—the attainment of the second, namely happiness, which is always conditional; indeed it may reduce it below zero without nature proceeding unpurposively in the matter, because reason, which cognizes its highest practical vocation in the establishment of a good will, in attaining this purpose is capable only of its own kind of satisfaction, namely from fulfilling an end which in turn only reason determines, even if this should be combined with many infringements upon the ends of inclination.

We have, then, to explicate the concept of a will that is to be esteemed in itself and that is good apart from any further purpose, as it already dwells in natural sound understanding and needs not so much to be taught as only to be clarified—this concept that always takes first place in estimating the total worth of our actions and constitutes the condition of all the rest. In order to do so, we shall set before ourselves the concept of **duty**, which contains that of a good will though under certain subjective limitations and hindrances, which, however, far from concealing it and making it unrecognizable, rather bring it out by contrast and make it shine forth all the more brightly.

I here pass over all actions that are already recognized as contrary to duty, even though they may be useful for this or that purpose; for in their case the question whether they might have been done *from duty* never arises, since they even conflict with it. I also set aside actions that are really in conformity with duty but to which human beings have *no inclination* immediately and which they still perform because they are impelled to do so through another inclination. For in this case it is easy to distinguish whether an action in conformity with duty is done *from duty* or from a self-seeking purpose. It is much more difficult to note this distinction when an action conforms with duty and the subject has, besides, an *immediate* inclination to it. For example, it certainly conforms with duty that a shopkeeper not overcharge an inexperienced customer, and where there is a good deal of trade a prudent merchant does not overcharge but keeps a fixed general price for everyone, so that a child can buy from him as well as everyone else. People are thus served *honestly*; but this is not nearly enough for us to believe that the merchant acted in this way from duty and basic principles of honesty; his advantage required it; it cannot be assumed here that he had, besides, an immediate inclination toward his customers, so as from love, as it were, to give no one preference over another in the matter of price. Thus the action was done neither from duty nor from immediate inclination but merely for purposes of self-interest.

On the other hand, to preserve one's life is a duty, and besides everyone has an immediate inclination to do so. But on this account the often anxious care that most people take of it still has no inner worth and their maxim has no moral content. They look after their lives *in conformity with duty* but not *from duty*. On the other hand, if adversity and hopeless grief have quite taken away the taste for life; if an unfortunate man, strong of soul and more indignant about his fate than despondent or dejected, wishes for death and yet preserves his life without loving it, not from inclination or fear but from duty, then his maxim has moral content.

To be beneficent where one can is a duty, and besides there are many souls so sympathetically attuned that, without any other motive of vanity or self-interest they find an inner satisfaction in spreading joy around them and can take delight in the satisfaction of others so far as it is their own work. But I assert that in such a case an action of this kind, however it may conform with duty and however amiable it may be, has nevertheless no true moral worth but is on the same footing with other inclinations, for example, the inclination to honor, which, if it fortunately lights upon what is in fact in the common interest and in conformity with duty and hence honorable, deserves praise and encouragement but not esteem; for the maxim lacks moral content, namely that of doing such actions not from inclination but *from duty*. Suppose, then, that the mind of this philanthropist were overclouded by his own grief, which extinguished all sympathy with the fate of others, and that while he still had the means to benefit others in distress their troubles did not move him because he had enough to do with his own; and suppose that now, when no longer incited to it by any inclination, he nevertheless tears himself out of this deadly insensibility

and does the action without any inclination, simply from duty; then the action first has its genuine moral worth. Still further: if nature had put little sympathy in the heart of this or that man; if (in other respects an honest man) he is by temperament cold and indifferent to the sufferings of others, perhaps because he himself is provided with the special gift of patience and endurance toward his own sufferings and presupposes the same in every other or even requires it; if nature had not properly fashioned such a man (who would in truth not be its worst product) for a philanthropist, would he not still find within himself a source from which to give himself a far higher worth than what a mere good-natured temperament might have? By all means! It is just then that the worth of character comes out, which is moral and incomparably the highest, namely that he is beneficent not from inclination but from duty.

To assure one's own happiness is a duty (at least indirectly); for, want of satisfaction with one's condition, under pressure from many anxieties and amid unsatisfied needs, could easily become a great *temptation to transgression of duty*. But in addition, without looking to duty here, all people have already, of themselves, the strongest and deepest inclination to happiness because it is just in this idea that all inclinations unite in one sum. However, the precept of happiness is often so constituted that it greatly infringes upon some inclinations, and yet one can form no determinate and sure concept of the sum of satisfaction of all inclinations under the name of happiness. Hence it is not to be wondered at that a single inclination, determinate both as to what it promises and as to the time within which it can be satisfied, can often outweigh a fluctuating idea, and that a man—for example, one suffering from gout—can choose to enjoy what he likes and put up with what he can since, according to his calculations, on this occasion at least he has not sacrificed the enjoyment of the present moment to the perhaps groundless expectation of a happiness that is supposed to lie in health. But even in this case, when the general; inclination to happiness did not determine his will; when health, at least for him, did not enter as so necessary into this calculation, there is still left over here, as in all other cases, a law, namely to promote his happiness not from inclination but from duty; and it is then that his conduct first has properly moral worth.

It is undoubtedly in this way, again, that we are to understand the passages from scripture in which we are commanded to love our neighbor, even our enemy. For, love as an inclination cannot be commanded, but beneficence from duty—even though no inclination impels us to it and, indeed, natural and unconquerable aversion opposes it—is *practical* and not *pathological* love, which lies in the will and not in the propensity of feeling, in principles of action and not in melting sympathy; and it alone can be commanded.

The second proposition is this: an action from duty has its moral worth *not in the purpose* to be attained by it but in the maxim in accordance with which it is decided upon, and therefore does not depend upon the realization of the object of the action but merely upon the *principle of volition* in accordance with which the action is done without regard for any object of the faculty of desire. That the purposes we may have for our actions, and their effects as ends and incentives of the will, can give actions no unconditional and moral worth is clear from what has gone before. In what, then, can this worth lie, if it is not to be in the will in relation to the hoped for effect of the action? It can lie nowhere else *than in the principle of the will* without regard for the ends that can be brought about by such an action. For, the will stands between its *a priori* principle, which is formal, and its *a posteriori* incentive, which is material, as at a crossroads; and since it must still be determined by something, it must be determined by the formal principle of volition as such when an action is done from duty, where every material principle has been withdrawn from it.

The third proposition, which is a consequence of the two preceding, I would express as follows: *duty is the necessity of an action from respect for law.* For an object as the effect of my proposed action I can indeed have *inclination* but *never respect*, just because it is merely an effect and not an activity of a will. In the same way I cannot have respect for inclination as such, whether it is mine or that of another; I can at most in the first case approve it and in the second sometimes even love it, that is, regard it as favorable to my own advantage. Only what is connected with my will merely as ground and never as effect, what does not serve my inclination but outweighs it or at least excludes it altogether from calculations in making a choice—hence the mere law for itself—can be an object of respect and so a command. Now, an action from duty is to put aside entirely the influence of inclination and with it every object of the will; hence there is left for the will nothing that could determine it except objectively the *law* and subjectively *pure respect* for this practical law, and so the maxim of complying with such a law even if it infringes upon all my inclinations.

Thus the moral worth of an action does not lie in the effect expected from it and so too does not lie in any principle of action that needs to borrow its motive from this expected effect. For, all these effects (agreeableness of one's condition, indeed even promotion of others' happiness) could have been also brought about by other causes, so that there would have been no need, for this, of the will of a rational being, in which, however, the highest and unconditional good alone can be found. Hence nothing other than *the representation of the law* in itself, *which can of course occur only in a rational being*, insofar as it and not the hoped-for effect is the determining ground of the will, can constitute the preeminent good we call moral, which is already present in the person himself who acts in accordance with this representation and need not wait upon the effect of his action.

But what kind of law can that be, the representation of which must determine the will, even without regard for the effect expected from it, in order for the will to be called good absolutely and without limitation? Since I have deprived the will of every impulse that could arise for it from obeying some law, nothing is left but the conformity of actions as such with universal law, which alone is to serve the will as its principle, that is, *I ought never to act except in such a way that I could also will that my maxim should become a universal law.* Here mere conformity to law as such, without having as its basis some law determined for certain actions, is what serves the will as its principle, and must so serve it, if duty is not to be everywhere an empty delusion and a chimerical concept. Common human reason also agrees completely with this in its practical appraisals and always has this principle before its eyes. Let the question be, for example: may I, when hard pressed, make a promise with the intention not to keep it? Here I easily distinguish two significations the question can have: whether it is prudent or whether it is in conformity with duty to make a false promise. The first can undoubtedly often be the case. I see very well that it is not enough to get out of a present difficulty by means of this subterfuge but that I must reflect carefully whether this lie may later give rise to much greater inconvenience for me than that from which I now extricate myself; and since, with all my supposed *cunning*, the results cannot be so easily foreseen but that once confidence in me is lost this could be far more prejudicial to me than all the troubles I now think to avoid, I must reflect whether the matter might be handled *more prudently* by proceeding on a general maxim and making it a habit to promise nothing except with the intention of keeping it. But it is soon clear to me that such a maxim will still be based only on results feared. To be truthful from duty, however, is something entirely different from being truthful from anxiety about detrimental results, since in the first case the concept of the action in itself already contains a law for me while in the second I must first look about elsewhere to see what effects on me might be combined with it. For, if I deviate from the principle of duty this is quite certainly evil; but if I am unfaithful to my maxim of prudence this can sometimes be very advantageous to me, although it is certainly safer to abide by it. However, to inform myself in the shortest and yet infallible way about the answer to this problem, whether a lying promise is in conformity with duty, I ask myself: would I indeed be content that my maxim (to get myself out of difficulties by a false promise) should hold as a universal law (for myself as well as for others)? and could I indeed say to myself that every one may make a false promise when he finds himself in a difficulty he can get out of in no other way? Then I soon become aware that I could indeed will the lie, but by no means a universal law to lie; for in accordance with such a law there would properly be no promises at all, since it would be futile to avow my will with regard to my future actions to others who would not believe this avowal or, if they rashly did so, would pay me back in like coin; and thus my maxim, as soon as it were made a universal law, would have to destroy itself.

I do not, therefore, need any penetrating acuteness to see what I have to do in order that my volition be morally good. Inexperienced in the course of the world, incapable of being prepared for whatever might come to pass in it, I ask myself only: can you also will that your maxim become a universal law? If not, then it is to be repudiated, and that not because of a disadvantage to you or even to others forthcoming from it but because it cannot fit as a principle into a possible giving of universal law, for which lawgiving reason, however, forces from me immediate respect. Although I do not yet *see* what this respect is based upon (this the philosopher may investigate), I at least understand this much: that it is an estimation of a worth that far outweighs any worth of what is recommended by inclination, and that the necessity of my action from *pure* respect for the practical law is what constitutes duty, to which every other motive must give way because it is the condition of a will good *in itself*, the worth of which surpasses all else.

Thus, then, we have arrived, within the moral cognition of common human reason, at its principle, which it admittedly does not think so abstractly in a universal form but which it actually has always before its eyes and uses as the norm for its appraisals. Here it would be easy to show how common human reason, with this compass in hand, knows very well how to distinguish in every case that comes up what is good and what is evil, what is in conformity with duty or contrary to duty, if, without in the least teaching it anything new, we only, as did Socrates, make it attentive to its own principle; and that there is, accordingly, no need of science and philosophy to know what one has to do in order to be honest and good, and even wise and virtuous. We might even have assumed in advance that cognizance of what it is incumbent upon everyone to do, and so also to know, would be the affair of every human being, even the most common.

Yet we cannot consider without admiration how great an advantage the practical faculty of appraising has over the theoretical in common human understanding. In the latter, if common reason ventures to depart from laws of experience and perceptions of the senses it falls into sheer incomprehensibilities and self-contradictions, at least into a chaos of uncertainty, obscurity, and instability. But in practical matters, it is just when common understanding excludes all sensible incentives from practical laws that its faculty of appraising first begins to show itself to advantage. It then becomes even subtle, whether in quibbling tricks with its own conscience or with other claims regarding what is to be called right, or in sincerely wanting to determine the worth of actions for its own instruction; and, what is most admirable, in the latter case it can even have as good a hope of hitting the mark as any philosopher can promise himself; indeed, it is almost more sure in this matter, because a philosopher, though he cannot have any other principle than that of common understanding, can easily confuse his judgment by a mass of considerations foreign and irrelevant to the matter and deflect it from the straight course. Would it not therefore be more advisable in moral matters to leave the judgment of common reason as it is and, at most, call in philosophy only to present the system of morals all the more completely and apprehensibly and to present its rules in a form more convenient for use (still more for disputation), but not to lead common human understanding, even in practical matters, away from its fortunate simplicity and to put it, by means of philosophy, on a new path of investigation and instruction?

There is something splendid about innocence; but what is bad about it, in turn, is that it cannot protect itself very well and is easily seduced. Because of this, even wisdom—which otherwise consists more in conduct than in knowledge—still needs science, not in order to learn from it but in order to provide access and durability for its precepts. The human being feels within himself a powerful counterweight to all the commands of duty, which reason represents to him as so deserving of the highest respect- the counterweight of his needs and inclinations, the entire satisfaction of which he sums up under the name happiness. Now reason issues its precepts unremittingly, without thereby promising anything to the inclinations, and so, as it were, with disregard and contempt for those claims, which are so impetuous and besides so apparently equitable (and refuse to be neutralized by any command). But from this there arises a *natural dialectic*, that is, a propensity to rationalize against those strict laws of duty and to cast doubt upon their validity, or at least upon their purity and strictness, and, where possible, to make them better suited to our wishes and inclinations, that is, to corrupt them at their basis and to destroy all their dignity—something that even common practical reason cannot, in the end, call good.

In this way *common human reason* is impelled, not by some need of speculation (which never touches it as long as it is content to be mere sound reason), but on practical grounds themselves, to go out of its sphere and to take a step into the field of *practical philosophy*, in order to obtain there information and distinct instruction regarding the source of its principle and the correct determination of this principle in comparison with maxims based on need and inclination, so that it may escape from its predicament about claims from both sides and not run the risk of being deprived of all genuine moral principles through the ambiguity into which it easily falls. So there develops unnoticed in common practical reason as well, when it cultivates itself, a *dialectic* that constrains it to seek help in philosophy, just as happens in its theoretical use; and the first will, accordingly, find no more rest than the other except in a complete critique of our reason.

SECTION II: TRANSITION FROM POPULAR MORAL PHILOSOPHY TO METAPHYSICS OF MORALS

If we have so far drawn our concept of duty from the common use of our practical reason, it is by no means to be inferred from this that we have treated it as a concept of experience. On the contrary, if we attend to experience of people's conduct we meet frequent and, as we ourselves admit, just complaints that no certain example can be cited of the disposition to act from pure duty; that, though much may be done *in conformity with* what *duty* commands, still it is always doubtful whether it is really done *from duty* and therefore has moral worth. Hence there have at all times been philosophers who have absolutely denied the reality of this disposition in human actions and ascribed everything to more or less refined self-love. They did not, on account of this, call into doubt the correctness of the concept of morality but rather spoke with deep regret of the frailty and impurity of human nature, which is indeed noble enough to take as its precept an idea so worthy of respect but at the same time is too weak to follow it, and uses reason, which should serve it for giving law, only to look after the interests of the inclinations, whether singly or, at most, in their greatest compatibility with one another.

In fact, it is absolutely impossible by means of experience to make out with complete certainty a single case in which the maxim of an action otherwise in conformity with duty rested simply on moral grounds and on the representation of one's duty. It is indeed sometimes the case that with the keenest self-examination we find nothing besides the moral ground of duty that could have been powerful enough to move us to this or that good action and to so great a sacrifice; but from this it cannot be inferred with certainty that no covert impulse of self-love, under the mere pretense of that idea, was not actually the real determining cause of the will; for we like to flatter ourselves by falsely attributing to ourselves a nobler motive, whereas in fact we can never, even by the most strenuous self-examination, get entirely behind our covert incentives, since, when moral worth is at issue, what counts is not actions, a which one sees, but those inner principles of actions that one does not see.

Moreover, one cannot better serve the wishes of those who ridicule all morality as the mere phantom of a human imagination overstepping itself through self-conceit than by granting them that concepts of duty must be drawn solely from experience (as, from indolence, people like to persuade themselves is the case with all other concepts as well); for then one prepares a sure triumph for them. From love of humankind I am willing to admit that even most of our actions are in conformity with duty; but if we look more closely at the intentions and aspirations in them we everywhere come upon the dear self, which is always turning up; and it is on this that their purpose is based, not on the strict command of duty, which would often require self-denial. One need not be an enemy of virtue but only a cool observer, who does not take the liveliest wish for the good straight-away as its reality, to become doubtful at certain moments (especially with increasing years, when experience has made one's judgment partly more shrewd and partly more acute in observation) whether any true virtue is to be found in the world. And then nothing can protect us against falling away completely from our ideas of duty and can preserve in our soul a well-grounded respect for its law other than the clear conviction that, even there never have been actions arising from such pure sources, what is at issue here is not whether this or that happened; that, instead, reason by itself and independently of all appearances commands what ought to happen; that, accordingly, actions of which the world has perhaps so far given no example, and whose very practicability might be very much doubted by one who bases everything on experience, are still inflexibly commanded by reason; and that, for example, pure sincerity in friendship can be no less required of everyone even if up to now there may never have been a sincere friend, because this duty—as duty in general—lies, prior to all experience, in the idea of a reason determining the will by means of *a priori* grounds.

If we add further that, unless we want to deny to the concept of morality any truth and any relation to some possible object, we cannot dispute that its law is so extensive in its import that it must hold not only for human beings but for all *rational beings as such*, not merely under contingent conditions and with exceptions but with *absolute necessity*, then it is clear that no experience could give occasion to infer even the possibility of such apodictic laws. For, by what right could we bring into unlimited respect, as a universal precept for every rational nature, what is perhaps valid only under the contingent conditions of humanity? And how should laws of the determination of *our* will be taken as laws of the determination of the will of rational beings as such, and for ours only as rational beings, if they were merely empirical and did not have their origin completely a priori in pure but practical reason?

Nor could one give worse advice to morality than by wanting to derive it from examples. For, every example of it represented to me must itself first be appraised in accordance with principles of morality, as to whether it is also worthy to serve as an original example, that

is, as a model; it can by no means authoritatively provide the concept of morality. Even the Holy One of the Gospel must first be compared with our ideal of moral perfection before he is cognized as such; even he says of himself: why do you call me (whom you see) good? none is good (the archetype of the good) but God only (whom you do not see). But whence have we the concept of God as the highest good? Solely from the *idea* of moral perfection that reason frames *a priori* and connects inseparably with the concept of a free will. Imitation has no place at all in matters of morality, and examples serve only for encouragement, that is, they put beyond doubt the practicability of what the law commands and make intuitive what the practical rule expresses more generally, but they can never justify setting aside their true original, which lies in reason, and guiding oneself by examples.

If there is, then, no genuine supreme basic principle of morality that does not have to rest only on pure reason independently of all experience, I believe it unnecessary even to ask whether it is a good thing to set forth in their generality (*in abstracto*) these concepts as they, along with the principles belonging to them, are fixed a priori, if this cognition is to be distinguished from the common and called philosophic. But in our day it may well be necessary to ask this. For if votes were collected as to which is to be preferred—pure rational cognition separated from anything empirical, hence metaphysics of morals, or popular practical philosophy—one can guess at once on which side the preponderance would fall.

This descending to popular concepts is certainly very commendable, provided the ascent to the principles of pure reason has first taken place and has been carried through to complete satisfaction. That would mean that the doctrine of morals is first *grounded* on metaphysics and afterwards, when it has been firmly established, is provided with *access* by means of popularity. But it is quite absurd to want to comply with popularity in the first investigation, on which all correctness of basic principles depends. Not only can this procedure never lay claim to the very rare merit of a true *philosophic popularity*, since there is no art in being commonly understandable if one thereby renounces any well-grounded insight; it also produces a disgusting hodge-podge of patchwork observations and half-rationalized principles, in which shallow pates revel because it is something useful for everyday chitchat, but the insightful, feeling confused and dissatisfied without being able to help themselves, avert their eyes—although philosophers, who see quite well through the deception, get little hearing when they call [moralists] away for a time from this alleged popularity, so that they may be rightly popular only after having acquired determinate insight.

One need only look at attempts at morality in that popular taste. One will find now the special determination of human nature (but occasionally the idea of a rational nature as such along with it), now perfection, now happiness, here moral feeling, there fear of God, a bit of this and also a bit of that in a marvelous mixture, without its occurring to them to ask whether the principles of morality are to be sought at all in acquaintance with human nature (which we can get only from experience) and, if this is not the case—if these principles are to be found altogether *a priori*, free from anything empirical, solely in pure rational concepts and nowhere else even to the slightest extent—instead to adopt the plan of quite separating this investigation as pure practical philosophy or (if one may use a name so decried) as metaphysics of morals, of bringing it all by itself to its full completeness, and of putting off the public, which demands popularity, pending the outcome of this undertaking.

But such a completely isolated metaphysics of morals, mixed with no anthropology, theology, physics, or hyperphysics and still less with occult qualities (which could be called hypophysical), is not only an indispensable substratum of all theoretical and surely determined cognition of duties; it is also a desideratum of utmost importance to the actual fulfillment of their precepts. For, the pure thought of duty and in general of the moral law, mixed with no foreign addition of empirical inducements, has by way of reason alone (which with this first becomes aware that it can of itself also be practical) an influence on the human heart so much more powerful than all other incentives, which may be summoned from the empirical field, that reason, in the consciousness of its dignity, despises the latter and can gradually become their master; on the other hand a mixed doctrine of morals, put together from incentives of feeling and inclination and also of rational concepts, must make the mind waver between motives that cannot be brought under any principle, that can lead only contingently to what is good and can very often also lead to what is evil.

From what has been said it is clear that all moral concepts have their seat and origin completely *a priori* in reason, and indeed in the most common reason just as in reason that is speculative in the highest degree; that they cannot be abstracted from any empirical and therefore merely contingent cognitions; that just in this purity of their origin lies their dignity, so that they can serve us as supreme practical principles; that in adding anything empirical to them one subtracts just that much from their genuine influence and from the unlimited worth of actions; that it is not only a requirement of the greatest necessity for theoretical purposes, when it is a matter merely of speculation, but also of the greatest practical importance to draw its concepts and laws from pure reason, to set them forth pure and unmixed, and indeed to determine the extent of this entire practical or pure rational cognition, that is, to determine the entire faculty of pure practical reason; and in so doing, it is of the greatest practical importance not to make its principles dependent upon the special nature of human reason—as speculative philosophy permits and even at times finds necessary—but instead, just because moral laws are to hold for every rational being as such, to derive them from the universal concept of a rational being as such, and in this way to set forth completely the whole of morals, which needs anthropology for its *application* to human beings, at first independently of this as pure philosophy, that is, as metaphysics (as can well be done in this kind of quite separated cognitions); [for we are] well aware that, unless we are in possession of this, it would be—I will not say futile to determine precisely for speculative appraisal the moral element of duty in all that conforms with duty, but—impossible to base morals on their genuine principles even for common and practical use, especially that of moral instruction, and thereby to bring about pure moral dispositions and engraft them onto people's minds for the highest good in the world.

However, in order to advance by natural steps in this study—not merely from common moral appraisal (which is here very worthy of respect) to philosophic, as has already been done, but—from a popular philosophy, which goes no further than it can by groping with the help of examples, to metaphysics (which no longer lets itself be held back by anything empirical and, since it must measure out the whole sum of rational cognition of this kind, goes if need be all the way to ideas, where examples themselves fail us), we must follow and present distinctly the practical faculty of reason, from its general rules of determination to the point where the concept of duty arises from it.

Everything in nature works in accordance with laws. Only a rational being has the capacity to act *in accordance with the representation* of laws, that is, in accordance with principles, or has a *will*. Since *reason* is required for the derivation of actions from laws, the will is nothing other than practical reason. If reason infallibly determines the will, the actions of such a being that are cognized as objectively necessary are also subjectively necessary, that is, the will is a capacity to choose *only that* which reason independently of inclination cognizes as practically necessary, that is, as good. However, if reason solely by itself does not adequately deter mine the will; if the will is exposed also to subjective conditions (certain incentives) that are not always in accord with the objective ones; in a word, if the will is not *in itself* completely in conformity with reason (as is actually the case with human beings), then actions that are cognized as objectively necessary are subjectively contingent, and the determination of such a will in conformity with objective laws is *necessitation*: that is to say, the relation of objective laws to a will that is not thoroughly good is represented as the determination of the will of a rational being through grounds of reason, indeed, but grounds to which this will is not by its nature necessarily obedient.

The representation of an objective principle, insofar as it is necessitating for a will, is called a command (of reason), and the formula of the command is called an **imperative**.

All imperatives are expressed by an *ought* and indicate by this the relation of an objective law of reason to a will that by its subjective constitution is not necessarily determined by it (a necessitation). They say that to do or to omit something would be good, but they say it to a will that does not always do something just because it is represented to it that it would be good to do that thing. Practical good, however, is that which determines the will by means of representations of reason, hence not by subjective causes but objectively, that is, from grounds that are valid for every rational being as such. It is distinguished from the *agreeable*, as that which influences the will only by means of feeling from merely subjective causes, which hold only for the senses of this or that one, and not as a principle of reason, which holds for everyone.

A perfectly good will would, therefore, equally stand under objective laws (of the good), but it could not on this account be represented as *necessitated* to actions in conformity with law since of itself, by its subjective constitution, it can be determined only through the representation of the good. Hence no imperatives

hold for the *divine* will and in general for a *holy* will: the "ought" is out of place here, because volition is of itself necessarily in accord with the law. Therefore imperatives are only formulae expressing the relation of objective laws of volition in general to the subjective imperfection of the will of this or that rational being, for example, of the human will.

Now, all imperatives command either *hypothetically* or *categorically*. The former represent the practical necessity of a possible action as a means to achieving something else that one wills (or that it is at least possible for one to will). The categorical imperative would be that which represented an action as objectively necessary of itself, without reference to another end.

Since every practical law represents a possible action as good and thus as necessary for a subject practically determinable by reason, all imperatives are formulae for the determination of action that is necessary in accordance with the principle of a will which is good in some way. Now, if the action would be good merely as a means *to something else* the imperative is *hypothetical*; if the action is represented as *in itself* good, hence as necessary in a will in itself conforming to reason, as its principle, *then it is categorical.*

The imperative thus says which action possible by me would be good, and represents a practical rule in relation to a will that does not straightaway do an action just because it is good, partly because the subject does not always know that it is good, partly because, even if he knows this, his maxims could still be opposed to the objective principles of a practical reason.

Hence the hypothetical imperative says only that the action is good for some *possible* or *actual* purpose. In the first case it is a **problematically** practical principle, in the second an **assertorically** practical principle. The categorical imperative, which declares the action to be of itself objectively necessary without reference to some purpose, that is, even apart from any other end, holds as an **apodictically** practical principle.

One can think of what is possible only through the powers of some rational being as also a possible purpose of some will; accordingly, principles of action, insofar as this is represented as necessary for attaining some possible purpose to be brought about by it, are in fact innumerable. All sciences have some practical part, consisting of problems [which suppose] that some end is possible for us and of imperatives as to how it can be attained. These can therefore be called, in general, imperatives of **skill**. Whether the end is rational and good is not at all the question here, but only what one must do in order to attain it. The precepts for a physician to make his man healthy in a well-grounded way, and for a poisoner to be sure of killing his, are of equal worth insofar as each serves perfectly to bring about his purpose. Since in early youth it is not known what ends might occur to us in the course of life, parents seek above all to have their children learn *a great many* things and to provide for *skill* in the use of means to all sorts of *discretionary* ends, about none of which can they determine whether it might in the future actually become their pupil's purpose, though it is always *possible* that he might at some time have it; and this concern is so great that they commonly neglect to form and correct their children's judgment about the worth of the things that they might make their ends.

There is, however, *one* end that can be presupposed as actual in the case of all rational beings (insofar as imperatives apply to them, namely as dependent beings), and therefore one purpose that they not merely *could* have but that we can safely presuppose they all actually *do have* by a natural necessity, and that purpose is *happiness*. The hypothetical imperative that represents the practical necessity of an action as a means to the promotion of happiness is **assertoric**. It may be set forth not merely as necessary to some uncertain, merely possible purpose but to a purpose that can be presupposed surely and a priori in the case of every human being, because it belongs to his essence. Now, skill in the choice of means to one's own greatest well-being can be called *prudence* in the narrowest sense. Hence the imperative that refers to the choice of means to one's own happiness, that is, the precept of prudence, is still always *hypothetical*; the action is not commanded absolutely but only as a means to another purpose.

Finally there is one imperative that, without being based upon and having as its condition any other purpose to be attained by certain conduct, commands this conduct immediately. This imperative is **categorical**. It has to do not with the matter of the action and what is to result from it, but with the form and the principle from which the action itself follows; and the essentially good in the action consists in the disposition, let the result be what it may. This imperative may be called the imperative of **morality**.

Volition in accordance with these three kinds of principles is also clearly distinguished by dissimilarity in the necessitation of the will. In order to make this

dissimilarity evident, I think they would be most suitably named in their order by being said to be either *rules* of skill, or *counsels* of prudence, or *commands* (*laws*) of morality. For, only law brings with it the concept of an *unconditional* and objective and hence universally valid necessity, and commands are laws that must be obeyed, that is, must be followed even against inclination. *Giving counsel* does involve necessity, which, however, can hold only under a subjective and contingent condition, whether this or that man counts this or that in his happiness; the categorical imperative, on the contrary, is limited by no condition and, as absolutely although practically necessary, can be called quite strictly a command. The first imperative could also be called *technical* (belonging to art), the second *pragmatic* (belonging to welfare), the third *moral* (belonging to free conduct as such, that is, to morals).

Now the question arises: how are all these imperatives possible? This question does not inquire how the performance of the action that the imperative commands can be thought, but only how the necessitation of the will, which the imperative expresses in the problem, can be thought. How an imperative of skill is possible requires no special discussion. Whoever wills the end also wills (insofar as reason has decisive influence on his actions) the indispensably necessary means to it that are within his power. This proposition is, as regards the volition, analytic; for in the volition of an object as my effect, my causality as acting cause, that is, the use of means, is already thought, and the imperative extracts the concept of actions necessary to this end merely from the concept of a volition of this end (synthetic propositions no doubt belong to determining the means themselves to a purpose intended, but they do not have to do with the ground for actualizing the act of will but for actualizing the object). That in order to divide a line into two equal parts on a sure principle I must make two intersecting arcs from its ends, mathematics admittedly teaches only by synthetic propositions; but when I know that only by such an action can the proposed effect take place, then it is an analytic proposition that if I fully will the effect I also will the action requisite to it; for, it is one and the same thing to represent something as an effect possible by me in a certain way and to represent myself as acting in this way with respect to it.

If only it were as easy to give a determinate concept of happiness, imperatives of prudence would agree entirely with those of skill and would be just as analytic. For it could be said, here just as there: who wills the end also wills (necessarily in conformity with reason) the sole means to it that are within his control. But it is a misfortune that the concept of happiness is such an indeterminate concept that, although every human being wishes to attain this, he can still never say determinately and consistently with himself what he really wishes and wills. The cause of this is that all the elements that belong to the concept of happiness are without exception empirical, that is, they must be borrowed from experience, and that nevertheless for the idea of happiness there is required an absolute whole, a maximum of well-being in my present condition and in every future condition. Now, it is impossible for the most insightful and at the same time most powerful but still finite being to frame for himself a determinate concept of what he really wills here. If he wills riches, how much anxiety, envy and intrigue might he not bring upon himself in this way! If he wills a great deal of cognition and insight, that might become only an eye all the more acute to show him, as all the more dreadful, ills that are now concealed from him and that cannot be avoided, or to burden his desires, which already give him enough to do, with still more needs. If he wills a long life, who will guarantee him that it would not be a long misery? If he at least wills health, how often has not bodily discomfort kept someone from excesses into which unlimited health would have let him fall, and so forth. In short, he is not capable of any principle by which to determine with complete certainty what would make him truly happy, because for this omniscience would be required. One cannot therefore act on determinate principles for the sake of being happy, but only on empirical counsels, for example, of a regimen, frugality, courtesy, reserve and so forth, which experience teaches are most conducive to well-being on the average. From this it follows that imperatives of prudence cannot, to speak precisely, command at all, that is, present actions objectively as practically *necessary*; that they are to be taken as counsels (*consilia*) rather than as commands (*praecepta*) of reason; that the problem of determining surely and universally which action would promote the happiness of a rational being is completely insoluble, so that there can be no imperative with respect to it that would, in the strict sense, command him to do what would make him happy; for happiness is not an ideal of reason but of imagination, resting merely upon empirical grounds, which it is futile to expect should determine an action by which the totality of a series of results in fact infinite would be attained. This imperative of prudence would, nevertheless, be an analytic practical proposition if it is supposed that the means to happiness can be

assigned with certainty; for it is distinguished from the imperative of skill only in this: that in the case of the latter the end is merely possible, whereas in the former it is given; but since both merely command the means to what it is presupposed one wills as an end, the imperative that commands volition of the means for him who wills the end is in both cases analytic. Hence there is also no difficulty with respect to the possibility of such an imperative.

On the other hand, the question of how the imperative of *morality* is possible is undoubtedly the only one needing a solution, since it is in no way hypothetical and the objectively represented necessity can therefore not be based on any presupposition, as in the case of hypothetical imperatives. Only we must never leave out of account, here, that it cannot be made out *by means of any example*, and so empirically, whether there is any such imperative at all, but it is rather to be feared that all imperatives which seem to be categorical may yet in some hidden way be hypothetical. For example, when it is said "you ought not to promise anything deceitfully," and one assumes that the necessity of this omission is not giving counsel for avoiding some other ill—in which case what is said would be "you ought not to make a lying promise lest if it comes to light you destroy your credit" -but that an action of this kind must be regarded as in itself evil and that the imperative of prohibition is therefore categorical: one still cannot show with certainty in any example that the will is here determined merely through the law, without another incentive, although it seems to be so; for it is always possible that covert fear of disgrace, perhaps also obscure apprehension of other dangers, may have had an influence on the will. Who can prove by experience the nonexistence of a cause when all that experience teaches is that we do not perceive it? In such a case, however, the so-called moral imperative, which as such appears to be categorical and unconditional, would in fact be only a pragmatic precept that makes us attentive to our advantage and merely teaches us to take this into consideration.

We shall thus have to investigate entirely *a priori* the possibility of a *categorical* imperative, since we do not here have the advantage of its reality being given in experience, so that the possibility would be necessary not to establish it but merely to explain it. In the meantime, how ever, we can see this much: that the categorical imperative alone has the tenor of a practical **law**; all the others can indeed be called *principles* of the will but not laws, since what it is necessary to do merely for achieving a discretionary purpose can be regarded as in itself contingent and we can always be released from the precept if we give up the purpose; on the contrary, the unconditional command leaves the will no discretion with respect to the opposite, so that it alone brings with it that necessity which we require of a law.

Second, in the case of this categorical imperative or law of morality the ground of the difficulty (of insight into its possibility) is also very great. It is an *a priori* synthetic practical proposition; and since it is so difficult to see the possibility of this kind of proposition in theoretical cognition, it can be readily gathered that the difficulty will be no less in practical cognition.

In this task we want first to inquire whether the mere concept of a categorical imperative may not also provide its formula containing the proposition which alone can be a categorical imperative. For, how such an absolute command is possible, even if we know its tenor, will still require special and difficult toil, which, however, we postpone to the last section.

When I think of a *hypothetical* imperative in general I do not know beforehand what it will contain; I do not know this until I am given the condition. But when I think of a *categorical* imperative I know at once what it contains. For, since the imperative contains, beyond the law, only the necessity that the maxim be in conformity with this law, while the law contains no condition to which it would be limited, nothing is left with which the maxim of action is to conform but the universality of a law as such; and this conformity alone is what the imperative properly represents as necessary.

There is, therefore, only a single categorical imperative and it is this: *act only in accordance with that maxim through which you can at the same time will that it become a universal law.*

Now, if all imperatives of duty can be derived from this single imperative as from their principle, then, even though we leave it undecided whether what is called duty is not as such an empty concept, we shall at least be able to show what we think by it and what the concept wants to say.

Since the universality of law in accordance with which effects take place constitutes what is properly called nature in the most general sense (as regards its form)— that is, the existence of things insofar as it is determined in accordance with universal laws—the universal imperative of duty can also go as follows: *act as if the maxim of your action were to become by your will a universal law of nature*.

We shall now enumerate a few duties in accordance with the usual division of them into duties to ourselves and to other human beings and into perfect and imperfect duties.

1. Someone feels sick of life because of a series of troubles that has grown to the point of despair, but is still so far in possession of his reason that he can ask himself whether it would not be contrary to his duty to himself to take his own life. Now he inquires whether the maxim of his action could indeed become a universal law of nature. His maxim, however, is: from self-love I make it my principle to shorten my life when its longer duration threatens more troubles than it promises agreeableness. The only further question is whether this principle of self-love could become a universal law of nature. It is then seen at once that a nature whose law it would be to destroy life itself by means of the same feeling whose destination is to impel toward the furtherance of life would contradict itself and would therefore not subsist as nature; thus that maxim could not possibly be a law of nature and, accordingly, altogether opposes the supreme principle of all duty.

2. Another finds himself urged by need to borrow money. He well knows that he will not be able to repay it but sees also that nothing will be lent him unless he promises firmly to repay it within a determinate time. He would like to make such a promise, but he still has enough conscience to ask himself: is it not forbidden and contrary to duty to help oneself out of need in such a way? Supposing that he still decided to do so, his maxim of action would go as follows: when I believe myself to be in need of money I shall borrow money and promise to repay it, even though I know that this will never happen. Now this principle of self-love or personal advantage is perhaps quite consistent with my whole future welfare, but the question now is whether it is right. I therefore turn the demand of self-love into a universal law and put the question as follows: how would it be if my maxim became a universal law? I then see at once that it could never hold as a universal law of nature and be consistent with itself, but must necessarily contradict itself. For, the universality of a law that everyone, when he believes himself to be in need, could promise whatever he pleases with the intention of not keeping it would

make the promise and the end one might have in it itself impossible, since no one would believe what was promised him but would laugh at all such expressions as vain pretenses.

3. A third finds in himself a talent that by means of some cultivation could make him a human being useful for all sorts of purposes. However, he finds himself in comfortable circumstances and prefers to give himself up to pleasure than to trouble himself with enlarging and improving his fortunate natural predispositions. But he still asks himself whether his maxim of neglecting his natural gifts, besides being consistent with his propensity to amusement, is also consistent with what one calls duty. He now sees that a nature could indeed always subsist with such a universal law, although . . . the human being should let his talents rust and be concerned with devoting his life merely to idleness, amusement, procreation—in a word, to enjoyment; only he cannot possibly **will** that this become a universal law or be put in us as such by means of natural instinct. For, as a rational being he necessarily wills that all the capacities in him be developed, since they serve him and are given to him for all sorts of possible purposes.

Yet a **fourth**, for whom things are going well while he sees that others (whom he could very well help) have to contend with great hardships, thinks: what is it to me? let each be as happy as heaven wills or as he can make himself; I shall take nothing from him nor even envy him; only I do not care to contribute anything to his welfare or to his assistance in need! Now, if such a way of thinking were to become a universal law the human race could admittedly very well subsist, no doubt even better than when everyone prates about sympathy and benevolence and even exerts himself to practice them occasionally, but on the other hand also cheats where he can, sells the right of human beings or otherwise infringes upon it. But although it is possible that a universal law of nature could very well subsist in accordance with such a maxim, it is still impossible to **will** that such a principle hold everywhere as a law of nature. For, a will that decided this would conflict with itself, since many cases could occur in which one would need the love and sympathy of others and in which, by such a law of nature arisen from his own will, he would rob himself of all hope of the assistance he wishes for himself.

These are a few of the many actual duties, or at least of what we take to be such, whose derivation from the one principle cited above is clear. We must *be able to*

will that a maxim of our action become a universal law: this is the canon of moral appraisal of action in general. Some actions are so constituted that their maxim cannot even be *thought* without contradiction as a universal law of nature, far less could one *will* that it *should* become such. In the case of others that inner impossibility is indeed not to be found, but it is still impossible to *will* that their maxim be raised to the universality of a law of nature because such a will would contradict itself. It is easy to see that the first is opposed to strict or narrower (unremitting); duty, the second only to wide (meritorious) duty; and so all duties, as far as the kind of obligation (not the object of their action) is concerned, have by these examples been set out completely in their dependence upon the one principle.

If we now attend to ourselves in any transgression of a duty, we find that we do not really will that our maxim should become a universal law, since that is impossible for us, but that the opposite of our maxim should instead remain a universal law, only we take the liberty of making an *exception* to it for ourselves (or just for this once) to the advantage of our inclination. Consequently, if we weighed all cases from one and the same point of view, namely that of reason, we would find a contradiction in our own will, namely that a certain principle be objectively necessary as a universal law and yet subjectively not hold universally but allow exceptions. Since, however, we at one time regard our action from the point of view of a will wholly conformed with reason but then regard the very same action from the point of view of a will affected by inclination, there is really no contradiction here but instead a resistance of inclination to the precept of reason (*antagonismus*), through which the universality of the principle (*universalitas*) is changed into mere generality (*generalitas*) and the practical rational principle is to meet the maxim half way. Now, even though this cannot be justified in our own impartially rendered judgment, it still shows that we really acknowledge the validity of the categorical imperative and permit ourselves (with all respect for it) only a few exceptions that, as it seems to us, are inconsiderable and wrung from us.

We have therefore shown at least this much: that if duty is a concept that is to contain significance and real lawgiving for our actions it can be expressed only in categorical imperatives and by no means in hypothetical ones; we have also—and this is already a great deal—set forth distinctly and as determined for every use the content of the categorical imperative, which must contain the principle of all duty (if there is such a thing at all). But we have not yet advanced so far as to prove a priori that there really is such an imperative, that there is a practical law, which commands absolutely of itself and without any incentives, and that the observance of this law is duty.

For the purpose of achieving this it is of the utmost importance to take warning that we must not let ourselves think of wanting to derive the reality of this principle from the *special property of human nature*. For, duty is to be practical unconditional necessity of action and it must therefore hold for all rational beings (to which alone an imperative can apply at all) and *only because of this* be also a law for all human wills. On the other hand, what is derived from the special natural constitution of humanity—what is derived from certain feelings and propensities and even, if possible, from a special tendency that would be peculiar to human reason and would not have to hold necessarily for the will of every rational being—that can indeed yield a maxim for us but not a law; it can yield a subjective principle on which we might act if we have the propensity and inclination, but not an objective principle on which we would be *directed* to act even though every propensity, inclination, and natural tendency of ours were against it—so much so that the sublimity and inner dignity of the command in a duty is all the more manifest the fewer are the subjective causes in favor of it and the more there are against it, without thereby weakening in the least the necessitation by the law or taking anything away from its validity.

Here, then, we see philosophy put in fact in a precarious position, which is to be firm even though there is nothing in heaven or on earth from which it depends or on which it is based. Here philosophy is to manifest its purity as sustainer of its own laws, not as herald of laws that an implanted sense or who knows what tutelary nature whispers to it, all of which—though they may always be better than nothing at all—can still never yield basic principles that reason dictates and that must have their source entirely and completely *a priori* and, at the same time, must have their commanding authority from this: that they expect nothing from the inclination of human beings but everything from the supremacy of the law and the respect owed it or, failing this, condemn the human being to contempt for himself and inner abhorrence.

Hence everything empirical, as an addition to the principle of morality, is not only quite inept for this; it is also highly prejudicial to the purity of morals, where

the proper worth of an absolutely good will—a worth raised above all price—consists just in the principle of action being free from all influences of contingent grounds, which only experience can furnish. One cannot give too many or too frequent warnings against this laxity, or even mean cast of mind, which seeks its principle among empirical motives and laws; for, human reason in its weariness gladly rests on this pillow and in a dream of sweet illusions (which allow it to embrace a cloud instead of Juno) it substitutes for morality a bastard patched up from limbs of quite diverse ancestry, which looks like whatever one wants to see in it but not like virtue for him who has once seen virtue in her true form.

The question is therefore this: is it a necessary law *for all rational beings* always to appraise their actions in accordance with such maxims as they themselves could will to serve as universal laws? If there is such a law, then it must already be connected (completely a priori) with the concept of the will of a rational being as such. But in order to discover this connection we must, however reluctantly, step forth, namely into metaphysics, although into a domain of it that is distinct from speculative philosophy, namely into metaphysics of morals. In a practical philosophy, where we have to do not with assuming grounds for what happens but rather laws for what ought to happen even if it never does, that is, objective practical laws, we do not need to undertake an investigation into the grounds on account of which something pleases or displeases; how the satisfaction of mere sensation differs from taste, and whether the latter differs from a general satisfaction of reason; upon what the feeling of pleasure or displeasure rests, and how from it desires and inclinations arise, and from them, with the cooperation of reason, maxims; for all that belongs to an empirical doctrine of the soul, which would constitute the second part of the doctrine of nature when this is regarded as philosophy of nature insofar as it is based on empirical laws. Here, however, it is a question of objective practical laws and hence of the relation of a will to itself insofar as it determines itself only by reason; for then everything that has reference to the empirical falls away of itself, since if reason entirely by itself determines conduct (and the possibility of this is just what we want now to investigate), it must necessarily do so *a priori*.

The will is thought as a capacity to determine itself to acting in conformity with the *representation of certain laws*. And such a capacity can be found only in rational beings. Now, what serves the will as the objective ground of its self-determination is an end, and this, if it is given by reason alone, must hold equally for all rational beings. What, on the other hand, contains merely the ground of the possibility of an action the effect of which is an end is called a *means*. The subjective ground of desire is an *incentive*; the objective ground of volition is a *motive*; hence the distinction between subjective ends, which rest on incentives, and objective ends, which depend on motives, which hold for every rational being. Practical principles are *formal* if they abstract from all subjective ends, whereas they are *material* if they have put these, and consequently certain incentives, at their basis. The ends that a rational being proposes at his discretion as *effects* of his actions (material ends) are all only relative; for only their mere relation to a specially constituted faculty of desire on the part of the subject gives them their worth, which can therefore furnish no universal principles, no principles valid and necessary for all rational beings and also for every volition, that is, no practical laws. Hence all these relative ends are only the ground of hypothetical imperatives.

But suppose there were something *the existence of which in itself* has an absolute worth, something which as *an end in itself* could be a ground of determinate laws; then in it, and in it alone, would lie the ground of a possible categorical imperative, that is, of a practical law.

Now I say that the human being and in general every rational being exists as an end in itself, *not merely as a means* to be used by this or that will at its discretion; instead he must in all his actions, whether directed to himself or also to other rational beings, always be regarded at the same time as an end. All objects of the inclinations have only a conditional worth; for, if there were not inclinations and the needs based on them, their object would be without worth. But the inclinations themselves, as sources of needs, are so far from having an absolute worth, so as to make one wish to have them, that it must instead be the universal wish of every rational being to be altogether free from them. Thus the worth of any object *to be acquired* by our action is always conditional. Beings the existence of which rests not on our will but on nature, if they are beings without reason, still have only a relative worth, as means, and are therefore called *things*, whereas rational beings are called *persons* because their nature already marks them out as an end in itself, that is, as something that may not be used merely as a means, and hence so far limits all choice (and is an object of

respect). These, therefore, are not merely subjective ends, the existence of which as an effect of our action has a worth *for us*, but rather *objective ends*, that is, beings the existence of which is in itself an end, and indeed one such that no other end, to which they would serve *merely* as means, can be put in its place, since without it nothing of *absolute worth* would be found anywhere; but if all worth were conditional and therefore contingent, then no supreme practical principle for reason could be found anywhere.

If, then, there is to be a supreme practical principle and, with respect to the human will, a categorical imperative, it must be one such that, from the representation of what is necessarily an end for everyone because it is an *end in itself*, it constitutes an *objective* principle of the will and thus can serve as a universal practical law. The ground of this principle is: *rational nature exists as an end in itself*. The human being necessarily represents his own existence in this way; so far it is thus a *subjective* principle of human actions. But every other rational being also represents his existence in this way consequent on just the same rational ground that also holds for me; thus it is at the same time an *objective* principle from which, as a supreme practical ground, it must be possible to derive all laws of the will. The practical imperative will therefore be the following: *So act that you use humanity, whether in your own person or in the person of any other, always at the same time as an end, never merely as a means.* We shall see whether this can be carried out.

To keep to the preceding examples:

> First, as regards the concept of necessary duty to oneself, someone who has suicide in mind will ask himself whether his action can be consistent with the idea of humanity *as an end in itself.* If he destroys himself in order to escape from a trying condition he makes use of a person *merely as a means* to maintain a tolerable condition up to the end of life. A human being, however, is not a thing and hence not something that can be used *merely* as a means, but must in all his actions always be regarded as an end in itself. I cannot, therefore, dispose of a human being in my own person by maiming, damaging or killing him. (I must here pass over a closer determination of this principle that would prevent any misinterpretation, e.g., as to having limbs amputated in order to preserve myself, or putting my life in danger

in order to preserve my life, and so forth; that belongs to morals proper.)

Second, as regards necessary duty to others or duty owed them, he who has it in mind to make a false promise to others sees at once that he wants to make use of another human being *merely as a means*, without the other at the same time containing in himself the end. For, he whom I want to use for my purposes by such a promise cannot possibly agree to my way of behaving toward him, and so himself contain the end of this action. This conflict with the principle of other human beings is seen more distinctly if examples of assaults on the freedom and property of others are brought forward. For then it is obvious that he who transgresses the rights of human beings intends to make use of the person of others merely as means, without taking into consideration that, as rational beings, they are always to be valued at the same time as ends, that is, only as beings who must also be able to contain in themselves the end of the very same action.

Third, with respect to contingent (meritorious) duty to oneself, it is not enough that the action does not conflict with humanity in our person as an end in itself; it must also *harmonize* with it. Now there are in humanity predispositions to greater perfection, which belong to the end of nature with respect to humanity in our subject; to neglect these might admittedly be consistent with the *preservation* of humanity as an end in itself but not with the *furtherance* of this end.

Fourth, concerning meritorious duty to others, the natural end that all human beings have is their own happiness. Now, humanity might indeed subsist if no one contributed to the happiness of others but yet did not intentionally withdraw anything from it; but there is still only a negative and not a positive agreement with *humanity as an end in itself* unless everyone also tries, as far as he can, to further the ends of others. For, the ends of a subject who is an end in itself must as far as possible be also *my* ends, if that representation is to have its *full* effect in me.

This principle of humanity, and in general of every rational nature, *as an end in itself* (which is the supreme limiting condition of the freedom of action of every human being) is not borrowed from experience; first because of its universality, since it applies to all

rational beings as such and no experience is sufficient to determine anything about them; second because in it humanity is represented not as an end of human beings (subjectively), that is, not as an object that we of ourselves actually make our end, but as an objective end that, whatever ends we may have, ought as law to constitute the supreme limiting condition of all subjective ends, so that the principle must arise from pure reason. That is to say, the ground of all practical lawgiving lies (in accordance with the first principle) *objectively in the rule* and the form of universality which makes it fit to be a law (possibly a law of nature); *subjectively*, however, it lies in the end; but the subject of all ends is every rational being as an end in itself (in accordance with the second principle); from this there follows now the third practical principle of the will, as supreme condition of its harmony with universal practical reason, the idea *of the will of every rational being as a will giving universal law.*

In accordance with this principle all maxims are repudiated that are inconsistent with the will's own giving of universal law. Hence the will is not merely subject to the law but subject to it in such a way that it must be viewed as also giving the law to itself" and just because of this as first subject to the law (of which it can regard itself as the author).

Imperatives as they were represented above—namely in terms of the conformity of actions with universal law similar to a *natural order* or of the universal *supremacy as ends* of rational beings in themselves—did exclude from their commanding authority any admixture of interest as incentive, just by their having been represented as categorical; but they were only assumed to be categorical because we had to make such an assumption if we wanted to explain the concept of duty. But that there are practical propositions which command categorically could not itself be proved, any more than it could be proved either here or anywhere else in this section; one thing, however, could still have been done: namely, to indicate in the imperative itself the renunciation of all interest, in volition from duty, by means of some determination the imperative contains, as the specific mark distinguishing categorical from hypothetical imperatives; and this is done in the present third formula of the principle, namely the idea of the will of every rational being as *a will giving universal law.*

For when we think of a will of this kind, then although a will that stands under law may be bound to this law by means of some interest, a will that is itself the supreme lawgiver cannot possibly, as such, depend upon some interest; for, a will that is dependent in this way would itself need yet another law that would limit the interest of its self-love to the condition of a validity for universal law.

Thus the *principle* of every human will as *a will giving universal law through all its maxims*, provided it is otherwise correct, would be very *well suited* to be the categorical imperative by this: that just because of the idea of giving universal law *it is based on no interest* and therefore, among all possible imperatives, can alone be *unconditional*; or still better, by converting the proposition, if there is a categorical imperative (i.e., a law for every will of a rational being) it can only command that everything be done from the maxim of one's will as a will that could at the same time have as its object itself as giving universal law; for only then is the practical principle, and the imperative that the will obeys, unconditional, since it can have no interest as its basis.

If we look back upon all previous efforts that have ever been made to discover the principle of morality, we need not wonder now why all of them had to fail. It was seen that the human being is bound to laws by his duty, but it never occurred to them that he is subject *only to laws given by himself but still universal* and that he is bound only to act in conformity with his own will, which, however, in accordance with nature's end is a will giving universal law. For, if one thought of him only as subject to a law (whatever it may be), this law had to carry with it some interest by way of attraction or constraint, since it did not as a law arise from his will; in order to conform with the law, his will had instead to be constrained by *something else* to act in a certain way. By this quite necessary consequence, however, all the labor to find a supreme ground of duty was irretrievably lost. For, one never arrived at duty but instead at the necessity of an action from a certain interest. This might be one's own or another's interest. But then the imperative had to turn out always conditional and could not be fit for a moral command. I will therefore call this basic principle the principle of the **autonomy** of the will in contrast with every other, which I accordingly count as **heteronomy**.

The concept of every rational being as one who must regard himself as giving universal law through all the maxims of his will, so as to appraise himself and his actions from this point of view, leads to a very fruitful concept dependent upon it namely that of *a kingdom of ends*.

By a *kingdom* I understand a systematic union of various rational beings through common laws. Now since laws determine ends in terms of their universal validity, if we abstract from the personal differences of rational beings as well as from all the content of their private ends we shall be able to think of a whole of all ends in systematic connection (a whole both of rational beings as ends in themselves and of the ends of his own that each may set himself), that is, a kingdom of ends, which is possible in accordance with the above principles.

For, all rational beings stand under the *law* that each of them is to treat himself and all others *never merely as means* but always *at the same time as ends in themselves*. But from this there arises a systematic union of rational beings through common objective laws, that is, a kingdom, which can be called a kingdom of ends (admittedly only an ideal) because what these laws have as their purpose is just the relation of these beings to one another as ends and means.

A rational being belongs as a *member* to the kingdom of ends when he gives universal laws in it but is also himself subject to these laws. He belongs to it as *sovereign* when, as lawgiving, he is not subject to the will of any other.

A rational being must always regard himself as lawgiving in a kingdom of ends possible through freedom of the will, whether as a member or as sovereign. He cannot, however, hold the position of sovereign merely by the maxims of his will but only in case he is a completely independent being, without needs and with unlimited resources adequate to his will.

Morality consists, then, in the reference of all action to the lawgiving by which alone a kingdom of ends is possible. This lawgiving must, however, be found in every rational being himself and be able to arise from his will, the principle of which is, accordingly: to do no action on any other maxim than one such that it would be consistent with it to be a universal law, and hence to act only *so that the will could regard itself as at the same time giving universal law through its maxim*. Now, if maxims are not already of their nature in agreement with this objective principle of rational beings as givers of universal law, the necessity of an action in accordance with this principle is called practical necessitation, that is, *duty*. Duty does not apply to the sovereign in the kingdom of ends, but it does apply to every member of it and indeed to all in equal measure.

The practical necessity of acting in accordance with this principle, that is, duty, does not rest at all on feelings, impulses, and inclinations but merely on the relation of rational beings to one another, in which the will of a rational being must always be regarded as at the same time lawgiving, since otherwise it could not be thought as an *end in itself*. Reason accordingly refers every maxim of the will as giving universal law to every other will and also to every action toward oneself, and does so not for the sake of any other practical motive or any future advantage but from the idea of the *dignity* of a rational being, who obeys no law other than that which he himself at the same time gives.

In the kingdom of ends everything has either a *price* or a *dignity*. What has a price can be replaced by something else as its *equivalent*; what on the other hand is raised above all price and therefore admits of no equivalent has a dignity.

What is related to general human inclinations and needs has a *market price*; that which, even without presupposing a need, conforms with a certain taste, that is, with a delight in the mere purposeless play of our mental powers, has a *fancy price*; but that which constitutes the condition under which alone something can be an end in itself has not merely a relative worth, that is, a price, but an inner worth, that is, *dignity*.

Now, morality is the condition under which alone a rational being can be an end in itself, since only through this is it possible to be a lawgiving member in the kingdom of ends. Hence morality, and humanity insofar as it is capable of morality, is that which alone has dignity. Skill and diligence in work have a market price; wit, lively imagination and humor have a fancy price; on the other hand, fidelity in promises and benevolence from basic principles (not from instinct) have an inner worth. Nature, as well as art, contains nothing that, lacking these, it could put in their place; for their worth does not consist in the effects arising from them, in the advantage and use they provide, but in dispositions, that is, in maxims of the will that in this way are ready to manifest themselves through actions, even if success does not favor them. Such actions also need no recommendation from any subjective disposition or taste, so as to be looked upon with immediate favor and delight, nor do they need any immediate propensity or feeling for them; they present the will that practices them as the object of an immediate respect, and nothing but reason is required to *impose* them upon the will, not to *coax* them from it, which latter would in any case

be a contradiction in the case of duties. This estimation therefore lets the worth of such a cast of mind be cognized as dignity and puts it infinitely above all price, with which it cannot be brought into comparison or competition at all without, as it were, assaulting its holiness.

And what is it, then, that justifies a morally good disposition, or virtue, in making such high claims? It is nothing less than the share it affords a rational being *in the giving of universal laws*, by which it makes him fit to be a member of a possible kingdom of ends, which he was already destined to be by his own nature as an end in itself and, for that very reason, as lawgiving in the kingdom of ends—as free with respect to all laws of nature, obeying only those which he himself gives and in accordance with which his maxims can belong to a giving of universal law (to which at the same time he subjects himself). For, nothing can have a worth other than that which the law determines for it. But the lawgiving itself, which determines all worth, must for that very reason have a dignity, that is, an unconditional, incomparable worth; and the word *respect* alone provides a becoming expression for the estimate of it that a rational being must give. *Autonomy* is therefore the ground of the dignity of human nature and of every rational nature.

The above three ways of representing the principle of morality are at bottom only so many formulae of the very same law, and any one of them of itself unites the other two in it. There is nevertheless a difference among them, which is indeed subjectively rather than objectively practical, intended namely to bring an idea of reason closer to intuition (by a certain analogy) and thereby to feeling. All maxims have, namely,

1. a *form*, which consists in universality; and in this respect the formula of the moral imperative is expressed thus: that maxims must be chosen' as if they were to hold as universal laws of nature;

2. a *matter*, namely an end, and in this respect the formula says that a rational being, as an end by its nature and hence as an end in itself, must in every maxim serve as the limiting condition of all merely relative and arbitrary ends;

3. a *complete determination* of all maxims by means of that formula, namely that all maxims from one's own lawgiving are to harmonize with a possible kingdom of ends as with a kingdom of nature. A progression takes place here, as through the categories

of the *unity* of the form of the will (its universality), the *plurality* of the matter (of objects, i.e., of ends), and the *all-ness* or totality of the system of these. But one does better always to proceed in moral *appraisal* by the strict method and put at its basis the universal formula of the categorical imperative: *act in accordance with a maxim that can at the same time make itself a universal law*. If, however, one wants also to provide *access* for the moral law, it is very useful to bring one and the same action under the three concepts mentioned above and thereby, as far as possible, bring it closer to intuition.

We can now end where we set out from at the beginning, namely with the concept of a will unconditionally good. *That will is absolutely good* which cannot be evil, hence whose maxim, if made a universal law, can never conflict with itself. This principle is, accordingly, also its supreme law: act always on that maxim whose universality as a law you can at the same time will; this is the sole condition under which a will can never be in conflict with itself, and such an imperative is categorical. Since the validity of the will as a universal law for possible actions has an analogy with the universal connection of the existence of things in accordance with universal laws, which is the formal aspect of nature in general, the categorical imperative can also be expressed thus: *act in accordance with maxims that can at the same time have as their object themselves as universal laws of nature*. In this way, then, the formula of an absolutely good will is provided.

Rational nature is distinguished from the rest of nature by this, that it sets itself an end. This end would be the matter of every good will. But since, in the idea of a will absolutely good without any limiting condition (attainment of this or that end) abstraction must be made altogether from every end to be *effected* (this would make every will only relatively good), the end must here be thought not as an end to be effected but as an *independently existing* end, and hence thought only negatively, that is, as that which must never be acted against and which must therefore in every volition be estimated never merely as a means but always at the same time as an end. Now, this end can be nothing other than the subject of all possible ends itself, because this subject is also the subject of a possible absolutely good will; for, such a will cannot without contradiction be subordinated to any other object. The principle, so act with reference to every rational being (yourself and others) that in your maxim it holds at the same time as an end in itself, is thus at bottom the

same as the basic principle, act on a maxim that at the same time contains in itself its own universal validity for every rational being. For, to say that in the use of means to any end I am to limit my maxim to the condition of its universal validity as a law for every subject is tantamount to saying that the subject of ends, that is, the rational being itself, must be made the basis of all maxims of actions, never merely as a means but as the supreme limiting condition in the use of all means, that is, always at the same time as an end.

Now, from this it follows incontestably that every rational being, as an end in itself, must be able to regard himself as also giving universal laws with respect to any law whatsoever to which he may be subject; for, it is just this fitness of his maxims for giving universal law that marks him out as an end in itself; it also follows that this dignity (prerogative) he has over all merely natural beings brings with it that he must always take his maxims from the point of view of himself, and likewise every other rational being, as lawgiving beings (who for this reason are also called persons). Now in this way a world of rational beings (*mundus intelligibilis*) as a kingdom of ends is possible, through the giving of their own laws by all persons as members. Consequently, every rational being must act as if he were by his maxims at all times a lawgiving member of the universal kingdom of ends. The formal principle of these maxims is, act as if your maxims were to serve at the same time as a universal law (for all rational beings). A kingdom of ends is thus possible only by analogy with a kingdom of nature; the former, however, is possible only through maxims, that is, rules imposed upon oneself, the latter only through laws of externally necessitated efficient causes. Despite this, nature as a whole, even though it is regarded as a machine, is still given the name "a kingdom of nature" insofar as and because it has reference to rational beings as its ends. Now, such a kingdom of ends would actually come into existence through maxims whose rule the categorical imperative prescribes to all rational beings *if they were universally followed*. It is true that, even though a rational being scrupulously follows this maxim himself, he cannot for that reason count upon every other to be faithful to the same maxim nor can he count upon the kingdom of nature and its purposive order to harmonize with him, as a fitting member, toward a kingdom of ends possible through himself, that is, upon its favoring his expectation of happiness; nevertheless that law, act in accordance with the maxims of a member giving universal laws for a merely possible kingdom of ends, remains in its full force because it commands categorically. And just in this lies the paradox that the mere dignity of humanity as rational nature, without any other end or advantage to be attained by it—hence respect for a mere idea—is yet to serve as an inflexible precept of the will, and that it is just in this independence of maxims from all such incentives that their sublimity consists, and the worthiness of every rational subject to be a lawgiving member in the kingdom of ends; for otherwise he would have to be represented only as subject to the natural law of his needs. Even if the kingdom of nature as well as the kingdom of ends were thought as united under one sovereign, so that the latter would no longer remain a mere idea but would obtain true reality, it would no doubt gain the increment of a strong incentive but never any increase of its inner worth; for, even this sole absolute lawgiver would, despite this, still have to be represented as appraising the worth of rational beings only by their disinterested conduct, prescribed to themselves merely from that idea. The essence of things is not changed by their external relations; and that which, without taking account of such relations, alone constitutes the worth of a human being is that in terms of which he must also be appraised by whoever does it, even by the supreme being. *Morality* is thus the relation of actions to the autonomy of the will, that is, to a possible giving of universal law through its maxims. An action that can coexist with the autonomy of the will is *permitted*; one that does not accord with it is *forbidden*. A will whose maxims necessarily harmonize with the laws of autonomy is a holy, absolutely good will. The dependence upon the principle of autonomy of a will that is not absolutely good (moral necessitation) is obligation. This, accordingly, cannot be attributed to a holy being. The objective necessity of an action from obligation is called *duty*.

From what has just been said it is now easy to explain how it happens that, although in thinking the concept of duty we think of subjection to the law, yet at the same time we thereby represent a certain sublimity and *dignity* in the person who fulfills all his duties. For there is indeed no sublimity in him insofar as he is *subject* to the moral law, but there certainly is insofar as he is at the same time *lawgiving* with respect to it and only for that reason subordinated to it. We have also shown above how neither fear nor inclination but simply respect for the law is that incentive which can give actions a moral worth. Our own will insofar as it would act only under the condition of a possible giving of universal law through its maxims—this will possible for us in idea—is the proper object of respect; and the dignity of humanity consists just in this capacity to give universal law, though with the condition of also being itself subject to this very lawgiving.

[Groundwork of the Metaphysics of Morals. Trans. by Mary Gregor. (Cambridge University Press, 1997).]

CHAPTER TEN

Bentham and Mill on Utility, Happiness, and Morality

Jeremy Bentham (1748–1832)

John Stuart Mill (1806–1873)

Courtesy of Library of Congress

SELECTED READINGS

▶ *An Introduction to the Principles of Morality and Legislation*—Jeremy Bentham
▶ *Utilitarianism*—John Stuart Mill

An Introduction to the Principles of Morality and Legislation

Jeremy Bentham
(Edited by Joseph R. Kirkland)

CHAPTER I: OF THE PRINCIPLE OF UTILITY

I.1

I. Nature has placed mankind under the governance of two sovereign masters, pain and pleasure. It is for them alone to point out what we ought to do, as well as to determine what we shall do. On the one hand the standard of right and wrong, on the other the chain of causes and effects, are fastened to their throne. They govern us in all we do, in all we say, in all we think: every effort we can make to throw off our subjection, will serve but to demonstrate and confirm it. In words a man may pretend to abjure their empire: but in reality he will remain subject to it all the while. The principle of utility recognizes this subjection, and assumes it for the foundation of that system, the object of which is to rear the fabric of felicity by the hands of reason and of law. Systems which attempt to question it, deal in sounds instead of sense, in caprice instead of reason, in darkness instead of light.

I.2

But enough of metaphor and declamation: it is not by such means that moral science is to be improved.

I.3

II. The principle of utility is the foundation of the present work: it will be proper therefore at the outset to give an explicit and determinate account of what is meant by it. By the principle of utility is meant that principle which approves or disapproves of every action whatsoever, according to the tendency it appears to have to augment or diminish the happiness of the party whose interest is in question: or, what is the same thing in other words, to promote or to oppose that happiness. I say of every action whatsoever, and therefore not only of every action of a private individual, but of every measure of government.

I.4

III. By utility is meant that property in any object, whereby it tends to produce benefit, advantage, pleasure, good, or happiness, (all this in the present case comes to the same thing) or (what comes again to the same thing) to prevent the happening of mischief, pain, evil, or unhappiness to the party whose interest is considered: if that party be the community in general, then the happiness of the community: if a particular individual, then the happiness of that individual.

I.5

IV. The interest of the community is one of the most general expressions that can occur in the phraseology of morals: no wonder that the meaning of it is often lost. When it has a meaning, it is this. The community is a fictitious body, composed of the individual persons who are considered as constituting as it were its members. The interest of the community then is, what?—the sum of the interests of the several members who compose it.

I.6

V. It is in vain to talk of the interest of the community, without understanding what is the interest of the individual. A thing is said to promote the interest, or to be for the interest, of an individual, when it tends to add to the sum total of his pleasures: or, what comes to the same thing, to diminish the sum total of his pains.

I.7

VI. An action then may be said to be conformable to the principle of utility, or, for shortness sake, to utility, (meaning with respect to the community at large) when the tendency it has to augment the happiness of the community is greater than any it has to diminish it.

I.8

VII. A measure of government (which is but a particular kind of action, performed by a particular person or persons) may be said to be conformable to or dictated by the principle of utility, when in like manner the tendency which it has to augment the happiness of the community is greater than any which it has to diminish it.

I.9

VIII. When an action, or in particular a measure of government, is supposed by a man to be conformable to the principle of utility, it may be convenient, for the purposes of discourse, to imagine a kind of law or dictate, called a law or dictate of utility: and to speak of the action in question, as being conformable to such law or dictate.

I.10

IX. A man may be said to be a partisan of the principle of utility, when the approbation or disapprobation he annexes to any action, or to any measure, is determined by and proportioned to the tendency which he conceives it to have to augment or to diminish the happiness of the community: or in other words, to its conformity or unconformity to the laws or dictates of utility.

I.11

X. Of an action that is conformable to the principle of utility one may always say either that it is one that ought to be done, or at least that it is not one that ought not to be done. One may say also, that it is right it should be done; at least that it is not wrong it should be done: that it is a right action; at least that it is not a wrong action. When thus interpreted, the words ought, and right and wrong and others of that stamp, have a meaning: when otherwise, they have none.

I.12

XI. Has the rectitude of this principle been ever formally contested? It should seem that it had, by those who have not known what they have been meaning. Is it susceptible of any direct proof? It should seem not: for that which is used to prove everything else, cannot itself be proved: a chain of proofs must have their commencement somewhere. To give such proof is as impossible as it is needless.

I.13

XII. Not that there is or ever has been that human creature at breathing, however stupid or perverse, who has not on many, perhaps on most occasions of his life, deferred to it. By the natural constitution of the human frame, on most occasions of their lives men in general embrace this principle, without thinking of it: if not for the ordering of their own actions, yet for the trying of their own actions, as well as of those of other men. There have been, at the same time, not many perhaps, even of the most intelligent, who have been disposed to embrace it purely and without reserve. There are even few who have not taken some occasion or other to quarrel with it, either on account of their not understanding always how to apply it, or on account of some prejudice or other which they were afraid to

examine into, or could not bear to part with. For such is the stuff that man is made of: in principle and in practice, in a right track and in a wrong one, the rarest of all human qualities is consistency.

I.14

XIII. When a man attempts to combat the principle of utility, it is with reasons drawn, without his being aware of it, from that very principle itself. His arguments, if they prove anything, prove not that the principle is wrong, but that, according to the applications he supposes to be made of it, it is misapplied. Is it possible for a man to move the earth? Yes; but he must first find out another earth to stand upon.

CHAPTER II: OF PRINCIPLES ADVERSE TO THAT OF UTILITY

II.1

I. If the principle of utility be a right principle to be governed by, and that in all cases, it follows from what has been just observed, that whatever principle differs from it in any case must necessarily be a wrong one. To prove any other principle, therefore, to be a wrong one, there needs no more than just to show it to be what it is, a principle of which the dictates are in some point or other different from those of the principle of utility: to state it is to confute it.

II.2

II. A principle may be different from that of utility in two ways: 1. By being constantly opposed to it: this is the case with a principle which may be termed the principle of asceticism. 2. By being sometimes opposed to it, and sometimes not, as it may happen: this is the case with another, which may be termed the principle of sympathy and antipathy.

II.3

III. By the principle of asceticism I mean that principle, which, like the principle of utility, approves or disapproves of any action, according to the tendency which it appears to have to augment or diminish the happiness of the party whose interest is in question; but in an inverse manner: approving of actions in as far as they tend to diminish his happiness; disapproving of them in as far as they tend to augment it.

II.4

IV. It is evident that anyone who reprobates any the least particle of pleasure, as such, from whatever source derived, is *pro tanto* a partisan of the principle of asceticism. It is only upon that principle, and not from the principle of utility, that the most abominable pleasure which the vilest of malefactors ever reaped from his crime would be to be reprobated, if it stood alone. The case is, that it never does stand alone; but is necessarily followed by such a quantity of pain (or, what comes to the same thing, such a chance for a certain quantity of pain) that the pleasure in comparison of it, is as nothing: and this is the true and sole, but perfectly sufficient, reason for making it a ground for punishment.

II.5

V. There are two classes of men of very different complexions, by whom the principle of asceticism appears to have been embraced; the one a set of moralists, the other a set of religionists. Different accordingly have been the motives which appear to have recommended it to the notice of these different parties. Hope, that is the prospect of pleasure, seems to have animated the former: hope, the aliment of philosophic pride: the hope of honor and reputation at the hands of men. Fear, that is, the prospect of pain, the latter: fear, the offspring of superstitious fancy: the fear of future punishment at the hands of a splenetic and revengeful Deity. I say in this case fear: for of the invisible future, fear is more powerful than hope. These circumstances characterize the two different parties among the partisans of the principle of asceticism; the parties and their motives different, the principle the same.

II.6

VI. The religious party, however, appear to have carried it farther than the philosophical: they have acted more consistently and less wisely. The philosophical party have scarcely gone farther than to reprobate pleasure: the religious party have frequently gone so far as to make it a matter of merit and of duty to court pain. The philosophical party have hardly gone farther than the making pain a matter of indifference. It is no evil, they have said: they have not said, it is a good. They have not so much as reprobated all pleasure in the lump. They have discarded only what they have called the gross; that is, such as are organical, or of which the origin is easily traced up to such as are organical: they have even cherished and magnified the refined. Yet this, however, not under the name of pleasure: to cleanse itself from the sordidness of its impure original, it was necessary it should change its name: the honorable, the glorious, the reputable, the becoming, the virtuous, the decorum it was to be called: in short, anything but pleasure.

II.7

VII. From these two sources have flowed the doctrines from which the sentiments of the bulk of mankind have all along received a tincture of this principle; some from the philosophical, some from the religious, some from both. Men of education more frequently from the philosophical, as more suited to the elevation of their sentiments: the vulgar more frequently from the superstitious, as more suited to the narrowness of their intellect, undilated by knowledge: and to the abjectness of their condition, continually open to the attacks of fear. The tinctures, however, derived from the two sources, would naturally intermingle, insomuch that a man would not always know by which of them he was most influenced: and they would often serve to corroborate and enliven one another. It was this conformity that made a kind of alliance between parties of a complexion otherwise so dissimilar: and disposed them to unite upon various occasions against the common enemy, the partisan of the principle of utility, whom they joined in branding with the odious name of Epicurean.

II.8

VIII. The principle of asceticism, however, with whatever warmth it may have been embraced by its partisans as a rule of private conduct, seems not to have been carried to any considerable length, when applied to the business of government. In a few instances it has been carried a little way by the philosophical party: witness the Spartan regimen. Though then, perhaps, it may be considered as having been a measure of security: and an application, though a precipitate and perverse application, of the principle of utility. Scarcely in any instances, to any considerable length, by the religious: for the various monastic orders, and the societies of the Quakers, Dumplers, Moravians, and other religionists, have been free societies, whose regimen no man has been restricted to without the intervention of his own consent. Whatever merit a man may have thought there would be in making himself miserable, no such notion seems ever to have occurred to any of them, that it may be a merit, much less a duty, to make others miserable: although it should seem, that if a certain quantity of misery were a thing so desirable, it would not matter much whether it were brought by each man upon himself, or by one man upon another. It is true, that from the same source from whence, among the religionists, the attachment to the principle of asceticism took its rise, flowed other doctrines and practices, from which misery in abundance was produced in one man by the instrumentality of another: witness the holy wars, and the persecutions for religion. But the passion for producing misery in these cases proceeded upon some special ground: the exercise of it was confined to persons of particular descriptions: they were tormented, not as men, but as heretics and infidels. To have inflicted the same miseries on their fellow believers and fellow-sectaries, would have been as blamable in the eyes even of these religionists, as in those of a partisan of the principle of utility. For a man to give himself a certain number of stripes was indeed meritorious: but to give the same number of stripes to another man, not consenting, would have been a sin. We read of saints, who for the good of their souls, and the mortification of their bodies, have voluntarily yielded themselves a prey to vermin: but though many persons of this class have wielded the reins of empire, we read of none who have set themselves to work, and made laws on purpose, with a view of stocking the body politic with the breed of highwaymen, housebreakers, or incendiaries. If at any time they have suffered the nation to be preyed upon by swarms of idle pensioners, or useless placemen, it has rather been from negligence and imbecility, than from any settled plan for oppressing and plundering of the people. If at any time they have sapped the sources of national wealth, by cramping commerce, and driving the inhabitants into emigration, it has been with other views, and in pursuit of other ends. If they have declaimed against the pursuit of pleasure, and the use of wealth, they have commonly stopped at declamation: they have not, like Lycurgus, made express ordinances for the purpose of banishing the precious metals. If they have established idleness by a law, it has been not because idleness, the mother of vice and misery, is itself a virtue, but because idleness (say they) is the road to holiness. If under the notion of fasting, they have joined in the plan of confining their subjects to a diet, thought by some to be of the most nourishing and prolific nature, it has been not for the sake of making them tributaries to the nations by whom that diet was to be supplied, but for the sake of manifesting their own power, and exercising the obedience of the people. If they have established, or suffered to be established, punishments for the breach of celibacy, they have done no more than comply with the petitions of those deluded rigorists, who, dupes to the ambitious and deep-laid policy of their rulers, first laid themselves under that idle obligation by a vow.

II.9

IX. The principle of asceticism seems originally to have been the reverie of certain hasty speculators, who having perceived, or fancied, that certain pleasures, when reaped in certain circumstances, have, at the long run, been attended with pains more than equivalent to them, took occasion to quarrel with every thing that offered itself under the name of pleasure. Having then got thus far, and having forgot the point which they set out from, they pushed on, and went so much further as to think it meritorious to fall in love with pain. Even this, we see, is at bottom but the principle of utility misapplied.

II.10

X. The principle of utility is capable of being consistently pursued; and it is but tautology to say, that the more consistently it is pursued, the better it must ever be for human-kind. The principle of asceticism never was, nor ever can be, consistently pursued by any living creature. Let but one tenth part of the inhabitants of this earth pursue it consistently, and in a day's time they will have turned it into a hell.

CHAPTER IV: VALUE OF A LOT OF PLEASURE OR PAIN, HOW TO BE MEASURED
IV.1

I. Pleasures then, and the avoidance of pains, are the ends that the legislator has in view; it behooves him therefore to understand their value. Pleasures and pains are the instruments he has to work with: it behooves him therefore to understand their force, which is again, in other words, their value.

IV.2

II. To a person considered by himself, the value of a pleasure or pain considered by itself, will be greater or less, according to the four following circumstances:

1. Its *intensity.*

2. Its *duration.*

3. Its *certainty* or *uncertainty.*

4. Its *propinquity* or *remoteness.*

IV.3

III. These are the circumstances which are to be considered in estimating a pleasure or a pain considered each of them by itself. But when the value of any pleasure or pain is considered for the purpose of estimating the tendency of any act by which it is produced, there are two other circumstances to be taken into the account; these are,

IV.4

5. Its *fecundity*, or the chance it has of being followed by sensations of the same kind: that is, pleasures, if it be a pleasure: pains, if it be a pain.

IV.5

6. Its *purity*, or the chance it has of not being followed by sensations of the opposite kind: that is, pains, if it be a pleasure: pleasures, if it be a pain.

IV.6

These two last, however, are in strictness scarcely to be deemed properties of the pleasure or the pain itself; they are not, therefore, in strictness to be taken into the account of the value of that pleasure or that pain. They are in strictness to be deemed properties only of the act, or other event, by which such pleasure or pain has been produced; and accordingly are only to be taken into the account of the tendency of such act or such event.

IV.7

IV. To a number of persons, with reference to each of whom to the value of a pleasure or a pain is considered, it will be greater or less, according to seven circumstances: to wit, the six preceding ones; viz.

1. Its *intensity*.

2. Its *duration*.

3. Its *certainty* or *uncertainty*.

4. Its *propinquity* or *remoteness*.

5. Its *fecundity*.

6. Its *purity*.

And one other; to wit:

7. Its *extent*; that is, the number of persons to whom it extends; or (in other words) who are affected by it.

IV.8

V. To take an exact account then of the general tendency of any act, by which the interests of a community are affected, proceed as follows. Begin with any one person of those whose interests seem most immediately to be affected by it: and take an account,

IV.9

1. Of the value of each distinguishable pleasure which appears to be produced by it in the first instance.

IV.10

2. Of the value of each pain which appears to be produced by it in the first instance.

IV.11

3. Of the value of each pleasure which appears to be produced by it after the first. This constitutes the fecundity of the first pleasure and the impurity of the first pain.

IV.12

4. Of the value of each pain which appears to be produced by it after the first. This constitutes the fecundity of the first pain, and the impurity of the first pleasure.

IV.13

5. Sum up all the values of all the pleasures on the one side, and those of all the pains on the other. The balance, if it be on the side of pleasure, will give the good tendency of the act upon the whole, with respect to the interests of that individual person; if on the side of pain, the bad tendency of it upon the whole.

IV.14

6. Take an account of the number of persons whose interests appear to be concerned; and repeat the above process with respect to each. Sum up the numbers expressive of the degrees of good tendency, which the act has, with respect to each individual, in regard to whom the tendency of it is good upon the whole: do this again with respect to each individual, in regard to whom the tendency of it is good upon the whole: do this again with respect to each individual, in regard to whom the tendency of it is bad upon the whole. Take the balance which if on the side of pleasure, will give the general good tendency of the act, with respect to the total number or community of individuals concerned; if on the side of pain, the general evil tendency, with respect to the same community.

IV.15

VI. It is not to be expected that this process should be strictly pursued previously to every moral judgment, or to every legislative or judicial operation. It may, however, be always kept in view: and as near as the process actually pursued on these occasions approaches to it, so near will such process approach to the character of an exact one.

IV.16

VII. The same process is alike applicable to pleasure and pain, in whatever shape they appear: and by whatever denomination they are distinguished: to pleasure, whether it be called good (which is properly the cause or instrument of pleasure) or profit (which is distant pleasure, or the cause or instrument of distant pleasure,) or convenience, or advantage, benefit, emolument, happiness, and so forth: to pain, whether it be called evil, (which corresponds to good) or mischief, or inconvenience, or disadvantage, or loss, or unhappiness, and so forth.

IV.17

VIII. Nor is this a novel and unwarranted, any more than it is. a useless theory. In all this there is nothing but what the practice of mankind, wheresoever they have a clear view of their own interest, is perfectly conformable to. An article of property, an estate in land, for instance, is valuable, on what account? On account of the pleasures of all kinds which it enables a man to produce, and what comes to the same thing the pains of all kinds which it enables him to avert. But the value of such an article of property is universally understood to rise or fall according to the length or shortness of the time which a man has in it: the certainty or uncertainty of its coming into possession: and the nearness or remoteness of the time at which, if at all, it is to come into possession. As to the intensity of the pleasures which a man may derive from it, this is never thought of, because it depends upon the use which each particular person may come to make of it; which cannot be estimated till the particular pleasures he may come to derive from it, or the particular pains he may come to exclude by means of it, are brought to view. For the same reason, neither does he think of the fecundity or purity of those pleasures.

[An Introduction to the Principles of Morals and Legislation. (London: W. Pickering, 1823)]

Utilitarianism

John Stuart Mill
(Edited by Joseph R. Kirkland)

CHAPTER I: GENERAL REMARKS

There are few circumstances among those which make up the present condition of human knowledge, more unlike what might have been expected, or more significant of the backward state in which speculation on the most important subjects still lingers, than the little progress which has been made in the decision of the controversy respecting the criterion of right and wrong. From the dawn of philosophy, the question concerning the *summum bonum*, or, what is the same thing, concerning the foundation of morality, has been accounted the main problem in speculative thought, has occupied the most gifted intellects, and divided them into sects and schools, carrying on a vigorous warfare against one another. And after more than two thousand years the same discussions continue, philosophers are still ranged under the same contending banners, and neither thinkers nor mankind at large seem nearer to being unanimous on the subject, than when the youth Socrates listened to the old Protagoras, and asserted (if Plato's dialogue be grounded on a real conversation) the theory of utilitarianism against the popular morality of the so-called sophist.

It is true that similar confusion and uncertainty, and in some cases similar discordance, exist respecting the first principles of all the sciences, not excepting that which is deemed the most certain of them, mathematics; without much impairing, generally indeed without impairing at all, the trustworthiness of the conclusions of those sciences. An apparent anomaly, the explanation of which is, that the detailed doctrines of a science are not usually deduced from, nor depend for their evidence upon, what are called its first principles. Were it not so, there would be no science more precarious, or whose conclusions were more insufficiently made out, than algebra; which derives none of its certainty from what are commonly taught to learners as its elements, since these, as laid down by some of its most eminent teachers, are as full of fictions as English law, and of mysteries as theology. The truths which are ultimately accepted as the first principles of a science, are really the last results of metaphysical analysis, practiced on the elementary notions with which the science is conversant; and their relation to the science is not that of

foundations to an edifice, but of roots to a tree, which may perform their office equally well though they be never dug down to and exposed to light. But though in science the particular truths precede the general theory, the contrary might be expected to be the case with a practical art, such as morals or legislation. All action is for the sake of some end, and rules of action, it seems natural to suppose, must take their whole character and color from the end to which they are subservient. When we engage in a pursuit, a clear and precise conception of what we are pursuing would seem to be the first thing we need, instead of the last we are to look forward to. A test of right and wrong must be the means, one would think, of ascertaining what is right or wrong, and not a consequence of having already ascertained it.

The difficulty is not avoided by having recourse to the popular theory of a natural faculty, a sense or instinct, informing us of right and wrong. For—besides that the existence of such a moral instinct is itself one of the matters in dispute—those believers in it who have any pretensions to philosophy, have been obliged to abandon the idea that it discerns what is right or wrong in the particular case in hand, as our other senses discern the sight or sound actually present. Our moral faculty, according to all those of its interpreters who are entitled to the name of thinkers, supplies us only with the general principles of moral judgments; it is a branch of our reason, not of our sensitive faculty; and must be looked to for the abstract doctrines of morality, not for perception of it in the concrete. The intuitive, no less than what may be termed the inductive, school of ethics, insists on the necessity of general laws. They both agree that the morality of an individual action is not a question of direct perception, but of the application of a law to an individual case. They recognize also, to a great extent, the same moral laws; but differ as to their evidence, and the source from which they derive their authority. According to the one opinion, the principles of morals are evident à priori, requiring nothing to command assent, except that the meaning of the terms be understood. According to the other doctrine, right and wrong, as well as truth and falsehood, are questions of observation and experience. But both hold equally that morality must be deduced from principles; and the intuitive school affirm as strongly as the inductive, that there is a science of morals. Yet they seldom attempt to make out a list of the à priori principles which are to serve as the premises of the science; still more rarely do they make any effort to reduce those various principles to one first principle, or common ground of obligation. They either assume the ordinary precepts of morals as of *a priori* authority, or they lay down as the common groundwork of those maxims, some generality much less obviously authoritative than the maxims themselves, and which has never succeeded in gaining popular acceptance. Yet to support their pretensions there ought either to be some one fundamental principle or law, at the root of all morality, or if there be several, there should be a determinate order of precedence among them; and the one principle, or the rule for deciding between the various principles when they conflict, ought to be self-evident.

To inquire how far the bad effects of this deficiency have been mitigated in practice, or to what extent the moral beliefs of mankind have been vitiated or made uncertain by the absence of any distinct recognition of an ultimate standard, would imply a complete survey and criticism of past and present ethical doctrine. It would, however, be easy to show that whatever steadiness or consistency these moral beliefs have attained, has been mainly due to the tacit influence of a standard not recognized. Although the non-existence of an acknowledged first principle has made ethics not so much a guide as a consecration of men's actual sentiments, still, as men's sentiments, both of favor and of aversion, are greatly influenced by what they suppose to be the effects of things upon their happiness, the principle of utility, or as Bentham latterly called it, the greatest happiness principle, has had a large share in forming the moral doctrines even of those who most scornfully reject its authority. Nor is there any school of thought which refuses to admit that the influence of actions on happiness is a most material and even predominant consideration in many of the details of morals, however unwilling to acknowledge it as the fundamental principle of morality, and the source of moral obligation. I might go much further, and say that to all those *a priori* moralists who deem it necessary to argue at all, utilitarian arguments are indispensable. It is not my present purpose to criticize these thinkers; but I cannot help referring, for illustration, to a systematic treatise by one of the most illustrious of them, the Metaphysics of Ethics, by Kant. This remarkable man, whose system of thought will long remain one of the landmarks in the history of philosophical speculation, does, in the treatise in question, lay down an universal first principle as the origin and ground of moral obligation; it is this:—'So act, that the rule on which thou actest would admit of being adopted as a law by all rational beings.' But when he begins to deduce from this precept any of the actual duties of morality, he fails, almost grotesquely, to show that there would be any contradiction, any logical (not to say physical) impossibility, in the adoption by all rational beings of the most outrageously immoral rules of conduct. All he shows is that the consequences of their universal adoption would be such as no one would choose to incur.

On the present occasion, I shall, without further discussion of the other theories, attempt to contribute something towards the understanding and appreciation of the Utilitarian or Happiness theory, and towards such proof as it is susceptible of. It is evident that this cannot be proof in the ordinary and popular meaning of the term. Questions of ultimate ends are not amenable to direct proof. Whatever can be proved to be good, must be so by being shown to be a means to something admitted to be good without proof. The medical art is proved to be good, by its conducing to health; but how is it possible to prove that health is good? The art of music is good, for the reason, among others, that it produces pleasure; but what proof is it possible to give that pleasure is good? If, then, it is asserted that there is a comprehensive formula, including all things which are in themselves good, and that whatever else is good, is not so as an end, but as a mean, the formula may be accepted or rejected, but is not a subject of what is commonly understood by proof. We are not, however, to infer that its acceptance or rejection must depend on blind impulse, or arbitrary choice. There is a larger meaning of the word proof, in which this question is as amenable to it as any other of the disputed questions of philosophy. The subject is within the cognizance of the rational faculty; and neither does that faculty deal with it solely in the way of intuition. Considerations may be presented capable of determining the intellect either to give or withhold its assent to the doctrine; and this is equivalent to proof.

We shall examine presently of what nature are these considerations; in what manner they apply to the case, and what rational grounds, therefore, can be given for accepting or rejecting the utilitarian formula. But it is a preliminary condition of rational acceptance or rejection, that the formula should be correctly understood. I believe that the very imperfect notion ordinarily formed of its meaning, is the chief obstacle which impedes its reception; and that could it be cleared, even from only the grosser misconceptions, the question would be greatly simplified, and a large proportion of its difficulties removed. Before, therefore, I attempt to enter into the philosophical grounds which can be given for assenting to the utilitarian standard, I shall offer some illustrations of the doctrine itself; with the view of showing more clearly what it is, distinguishing it from what it is not, and disposing of such of the practical objections to it as either originate in, or are closely connected with, mistaken interpretations of its meaning. Having thus prepared the ground, I shall afterwards endeavor to throw such light as I can upon the question, considered as one of philosophical theory.

CHAPTER II: WHAT UTILITARIANISM IS

A passing remark is all that needs be given to the ignorant blunder of supposing that those who stand up for utility as the test of right and wrong, use the term in that restricted and merely colloquial sense in which utility is opposed to pleasure. An apology is due to the philosophical opponents of utilitarianism, for even the momentary appearance of confounding them with any one capable of so absurd a misconception; which is the more extraordinary, inasmuch as the contrary accusation, of referring everything to pleasure, and that too in its grossest form, is another of the common charges against utilitarianism: and, as has been pointedly remarked by an able writer, the same sort of persons, and often the very same persons, denounce the theory "as impracticably dry when the word utility precedes the word pleasure, and as too practically voluptuous when the word pleasure precedes the word utility." Those who know anything about the matter are aware that every writer, from Epicurus to Bentham, who maintained the theory of utility, meant by it, not something to be contradistinguished from pleasure, but pleasure itself, together with exemption from pain; and instead of opposing the useful to the agreeable or the ornamental, have always declared that the useful means these, among other things. Yet the common herd, including the herd of writers, not only in newspapers and periodicals, but in books of weight and pretension, are perpetually falling into this shallow mistake. Having caught up the word utilitarian, while knowing nothing whatever about it but its sound, they habitually express by it the rejection, or the neglect, of pleasure in some of its forms; of beauty, of ornament, or of amusement. Nor is the term thus ignorantly misapplied solely in disparagement, but occasionally in compliment; as though it

implied superiority to frivolity and the mere pleasures of the moment. And this perverted use is the only one in which the word is popularly known, and the one from which the new generation are acquiring their sole notion of its meaning. Those who introduced the word, but who had for many years discontinued it as a distinctive appellation, may well feel themselves called upon to resume it, if by doing so they can hope to contribute anything towards rescuing it from this utter degradation.

The creed which accepts as the foundation of morals, Utility, or the Greatest Happiness Principle, holds that actions are right in proportion as they tend to promote happiness, wrong as they tend to produce the reverse of happiness. By happiness is intended pleasure, and the absence of pain; by unhappiness, pain, and the privation of pleasure. To give a clear view of the moral standard set up by the theory, much more requires to be said; in particular, what things it includes in the ideas of pain and pleasure; and to what extent this is left an open question. But these supplementary explanations do not affect the theory of life on which this theory of morality is grounded—namely, that pleasure, and freedom from pain, are the only things desirable as ends; and that all desirable things (which are as numerous in the utilitarian as in any other scheme) are desirable either for the pleasure inherent in themselves, or as means to the promotion of pleasure and the prevention of pain.

Now, such a theory of life excites in many minds, and among them in some of the most estimable in feeling and purpose, inveterate dislike. To suppose that life has (as they express it) no higher end than pleasure—no better and nobler object of desire and pursuit—they designate as utterly mean and groveling; as a doctrine worthy only of swine, to whom the followers of Epicurus were, at a very early period, contemptuously likened; and modern holders of the doctrine are occasionally made the subject of equally polite comparisons by its German, French, and English assailants.

When thus attacked, the Epicureans have always answered, that it is not they, but their accusers, who represent human nature in a degrading light; since the accusation supposes human beings to be capable of no pleasures except those of which swine are capable. If this supposition were true, the charge could not be gainsaid, but would then be no longer an imputation; for if the sources of pleasure were precisely the same to human beings and to swine, the rule of life which is good enough for the one would be good enough for the other. The comparison of the Epicurean life to that of beasts is felt as degrading, precisely because a beast's pleasures do not satisfy a human being's conceptions of happiness. Human beings have faculties more elevated than the animal appetites, and when once made conscious of them, do not regard anything as happiness which does not include their gratification. I do not, indeed, consider the Epicureans to have been by any means faultless in drawing out their scheme of consequences from the utilitarian principle. To do this in any sufficient manner, many Stoic, as well as Christian elements require to be included. But there is no known Epicurean theory of life which does not assign to the pleasures of the intellect; of the feelings and imagination, and of the moral sentiments, a much higher value as pleasures than to those of mere sensation. It must be admitted, however, that utilitarian writers in general have placed the superiority of mental over bodily pleasures chiefly in the greater permanency, safety, uncostliness, etc., of the former— that is, in their circumstantial advantages rather than in their intrinsic nature. And on all these points utilitarians have fully proved their case; but they might have taken the other, and, as it may be called, higher ground, with entire consistency. It is quite compatible with the principle of utility to recognize the fact, that some kinds of pleasure are more desirable and more valuable than others. It would be absurd that while, in estimating all other things, quality is considered as well as quantity, the estimation of pleasures should be supposed to depend on quantity alone.

If I am asked, what I mean by difference of quality in pleasures, or what makes one pleasure more valuable than another, merely as a pleasure, except its being greater in amount, there is but one possible answer. Of two pleasures, if there be one to which all or almost all who have experience of both give a decided preference, irrespective of any feeling of moral obligation to prefer it, that is the more desirable pleasure. If one of the two is, by those who are competently acquainted with both, placed so far above the other that they prefer it, even though knowing it to be attended with a greater amount of discontent, and would not resign it for any quantity of the other pleasure which their nature is capable of, we are justified in ascribing to the preferred enjoyment a superiority in quality, so far outweighing quantity as to render it, in comparison, of small account.

Now it is an unquestionable fact that those who are equally acquainted with, and equally capable of appreciating and enjoying, both, do give a most marked preference to the manner of existence which employs their higher faculties. Few human creatures would consent to be changed into any of the lower animals, for a promise of the fullest allowance of a beast's pleasures; no intelligent human being would consent to be a fool, no instructed person would be an ignoramus, no person of feeling and conscience would be selfish and base, even though they should be persuaded that the fool, the dunce, or the rascal is better satisfied with his lot than they are with theirs. They would not resign what they possess more than he, for the most complete satisfaction of all the desires which they have in common with him. If they ever fancy they would, it is only in cases of unhappiness so extreme, that to escape from it they would exchange their lot for almost any other, however undesirable in their own eyes. A being of higher faculties requires more to make him happy, is capable probably of more acute suffering, and is certainly accessible to it at more points, than one of an inferior type; but in spite of these liabilities, he can never really wish to sink into what he feels to be a lower grade of existence. We may give what explanation we please of this unwillingness; we may attribute it to pride, a name which is given indiscriminately to some of the most and to some of the least estimable feelings of which mankind are capable; we may refer it to the love of liberty and personal independence, an appeal to which was with the Stoics one of the most effective means for the inculcation of it; to the love of power, or to the love of excitement, both of which do really enter into and contribute to it: but its most appropriate appellation is a sense of dignity, which all human beings possess in one form or other, and in some, though by no means in exact, proportion to their higher faculties, and which is so essential a part of the happiness of those in whom it is strong, that nothing which conflicts with it could be, otherwise than momentarily, an object of desire to them. Whoever supposes that this preference takes place at a sacrifice of happiness-that the superior being, in anything like equal circumstances, is not happier than the inferior-confounds the two very different ideas, of happiness, and content. It is indisputable that the being whose capacities of enjoyment are low, has the greatest chance of having them fully satisfied; and a highly-endowed being will always feel that any happiness which he can look for, as the world is constituted, is imperfect. But he can learn to bear its imperfections, if they are at all bearable; and they will not make him envy the being who is indeed unconscious of the imperfections, but only because he feels not at all the good which those imperfections qualify. It is better to be a human being dissatisfied than a pig satisfied; better to be Socrates dissatisfied than a fool satisfied. And if the fool, or the pig, is of a different opinion, it is because they only know their own side of the question. The other party to the comparison knows both sides.

It may be objected, that many who are capable of the higher pleasures, occasionally, under the influence of temptation, postpone them to the lower. But this is quite compatible with a full appreciation of the intrinsic superiority of the higher. Men often, from infirmity of character, make their election for the nearer good, though they know it to be the less valuable; and this no less when the choice is between two bodily pleasures, than when it is between bodily and mental. They pursue sensual indulgences to the injury of health, though perfectly aware that health is the greater good. It may be further objected, that many who begin with youthful enthusiasm for everything noble, as they advance in years sink into indolence and selfishness. But I do not believe that those who undergo this very common change, voluntarily choose the lower description of pleasures in preference to the higher. I believe that before they devote themselves exclusively to the one, they have already become incapable of the other. Capacity for the nobler feelings is in most natures a very tender plant, easily killed, not only by hostile influences, but by mere want of sustenance; and in the majority of young persons it speedily dies away if the occupations to which their position in life has devoted them, and the society into which it has thrown them, are not favorable to keeping that higher capacity in exercise. Men lose their high aspirations as they lose their intellectual tastes, because they have not time or opportunity for indulging them; and they addict themselves to inferior pleasures, not because they deliberately prefer them, but because they are either the only ones to which they have access, or the only ones which they are any longer capable of enjoying. It may be questioned whether anyone who has remained equally susceptible to both classes of pleasures, ever knowingly and calmly preferred the lower; though many, in all ages, have broken down in an ineffectual attempt to combine both.

From this verdict of the only competent judges, I apprehend there can be no appeal. On a question which is the best worth having of two pleasures, or which of two modes of existence is the most grateful to the feelings, apart from its moral attributes and from its consequences, the judgment of those who are qualified by knowledge of both, or, if they differ, that of the majority among them, must be admitted as final. And there

needs be the less hesitation to accept this judgment respecting the quality of pleasures, since there is no other tribunal to be referred to even on the question of quantity. What means are there of determining which is the acutest of two pains, or the most intense of two pleasurable sensations, except the general suffrage of those who are familiar with both? Neither pains nor pleasures are homogeneous, and pain is always heterogeneous with pleasure. What is there to decide whether a particular pleasure is worth purchasing at the cost of a particular pain, except the feelings and judgment of the experienced? When, therefore, those feelings and judgment declare the pleasures derived from the higher faculties to be preferable in kind, apart from the question of intensity, to those of which the animal nature, disjoined from the higher faculties, is susceptible, they are entitled on this subject to the same regard.

I have dwelt on this point, as being a necessary part of a perfectly just conception of Utility or Happiness, considered as the directive rule of human conduct. But it is by no means an indispensable condition to the acceptance of the utilitarian standard; for that standard is not the agent's own greatest happiness, but the greatest amount of happiness altogether; and if it may possibly be doubted whether a noble character is always the happier for its nobleness, there can be no doubt that it makes other people happier, and that the world in general is immensely a gainer by it. Utilitarianism, therefore, could only attain its end by the general cultivation of nobleness of character, even if each individual were only benefited by the nobleness of others, and his own, so far as happiness is concerned, were a sheer deduction from the benefit. But the bare enunciation of such an absurdity as this last, renders refutation superfluous.

According to the Greatest Happiness Principle, as above explained, the ultimate end, with reference to and for the sake of which all other things are desirable (whether we are considering our own good or that of other people), is an existence exempt as far as possible from pain, and as rich as possible in enjoyments, both in point of quantity and quality; the test of quality, and the rule for measuring it against quantity, being the preference felt by those who, in their opportunities of experience, to which must be added their habits of self-consciousness and self-observation, are best furnished with the means of comparison. This, being, according to the utilitarian opinion, the end of human action, is necessarily also the standard of morality; which may accordingly be defined, the rules and precepts for human conduct, by the observance of which an existence such as has been described might be, to the greatest extent possible, secured to all mankind; and not to them only, but, so far as the nature of things admits, to the whole sentient creation.

Against this doctrine, however, arises another class of objectors, who say that happiness, in any form, cannot be the rational purpose of human life and action; because, in the first place, it is unattainable: and they contemptuously ask, "What right hast thou to be happy?"—a question which Mr. Carlyle clenches by the addition, "What right, a short time ago, hadst thou even to be?" Next, they say, that men can do without happiness; that all noble human beings have felt this, and could not have become noble but by learning the lesson of Entsagen, or renunciation; which lesson, thoroughly learnt and submitted to, they affirm to be the beginning and necessary condition of all virtue.

The first of these objections would go to the root of the matter were it well founded; for if no happiness is to be had at all by human beings, the attainment of it cannot be the end of morality, or of any rational conduct. Though, even in that case, something might still be said for the utilitarian theory; since utility includes not solely the pursuit of happiness, but the prevention or mitigation of unhappiness; and if the former aim be chimerical, there will be all the greater scope and more imperative need for the latter, so long at least as mankind think fit to live, and do not take refuge in the simultaneous act of suicide recommended under certain conditions by Novalis. When, however, it is thus positively asserted to be impossible that human life should be happy, the assertion, if not something like a verbal quibble, is at least an exaggeration. If by happiness be meant a continuity of highly pleasurable excitement, it is evident enough that this is impossible. A state of exalted pleasure lasts only moments, or in some cases, and with some intermissions, hours or days, and is the occasional brilliant flash of enjoyment, not its permanent and steady flame. Of this the philosophers who have taught that happiness is the end of life were as fully aware as those who taunt them. The happiness which they meant was not a life of rapture, but moments of such, in an existence made up of few and transitory pains, many and various pleasures, with a decided predominance of the active over the passive, and having as the foundation of the whole, not to expect more from life than it is capable of bestowing. A life thus composed, to those who have been fortunate enough to obtain it, has always appeared worthy of the name of happiness. And such an existence is even now the lot of

many, during some considerable portion of their lives. The present wretched education, and wretched social arrangements, are the only real hindrance to its being attainable by almost all.

The objectors perhaps may doubt whether human beings, if taught to consider happiness as the end of life, would be satisfied with such a moderate share of it. But great numbers of mankind have been satisfied with much less. The main constituents of a satisfied life appear to be two, either of which by itself is often found sufficient for the purpose: tranquility, and excitement. With much tranquility, many find that they can be content with very little pleasure: with much excitement, many can reconcile themselves to a considerable quantity of pain. There is assuredly no inherent impossibility in enabling even the mass of mankind to unite both; since the two are so far from being incompatible that they are in natural alliance, the prolongation of either being a preparation for, and exciting a wish for, the other. It is only those in whom indolence amounts to a vice, that do not desire excitement after an interval of repose; it is only those in whom the need of excitement is a disease, that feel the tranquility which follows excitement dull and insipid, instead of pleasurable in direct proportion to the excitement which preceded it. When people who are tolerably fortunate in their outward lot do not find in life sufficient enjoyment to make it valuable to them, the cause generally is, caring for nobody but themselves. To those who have neither public nor private affections, the excitements of life are much curtailed, and in any case dwindle in value as the time approaches when all selfish interests must be terminated by death: while those who leave after them objects of personal affection, and especially those who have also cultivated a fellow-feeling with the collective interests of mankind, retain as lively an interest in life on the eve of death as in the vigor of youth and health. Next to selfishness, the principal cause which makes life unsatisfactory, is want of mental cultivation. A cultivated mind—I do not mean that of a philosopher, but any mind to which the fountains of knowledge have been opened, and which has been taught, in any tolerable degree, to exercise its faculties—finds sources of inexhaustible interest in all that surrounds it; in the objects of nature, the achievements of art, the imaginations of poetry, the incidents of history, the ways of mankind past and present, and their prospects in the future. It is possible, indeed, to become indifferent to all this, and that too without having exhausted a thousandth part of it; but only when one has had from the beginning no moral or human interest in these things, and has sought in them only the gratification of curiosity.

Now there is absolutely no reason in the nature of things why an amount of mental culture sufficient to give an intelligent interest in these objects of contemplation, should not be the inheritance of every one born in a civilized country. As little is there an inherent necessity that any human being should be a selfish egotist, devoid of every feeling or care but those which center in his own miserable individuality. Something far superior to this is sufficiently common even now, to give ample earnest of what the human species may be made. Genuine private affections, and a sincere interest in the public good, are possible, though in unequal degrees, to every rightly brought-up human being. In a world in which there is so much to interest, so much to enjoy, and so much also to correct and improve, everyone who has this moderate amount of moral and intellectual requisites is capable of an existence which may be called enviable; and unless such a person, through bad laws, or subjection to the will of others, is denied the liberty to use the sources of happiness within his reach, he will not fail to find this enviable existence, if he escape the positive evils of life, the great sources of physical and mental suffering—such as indigence, disease, and the unkindness, worthlessness, or premature loss of objects of affection. The main stress of the problem lies, therefore, in the contest with these calamities, from which it is a rare good fortune entirely to escape; which, as things now are, cannot be obviated, and often cannot be in any material degree mitigated. Yet no one whose opinion deserves a moment's consideration can doubt that most of the great positive evils of the world are in themselves removable, and will, if human affairs continue to improve, be in the end reduced within narrow limits. Poverty, in any sense implying suffering, may be completely extinguished by the wisdom of society, combined with the good sense and providence of individuals. Even that most intractable of enemies, disease, may be indefinitely reduced in dimensions by good physical and moral education, and proper control of noxious influences; while the progress of science holds out a promise for the future of still more direct conquests over this detestable foe. And every advance in that direction relieves us from some, not only of the chances which cut short our own lives, but, what concerns us still more, which deprive us of those in whom our happiness is wrapped up. As for vicissitudes of fortune, and other disappointments connected with worldly circumstances, these are principally the effect either of gross imprudence, of ill-regulated desires, or of bad or imperfect social institutions. All the grand sources, in short, of human suffering are in a great degree, many of them almost entirely, conquerable by human care and effort; and though their removal is grievously slow—though a long succession of generations will perish in the breach before the conquest is completed, and this world becomes all that, if will and knowledge were not wanting, it might easily be made—yet every mind sufficiently intelligent and generous to bear a part, however small and inconspicuous, in the endeavor, will draw a noble enjoyment from the contest itself, which he would not for any bribe in the form of selfish indulgence consent to be without.

And this leads to the true estimation of what is said by the objectors concerning the possibility, and the obligation, of learning to do without happiness. Unquestionably it is possible to do without happiness; it is done involuntarily by nineteen-twentieths of mankind, even in those parts of our present world which are least deep in barbarism; and it often has to be done voluntarily by the hero or the martyr, for the sake of something which he prizes more than his individual happiness. But this something, what is it, unless the happiness of others, or some of the requisites of happiness? It is noble to be capable of resigning entirely one's own portion of happiness, or chances of it: but, after all, this self-sacrifice must be for some end; it is not its own end; and if we are told that its end is not happiness, but virtue, which is better than happiness, I ask, would the sacrifice be made if the hero or martyr did not believe that it would earn for others immunity from similar sacrifices? Would it be made, if he thought that his renunciation of happiness for himself would produce no fruit for any of his fellow creatures, but to make their lot like his, and place them also in the condition of persons who have renounced happiness? All honor to those who can abnegate for themselves the personal enjoyment of life, when by such renunciation they contribute worthily to increase the amount of happiness in the world; but he who does it, or professes to do it, for any other purpose, is no more deserving of admiration than the ascetic mounted on his pillar. He may be an inspiriting proof of what men can do, but assuredly not an example of what they should.

Though it is only in a very imperfect state of the world's arrangements that anyone can best serve the happiness of others by the absolute sacrifice of his own, yet so long as the world is in that imperfect state, I fully acknowledge that the readiness to make such a sacrifice is the highest virtue which can be found in man. I will add, that in this condition of the world, paradoxical as the assertion may be, the conscious ability to do without happiness gives the best prospect of realizing such happiness as is attainable. For nothing except that consciousness can raise a person above the chances of life, by making him feel that, let fate and fortune do their worst, they have not power to subdue him: which, once felt, frees him from excess of anxiety concerning the evils of life, and enables him, like many a Stoic in the worst times of the Roman Empire, to cultivate in tranquility the sources of satisfaction accessible to him, without concerning himself about the uncertainty of their duration, any more than about their inevitable end.

Meanwhile, let utilitarians never cease to claim the morality of self-devotion as a possession which belongs by as good a right to them, as either to the Stoic or to the Transcendentalist. The utilitarian morality does recognize in human beings the power of sacrificing their own greatest good for the good of others. It only refuses to admit that the sacrifice is itself a good. A sacrifice which does not increase, or tend to increase, the sum total of happiness, it considers as wasted. The only self-renunciation which it applauds, is devotion to the happiness, or to some of the means of happiness, of others; either of mankind collectively, or of individuals within the limits imposed by the collective interests of mankind.

I must again repeat, what the assailants of utilitarianism seldom have the justice to acknowledge, that the happiness which forms the utilitarian standard of what is right in conduct, is not the agent's own happiness, but that of all concerned. As between his own happiness and that of others, utilitarianism requires him to be as strictly impartial as a disinterested and benevolent spectator. In the golden rule of Jesus of Nazareth, we read the complete spirit of the ethics of utility. To do as one would be done by, and to love one's neighbor as oneself, constitute the ideal perfection of utilitarian morality. As the means of making the nearest approach to this ideal, utility would enjoin, first, that laws and social arrangements should place the happiness, or (as speaking practically it may be called) the interest, of every individual, as nearly as possible in harmony with the interest of the whole; and secondly, that education and opinion, which have so vast a power over human character, should so use that power as to establish in the mind of every individual an indissoluble association between his own happiness and the good of the

whole; especially between his own happiness and the practice of such modes of conduct, negative and positive, as regard for the universal happiness prescribes: so that not only he may be unable to conceive the possibility of happiness to himself, consistently with conduct opposed to the general good, but also that a direct impulse to promote the general good may be in every individual one of the habitual motives of action, and the sentiments connected therewith may fill a large and prominent place in every human being's sentient existence. If the impugners of the utilitarian morality represented it to their own minds in this its true character, I know not what recommendation possessed by any other morality they could possibly affirm to be wanting to it: what more beautiful or more exalted developments of human nature any other ethical system can be supposed to foster, or what springs of action, not accessible to the utilitarian, such systems rely on for giving effect to their mandates.

The objectors to utilitarianism cannot always be charged with representing it in a discreditable light. On the contrary, those among them who entertain anything like a just idea of its disinterested character, sometimes find fault with its standard as being too high for humanity. They say it is exacting too much to require that people shall always act from the inducement of promoting the general interests of society. But this is to mistake the very meaning of a standard of morals, and to confound the rule of action with the motive of it. It is the business of ethics to tell us what are our duties, or by what test we may know them; but no system of ethics requires that the sole motive of all we do shall be a feeling of duty; on the contrary, ninety-nine hundredths of all our actions are done from other motives, and rightly so done, if the rule of duty does not condemn them. It is the more unjust to utilitarianism that this particular misapprehension should be made a ground of objection to it, inasmuch as utilitarian moralists have gone beyond almost all others in affirming that the motive has nothing to do with the morality of the action, though much with the worth of the agent. He who saves a fellow creature from drowning does what is morally right, whether his motive be duty, or the hope of being paid for his trouble: he who betrays the friend that trusts him, is guilty of a crime, even if his object be to serve another friend to whom he is under greater obligations.[B] But to speak only of actions done from the motive of duty, and in direct obedience to principle: it is a misapprehension of the utilitarian mode of thought, to conceive it as implying that people should fix their minds upon so wide a generality as the world, or society at large. The great majority of good actions are intended, not for the benefit of the world, but for that of individuals, of which the good of the world is made up; and the thoughts of the most virtuous man need not on these occasions travel beyond the particular persons concerned, except so far as is necessary to assure himself that in benefiting them he is not violating the rights—that is, the legitimate and authorized expectations—of anyone else. The multiplication of happiness is, according to the utilitarian ethics, the object of virtue: the occasions on which any person (except one in a thousand) has it in his power to do this on an extended scale, in other words, to be a public benefactor, are but exceptional; and on these occasions alone is he called on to consider public utility; in every other case, private utility, the interest or happiness of some few persons, is all he has to attend to. Those alone the influence of whose actions extends to society in general, need concern themselves habitually about so large an object. In the case of abstinences indeed—of things which people forbear to do, from moral considerations, though the consequences in the particular case might be beneficial—it would be unworthy of an intelligent agent not to be consciously aware that the action is of a class which, if practiced generally, would be generally injurious, and that this is the ground of the obligation to abstain from it. The amount of regard for the public interest implied in this recognition, is no greater than is demanded by every system of morals; for they all enjoin to abstain from whatever is manifestly pernicious to society.

The same considerations dispose of another reproach against the doctrine of utility, founded on a still grosser misconception of the purpose of a standard of morality, and of the very meaning of the words right and wrong. It is often affirmed that utilitarianism renders men cold and unsympathizing; that it chills their moral feelings towards individuals; that it makes them regard only the dry and hard consideration of the consequences of actions, not taking into their moral estimate the qualities from which those actions emanate. If the assertion means that they do not allow their judgment respecting the rightness or wrongness of an action to be influenced by their opinion of the qualities of the person who does it, this is a complaint not against utilitarianism, but against having any standard of morality at all; for certainly no known ethical standard decides an action to be good or bad because it is done by a good or a bad man, still less because done by an amiable,

a brave, or a benevolent man or the contrary. These considerations are relevant, not to the estimation of actions, but of persons; and there is nothing in the utilitarian theory inconsistent with the fact that there are other things which interest us in persons besides the rightness and wrongness of their actions. The Stoics, indeed, with the paradoxical misuse of language which was part of their system, and by which they strove to raise themselves above all concern about anything but virtue, were fond of saying that he who has that has everything; that he, and only he, is rich, is beautiful, is a king. But no claim of this description is made for the virtuous man by the utilitarian doctrine. Utilitarians are quite aware that there are other desirable possessions and qualities besides virtue, and are perfectly willing to allow to all of them their full worth. They are also aware that a right action does not necessarily indicate a virtuous character, and that actions which are blamable often proceed from qualities entitled to praise. When this is apparent in any particular case, it modifies their estimation, not certainly of the act, but of the agent. I grant that they are, notwithstanding, of opinion, that in the long run the best proof of a good character is good actions; and resolutely refuse to consider any mental disposition as good, of which the predominant tendency is to produce bad conduct. This makes them unpopular with many people; but it is an unpopularity which they must share with everyone who regards the distinction between right and wrong in a serious light; and the reproach is not one which a conscientious utilitarian need be anxious to repel.

If no more be meant by the objection than that many utilitarians look on the morality of actions, as measured by the utilitarian standard, with too exclusive a regard, and do not lay sufficient stress upon the other beauties of character which go towards making a human being loveable or admirable, this may be admitted. Utilitarians who have cultivated their moral feelings, but not their sympathies nor their artistic perceptions, do fall into this mistake; and so do all other moralists under the same conditions. What can be said in excuse for other moralists is equally available for them, namely, that if there is to be any error, it is better that it should be on that side. As a matter of fact, we may affirm that among utilitarians as among adherents of other systems, there is every imaginable degree of rigidity and of laxity in the application of their standard: some are even puritanically rigorous, while others are as indulgent as can possibly be desired by sinner or by sentimentalist. But on the whole, a doctrine which brings prominently forward the interest that mankind have in the repression and prevention of conduct which violates the moral law, is likely to be inferior to no other in turning the sanctions of opinion against such violations. It is true, the question: "What does violate the moral law?" is one on which those who recognize different standards of morality are likely now and then to differ. But difference of opinion on moral questions was not first introduced into the world by utilitarianism, while that doctrine does supply, if not always an easy, at all events a tangible and intelligible mode of deciding such differences.

It may not be superfluous to notice a few more of the common misapprehensions of utilitarian ethics, even those which are so obvious and gross that it might appear impossible for any person of candor and intelligence to fall into them: since persons, even of considerable mental endowments, often give themselves so little trouble to understand the bearings of any opinion against which they entertain a prejudice, and men are in general so little conscious of this voluntary ignorance as a defect, that the most vulgar misunderstandings of ethical doctrines are continually met with in the deliberate writings of persons of the greatest pretensions both to high principle and to philosophy. We not uncommonly hear the doctrine of utility inveighed against as a godless doctrine. If it be necessary to say anything at all against so mere an assumption, we may say that the question depends upon what idea we have formed of the moral character of the Deity. If it be a true belief that God desires, above all things, the happiness of his creatures, and that this was his purpose in their creation, utility is not only not a godless doctrine, but more profoundly religious than any other. If it be meant that utilitarianism does not recognize the revealed will of God as the supreme law of morals, I answer, that a utilitarian who believes in the perfect goodness and wisdom of God, necessarily believes that whatever God has thought fit to reveal on the subject of morals, must fulfil the requirements of utility in a supreme degree. But others besides utilitarians have been of opinion that the Christian revelation was intended, and is fitted, to inform the hearts and minds of mankind with a spirit which should enable them to find for themselves what is right, and incline them to do it when found, rather than to tell them, except in a very general way, what it is: and that we need a doctrine of ethics, carefully followed out, to interpret to us the will of God. Whether this opinion is correct or not, it is superfluous here to discuss; since whatever aid

religion, either natural or revealed, can afford to ethical investigation, is as open to the utilitarian moralist as to any other. He can use it as the testimony of God to the usefulness or hurtfulness of any given course of action, by as good a right as others can use it for the indication of a transcendental law, having no connection with usefulness or with happiness.

Again, Utility is often summarily stigmatized as an immoral doctrine by giving it the name of Expediency, and taking advantage of the popular use of that term to contrast it with Principle. But the Expedient, in the sense in which it is opposed to the Right, generally means that which is expedient for the particular interest of the agent himself: as when a minister sacrifices the interest of his country to keep himself in place. When it means anything better than this, it means that which is expedient for some immediate object, some temporary purpose, but which violates a rule whose observance is expedient in a much higher degree. The Expedient, in this sense, instead of being the same thing with the useful, is a branch of the hurtful. Thus, it would often be expedient, for the purpose of getting over some momentary embarrassment, or attaining some object immediately useful to ourselves or others, to tell a lie. But inasmuch as the cultivation in ourselves of a sensitive feeling on the subject of veracity, is one of the most useful, and the enfeeblement of that feeling one of the most hurtful, things to which our conduct can be instrumental; and inasmuch as any, even unintentional, deviation from truth, does that much towards weakening the trustworthiness of human assertion, which is not only the principal support of all present social well-being, but the insufficiency of which does more than any one thing that can be named to keep back civilization, virtue, everything on which human happiness on the largest scale depends; we feel that the violation, for a present advantage, of a rule of such transcendent expediency, is not expedient, and that he who, for the sake of a convenience to himself or to some other individual, does what depends on him to deprive mankind of the good, and inflict upon them the evil, involved in the greater or less reliance which they can place in each other's word, acts the part of one of their worst enemies. Yet that even this rule, sacred as it is, admits of possible exceptions, is acknowledged by all moralists; the chief of which is when the withholding of some fact (as of information from a male-factor, or of bad news from a person dangerously ill) would preserve some one (especially a person other than oneself) from great and unmerited evil, and when the withholding can only be effected by denial. But in order that the exception may not extend itself beyond the need, and may have the least possible effect in weakening reliance on veracity, it ought to be recognized, and, if possible, its limits defined; and if the principle of utility is good for anything, it must be good for weighing these conflicting utilities against one another, and marking out the region within which one or the other preponderates.

Again, defenders of utility often find themselves called upon to reply to such objections as this—that there is not time, previous to action, for calculating and weighing the effects of any line of conduct on the general happiness. This is exactly as if any one were to say that it is impossible to guide our conduct by Christianity, because there is not time, on every occasion on which anything has to be done, to read through the Old and New Testaments. The answer to the objection is, that there has been ample time, namely, the whole past duration of the human species. During all that time mankind have been learning by experience the tendencies of actions; on which experience all the prudence, as well as all the morality of life, is dependent. People talk as if the commencement of this course of experience had hitherto been put off, and as if, at the moment when some man feels tempted to meddle with the property or life of another, he had to begin considering for the first time whether murder and theft are injurious to human happiness. Even then I do not think that he would find the question very puzzling; but, at all events, the matter is now done to his hand. It is truly a whimsical supposition, that if mankind were agreed in considering utility to be the test of morality, they would remain without any agreement as to what is useful, and would take no measures for having their notions on the subject taught to the young, and enforced by law and opinion. There is no difficulty in proving any ethical standard whatever to work ill, if we suppose universal idiocy to be conjoined with it, but on any hypothesis short of that, mankind must by this time have acquired positive beliefs as to the effects of some actions on their happiness; and the beliefs which have thus come down are the rules of morality for the multitude, and for the philosopher until he has succeeded in finding better. That philosophers might easily do this, even now, on many subjects; that the received code of ethics is by no means of divine right; and that mankind have still much to learn as to the effects of actions on the general happiness, I admit, or rather, earnestly maintain. The corollaries from the principle of utility, like the precepts of every practical art, admit of indefinite

improvement, and, in a progressive state of the human mind, their improvement is perpetually going on. But to consider the rules of morality as improvable, is one thing; to pass over the intermediate generalizations entirely, and endeavor to test each individual action directly by the first principle, is another. It is a strange notion that the acknowledgment of a first principle is inconsistent with the admission of secondary ones. To inform a traveler respecting the place of his ultimate destination, is not to forbid the use of landmarks and direction-posts on the way. The proposition that happiness is the end and aim of morality, does not mean that no road ought to be laid down to that goal, or that persons going thither should not be advised to take one direction rather than another. Men really ought to leave off talking a kind of nonsense on this subject, which they would neither talk nor listen to on other matters of practical concernment. Nobody argues that the art of navigation is not founded on astronomy, because sailors cannot wait to calculate the Nautical Almanac. Being rational creatures, they go to sea with it ready calculated; and all rational creatures go out upon the sea of life with their minds made up on the common questions of right and wrong, as well as on many of the far more difficult questions of wise and foolish. And this, as long as foresight is a human quality, it is to be presumed they will continue to do. Whatever we adopt as the fundamental principle of morality, we require subordinate principles to apply it by: the impossibility of doing without them, being common to all systems, can afford no argument against any one in particular: but gravely to argue as if no such secondary principles could be had, and as if mankind had remained till now, and always must remain, without drawing any general conclusions from the experience of human life, is as high a pitch, I think, as absurdity has ever reached in philosophical controversy.

The remainder of the stock arguments against utilitarianism mostly consist in laying to its charge the common infirmities of human nature, and the general difficulties which embarrass conscientious persons in shaping their course through life. We are told that a utilitarian will be apt to make his own particular case an exception to moral rules, and, when under temptation, will see an utility in the breach of a rule, greater than he will see in its observance. But is utility the only creed which is able to furnish us with excuses for evil doing, and means of cheating our own conscience? They are afforded in abundance by all doctrines which recognize as a fact in morals the existence of conflicting considerations; which all doctrines do, that have been believed by sane persons. It is not the fault of any creed, but of the complicated nature of human affairs, that rules of conduct cannot be so framed as to require no exceptions, and that hardly any kind of action can safely be laid down as either always obligatory or always condemnable. There is no ethical creed which does not temper the rigidity of its laws, by giving a certain latitude, under the moral responsibility of the agent, for accommodation to peculiarities of circumstances; and under every creed, at the opening thus made, self-deception and dishonest casuistry get in. There exists no moral system under which there do not arise unequivocal cases of conflicting obligation. These are the real difficulties, the knotty points both in the theory of ethics, and in the conscientious guidance of personal conduct. They are overcome practically with greater or with less success according to the intellect and virtue of the individual; but it can hardly be pretended that any one will be the less qualified for dealing with them, from possessing an ultimate standard to which conflicting rights and duties can be referred. If utility is the ultimate source of moral obligations, utility may be invoked to decide between them when their demands are incompatible. Though the application of the standard may be difficult, it is better than none at all: while in other systems, the moral laws all claiming independent authority, there is no common umpire entitled to interfere between them; their claims to precedence one over another rest on little better than sophistry, and unless determined, as they generally are, by the unacknowledged influence of considerations of utility, afford a free scope for the action of personal desires and partialities. We must remember that only in these cases of conflict between secondary principles is it requisite that first principles should be appealed to. There is no case of moral obligation in which some secondary principle is not involved; and if only one, there can seldom be any real doubt which one it is, in the mind of any person by whom the principle itself is recognized.

FOOTNOTE:

An opponent, whose intellectual and moral fairness it is a pleasure to acknowledge (the Rev. J. Llewellyn Davis), has objected to this passage, saying, "Surely the rightness or wrongness of saving a man from drowning does depend very much upon the motive with which it is done. Suppose that a tyrant, when his enemy jumped into the sea to escape from him, saved him from drowning simply in order that he might inflict upon him more exquisite tortures, would it tend to clearness to speak of that rescue as 'a morally right action?' Or suppose again, according to one of the stock illustrations of ethical inquiries, that a man betrayed a trust received from a friend, because the discharge of it would fatally injure that friend himself or someone belonging to him, would utilitarianism compel one to call the betrayal 'a crime' as much as if it had been done from the meanest motive?"

I submit, that he who saves another from drowning in order to kill him by torture afterwards, does not differ only in motive from him who does the same thing from duty or benevolence; the act itself is different. The rescue of the man is, in the case supposed, only the necessary first step of an act far more atrocious than leaving him to drown would have been. Had Mr. Davis said, "The rightness or wrongness of saving a man from drowning does depend very much"—not upon the motive, but—"upon the intention" no utilitarian would have differed from him. Mr. Davis, by an oversight too common not to be quite venial, has in this case confounded the very different ideas of Motive and Intention. There is no point which utilitarian thinkers (and Bentham pre-eminently) have taken more pains to illustrate than this. The morality of the action depends entirely upon the intention—that is, upon what the agent wills to do. But the motive, that is, the feeling which makes him will so to do, when it makes no difference in the act, makes none in the morality: though it makes a great difference in our moral estimation of the agent, especially if it indicates a good or a bad habitual disposition—a bent of character from which useful, or from which hurtful actions are likely to arise.

CHAPTER III: OF THE ULTIMATE SANCTION OF THE PRINCIPLE OF UTILITY

The question is often asked, and properly so, in regard to any supposed moral standard: "What is its sanction? What are the motives to obey it?" or, more specifically, "What is the source of its obligation? Whence does it derive its binding force?" It is a necessary part of moral philosophy to provide the answer to this question; which, though frequently assuming the shape of an objection to the utilitarian morality, as if it had some special applicability to that above others, really arises in regard to all standards. It arises, in fact, whenever a person is called on to adopt a standard or refer morality to any basis on which he has not been accustomed to rest it. For the customary morality, that which education and opinion have consecrated, is the only one which presents itself to the mind with the feeling of being in itself obligatory; and when a person is asked to believe that this morality derives its obligation from some general principle round which custom has not thrown the same halo, the assertion is to him a paradox; the supposed corollaries seem to have a more binding force than the original theorem; the superstructure seems to stand better without, than with, what is represented as its foundation. He says to himself, I feel that I am bound not to rob or murder, betray or deceive; but why am I bound to promote the general happiness? If my own happiness lies in something else, why may I not give that the preference?

If the view adopted by the utilitarian philosophy of the nature of the moral sense be correct, this difficulty will always present itself, until the influences which form moral character have taken the same hold of the principle which they have taken of some of the consequences— until, by the improvement of education, the feeling of unity with our fellow creatures shall be (what it cannot be doubted that Christ intended it to be) as deeply rooted in our character, and to our own consciousness as completely a part of our nature, as the horror of crime is in an ordinarily well-brought-up young person. In the meantime, however, the difficulty has no peculiar application to the doctrine of utility, but is inherent in every attempt to analyze morality and reduce it to principles; which, unless the principle is already in men's minds invested with as much sacredness as any of its applications, always seems to divest them of a part of their sanctity.

The principle of utility either has, or there is no reason why it might not have, all the sanctions which belong to any other system of morals. Those sanctions are either external or internal. Of the external sanctions it is not necessary to speak at any length. They are, the hope of favor and the fear of displeasure from our fellow creatures or from the Ruler of the Universe, along with whatever we may have of sympathy or affection for them or of love and awe of Him, inclining us to do His will independently of selfish consequences. There is evidently no reason why all these motives for observance should not attach themselves to the utilitarian morality, as completely and as powerfully as to any other. Indeed, those of them which refer to our fellow creatures are sure to do so, in proportion to the amount of general intelligence; for whether there be any other ground of moral obligation than the general happiness or not, men do desire happiness; and however imperfect may be their own practice, they desire and commend all conduct in others towards themselves, by which they think their happiness is promoted. With regard to the religious motive, if men believe, as most profess to do, in the goodness of God, those who think that conduciveness to the general happiness is the essence, or even only the criterion, of good, must necessarily believe that it is also that which God approves. The whole force therefore of external reward and punishment, whether physical or moral, and whether proceeding from God or from our fellow men, together with all that the capacities of human nature admit, of disinterested devotion to either, become available to enforce the utilitarian morality, in proportion as that morality is recognized; and the more powerfully, the more the appliances of education and general cultivation are bent to the purpose.

So far as to external sanctions. The internal sanction of duty, whatever our standard of duty may be, is one and the same—a feeling in our own mind; a pain, more or less intense, attendant on violation of duty, which in properly cultivated moral natures rises, in the more serious cases, into shrinking from it as an impossibility. This feeling, when disinterested, and connecting itself with the pure idea of duty, and not with some particular form of it, or with any of the merely accessory circumstances, is the essence of Conscience; though in that complex phenomenon as it actually exists, the simple fact is in general all encrusted over with collateral associations, derived from sympathy, from love, and still more from fear; from all the forms of religious feeling; from the recollections of childhood and of all our past life; from self-esteem, desire of the esteem of others, and occasionally even self-abasement. This extreme complication is, I apprehend, the origin of the sort of mystical character which, by a tendency of the human mind of which there are many other examples, is apt to be attributed to the idea of moral obligation, and which leads people to believe that the idea cannot possibly attach itself to any other objects than those which, by a supposed mysterious law, are found in our present experience to excite it. Its binding force, however, consists in the existence of a mass of feeling which must be broken through in order to do what violates our standard of right, and which, if we do nevertheless violate that standard, will probably have to be encountered afterwards in the form of remorse. Whatever theory we have of the nature or origin of conscience, this is what essentially constitutes it.

The ultimate sanction, therefore, of all morality (external motives apart) being a subjective feeling in our own minds, I see nothing embarrassing to those whose standard is utility, in the question, what is the sanction of that particular standard? We may answer, the same as of all other moral standards—the conscientious feelings of mankind. Undoubtedly this sanction has no binding efficacy on those who do not possess the feelings it appeals to; but neither will these persons be more obedient to any other moral principle than to the utilitarian one. On them morality of any kind has no hold but through the external sanctions. Meanwhile the feelings exist, a feat in human nature, the reality of which, and the great power with which they are capable of acting on those in whom they have been duly cultivated, are proved by experience. No reason has ever been shown why they may not be cultivated to as great intensity in connection with the utilitarian, as with any other rule of morals.

There is, I am aware, a disposition to believe that a person who sees in moral obligation a transcendental fact, an objective reality belonging to the province of "Things in themselves," is likely to be more obedient to it than one who believes it to be entirely subjective, having its seat in human consciousness only. But whatever a person's opinion may be on this point of Ontology, the force he is really urged by is his own subjective feeling, and is exactly measured by its strength. No one's belief that Duty is an objective reality is stronger than the belief that God is so; yet the belief in God, apart from the expectation of actual reward and punishment, only operates on conduct through, and in proportion to, the subjective religious feeling. The sanction, so far as it is disinterested, is always in the mind itself; and the notion, therefore, of the transcendental moralists must be, that this sanction will not exist in the mind unless it is believed to have its root out of the mind; and that if a person is able to say to himself, That which is restraining me, and which is called my conscience, is only a feeling in my own mind, he may possibly draw the conclusion that when the feeling ceases the obligation ceases, and that if he find the feeling inconvenient, he may disregard it, and endeavor to get rid of it. But is this danger confined to the utilitarian morality? Does the belief that moral obligation has its seat outside the mind make the feeling of it too strong to be got rid of? The fact is so far otherwise, that all moralists admit and lament the ease with which, in the generality of minds, conscience can be silenced or stifled. The question: "Need I obey my conscience?" is quite as often put to

themselves by persons who never heard of the principle of utility, as by its adherents. Those whose conscientious feelings are so weak as to allow of their asking this question, if they answer it affirmatively, will not do so because they believe in the transcendental theory, but because of the external sanctions.

It is not necessary, for the present purpose, to decide whether the feeling of duty is innate or implanted. Assuming it to be innate, it is an open question to what objects it naturally attaches itself; for the philosophic supporters of that theory are now agreed that the intuitive perception is of principles of morality, and not of the details. If there be anything innate in the matter, I see no reason why the feeling which is innate should not be that of regard to the pleasures and pains of others. If there is any principle of morals which is intuitively obligatory, I should say it must be that. If so, the intuitive ethics would coincide with the utilitarian, and there would be no further quarrel between them. Even as it is, the intuitive moralists, though they believe that there are other intuitive moral obligations, do already believe this to be one; for they unanimously hold that a large portion of morality turns upon the consideration due to the interests of our fellow creatures. Therefore, if the belief in the transcendental origin of moral obligation gives any additional efficacy to the internal sanction, it appears to me that the utilitarian principle has already the benefit of it.

On the other hand, if, as is my own belief, the moral feelings are not innate, but acquired, they are not for that reason the less natural. It is natural to man to speak, to reason, to build cities, to cultivate the ground, though these are acquired faculties. The moral feelings are not indeed a part of our nature, in the sense of being in any perceptible degree present in all of us; but this, unhappily, is a fact admitted by those who believe the most strenuously in their transcendental origin. Like the other acquired capacities above referred to, the moral faculty, if not a part of our nature, is a natural outgrowth from it; capable, like them, in a certain small degree, of springing up spontaneously; and susceptible of being brought by cultivation to a high degree of development. Unhappily it is also susceptible, by a sufficient use of the external sanctions and of the force of early impressions, of being cultivated in almost any direction: so that there is hardly anything so absurd or so mischievous that it may not, by means of these influences, be made to act on the human mind with all the authority of conscience. To doubt that the same potency might be given by the same means to the principle of utility, even if it had no foundation in human nature, would be flying in the face of all experience.

But moral associations which are wholly of artificial creation, when intellectual culture goes on, yield by degrees to the dissolving force of analysis: and if the feeling of duty, when associated with utility, would appear equally arbitrary; if there were no leading department of our nature, no powerful class of sentiments, with which that association would harmonize, which would make us feel it congenial, and incline us not only to foster it in others (for which we have abundant interested motives), but also to cherish it in ourselves; if there were not, in short, a natural basis of sentiment for utilitarian morality, it might well happen that this association also, even after it had been implanted by education, might be analyzed away.

But there is this basis of powerful natural sentiment; and this it is which, when once the general happiness is recognized as the ethical standard, will constitute the strength of the utilitarian morality. This firm foundation is that of the social feelings of mankind; the desire to be in unity with our fellow creatures, which is already a powerful principle in human nature, and happily one of those which tend to become stronger, even without express inculcation, from the influences of advancing civilization. The social state is at once so natural, so necessary, and so habitual to man, that, except in some unusual circumstances or by an effort of voluntary abstraction, he never conceives himself otherwise than as a member of a body; and this association is riveted more and more, as mankind are further removed from the state of savage independence. Any condition, therefore, which is essential to a state of society, becomes more and more an inseparable part of every person's conception of the state of things which he is born into, and which is the destiny of a human being. Now, society between human beings, except in the relation of master and slave, is manifestly impossible on any other footing than that the interests of all are to be consulted. Society between equals can only exist on the understanding that the interests of all are to be regarded equally. And since in all states of civilization, every person, except an absolute monarch, has equals, everyone is obliged to live on these terms with somebody; and in every age some advance is made towards a state in which it will be impossible to live permanently on other terms with anybody. In this way people grow up unable to conceive as possible to them a state of total disregard of other people's interests. They are under a necessity of conceiving themselves as

at least abstaining from all the grosser injuries, and (if only for their own protection.) living in a state of constant protest against them. They are also familiar with the fact of co-operating with others, and proposing to themselves a collective, not an individual, interest, as the aim (at least for the time being) of their actions. So long as they are co-operating, their ends are identified with those of others; there is at least a temporary feeling that the interests of others are their own interests. Not only does all strengthening of social ties, and all healthy growth of society, give to each individual a stronger personal interest in practically consulting the welfare of others; it also leads him to identify his feelings more and more with their good, or at least with an ever greater degree of practical consideration for it. He comes, as though instinctively, to be conscious of himself as a being who of course pays regard to others. The good of others becomes to him a thing naturally and necessarily to be attended to, like any of the physical conditions of our existence. Now, whatever amount of this feeling a person has, he is urged by the strongest motives both of interest and of sympathy to demonstrate it, and to the utmost of his power encourage it in others; and even if he has none of it himself, he is as greatly interested as anyone else that others should have it. Consequently, the smallest germs of the feeling are laid hold of and nourished by the contagion of sympathy and the influences of education; and a complete web of corroborative association is woven round it, by the powerful agency of the external sanctions. This mode of conceiving ourselves and human life, as civilization goes on, is felt to be more and more natural. Every step in political improvement renders it more so, by removing the sources of opposition of interest, and levelling those inequalities of legal privilege between individuals or classes, owing to which there are large portions of mankind whose happiness it is still practicable to disregard. In an improving state of the human mind, the influences are constantly on the increase, which tend to generate in each individual a feeling of unity with all the rest; which feeling, if perfect, would make him never think of, or desire, any beneficial condition for himself, in the benefits of which they are not included. If we now suppose this feeling of unity to be taught as a religion, and the whole force of education, of institutions, and of opinion, directed, as it once was in the case of religion, to make every person grow up from infancy surrounded on all sides both by the profession and by the practice of it, I think that no one, who can realize this conception, will feel any misgiving about the sufficiency of the ultimate sanction for the Happiness morality. To any ethical student who finds the realization difficult, I recommend, as a means of facilitating it, the second of M. Comte's two principal works, the *Système de Politique Positive*. I entertain the strongest objections to the system of politics and morals set forth in that treatise; but I think it has superabundantly shown the possibility of giving to the service of humanity, even without the aid of belief in a Providence, both the physical power and the social efficacy of a religion; making it take hold of human life, and color all thought, feeling, and action, in a manner of which the greatest ascendency ever exercised by any religion may be but a type and foretaste; and of which the danger is, not that it should be insufficient, but that it should be so excessive as to interfere unduly with human freedom and individuality.

Neither is it necessary to the feeling which constitutes the binding force of the utilitarian morality on those who recognize it, to wait for those social influences which would make its obligation felt by mankind at large. In the comparatively early state of human advancement in which we now live, a person cannot indeed feel that entireness of sympathy with all others, which would make any real discordance in the general direction of their conduct in life impossible; but already a person in whom the social feeling is at all developed, cannot bring himself to think of the rest of his fellow creatures as struggling rivals with him for the means of happiness, whom he must desire to see defeated in their object in order that he may succeed in his. The deeply-rooted conception which every individual even now has of himself as a social being, tends to make him feel it one of his natural wants that there should be harmony between his feelings and aims and those of his fellow creatures. If differences of opinion and of mental culture make it impossible for him to share many of their actual feelings-perhaps make him denounce and defy those feelings-he still needs to be conscious that his real aim and theirs do not conflict; that he is not opposing himself to what they really wish for, namely, their own good, but is, on the contrary, promoting it. This feeling in most individuals is much inferior in strength to their selfish feelings, and is often wanting altogether. But to those who have it, it possesses all the characters of a natural feeling. It does not present itself to their minds as a superstition of education, or a law despotically imposed by the power of society, but as an attribute which it would not be well for them to be without. This conviction is the ultimate sanction of the greatest-happiness morality. This

it is which makes any mind, of well-developed feelings, work with, and not against, the outward motives to care for others, afforded by what I have called the external sanctions; and when those sanctions are wanting, or act in an opposite direction, constitutes in itself a powerful internal binding force, in proportion to the sensitiveness and thoughtfulness of the character; since few but those whose mind is a moral blank, could bear to lay out their course of life on the plan of paying no regard to others except so far as their own private interest compels.

CHAPTER IV: OF WHAT SORT OF PROOF THE PRINCIPLE OF UTILITY IS SUSCEPTIBLE

It has already been remarked, that questions of ultimate ends do not admit of proof, in the ordinary acceptation of the term. To be incapable of proof by reasoning is common to all first principles; to the first premises of our knowledge, as well as to those of our conduct. But the former, being matters of fact, may be the subject of a direct appeal to the faculties which judge of fact—namely, our senses, and our internal consciousness. Can an appeal be made to the same faculties on questions of practical ends? Or by what other faculty is cognizance taken of them?

Questions about ends are, in other words, questions what things are desirable. The utilitarian doctrine is, that happiness is desirable, and the only thing desirable, as an end; all other things being only desirable as means to that end. What ought to be required of this doctrine—what conditions is it requisite that the doctrine should fulfil—to make good its claim to be believed?

The only proof capable of being given that an object is visible, is that people actually see it. The only proof that a sound is audible, is that people hear it: and so of the other sources of our experience. In like manner, I apprehend, the sole evidence it is possible to produce that anything is desirable, is that people do actually desire it. If the end which the utilitarian doctrine proposes to itself were not, in theory and in practice, acknowledged to be an end, nothing could ever convince any person that it was so. No reason can be given why the general happiness is desirable, except that each person, so far as he believes it to be attainable, desires his own happiness. This, however, being a fact, we have not only all the proof which the case admits of, but all which it is possible to require, that happiness is a good: that each person's happiness is a good to that person, and the general happiness, therefore, a good to the aggregate of all persons. Happiness has made out its title as one of the ends of conduct, and consequently one of the criteria of morality.

But it has not, by this alone, proved itself to be the sole criterion. To do that, it would seem, by the same rule, necessary to show, not only that people desire happiness, but that they never desire anything else. Now it is palpable that they do desire things which, in common language, are decidedly distinguished from happiness. They desire, for example, virtue, and the absence of vice, no less really than pleasure and the absence of pain. The desire of virtue is not as universal, but it is as authentic a fact, as the desire of happiness. And hence the opponents of the utilitarian standard deem that they have a right to infer that there are other ends of human action besides happiness, and that happiness is not the standard of approbation and disapprobation.

But does the utilitarian doctrine deny that people desire virtue, or maintain that virtue is not a thing to be desired? The very reverse. It maintains not only that virtue is to be desired, but that it is to be desired disinterestedly, for itself. Whatever may be the opinion of utilitarian moralists as to the original conditions by which virtue is made virtue; however they may believe (as they do) that actions and dispositions are only virtuous because they promote another end than virtue; yet this being granted, and it having been decided, from considerations of this description, what is virtuous, they not only place virtue at the very head of the things which are good as means to the ultimate end, but they also recognize as a psychological fact the possibility of its being, to the individual, a good in itself, without looking to any end beyond it; and hold, that the mind is not in a right state, not in a state conformable to Utility, not in the state most conducive to the general happiness, unless it does love virtue in this manner—as a thing desirable in itself, even although, in the individual instance, it should not produce those other desirable consequences which it tends to produce, and on account of which it is held to be virtue. This opinion is not, in the smallest degree, a departure from the Happiness principle. The ingredients of happiness are very various, and each of them is desirable in itself, and not merely when considered as swelling an aggregate. The principle of utility does not mean that any given pleasure, as music, for instance, or any given exemption from pain, as for example health, are to be looked upon as means to a collective something termed happiness, and to be desired on that account. They are desired and

desirable in and for themselves; besides being means, they are a part of the end. Virtue, according to the utilitarian doctrine, is not naturally and originally part of the end, but it is capable of becoming so; and in those who love it disinterestedly it has become so, and is desired and cherished, not as a means to happiness, but as a part of their happiness.

To illustrate this farther, we may remember that virtue is not the only thing, originally a means, and which if it were not a means to anything else, would be and remain indifferent, but which by association with what it is a means to, comes to be desired for itself, and that too with the utmost intensity. What, for example, shall we say of the love of money? There is nothing originally more desirable about money than about any heap of glittering pebbles. Its worth is solely that of the things which it will buy; the desires for other things than itself, which it is a means of gratifying. Yet the love of money is not only one of the strongest moving forces of human life, but money is, in many cases, desired in and for itself; the desire to possess it is often stronger than the desire to use it, and goes on increasing when all the desires which point to ends beyond it, to be compassed by it, are falling off. It may be then said truly, that money is desired not for the sake of an end, but as part of the end. From being a means to happiness, it has come to be itself a principal ingredient of the individual's conception of happiness. The same may be said of the majority of the great objects of human life—power, for example, or fame; except that to each of these there is a certain amount of immediate pleasure annexed, which has at least the semblance of being naturally inherent in them; a thing which cannot be said of money. Still, however, the strongest natural attraction, both of power and of fame, is the immense aid they give to the attainment of our other wishes; and it is the strong association thus generated between them and all our objects of desire, which gives to the direct desire of them the intensity it often assumes, so as in some characters to surpass in strength all other desires. In these cases the means have become a part of the end, and a more important part of it than any of the things which they are means to. What was once desired as an instrument for the attainment of happiness, has come to be desired for its own sake. In being desired for its own sake it is, however, desired as part of happiness. The person is made, or thinks he would be made, happy by its mere possession; and is made unhappy by failure to obtain it. The desire of it is not a different thing from the desire of happiness, any more than the love of music, or the desire of health. They are included in happiness. They are some of the elements of which the desire of happiness is made up. Happiness is not an abstract idea, but a concrete whole; and these are some of its parts. And the utilitarian standard sanctions and approves their being so. Life would be a poor thing, very ill provided with sources of happiness, if there were not this provision of nature, by which things originally indifferent, but conducive to, or otherwise associated with, the satisfaction of our primitive desires, become in themselves sources of pleasure more valuable than the primitive pleasures, both in permanency, in the space of human existence that they are capable of covering, and even in intensity. Virtue, according to the utilitarian conception, is a good of this description. There was no original desire of it, or motive to it, save its conduciveness to pleasure, and especially to protection from pain. But through the association thus formed, it may be felt a good in itself, and desired as such with as great intensity as any other good; and with this difference between it and the love of money, of power, or of fame, that all of these may, and often do, render the individual noxious to the other members of the society to which he belongs, whereas there is nothing which makes him so much a blessing to them as the cultivation of the disinterested, love of virtue. And consequently, the utilitarian standard, while it tolerates and approves those other acquired desires, up to the point beyond which they would be more injurious to the general happiness than promotive of it, enjoins and requires the cultivation of the love of virtue up to the greatest strength possible, as being above all things important to the general happiness.

It results from the preceding considerations, that there is in reality nothing desired except happiness. Whatever is desired otherwise than as a means to some end beyond itself, and ultimately to happiness, is desired as itself a part of happiness, and is not desired for itself until it has become so. Those who desire virtue for its own sake, desire it either because the consciousness of it is a pleasure, or because the consciousness of being without it is a pain, or for both reasons united; as in truth the pleasure and pain seldom exist separately, but almost always together, the same person feeling pleasure in the degree of virtue attained, and pain in not having attained more. If one of these gave him no pleasure, and the other no pain, he would not love or desire virtue, or would desire it only for the other benefits which it might produce to himself or to persons whom he cared for.

We have now, then, an answer to the question, of what sort of proof the principle of utility is susceptible. If

the opinion which I have now stated is psychologically true—if human nature is so constituted as to desire nothing which is not either a part of happiness or a means of happiness, we can have no other proof, and we require no other, that these are the only things desirable. If so, happiness is the sole end of human action, and the promotion of it the test by which to judge of all human conduct; from whence it necessarily follows that it must be the criterion of morality, since a part is included in the whole.

And now to decide whether this is really so; whether mankind do desire nothing for itself but that which is a pleasure to them, or of which the absence is a pain; we have evidently arrived at a question of fact and experience, dependent, like all similar questions, upon evidence. It can only be determined by practiced self-consciousness and self-observation, assisted by observation of others. I believe that these sources of evidence, impartially consulted, will declare that desiring a thing and finding it pleasant, aversion to it and thinking of it as painful, are phenomena entirely inseparable, or rather two parts of the same phenomenon; in strictness of language, two different modes of naming the same psychological fact: that to think of an object as desirable (unless for the sake of its consequences), and to think of it as pleasant, are one and the same thing; and that to desire anything, except in proportion as the idea of it is pleasant, is a physical and metaphysical impossibility.

So obvious does this appear to me, that I expect it will hardly be disputed: and the objection made will be, not that desire can possibly be directed to anything ultimately except pleasure and exemption from pain, but that the will is a different thing from desire; that a person of confirmed virtue, or any other person whose purposes are fixed, carries out his purposes without any thought of the pleasure he has in contemplating them, or expects to derive from their fulfilment; and persists in acting on them, even though these pleasures are much diminished, by changes in his character or decay of his passive sensibilities, or are outweighed by the pains which the pursuit of the purposes may bring upon him. All this I fully admit, and have stated it elsewhere, as positively and emphatically as any one. Will, the active phenomenon, is a different thing from desire, the state of passive sensibility, and though originally an offshoot from it, may in time take root and detach itself from the parent stock; so much so, that in the case of an habitual purpose, instead of willing the thing because we desire it, we often desire it only because we will it.

This, however, is but an instance of that familiar fact, the power of habit, and is nowise confined to the case of virtuous actions. Many indifferent things, which men originally did from a motive of some sort, they continue to do from habit. Sometimes this is done unconsciously, the consciousness coming only after the action: at other times with conscious volition, but volition which has become habitual, and is put into operation by the force of habit, in opposition perhaps to the deliberate preference, as often happens with those who have contracted habits of vicious or hurtful indulgence. Third and last comes the case in which the habitual act of will in the individual instance is not in contradiction to the general intention prevailing at other times, but in fulfilment of it; as in the case of the person of confirmed virtue, and of all who pursue deliberately and consistently any determinate end. The distinction between will and desire thus understood, is an authentic and highly important psychological fact; but the fact consists solely in this—that will, like all other parts of our constitution, is amenable to habit, and that we may will from habit what we no longer desire for itself, or desire only because we will it. It is not the less true that will, in the beginning, is entirely produced by desire; including in that term the repelling influence of pain as well as the attractive one of pleasure. Let us take into consideration, no longer the person who has a confirmed will to do right, but him in whom that virtuous will is still feeble, conquerable by temptation, and not to be fully relied on; by what means can it be strengthened? How can the will to be virtuous, where it does not exist in sufficient force, be implanted or awakened? Only by making the person desire virtue—by making him think of it in a pleasurable light, or of its absence in a painful one. It is by associating the doing right with pleasure, or the doing wrong with pain, or by eliciting and impressing and bringing home to the person's experience the pleasure naturally involved in the one or the pain in the other, that it is possible to call forth that will to be virtuous, which, when confirmed, acts without any thought of either pleasure or pain. Will is the child of desire, and passes out of the dominion of its parent only to come under that of habit. That which is the result of habit affords no presumption of being intrinsically good; and there would be no reason for wishing that the purpose of virtue should become independent of pleasure and pain, were it not that the influence of the pleasurable and painful associations which prompt to virtue is not sufficiently to be depended on for unerring constancy of action until it has acquired the support of habit. Both in feeling and in conduct, habit is the only thing which imparts certainty; and it is because of the importance to others of being able to rely absolutely on one's feelings and conduct, and to oneself of being able to rely on one's own, that the will to do right ought to be cultivated into this habitual independence. In other words, this state of the will is a means to good, not intrinsically a good; and does not contradict the doctrine that nothing is a good to human beings but in so far as it is either itself pleasurable, or a means of attaining pleasure or averting pain.

But if this doctrine be true, the principle of utility is proved. Whether it is so or not, must now be left to the consideration of the thoughtful reader. . . .

[*Utilitarianism.* (7th ed. London: Longmans, Green, Reader, and Dyer, 1879).]

CHAPTER ELEVEN

James and Clifford on the Ethics of Belief

Image © Marta Paniti, 2014. Used under license from Shutterstock, Inc.

William James (1842–1910)

SELECTED READINGS

▶ "The Will to Believe"—William James

▶ "The Ethics of Belief" from *Lectures and Essays* —W.K. Clifford

"The Will to Believe"

William James
(Edited by Joseph R. Kirkland)

In the recently published *Life* by Leslie Stephen of his brother, Fitz-James, there is an account of a school to which the latter went when he was a boy. The teacher, a certain Mr. Guest, used to converse with his pupils in this wise: "Gurney, what is the difference between justification and sanctification?" "Stephen, prove the omnipotence of God," etc. In the midst of our Harvard freethinking and indifference we are prone to imagine that here at your good old orthodox College conversation continues to be somewhat upon this order; and to show you that we at Harvard have not lost all interest in these vital subjects, I have brought with me tonight something like a sermon on justification by faith to read to you,—I mean an essay in justification of faith, a defense of our right to adopt a believing attitude in religious matters, in spite of the fact that our merely logical intellect may not have been coerced. "The Will to Believe," accordingly, is the title of my paper.

I have long defended to my own students the lawfulness of voluntarily adopted faith; but as soon as they have got well imbued with the logical spirit, they have as a rule refused to admit my contention to be lawful philosophically, even though in point of fact they were personally all the time chock-full of some faith or other themselves. I am all the while, however, so profoundly convinced that my own position is correct, that your invitation has seemed to me a good occasion to make my statements more clear. Perhaps your minds will be more open than those with which I have hitherto had to deal. I will be as little technical as I can, though I must begin by setting up some technical distinctions that will help us in the end.

I.

Let us give the name of hypothesis to anything that may be proposed to our belief; and just as the electricians speak of live and dead wires, let us speak of any hypothesis as either live or dead A live hypothesis is one which appeals as a real possibility to him to whom it is proposed. If I ask you to believe in the Mahdi, the notion makes no electric connection with your nature; it refuses to scintillate with any credibility at all. As a hypothesis it is completely dead. To an Arab, however (even if he be not one of the Madhi's followers), the

hypothesis is among the mind's possibilities: it is alive. This shows that deadness and liveness in a hypothesis are not intrinsic properties, but relations to the individual thinker. They are measured by his willingness to act. The maximum of liveness in hypothesis means willingness to act irrevocably. Practically, that means belief; but there is some believing tendency wherever there is willingness to act at all.

Next, let us call the decision between two hypotheses an option. Options may be of several kinds. They may be:

1. living or dead;

2. forced or avoidable;

3. momentous or trivial;

and for our purpose we may call an option a genuine option when it of the forced, living, and momentous kind.

1. A living option is one in which both hypotheses are live ones. If I say to you: "Be a theosophist or be a Mohammedan," it is probably a dead option, because for you neither hypothesis is likely to be alive. But if I say: "Be an agnostic or be Christian," it is otherwise: trained as you are, each hypothesis makes some appeal, however small, to your belief.

2. Next, if I say to you: "Choose between going out with your umbrella or without it," I do not offer you a genuine option, for it is not forced. You can easily avoid it by not going out at all. Similarly, if I say, "Either love me or hate me," [or] "Either call my theory true or call it false," your option is avoidable. You may remain indifferent to me, neither loving nor hating, and you may decline to offer any judgment as to my theory. But if I say, "Either accept this truth or go without it," I put on you a forced option, for there is no standing place outside of the alternative. Every dilemma based on a complete logical disjunction, with no possibility of not choosing, is an option of this forced kind.

3. Finally, if I were Dr. Nansen and proposed to you to join my North Pole expedition, your option would be momentous; for this would probably be

your only similar opportunity, and your choice now would either exclude you from the North Pole sort of immortality altogether or put at least the chance of it into your hands. He who refuses to embrace a unique opportunity loses the prize as surely as if he tried and failed. Per contra, the option is trivial when the opportunity is not unique, when the stake is insignificant, or when the decision is reversible if it later prove unwise. Such trivial options abound in the scientific life. A chemist finds an hypothesis live enough to spend a year in its verification: he believes in it to that extent. But if his experiments prove inconclusive either way, he is quit for his loss of time, no vital harm being done.

It will facilitate our discussion if we keep all these distinctions well in mind.

II.

The next matter to consider is the actual psychology of human opinion. When we look at certain facts, it seems as if our passional and volitional nature lay at the root of all our convictions. When we look at others, it seems as if they could do nothing when the intellect had once said its say. Let us take the latter facts up first.

Does it not seem preposterous on the very face of it to talk of our opinions being modifiable at will? Can our will either help or hinder our intellect in its perceptions of truth? Can we, by just willing it, believe that Abraham Lincoln's existence is a myth, and that the portraits of him in McClure's Magazine are all of someone else? Can we, by any effort of our will, or by any strength of wish that it were true, believe ourselves well and about when we are roaring with rheumatism in bed, or feel certain that the sum of the two one-dollar bills in our pocket must be a hundred dollars? We can say any of these things, but we are absolutely impotent to believe them; and of just such things is the whole fabric of the truths that we do believe in made up, matters of fact, immediate or remote, as Hume said, and relations between ideas, which are either there or not there for us if we see them so, and which if not there cannot be put there by any action of our own.

In Pascal's *Thoughts* there is a celebrated passage known in literature as Pascal's wager. In it he tries to force us into Christianity by reasoning as if our concern with truth resembled our concern with the stakes in a game of chance. Translated freely his words are these: You must either believe or not believe that God is: which will you do? Your human reason cannot say. A game is going on

between you and the nature of things which at the day of judgment will bring out either heads or tails. Weigh what your gains and your losses would be if you should stake all you have on heads, or God's existence: if you win in such case, you gain eternal beatitude; if you lose, you lose nothing at all. If there were an infinity of chances, and only one for God in this wager, still you ought to stake your all on God; for though you surely risk a finite loss by this procedure, any finite loss is reasonable, even a certain one is reasonable, if there is but the possibility of infinite gain. Go, then, and take holy water, and have masses said; belief will come and stupefy your scruples, *Cela vous fera croire et vous abetira.* Why should you not? At bottom, what have you to lose?

You probably feel that when religious faith expresses itself thus, in the language of the gaming-table, it is put to its last trumps. Surely Pascal's own personal belief in masses and holy water had far other springs; and this celebrated page of his is but an argument for others, a last desperate snatch at a weapon against the hardness of the unbelieving heart. We feel that a faith in masses and holy water adopted willfully after such a mechanical calculation lack the inner soul of faith's reality; and if we were of the Deity, we should probably take pleasure in cutting off believers from their infinite reward. It is evident that unless there be some preexisting tendency to believe in masses and holy water, the option offered to the will by Pascal is not a living option. Certainly no Turk ever took to masses and holy water on its account; and even to us Protestants these seem such foregone impossibilities that Pascal's logic, invoked for them specifically, leaves us unmoved. As well might the Mahdi write to us, saying, "I am the Expected One whom God has created in his effulgence. You shall be infinitely happy if you confess me; otherwise you shall be cut off from the light of the sun. Weigh, then, your infinite gain if I am genuine against your finite sacrifice if I am not!" His logic would be that of Pascal; but he would vainly use it on us, for the hypothesis he offers us is dead. No tendency to act on it exists in us to any degree.

The talk of believing by our volition seems, then, from one point of view, simply silly. From another point of view it is worse than silly, it is vile. When one turns to the magnificent edifice of the physical sciences, and sees how it was reared; what thousands of disinterested moral lives of men lie buried in its mere foundations; what patience and postponement, what choking down of preference, what submission to the icy laws of outer fact are wrought into its very stones and mortar; how absolutely impersonal it stands in its vast augustness,--then how besotted and contemptible seems every little sentimentalist who comes blowing his voluntary smoke-wreaths, and pretending to decide things from out of his private dream! Can we wonder if those bred in the rugged and manly school of science should feel like spewing such subjectivism out of their mouths? The whole system of loyalties which grow up in the schools of science go dead against its toleration; so that it is only natural that those who have caught the scientific fever should pass over to the opposite extreme, and write sometimes as if the incorruptibly truthful intellect ought positively to prefer bitterness and unacceptableness to the heart in its cup.

"It fortifies my soul to know / That, thou I perish, Truth is so," sings Clough, while Huxley exclaims: "My only consolation lies in the reflection that, however bad our posterity may become, so far as they hold by the plain rule of not pretending to believe what they have no reason to believe, because it may be to their advantage so to pretend [the word 'pretend' is surely here redundant], they will not have reached the lowest depth of immorality." And that delicious enfant terrible Clifford writes: "Belief is desecrated when given to unproved and unquestioned statements for the solace and private pleasure of the believer. . . . Whoso would deserve well of his fellows in this matter will guard the purity of his belief with a very fanaticism of jealous care, lest at any time it should rest on an unworthy object, and catch a stain which can never be wiped away. . . . If [a] belief has been accepted on insufficient evidence [even though the belief be true, as Clifford on the same page explains] the pleasure is a stolen one. . . . It is sinful because it is stolen in defiance of our duty to mankind. That duty is to guard ourselves from such beliefs as from a pestilence which may shortly master our own body and then spread to the rest of the town. . . . It is wrong always, everywhere, and for everyone, to believe anything upon insufficient evidence."

III.

All this strikes one as healthy, even when expressed, as by Clifford, with somewhat too much of robust pathos in the voice. Free-will and simple wishing do seem, in the matter of our credences, to be only fifth wheels to the coach. Yet if anyone should thereupon assume that intellectual insight is what remains after wish and will and sentimental preference have taken wing, or that pure reason is what then settles our opinions, he would fly quite as directly in the teeth of the facts.

It is only our already dead hypotheses that our willing nature is unable to bring to life again. But what has made them dead for us is for the most part a previous action of our willing nature of an antagonistic kind. When I say "willing nature," I do not mean only such deliberate volitions as may have set up habits of belief that we cannot now escape from, I mean all such factors of belief as fear and hope, prejudice and passion, imitation and partisanship, the circumpressure of our caste and set. As a matter of fact we find ourselves believing, we hardly know how or why. Mr. Balfour gives the name of "authority" to all those influences, born of the intellectual climate, that make hypotheses possible or impossible for us, alive or dead. Here in this room, we all of us believe in molecules and the conservation of energy, in democracy and necessary progress, in Protestant Christianity and the duty of fighting for "the doctrine of the immortal Monroe," all for no reasons worthy of the name. We see into these matters with no more inner clearness, and probably with much less, than any disbeliever in them might possess. His unconventionality would probably have some grounds to show for its conclusions; but for us, not insight, but the prestige of the opinions, is what makes the spark shoot from them and light up our sleeping magazines of faith. Our reason is quite satisfied, in nine hundred and ninety-nine cases out of every thousand of us, if it can find a few arguments that will do to recite in case our credulity is criticized by someone else. Our faith is faith in someone else's faith, and in the greatest matters this is most the case. Our belief in truth itself, for instance, that there is a truth, and that our minds and it are made for each other, what is it but a passionate affirmation of desire, in which our social system backs us up? We want to have a truth; we want to believe that our experiments and studies and discussions must put us in a continually better and better position towards it; and on this line we agree to fight out our thinking lives. But if a pyrrhonistic sceptic asks us how we know all this, can our logic find a reply? No! Certainly it cannot. It is just one volition against another, we willing to go in for life upon a trust or assumption which he, for his part, does not care to make.

As a rule we disbelieve all facts and theories for which we have no use. Clifford's cosmic emotions find no use for Christian feelings. Huxley belabors the bishops because there is no use for sacerdotalism in his scheme of life. Newman, on the contrary, goes over to Romanism, and finds all sorts of reasons good for staying there, because a priestly system is for him an organic need and delight. Why do so few "scientists" even look at the evidence for telepathy, so called? Because they think, as a leading biologist, now dead, once said to me, that even if such a thing were true, scientists ought to band together to keep it suppressed and concealed. It would undo the uniformity of Nature and all sorts of other things without which scientists cannot carry on their pursuits. But if this very man had been shown something which as a scientist he might do with telepathy, he might not only have examined the evidence, but even have found it good enough. This very law which the logicians would impose upon us—if I may give the name of logicians to those who would rule out our willing nature here – is based on nothing but their own natural wish to exclude all elements for which they, in their professional quality of logicians, can find no use.

Evidently, then, our non-intellectual nature does influence our convictions. There are passional tendencies and volitions which run before and others which come after belief, and it is only the latter that are too late for the fair; and they are not too late when the previous passional work has been already in their own direction. Pascal's argument, instead of being powerless, then seems a regular clincher, and is the last stroke needed to make our faith in masses and holy water complete. The state of things is evidently far from simple; and pure insight and logic, whatever they might do ideally, are not the only things that really do produce our creeds.

IV.

Our next duty, having recognized this mixed-up state of affairs, is to ask whether it be simply reprehensible and pathological, or whether, on the contrary, we must treat it as a normal element in making up our minds. The thesis I defend is, briefly stated, this: Our passional nature not only lawfully may, but must, decide an option between propositions, whenever it is a genuine option that cannot by its nature be decided on intellectual grounds; for to say, under such circumstances, "Do not decide, but leave the question open," is itself a passional decision, just like deciding yes or no, and is attended with the same risk of losing the truth. The thesis thus abstractly expressed will, I trust, soon become quite clear. But I must first indulge in a bit more of preliminary work.

V.

It will be observed that for the purposes of this discussion we are on "dogmatic" ground,—ground, I mean, which leaves systematic philosophical skepticism altogether out of account. The postulate that there is truth, and that it is the destiny of our minds to attain it, we are deliberately resolving to make, though the skeptic will not make it. We part company with him, therefore, absolutely, at this point. But the faith that truth exists, and that our minds can find it, may be held in two ways. We may talk of the empiricist way and of the absolutist way of believing in truth. The absolutists in this matter say that we not only can attain to knowing truth, but we can know when we have attained to knowing it; while the empiricists think that although we may attain it, we cannot infallibly know when. To know is one thing, and to know for certain that we know is another. One may hold to the first being possible without the second; hence the empiricists and the absolutists, although neither of them is a skeptic in the usual philosophic sense of the term, show very different degrees of dogmatism in their lives.

If we look at the history of opinions, we see that the empiricist tendency has largely prevailed in science, while in philosophy the absolutist tendency has had everything its own way. The characteristic sort of happiness, indeed, which philosophies yield has mainly consisted in the conviction felt by each successive school or system that by it bottom-certitude had been attained. "Other philosophies are collections of opinions, mostly false; my philosophy gives standing-ground forever,"—who does not recognize in this the key-note of every system worthy of the name? A system, to be a system at all, must come as a closed system, reversible in this or that detail, perchance, but in its essential features never!

Scholastic orthodoxy, to which one must always go when one wishes to find perfectly clear statement, has beautifully elaborated this absolutist conviction in a doctrine which it calls that of "objective evidence." If, for example, I am unable to doubt that I now exist before you, that two is less than three, or that if all men are mortal then I am mortal too, it is because these things illumine my intellect irresistibly. The final ground of this objective evidence possessed by certain propositions is *the adequatio intellectus nostri cum re* [i.e., the agreement of our intellect with the thing known]. The certitude it brings involves an *aptitudinem ad extorquendam certum assensum* [i.e., an aptitude for extorting a certain assent from our intellect] on the part of the truth envisaged, and on the side of the subject a *quietem in cognitione* [i.e., a quiet rest in knowledge], when once the object is mentally received, that leaves no possibility of doubt behind; and in the whole transaction nothing operates but the *entitas ipsa* [i.e., entity itself] of the object and the *entitas ipsa* of the mind. We slouchy modern thinkers dislike to talk in Latin, indeed, we dislike to talk in set terms at all; but at bottom our own state of mind is very much like this whenever we uncritically abandon ourselves: You believe in objective evidence, and I do. Of some things we feel that we are certain: we know, and we know that we do know. There is something that gives a click inside of us, a bell that strikes twelve, when the hands of our mental clock have swept the dial and meet over the meridian hour. The greatest empiricists among us are only empiricists on reflection: when left to their instincts, they dogmatize like infallible popes. When the Cliffords tell us how sinful it is to be Christians on such "insufficient evidence," insufficiency is really the last thing they have in mind. For them the evidence is absolutely sufficient, only it makes the other way. They believe so completely in an anti-christian order of the universe that there is no living option: Christianity is a dead hypothesis from the start.

VI.

But now, since we are all such absolutists by instinct, what in our quality of students of philosophy ought we to do about the fact? Shall we espouse and indorse it? Or shall we treat it as a weakness of our nature from which we must free ourselves, if we can?

I sincerely believe that the latter course is the only one we can follow as reflective men. Objective evidence and certitude are doubtless very fine ideals to play with, but where on this moonlit and dream-visited planet are they found? I am, therefore, myself a complete empiricist so far as my theory of human knowledge goes. I live, to be sure, by the practical faith that we must go on experiencing and thinking over our experience, for only thus can our opinions grow more true; but to hold any one of them—I absolutely do not care which—as if it never could be reinterpretable or corrigible, I believe to be a tremendously mistaken attitude, and I think that the whole history of philosophy will bear me out. There is but one indefectibly certain truth, and that is the truth that pyrrhonistic skepticism itself leaves standing,—the truth that the present phenomenon of consciousness exists. That, however, is the bare starting-point of knowledge, the mere admission of a stuff to be philosophized about. The various philosophies are but so many attempts at expressing what this stuff really is. And if we repair to our libraries what

disagreement do we discover! Where is a certainly true answer found? Apart from abstract propositions of comparison (such as two and two are the same as four), propositions which tell us nothing by themselves about concrete reality, we find no proposition ever regarded by any one as evidently certain that has not either been called a falsehood, or at least had its truth sincerely questioned by someone else. The transcending of the axioms of geometry, not in play but in earnest, by certain of our contemporaries (as Zöllner and Charles H. Hinton), and the rejection of the whole Aristotelian logic by the Hegelians, are striking instances in point.

No concrete test of what is really true has ever been agreed upon. Some make the criterion external to the moment of perception, putting it either in revelation, the *consensus gentium* [i.e., the agreement of all nations], the instincts of the heart, or the systematized experience of the race. Others make the perceptive moment its own test,—Descartes, for instance, with his clear and distinct ideas guaranteed by the veracity of God; Reid with his "common-sense," and Kant with his forms of synthetic judgment *a priori*. The inconceivability of the opposite; the capacity to be verified by sense; the possession of complete organic unity or self-relation, realized when a thing is its own other,— are standards which, in turn, have been used. The much lauded objective evidence is never triumphantly there; it is a mere aspiration or *Grenzbegriff* [i.e., limit or boundary] marking the infinitely remote ideal of our thinking life. To claim that certain truths now possess it, is simply to say that when you think them true and they are true, then their evidence is objective, otherwise it is not. But practically one's conviction that the evidence one goes by is of the real objective brand, is only one more subjective opinion added to the lot. For what a contradictory array of opinions have objective evidence and absolute certitude been claimed! The world is rational through and through,—its existence is an ultimate brute fact; there is a personal God,—a personal God is inconceivable; there is an extra-mental physical world immediately known,—the mind can only know its own ideas; a moral imperative exists,—obligation is only the result of desires; a permanent spiritual principle is in every one,—there are only shifting states of mind; there is an endless chain of causes,—there is an absolute first cause; an eternal necessity,—a freedom; a purpose,—no purpose; a primal One,—a primal Many; a universal continuity,—an essential discontinuity in things; an infinity,—no infinity. There is this,—there is that: there is indeed nothing which someone has not thought absolutely true, while his neighbor deemed it absolutely false; and not an absolutist among them seems ever to have considered that the trouble may all the time be essential, and that the intellect, even with truth directly in its grasp, may have no infallible signal for knowing whether it be truth or no. When, indeed, one remembers that the most striking practical application to life of the doctrine of objective certitude has been the conscientious labors of the Holy Office of the Inquisition, one feels less tempted than ever to lend the doctrine a respectful ear.

But please observe, now, that when as empiricists we give up the doctrine of objective certitude, we do not thereby give up the quest or hope of truth itself. We still pin our faith on its existence, and still believe that we gain an ever better position towards it by systematically continuing to roll up experiences and think. Our great difference from the scholastic lies in the way we face. The strength of his system lies in the principles, the origin, the *terminus a quo* [i.e., the beginning point] of his thought; for us the strength is in the outcome, the upshot, the *terminus ad quem* [i.e., the end result]. Not where it comes from but what it leads to is to decide. It matters not to an empiricist from what quarter a hypothesis may come to him: he may have acquired it by fair means or by foul; passion may have whispered or accident suggested it; but if the total drift of thinking continues to confirm it, that is what he means by its being true.

VII.

One more point, small but important, and our preliminaries are done. There are two ways of looking at our duty in the matter of opinion, --ways entirely different, and yet ways about whose difference the theory of knowledge seems hitherto to have shown very little concern. We must know the truth; and we must avoid error,—these are our first and great commandments as would-be knowers; but they are not two ways of stating an identical commandment, they are two separable laws. Although it may indeed happen that when we believe the truth A, we escape as an incidental consequence from believing the falsehood B, it hardly ever happens that by merely disbelieving B we necessarily believe A. We may in escaping B fall into believing other falsehoods, C or D, just as bad as B; or we may escape B by not believing anything at all, not even A.

"Believe truth! Shun error!" These, we see, are two materially different laws; and by choosing between them we may end by coloring differently our whole

intellectual life. We may regard the chase for truth as paramount, and the avoidance of error as secondary; or we may, on the other hand, treat the avoidance of error as more imperative, and let truth take its chance. Clifford, in the instructive passage which I have quoted, exhorts us to the latter course. Believe nothing, he tells us, keep your mind in suspense forever, rather than by closing it on insufficient evidence incur the awful risk of believing lies. You, on the other hand, may think that the risk of being in error is a very small matter when compared with the blessings of real knowledge, and be ready to be duped many times in your investigation rather than postpone indefinitely the chance of guessing true. I myself find it impossible to go with Clifford. We must remember that these feelings of our duty about either truth or error are in any case only expressions of our passional life. Biologically considered, our minds are as ready to grind out falsehood as veracity, and he who says, "Better go without belief forever than believe a lie!" merely shows his own preponderant private horror of becoming a dupe. He may be critical of many of his desires and fears, but this fear he slavishly obeys. He cannot imagine any one questioning its binding force. For my own part, I have also a horror of being duped; but I can believe that worse things than being duped may happen to a man in this world: so Clifford's exhortation has to my ears a thoroughly fantastic sound. It is like a general informing his soldiers that it is better to keep out of battle forever than to risk a single wound. Not so are victories either over enemies or over nature gained. Our errors are surely not such awfully solemn things. In a world where we are so certain to incur them in spite of all our caution, a certain lightness of heart seems healthier than this excessive nervousness on their behalf. At any rate, it seems the fittest thing for the empiricist philosopher.

VIII.

And now, after all this introduction, let us go straight at our question. I have said, and now repeat it, that not only as a matter of fact do we find our passional nature influencing us in our opinions, but that there are some options between opinions in which this influence must be regarded both as an inevitable and as a lawful determinant of our choice.

I fear here that some of you my hearers will begin to scent danger, and lend an inhospitable ear. Two first steps of passion you have indeed had to admit as necessary,—we must think so as to avoid dupery, and we must think so as to gain truth; but the surest path to those ideal consummations, you will probably consider, is from now onwards to take no further passional step.

Well, of course, I agree as far as the facts will allow. Wherever the option between losing truth and gaining it is not momentous, we can throw the chance of gaining truth away, and at any rate save ourselves from any chance of believing falsehood, by not making up our minds at all till objective evidence has come. In scientific questions, this is almost always the case; and even in human affairs in general, the need of acting is seldom so urgent that a false belief to act on is better than no belief at all. Law courts, indeed, have to decide on the best evidence attainable for the moment, because a judge's duty is to make law as well as to ascertain it, and (as a learned judge once said to me) few cases are worth spending much time over: the great thing is to have them decided on any acceptable principle, and got out of the way. But in our dealings with objective nature we obviously are recorders, not makers, of the truth; and decisions for the mere sake of deciding promptly and getting on to the next business would be wholly out of place. Throughout the breadth of physical nature facts are what they are quite independently of us, and seldom is there any such hurry about them that the risks of being duped by believing a premature theory need be faced. The questions here are always trivial options, the hypotheses are hardly living (at any rate not living for us spectators), the choice between believing truth or falsehood is seldom forced. The attitude of skeptical balance is therefore the absolutely wise one if we would escape mistakes. What difference, indeed, does it make to most of us whether we have or have not a theory of the Röntgen rays [i.e., x-rays], whether we believe or not in mind-stuff, or have a conviction about the causality of conscious states? It makes no difference. Such options are not forced on us. On every account it is better not to make them, but still keep weighing reasons *pro et contra* with an indifferent hand.

I speak, of course, here of the purely judging mind. For purposes of discovery such indifference is to be less highly recommended, and science would be far less advanced than she is if the passionate desires of individuals to get their own faiths confirmed had been kept out of the game. See for example the sagacity which Spencer and Weismann now display. On the other hand, if you want an absolute duffer in an investigation, you must, after all, take the man who has no interest whatever in its results: he is the warranted incapable, the positive fool. The most useful investigator, because the most sensitive observer, is always he whose eager interest in one side of the question is balanced by an equally keen nervousness lest he become deceived. Science has organized this nervousness into a regular technique, her so-called method of verification; and she has fallen so deeply in love with the method that one may even say she has ceased to care for truth by itself at all. It is only truth as technically verified that interests her. The truth of truths might come in merely affirmative form, and she would decline to touch it. Such truth as that, she might repeat with Clifford, would be stolen in defiance of her duty to mankind. Human passions, however, are stronger than technical rules. "*Le coeur a ses raisons,*" as Pascal says, "*que la raison ne connait pas* [i.e., the heart has its reasons of which reason knows not]," and however indifferent to all but the bare rules of the game the umpire, the abstract intellect, may be, the concrete players who furnish him the materials to judge of are usually, each one of them, in love with some pet "live hypothesis" of his own. Let us agree, however, that wherever there is no forced option, the dispassionately judicial intellect with no pet hypothesis, saving us, as it does, from dupery at any rate, ought to be our ideal.

The question next arises: Are there not somewhere forced options in our speculative questions, and can we (as men who may be interested at least as much in positively gaining truth as in merely escaping dupery) always wait with impunity till the coercive evidence shall have arrived? It seems *a priori* improbable that the truth should be so nicely adjusted to our needs and powers as that. In the great boarding-house of nature, the cakes and the butter and the syrup seldom come out so even and leave the plates so clean. Indeed, we should view them with scientific suspicion if they did.

IX.

Moral questions immediately present themselves as questions whose solution cannot wait for sensible proof. A moral question is a question not of what sensibly exists, but of what is good, or would be good if it did exist. Science can tell us what exists; but to compare the worth, both of what exists and of what does not exist, we must consult not science, but what Pascal calls our heart. Science herself consults her heart when she lays it down that the infinite ascertainment of fact and correction of false belief are the supreme goods for man. Challenge the statement, and science can only repeat it oracularly, or else prove it by showing that such ascertainment and correction bring man all sorts of other goods which man's heart in turn declares.

The question of having moral beliefs at all or not having them is decided by our will. Are our moral preferences true or false, or are they only odd biological phenomena, making things good or bad for us, but in themselves indifferent? How can your pure intellect decide? If your heart does not want a world of moral reality, your head will assuredly never make you believe in one. Mephistophelian skepticism, indeed, will satisfy the head's play-instincts much better than any rigorous idealism can. Some men (even at the student age) are so naturally cool-hearted that the moralistic hypothesis never has for them any pungent life, and in their supercilious presence the hot young moralist always feels strangely ill at ease. The appearance of knowingness is on their side, of naïveté and gullibility on his. Yet, in the inarticulate heart of him, he clings to it that he is not a dupe, and that there is a realm in which (as Emerson says) all their wit and intellectual superiority is no better than the cunning of a fox. Moral skepticism can no more be refuted or proved by logic than intellectual skepticism can. When we stick to it that there is truth (be it of either kind), we do so with our whole nature, and resolve to stand or fall by the results. The sceptic with his whole nature adopts the doubting attitude; but which of us is the wiser, Omniscience only knows.

Turn now from these wide questions of good to a certain class of questions of fact, questions concerning personal relations, states of mind between one man and another. Do you like me or not?—for example. Whether you do or not depends, in countless instances, on whether I meet you half-way, am willing to assume that you must like me, and show you trust and expectation. The previous faith on my part in your liking's existence is in such cases what makes your liking come. But if I stand aloof, and refuse to budge an inch until I have objective evidence, until you shall have done something apt, as the absolutists say, *ad extorquendum assensum meum*, ten to one your liking never comes. How many women's hearts are vanquished by the mere sanguine insistence of some man that they must love him! He will not consent to the hypothesis that they cannot. The desire for a certain kind of truth here brings about that special truth's existence; and so it is in innumerable cases of other sorts. Who gains promotions, boons, appointments, but the man in whose life they are seen to play the part of live hypotheses, who discounts them, sacrifices other things for their sake before they have come, and takes risks for them in advance? His faith acts on the powers above him as a claim, and creates its own verification.

A social organism of any sort whatever, large or small, is what it is because each member proceeds to his own duty with a trust that the other members will simultaneously do theirs. Wherever a desired result is achieved by the co-operation of many independent persons, its existence as a fact is a pure consequence of the precursive faith in one another of those immediately concerned. A government, an army, a commercial system, a ship, a college, an athletic team, all exist on this condition, without which not only is nothing achieved, but nothing is even attempted. A whole train of passengers (individually brave enough) will be looted by a few highwaymen, simply because the latter can count on one another, while each passenger fears that if he makes a movement of resistance, he will be shot before anyone else backs him up. If we believed that the whole car-full would rise at once with us, we should each severally rise, and train-robbing would never even be attempted. There are, then, cases where a fact cannot come at all unless a preliminary faith exists in its coming. And where faith in a fact can help create the fact, that would be an insane logic which should say that faith running ahead of scientific evidence is the "lowest kind of immorality" into which a thinking being can fall. Yet such is the logic by which our scientific absolutists pretend to regulate our lives!

X.

In truths dependent on our personal action, then, faith based on desire is certainly a lawful and possibly an indispensable thing.

But now, it will be said, these are all childish human cases, and have nothing to do with great cosmic matters, like the question of religious faith. Let us then pass on to that. Religions differ so much in their accidents [i.e., details] that in discussing the religious question we must make it very generic and broad. What then do we now mean by the religious hypothesis? Science says things are; morality says some things are better than other things; and religion says essentially two things.

First, she says that the best things are the more eternal things, the overlapping things, the things in the universe that throw the last stone, so to speak, and say the final word. "Perfection is eternal,"—this phrase of Charles Secretan seems a good way of putting this first affirmation of religion, an affirmation which obviously cannot yet be verified scientifically at all.

The second affirmation of religion is that we are better off even now if we believe her first affirmation to be true.

Now, let us consider what the logical elements of this situation are in case the religious hypothesis in both its branches be really true. (Of course, we must admit that possibility at the outset. If we are to discuss the question at all, it must involve a living option. If for any of you religion be a hypothesis that cannot, by any living possibility be true, then you need go no farther. I speak to the "saving remnant" alone.) So proceeding, we see, first that religion offers itself as a momentous option. We are supposed to gain, even now, by our belief, and to lose by our nonbelief, a certain vital good. Secondly, religion is a forced option, so far as that good goes. We cannot escape the issue by remaining skeptical and waiting for more light, because, although we do avoid error in that way if religion be untrue, we lose the good, if it be true, just as certainly as if we positively chose to disbelieve. It is as if a man should hesitate indefinitely to ask a certain woman to marry him because he was not perfectly sure that she would prove an angel after he brought her home. Would he not cut himself off from that particular angel-possibility as decisively as if he went and married someone else? Skepticism, then, is not avoidance of option; it is option of a certain particular kind of risk. Better risk loss of truth than chance of error,—that is your faith-vetoer's exact position. He is actively playing his stake as much as the believer is; he is backing the field against the religious hypothesis, just as the believer is backing the religious hypothesis against the field. To preach skepticism to us as a duty until "sufficient evidence" for religion be found, is tantamount therefore to telling us, when in presence of the religious hypothesis, that to yield to our fear of its being error is wiser and better than to yield to our hope that it may be true. It is not intellect against all passions, then; it is only intellect with one passion laying down its law. And by what, forsooth, is the supreme wisdom of this passion warranted? Dupery for dupery, what proof is there that dupery through hope is so much worse than dupery through fear? I, for one, can see no proof; and I simply refuse obedience to the scientist's command to imitate his kind of option, in a case where my own stake is important enough to give me the right to choose my own form of risk. If religion be true and the evidence for it be still insufficient, I do not wish, by putting your extinguisher upon my nature (which feels to me as if it had after all some business in this matter), to forfeit my sole chance in life of getting upon the winning side,—that chance depending, of course, on my willingness to run the risk of acting as if my passional need of taking the world religiously might be prophetic and right.

All this is on the supposition that it really may be prophetic and right, and that, even to us who are discussing the matter, religion is a live hypothesis which may be true. Now, to most of us religion comes in a still further way that makes a veto on our active faith even more illogical. The more perfect and more eternal aspect of the universe is represented in our religions as having personal form. The universe is no longer a mere It to us, but a Thou, if we are religious; and any relation that may be possible from person to person might be possible here. For instance, although in one sense we are passive portions of the universe, in another we show a curious autonomy, as if we were small active centers on our own account. We feel, too, as if the appeal of religion to us were made to our own active good-will, as if evidence might be forever withheld from us unless we met the hypothesis half-way. To take a trivial illustration: just as a man who in a company of gentlemen made no advances, asked a warrant for every concession, and believed no one's word without proof, would cut himself off by such churlishness from all the social rewards that a more trusting spirit would earn,—so here, one who should shut himself up in snarling logicality and try to make the gods extort his recognition willy-nilly, or not get it at all, might cut himself off forever from his only opportunity of making the gods' acquaintance. This feeling, forced on us we know not whence, that by obstinately believing that there are gods (although not to do so would be so easy both for our logic and our life) we are doing the universe the deepest service we can, seems part of the living essence of the religious hypothesis. If the hypothesis were true in all its parts, including this one, then pure intellectualism, with its veto on our making willing advances, would be an absurdity; and some participation of our sympathetic nature would be logically required. I, therefore, for one, cannot see my way to accepting the agnostic rules for truth-seeking, or wilfully agree to keep my willing nature out of the game. I cannot do so for this plain reason, that a rule of thinking which would absolutely prevent me from acknowledging certain kinds of truth if those kinds of truth were really there, would be an irrational rule. That for me is the long and short of the formal logic of the situation, no matter what the kinds of truth might materially be.

I confess I do not see how this logic can be escaped. But sad experience makes me fear that some of you may still shrink from radically saying with me, *in abstracto*, that we have the right to believe at our own risk any hypothesis that is live enough to tempt our will.

I suspect, however, that if this is so, it is because you have got away from the abstract logical point of view altogether, and are thinking (perhaps without realizing it) of some particular religious hypothesis which for you is dead. The freedom to "believe what we will" you apply to the case of some patent superstition; and the faith you think of is the faith defined by the schoolboy when he said, "Faith is when you believe something that you know ain't true." I can only repeat that this is misapprehension. *In concreto*, the freedom to believe can only cover living options which the intellect of the individual cannot by itself resolve; and living options never seem absurdities to him who has them to consider. When I look at the religious question as it really puts itself to concrete men, and when I think of all the possibilities which both practically and theoretically it involves, then this command that we shall put a stopper on our heart, instincts, and courage, and wait—acting of course meanwhile more or less as if religion were not true 'til doomsday, or till such time as our intellect and senses working together may have raked in evidence enough, --this command, I say, seems to me the queerest idol ever manufactured in the philosophic cave. Were we scholastic absolutists, there might be more excuse. If we had an infallible intellect with its objective certitudes, we might feel ourselves disloyal to such a perfect organ of knowledge in not trusting to it exclusively, in not waiting for its releasing word. But if we are empiricists, if we believe that no bell in us tolls to let us know for certain when truth is in our grasp, then it seems a piece of idle fantasticality to preach so solemnly our duty of waiting for the bell. Indeed we may wait if we will,—I hope you do not think that I am denying that,—but if we do so, we do so at our peril as much as if we believed. In either case we act, taking our life in our hands. No one of us ought to issue vetoes to the other, nor should we bandy words of abuse. We ought, on the contrary, delicately and profoundly to respect one another's mental freedom: then only shall we bring about the intellectual republic; then only shall we have that spirit of inner tolerance without which all our outer tolerance is soulless, and which is empiricism's glory; then only shall we live and let live, in speculative as well as in practical things.

I began by a reference to Fitz James Stephen; let me end by a quotation from him:

"What do you think of yourself? What do you think of the world? . . . These are questions with which all must deal as it seems good to them. They are riddles of the Sphinx, and in some way or other we must deal with them. . . . In all important transactions of life we have to take a leap in the dark. . . . If we decide to leave the riddles unanswered, that is a choice; if we waver in our answer, that, too, is a choice: but whatever choice we make, we make it at our peril. If a man chooses to turn his back altogether on God and the future, no one can prevent him; no one can show beyond reasonable doubt that he is mistaken. If a man thinks otherwise and acts as he thinks, I do not see that anyone can prove that he is mistaken. Each must act as he thinks best; and if he is wrong, so much the worse for him. We stand on a mountain pass in the midst of whirling snow and blinding mist through which we get glimpses now and then of paths which may be deceptive. If we stand still we shall be frozen to death. If we take the wrong road we shall be dashed to pieces. We do not certainly know whether there is any right one. What must we do? 'Be strong and of a good courage.' Act for the best, hope for the best, and take what comes. . . . If death ends all, we cannot meet death better."

[An Address to the Philosophical Clubs of Yale and Brown Universities. Published in the New World. June, 1896.]

"The Ethics of Belief" from
Lectures and Essays

W. K. Clifford
(Edited by Joseph R. Kirkland)

I. THE DUTY OF INQUIRY

A ship-owner was about to send to sea an emigrant-ship. He knew that she was old, and not over-well built at the first; that she had seen many seas and climes, and often had needed repairs.

Doubts had been suggested to him that possibly she was not seaworthy. These doubts preyed upon his mind, and made him unhappy; he thought that perhaps he ought to have her thoroughly overhauled and refitted, even though this should put him at great expense. Before the ship sailed, however, he succeeded in overcoming these melancholy reflections. He said to himself that she had gone safely through so many voyages and weathered so many storms that it was idle to suppose she would not come safely home from this trip also. He would put his trust in

Providence, which could hardly fail to protect all these unhappy families that were leaving their fatherland to seek for better times elsewhere. He would dismiss from his mind all ungenerous suspicions about the honesty of builders and contractors. In such ways he acquired a sincere and comfortable conviction that his vessel was thoroughly safe and seaworthy; he watched her departure with a light heart, and benevolent wishes for the success of the exiles in their strange new home that was to be; and he got his insurance-money when she went down in mid-ocean and told no tales.

What shall we say of him? Surely this, that he was verily guilty of the death of those men. It is admitted that he did sincerely believe in the soundness of his ship; but the sincerity of his conviction can in no wise help him, because he had no right to believe on such evidence as was before him. He had acquired his belief not by honestly earning it in patient investigation, but by stifling his doubts. And although in the end he may have felt so sure about it that he could not think otherwise, yet inasmuch as he had knowingly and willingly worked himself into that frame of mind, he must be held responsible for it.

Let us alter the case a little, and suppose that the ship was not unsound after all; that she made her voyage safely, and many others after it. Will that diminish the guilt of her owner? Not one jot. When an action is once done, it is right or wrong for ever; no accidental failure of its good or evil fruits can possibly alter that. The man would not have been innocent, he would only have been not found out. The question of right or wrong has to do with the origin of his belief, not the matter of it; not what it was, but how he got it; not whether it turned out to be true or false, but whether he had a right to believe on such evidence as was before him. There was once an island in which some of the inhabitants professed a religion teaching neither the doctrine of original sin nor that of eternal punishment. A suspicion got abroad that the professors of this religion had made use of unfair means to get their doctrines taught to children.

They were accused of wresting the laws of their country in such a way as to remove children from the care of their natural and legal guardians; and even of stealing them away and keeping them concealed from their friends and relations. A certain number of men formed themselves into a society for the purpose of agitating the public about this matter. They published grave accusations against individual citizens of the highest position and character, and did all in their power to injure these citizens in their exercise of their professions. So great was the noise they made, that a Commission was appointed to investigate the facts; but after the Commission had carefully inquired into all the evidence that could be got, it appeared that the accused were innocent. Not only had they been accused of insufficient evidence, but the evidence of their innocence was such as the agitators might easily have obtained, if they had attempted a fair inquiry. After these disclosures the inhabitants of that country looked upon the members of the agitating society, not only as persons whose judgment was to be distrusted, but also as no longer to be counted honorable men. For although they had sincerely and conscientiously believed in the charges they had made, yet they had no right to believe on such evidence as was before them.

Their sincere convictions, instead of being honestly earned by patient inquiring, were stolen by listening to the voice of prejudice and passion.

Let us vary this case also, and suppose, other things remaining as before, that a still more accurate investigation proved the accused to have been really guilty. Would this make any difference in the guilt of the accusers? Clearly not; the question is not whether their belief was true or false, but whether they entertained it on wrong grounds. They would no doubt say, "Now you see that we were right after all; next time perhaps you will believe us." And they might be believed, but they would not thereby become honorable men. They would not be innocent, they would only be not found out. Every one of them, if he chose to examine himself *in foro conscientiae*, would know that he had acquired and nourished a belief, when he had no right to believe on such evidence as was before him; and therein he would know that he had done a wrong thing.

It may be said, however, that in both these supposed cases it is not the belief which is judged to be wrong, but the action following upon it. The ship-owner might say, "I am perfectly certain that my ship is sound, but still I feel it my duty to have her examined, before trusting the lives of so many people to her." And it might be said to the agitator, "However convinced you were of the justice of your cause and the truth of your convictions, you ought not to have made a public attack upon any man's character until you had examined the evidence on both sides with the utmost patience and care."

In the first place, let us admit that, so far as it goes, this view of the case is right and necessary; right, because even when a man's belief is so fixed that he cannot think otherwise, he still has a choice in the action suggested by it, and so cannot escape the duty of investigating on the ground of the strength of his convictions; and necessary, because those who are not yet capable of controlling their feelings and thoughts must have a plain rule dealing with overt acts." But this being premised as necessary, it becomes clear that it is not sufficient, and that our previous judgment is required to supplement it. For it is not possible so to sever the belief from the action it suggests as to condemn the one without condemning the other. No man holding a strong belief on one side of a question, or even wishing to hold a belief on one side, can investigate it with such fairness and completeness as if he were really in doubt and unbiased; so that the existence of a belief not founded on fair inquiry unfits a man for the performance of this necessary duty.

Nor is it that truly a belief at all which has not some influence upon the actions of him who holds it. He who truly believes that which prompts him to an action has looked upon the action to lust after it, he has committed it already in his heart. If a belief is not realized immediately in open deeds, it is stored up for the guidance of the future. It goes to make a part of that aggregate of beliefs which is the link between sensation and action at every moment of all our lives, and which is so organized and compacted together that no part of it can be isolated from the rest, but every new addition modifies the structure of the whole. No real belief, however trifling and fragmentary it may seem, is ever truly insignificant; it prepares us to receive more of its like, confirms those which resembled it before, and weakens others; and so gradually it lays a stealthy train in our inmost thoughts, which may someday explode into overt action, and leave its stamp upon our character forever.

And no one man's belief is in any case a private matter which concerns himself alone. Our lives our guided by that general conception of the course of things which has been created by society for social purposes. Our words, our phrases, our forms and processes and modes of thought, are common property, fashioned and perfected from age to age; an heirloom which every succeeding generation inherits as a precious deposit and a sacred trust to be handled on to the next one, not unchanged but enlarged and purified, with some clear marks of its proper handiwork. Into this, for good or ill, is woven every belief of every man who has speech of his fellows. An awful privilege, and an awful responsibility, that we should help to create the world in which posterity will live.

In the two supposed cases which have been considered, it has been judged wrong to believe on insufficient evidence, or to nourish belief by suppressing doubts and avoiding investigation. The reason of this judgment is not far to seek: it is that in both these cases the belief held by one man was of great importance to other men. But forasmuch as no belief held by one man, however seemingly trivial the belief, and however obscure the believer, is ever actually insignificant or without its effect on the fate of mankind, we have no choice but to extend our judgment to all cases of belief whatever. Belief, that sacred faculty which prompts the decisions of our will, and knits into harmonious working all the compacted energies of our being, is ours not for ourselves but for humanity. It is rightly used on truths which have been established by long experience and waiting toil, and which have stood in the fierce light of free and fearless questioning. Then it helps to bind men together, and to strengthen and direct their common action. It is desecrated when given to unproved and unquestioned statements, for the solace and private pleasure of the believer; to add a tinsel splendor to the plain straight road of our life and display a bright mirage beyond it; or even to drown the common sorrows of our kind by a self-deception which allows them not only to cast down, but also to degrade us. Whoso would deserve well of his fellows in this matter will guard the purity of his beliefs with a very fanaticism of jealous care, lest at any time it should rest on an unworthy object, and catch a stain which can never be wiped away.

It is not only the leader of men, statesmen, philosopher, or poet, who owes this bounden duty to mankind. Every rustic who delivers in the village alehouse his slow, infrequent sentences, may help to kill or keep alive the fatal superstitions which clog his race. Every hard-worked wife of an artisan may transmit to her children beliefs which shall knit society together, or rend it in pieces. No simplicity of mind, no obscurity of station, can escape the universal duty of questioning all that we believe.

It is true that this duty is a hard one, and the doubt which comes out of it is often a very bitter thing. It leaves us bare and powerless where we thought that we were safe and strong. To know all about anything is to know how to deal with it under all circumstances. We feel much happier and more secure when we think we know precisely what to do, no matter what happens, then when we have lost our way and do not know where to turn. And if we have supposed ourselves to know all about anything, and to be capable of doing what is fit in regard to it, we naturally do not like to find that we are really ignorant and powerless, that we have to begin again at the beginning, and try to learn what the thing is and how it is to be dealt with--if indeed anything can be learnt about it. It is the sense of power attached to a sense of knowledge that makes men desirous of believing, and afraid of doubting.

This sense of power is the highest and best of pleasures when the belief on which it is founded is a true belief, and has been fairly earned by investigation. For then we may justly feel that it is common property, and hold good for others as well as for ourselves. Then we may be glad, not that I have learned secrets by which I am safer and stronger, but that we men have got mastery over more of the world; and we shall be strong, not for ourselves but in the name of Man and his strength. But if the belief has been accepted on insufficient evidence, the pleasure is a stolen one.

Not only does it deceive ourselves by giving us a sense of power which we do not really possess, but it is sinful, because it is stolen in defiance of our duty to mankind. That duty is to guard ourselves from such beliefs as from pestilence, which may shortly master our own body and then spread to the rest of the town. What would be thought of one who, for the sake of a sweet fruit, should deliberately run the risk of delivering a plague upon his family and his neighbors?

And, as in other such cases, it is not the risk only which has to be considered; for a bad action is always bad at the time when it is done, no matter what happens afterwards. Every time we let ourselves believe for unworthy reasons, we weaken our powers of self-control, of doubting, of judicially and fairly weighing evidence. We all suffer severely enough from the maintenance and support of false beliefs and the fatally wrong actions which they lead to, and the evil born when one such belief is entertained is great and wide. But a greater and wider evil arises when the credulous character is maintained and supported, when a habit of believing for unworthy reasons is fostered and made permanent. If I steal money from any person, there may be no harm done from the mere transfer of possession; he may not feel the loss, or it may prevent him from using the money badly. But I cannot help doing this great wrong towards Man, that I make myself dishonest. What hurts society is not that it should lose its property, but that it should become a den of thieves, for then it must cease to be society. This is why we ought not to do evil, that good may come; for at any rate this great evil has come, that we have done evil and are made wicked thereby. In like manner, if I let myself believe anything on insufficient evidence, there may be no great harm done by the mere belief; it may be true after all, or I may never have occasion to exhibit it in outward acts. But I cannot help doing this great wrong towards Man, that I make myself credulous. The danger to society is not merely that it should believe wrong things, though that is great enough; but that it should become credulous, and lose the habit of testing things and inquiring into them; for then it must sink back into savagery.

The harm which is done by credulity in a man is not confined to the fostering of a credulous character in others, and consequent support of false beliefs. Habitual want of care about what I believe leads to habitual want of care in others about the truth of what is told to me. Men speak the truth of one another when each reveres the truth in his own mind and in the other's mind; but how shall my friend revere the truth in my mind when I myself am careless about it, when I believe thing because I want to believe them, and because they are comforting and pleasant? Will he not learn to cry, "Peace," to me, when there is no peace? By such a course I shall surround myself with a thick atmosphere of falsehood and fraud, and in that I must live. It may matter little to me, in my cloud-castle of sweet illusions and darling lies; but it matters much to Man that I have made my neighbors ready to deceive. The credulous man is father to the liar and the cheat; he lives in the bosom of this his family, and it is no marvel if he should become even as they are. So closely are our duties knit together, that whoso shall keep the whole law, and yet offend in one point, he is guilty of all.

To sum up: it is wrong always, everywhere, and for anyone, to believe anything upon insufficient evidence.

If a man, holding a belief which he was taught in childhood or persuaded of afterwards, keeps down and pushes away any doubts which arise about it in his mind, purposely avoids the reading of books and the company of men that call into question or discuss it, and regards as impious those questions which cannot easily be asked without disturbing it—the life of that man is one long sin against mankind.

[*"The Ethics of Belief" from Lectures and Essays*. (London: Macmillan, 1879).]

An Introduction to Logical Argument

Logic is the branch of philosophy dedicated to the study of correct reasoning and the rules and principles that govern proper logical argument. It is important to note that, in this context, an *argument* is not to be confused with merely *arguing* with someone over some matter. A logical argument is not the same thing as a dispute. Put simply, a logical argument involves the attempt to support the truth of *one* proposition (i.e., belief, opinion, claim, etc.) by appealing to the truth of *other*, logically related, propositions. We call the proposition whose truth we seek to support a **conclusion**. We call any proposition cited to support the truth of the conclusion a **premise**. You can think of the conclusion of an argument as its main point, while its premises are reasons to accept the truth of the main point.

Often, the author of an argument will flag the premise(s) and/or conclusion of their argument with **indicator words** or **phrases**. These are word or phrases used to distinguish the conclusion of an argument from its premise(s). Please note the list of some commonly occurring indicators, below.

Conclusion Indicators: therefore / wherefore / accordingly / we may conclude / entails that / hence / thus / consequently / we may infer / it must be that / whence / so / it follows that / implies that / as a result / etc.

Premise Indicators: since / as / insofar as / in that / because / for / given that / for the reason that / owing to / inasmuch as / etc.

It is also important to note that a proper logical argument requires *both* a conclusion and one or more premises. A single, stand-alone "conclusion" is not an argument; in fact, it's not even a proper conclusion. A lone proposition is called an **assertion**. Assertions may very well be true, but without any further reasons "backing them up," we have no good reason for accepting them as true. For example, I may assert: "The Detroit Tigers are the best team in baseball," but if I don't provide further reasons to back up my claim, it remains a mere assertion. If, instead, I bolster my claim by pointing to the team's win–loss record, their superior statistics in pitching and hitting compared with other teams, and so forth, my assertion becomes a proper argument.

Assertion: "The Detroit Tigers are the best team in baseball."

Argument: "The best team in baseball is the team with the best record. The Detroit Tigers have the best record. Therefore, the Detroit Tigers are the best team in baseball."

However, not all propositions are relevant to the truth of a particular conclusion, logically speaking. Consider:

"The best team in baseball is any team with white and blue jerseys. The Detroit Tigers have white and blue jerseys. Therefore, the Detroit Tigers are the best team in baseball."

There is something logically suspect about this reasoning, and you do not have to be a fan of baseball (or its sartorial conventions) to spot it. Of what logical *relevance* is a team's colors to that team's performance? Thus, in assessing the quality of a logical argument, we need to do more than merely assess the truth of its premise(s) and/or its conclusion. We also need to assess the quality of the underlying logical *structure* of an argument: that is, the logical connections (or lack thereof) between the premise(s) and the conclusion. In logic, we employ the concept of **validity** to describe the structure or form of an argument. An argument is logically valid when the truth of the premise(s) would conclusively guarantee the truth of the conclusion. In other words, a valid argument is an argument whose conclusion *must* be true if its premise(s) were true. We may very well use the word "valid" in a looser sense in casual conversation (e.g., "You make a valid point!"), but, in logic, "valid" is a more precise term of art. Individual propositions (e.g., premises and conclusions) are either *true* or *false*, not valid or invalid. Logical arguments, on the other hand, are never true or false, but *valid* or *invalid*. Validity is a formal or structural property of logical arguments. This means that, as odd as it may seem, an argument with a false premise—or even a false conclusion!—may nonetheless be valid. Let's see why.

Premise 1: All men are mortal.

Premise 2: Socrates is a man.

Conclusion: Socrates is mortal.

The above is a (classic) example of a logically valid argument. *If* it is true that all men are mortal, and *if* it is true that Socrates is a man, then it would follow logically that Socrates is mortal. Moreover, the truth of the conclusion of any logically valid argument follows with strict logical necessity. That is, there is no possible way for a valid argument to have true premises and a false conclusion. In logic, we say the truth of the conclusion of a valid argument *follows from* the truth of its premises. But compare:

Premise 1: All fnorbs are conbloozable.

Premise 2: Bsnord is a fnorb.

Conclusion: Bsnord is conbloozable.

It may seem bizarre to describe the above (intentionally obscure) argument as valid, but it is. Remember: validity is a structural or formal property of logical arguments and thus does not depend on the actual truth of any particular premise. *If* it were true that all fnobrs are conbloozable, and *if* it were true that Bsnord is a fnorb, then it would follow logically that Bsnord is conbloozable—whatever any of that might mean! Just as a valid argument may nonetheless have false premises, it is also possible for a valid argument to have a false conclusion:

Premise 1: All dogs are cats.

Premise 2: Professor Kirkland is a dog.

Conclusion: Professor Kirkland is a cat.

Here we have an argument with false premises *and* a false conclusion that, nevertheless, is valid. *If* it were true that all dogs are cats, and *if* it were true that Professor Kirkland is a dog, then it would follow logically that Professor Kirkland is a cat. Clearly, then, we need an additional concept to describe those arguments with a valid structure whose premises are *in fact* true. This is the concept of **soundness**. A logically sound argument is a logically valid argument whose premises are *actually* (not just presumably) true. In logic, it does not get any better than a sound argument. For, with a sound argument, we can confidently conclude that its conclusion is *necessarily true*:

Premise 1: All circles are round.

Premise 2: No squares are round.

Conclusion: No squares are circles.

As you might imagine, logically sound arguments are relatively rare in discourse. It is often the case that we cannot provide the sort of *conclusive* proof that sound arguments both require and guarantee. Fortunately, we have other options, logically speaking.

DEDUCTION AND INDUCTION

In logic, it is useful to distinguish between **deductive** and **inductive** reasoning. In the case of deductive reasoning, we attempt to construct an argument that is both valid and sound—that is, an argument with a structure such that the actual truth of its premises guarantees the actual truth of its conclusion. Any logical argument that fails to meet this high bar can be classified as inductive. In an inductive argument, the truth of the premise(s) provides less-than-definitive reasons for accepting the truth of the conclusion. We may think of the concepts of probability or likelihood, here. An inductive argument that is well constructed gives us good reasons for accepting the *probable* or *likely* truth of the conclusion. For example, if you developed heartburn shortly after every time you happened to drink a cup of coffee to date, it is reasonable to conclude that the coffee may have something to do with your symptoms. From this may we *definitively* conclude that *every* time you drink a cup of coffee in the future you will develop heartburn? We may not. It is possible? Sure. It is *necessary*, in the logical sense? It is not. Philosopher Bertrand Russell was fond of the following anecdote to illustrate this aspect of inductive reasoning. Every morning a chicken sees the screen of the chicken coop slide open as the farmer deposits the chicken's feed into the coop. This happens without fail, every morning, for years. In fact, the chicken comes to associate the opening of the screen with the pleasant experience of being fed. It is reasonable to infer that when, the screen swings open tomorrow morning, the chicken will be fed? Sure. Unless, of course, tomorrow is the ill-fated day that chicken soup is on the farmhouse menu!

Since the truth of the conclusion of an inductive argument is never guaranteed, we will need a different concept to evaluate the relative quality of inductive arguments. The concepts of validity and soundness are reserved for deductive arguments. With respect to inductive arguments, then, we speak of their relative **strength**. Any particular inductive argument is either more or less strong (or weak). The way to improve the strength of an inductive argument is to provide premises that increase the likelihood that the conclusion is true. But note: the moment that the truth of an argument's premises actually *guarantees* the truth of its conclusion, it is no longer an inductive argument but a deductively sound one. Thus, when it comes to induction, it is always possible for an inductive argument to have true premises and a very strong structure, but with a false conclusion all the same. A helpful analogy here can be drawn from the sphere of justice and criminal law. In a criminal courtroom, the prosecutor may try to prove the guilt of a defendant beyond all reasonable doubt by introducing evidence that bolsters her claim that the defendant is, in fact, guilty. That said, no matter how much evidence a prosecutor cites in making her case, it always remains logically possible that the defendant is not, in fact, guilty. Maybe it's a case of mistaken identity. Maybe his evil twin did it! When it comes to inductive reasoning, the most we can strive for are highly probable or likely conclusions. Certain truth is the province of deduction, not induction.

LOGICAL FALLACIES

In logic, a **fallacy** is an error in reasoning. Thus, a fallacious argument is a logical argument that suffers from one or more serious defects. Logical fallacies are therefore best avoided wherever possible in our reasoning. Logical fallacies may be *intentional*—that is, deliberately committed, perhaps as a rhetorical tactic to "win" a dispute by whatever means necessary, logical or not—or *unintentional* in nature. Intentional or otherwise, we should avoid fallacious reasoning in our own arguments, and we should be attentive to fallacious reasoning in the arguments of others. Provided below is a list of some unfortunately common informal logical fallacies. This is far from a complete list, but it can serve as a useful reference for when we encounter an aspect of someone's argument that seems suspect for reasons we perhaps cannot initially put our finger on.

Straw Man: When a person's position or claims are mischaracterized in an uncharitable fashion so as to make them easier to address and/or refute. It takes its name from the image of a scarecrow. Just as a scarecrow is easier to topple than an actual person, a caricatured version of one's views can be easier to "knock over," as well. This is fallacious because the straw man fallacy amounts to changing the subject to a different, and therefore irrelevant, claim or set of claims.

> *"Anyone who supports a raise in the minimum wage hates capitalism and thus is a Communist."*

Slippery Slope: When it is erroneously claimed that a particular position, policy, etc., (A) will inexorably lead to terrible and/or unacceptable consequences in the future (X, Y, Z). Not all invocations of a "slippery slope" are fallacious, however, as it is possible that A will in fact make it more likely that X, Y, and/or Z will occur. The invocation of a slippery slope is fallacious when it is unclear or unlikely that A will in fact lead to X, Y, and Z.

> *"If we lower the legal voting age to 18, then eventually babies will demand the right to vote!"*

Post hoc ergo propter hoc: From the Latin: "After this, therefore because of this." When one event is assumed to be the effect of another, prior event on insufficient causal evidence. Just because event A precedes event B in time does not necessarily mean that A was the cause of B. The likely source of many superstitious beliefs.

> *"A black cat crossed my path and then I received a phone call with bad news. Black cats are bad luck."*

Circular Argument: When an argument merely asserts the truth of the conclusion it is supposed to prove instead of providing premises that actually support the truth of the conclusion; also known as "begging the question."

> *"There ought to be a law against gambling because gambling should be illegal."*

Argumentum ad Hominem: From the Latin: "Against the man." An irrelevant personal attack, critiquing some aspect of the person espousing a position instead of their position itself. If someone's character or personal history is in fact relevant to a discussion, then invocations of the same are not irrelevant and therefore not fallacious. However, the Argumentum ad Hominem fallacy is comparable to the Straw Man fallacy in that it effectively changes the subject and can be construed as a gesture of argumentative surrender.

> *"Professor Kirkland supports a raise for adjunct lecturers, but of course he would. Have you seen his stupid hat? Only an idiot would wear a hat like that, so we can safely ignore his concerns."*

Argumentum ad Populum: An irrelevant appeal to the popularity of a position, view, or practice; that is, an appeal to the majority. This appeal can be fallacious insofar as the truth does not always reside with the majority.

> *"More Americans smoke Marlboros than any other brand. Smoking Marlboros is good for you!"*

False Dilemma: When one presumes that there are only two mutually exclusive options in a particular scenario, when in fact there are more than two. Not all dilemmas are false: when you flip a coin, it's going to turn up either heads or tails. A dilemma becomes fallacious when there are legitimately more than two possible outcomes (i.e., possibilities, options, etc.) but the author or speaker in question unreasonably insists there are not.

> *"America: Love it or leave it!"*

Fallacy of Composition: When one presumes that something true of one part of a whole must also be true of the whole itself.

> *"Students are an important part of the University. Students have arms and legs. Therefore, the University has arms and legs."*

Fallacy of Division: When one presumes that something true of the whole must also be true of parts of the whole.

> *"Water is wet, and water consists of hydrogen and oxygen. Thus, hydrogen and oxygen are wet."*

Appeal to Authority: When no further reasons to support the truth of a conclusion are provided, save for the invocation of one's authority. Not all appeals to authority are fallacious, as some people do in fact have more expertise than others in certain areas. However, any nonfallacious appeal to authority will feature additional reasons justifying *why* a given authority accepts a particular claim. Be on guard for authorities in one area claiming to speak as authorities in another area unrelated to their expertise (e.g., celebrity endorsements in advertising).

> *"Because I said so."*

Logical Exercises

Name: _____

For each of the following logical arguments, indicate whether they are valid and/or sound. If an argument is invalid and/or unsound, explain why in the space provided.

1. All whales are mammals, and Shamu is a whale. Thus, Shamu is a mammal.

2. If it rains, then the sidewalks will be wet. Since the sidewalks are wet, we can infer that it rained.

3. Because it rained, we can conclude that the sidewalks are wet. That's because, if it rains then the sidewalks will be wet.

4. Most people are right handed and Kurt Cobain was a person, so we can infer that Kurt Cobain was right handed.

5. All people are left handed and Kurt Cobain was a person, so we can conclude that Kurt Cobain was left handed.

6. Insofar as all unicorns have horns and all bulls have horns, then it follows that all bulls are unicorns.

7. Eighty-two percent of all Americans who have died from liver complications consumed tomatoes at some point in their life. From this we may conclude that eating tomatoes causes liver damage.

8. The Bible claims that God exists, and the Bible is true because it was inspired by God. Therefore, God exists.

9. If we legalize marijuana for recreational use, then what's stopping us from repealing the laws prohibiting theft and murder? Hence, legalizing marijuana for recreational use is a terrible idea.

10. Either you love chocolate ice cream or you love vanilla ice cream. You do not love vanilla ice cream, therefore we can infer that you love chocolate ice cream.